American
PHILOSOPHERS
AT WORK

American PHILOSOPHERS AT WORK

The Philosophic Scene *in the* United States

Edited by
SIDNEY HOOK

CRITERION BOOKS   NEW YORK

Contents

THREE. Ethics and Social Philosophy

Introduction

In his classic study of American democracy, Alexis de Tocqueville observed that "in no country of the civilized world is less attention paid to philosophy than in the United States." De Tocqueville's reference was to the formal philosophy of the schools and to technical doctrines in which visions of life and judgments of value are expressed, but so obscurely that their vital bearing is missed. He went on, however, to pay a remarkably perceptive and generous tribute to the philosophical attitudes which he found embodied in American habits of understanding and conduct. At a time when the population of the United States was ethnically much more homogeneous than it is today, de Tocqueville found "common to the whole people" the following rules of philosophical method:

> To evade the bondage of system and habit, of family-maxims, class-opinions, and, in some degree, of national prejudices: to accept tradition only as a means of information, and existing facts only as a lesson used in doing otherwise, and doing better; to seek the reason of things for one's self, and one's self alone; to tend to results without being bound to means, and to aim at the substance through the form—such are the principal characteristics of what I shall call the philosophical method of the Americans. But if I go further, and if I seek among these characteristics that which predominates over and includes almost all the rest, I discover that in most of the operations of the mind each American appeals to the individual exercise of his own understanding alone. America is therefore one of the countries in the world where philosophy is least studied, and where the precepts of Descartes are best applied.

One is tempted to observe that a people whose mode of thought is so gifted, so independent, so sensitive to differences in person, place, and thing hardly needs a formal school philosophy to give direction to its thinking. It is an interesting question to speculate upon whether if de Tocqueville were to revisit America today he would find his judgments about popular judgment confirmed. As in all other things, he would probably find less individualism both in thought and action. And he would discover that it is not so much the precepts of Descartes which are applied but rather "the argument from Missouri" which stresses not professions but actions, not promises but consequences and fruits.

With respect to philosophy as a discipline and body of specialized thought, however, there is little doubt that de Tocqueville's judgment remains substantially true. The United States is still a country in which philosophy is least studied, in which proportionately fewer books on philosophy are bought and read, in which the views of philosophers are considered less relevant to the concerns of nonphilosophers, even less newsworthy, than in most European countries. Philosophy creates a stir only where its implications seem to impinge directly upon matters of public interest like education and law. The reasons for this are variously interpreted. It may testify to the fact that philosophy has come of age, that it is no longer the queen of the sciences, that it is no longer in pursuit of wisdom, or salvation or intellectual comfort but a specialized science itself. From this point of view philosophy should no more be expected to provide intellectual leadership or a unifying point of view for a culture than theoretical physics or comparative philology. It may, however, also testify to the fact that philosophy is forging the tools and concepts which are required to take a fresh grip on perennial problems that have defied resolution—even if the resolution consists in showing that perennial problems are not genuine—and on new problems that are not perennial but genuine.

Whatever the reasons, the existence of American civilization, rooted in a European heritage but an outgrowth of a unique historical experience, calls for some philosophical interpretation of its dominant values and ideals. Failing to find it, it is natural to look at the character and contributions of professional philosophy as a possible clue to styles of thought, feeling, and interest—the intellectual passions of an age. On numerous occasions, especially at transoceanic meetings and conferences in which are found differences in points of view, value, and color of thought far more marked than differences in language or color or skin, there is invariably manifested an intense curiosity about the nature of the American scene, especially of the current philosophic scene. Whether out of fear or friendship, the literate representatives of nations who see their destinies involved for good or evil in those of the United States are eager to fathom the depths or shallows of American culture. Impressionistic beliefs abroad about American culture indicate that by and large the United States is still an undiscovered country. The same may be said of impressionistic beliefs about American philosophy, only more so.

This volume has grown out of an attempt to meet the natural and almost universal curiosity about what American philosophers are doing, about what lies at the center of their contemporary intellectual concern. And it should be as instructive to those who live in America as to those who live elsewhere.

Instead of offering a summary and interpretation of the doctrine, allegiances and classifications of American philosophers, which inevitably reflects an editorial bias, it seems desirable, and a welcome departure from previous accounts of American philosophy, to give representative American philosophers an opportunity to present their own selections from their writings, to reveal them, so to speak, at work. The fact that it shows American philosophers in work clothes rather than holiday dress makes more authentic the evidence of what they are thinking about and how.

All important philosophical movements are represented in this collection as well as all the major regions of the country, but in the nature of the case it was impossible to include all important individual thinkers. Nothing is to be inferred about the philosophic distinction of any thinker from his absence in this book. Whatever the philosophical status of space and time no editor can abridge their tyranny in the world of everyday existence.

I permit myself a few observations about the character of American philosophy as evinced in these self-selections, observations, the validity of which the reader may judge in the light of his own reading.

American philosophy is no parochial affair but an integral part of the Continental, and especially the English tradition in philosophy. American philosophers are much better informed of philosophical movements in foreign countries, the nature of their problems and interests than are their colleagues in foreign countries about American philosophy. To this day William James is almost the only great American figure known abroad and even he is judged in terms of antecedently held views about the nature of pragmatism rather than in the light of a fresh and sympathetic reading of his work.

American philosophers, with some notable exceptions, no longer practice philosophy in the grand *tradition,* essaying wholesale views about the nature of man, existence, and eternity. Inspired by the results won in the sciences, they do not even practice philosophy in the grand *manner* but concentrate on the patient analysis of specific problems aiming at results which although piecemeal are more likely to withstand criticism. The natural consequence is an estrangement from the interests of educated laymen who feel that technical philosophy is remote from their concerns. And to be sure, no longer can he who runs read philosophy. He must study it, sometimes with pencil and paper in hand. On the other hand, scientists who are not philosophically trained find little illumination in the scientific analysis of philosophers whom they tend to regard as mere camp followers of scientific progress. This, despite the fact that in the absence of philosophical sophistication the report the scientist makes to the nonscientist of the strange new world discovered by modern science is apt to generate confusion and needless paradox.

Recent years have witnessed an impressive shift of attention to theoretical problems of value and ethical theory. But few philosophers have attempted to come to grips with specific social problems, involving conflicts of specific sets of value, in a philosophical way. And by a philosophical way I mean clarifying the issues in dispute, separating the purely verbal from the factual issues, explicating what is at stake, the degree of difference, what specific cognitive truths differences in specific value judgments depend upon, and which of the proposals in sight is more likely to lead to a satisfactory resolution of the difficulty. There are many concrete problems in law and morals, in social, political and educational philosophy which cry out for the illumination a rigorous analysis can throw upon them. In this way, if philosophy leaves salvation to religion, and the accumulation of knowledge and the construction of better-made scientific languages to the scientist, philosophy on a modest scale can contribute to human wisdom and take its rightful place in the community. It will at least be listened to. For, in the end professional philosophers exist not for each other alone but for those who are not professional philosophers, also.

Finally, the trait which de Tocqueville saw as characteristic of philosophically innocent Americans, is conspicuous among the sophisticated professional philosophers. Each is an independent thinker even when he voluntarily adheres to a school of thought, and most of them adhere to no school. There is no state philosophy in America and no authority is recognized except good argument and cogent evidence. The continuous disagreements among American philosophers may show that philosophy is still far from being a science or even scientific, but it also proves that American philosophers are free. Ultimately it is more important that they be free than that they agree.

SIDNEY HOOK

PART ONE

Logic and Scientific Method

ALICE AMBROSE

Justifying Inductive Inference

I wish to begin with a matter about which, to quote Russell, "none of us, in fact, feel the slightest doubt."[1] I then propose to discuss doubts of that curious academic kind with which philosophers have challenged common sense, with a view to seeing through them clearly enough to find the way back to the common-sense, non-skeptical position. It is not intellectually satisfactory to indulge in the ordinary man's reaction of brushing aside these doubts as trivial or unreal. But it may be possible to cope with them without having to relinquish the common-sense position.

Consider the following quotation from Russell's *Problems of Philosophy:*

> We are all convinced that the sun will rise tomorrow. Why? Is this belief a mere blind outcome of past experience, or can it be justified as a reasonable belief? . . . If we are asked why we believe [this], we shall naturally answer, "Because it always has risen every day." We have a firm belief that it will rise in the future, because it has risen in the past.[2] . . . The problem

we have to discuss is whether there is any reason for believing in what is called "the uniformity of nature."[3] . . . Do *any* number of cases of a law being fulfilled in the past afford evidence that it will be fulfilled in the future?[4] . . . When two things have been found to be often associated, and no instance is known of the one occurring without the other, does the occurrence of one of the two, in a fresh instance, give any good ground for expecting the other?[5] . . . If not, it becomes plain that we have no ground whatever for expecting the sun to rise tomorrow, or for expecting the bread we shall eat at our next meal not to poison us.[6]

Russell makes clear that in raising these questions he is not suggesting we seek for a proof that these expectations "*must* be fulfilled, but only for some reason in favour of the view that they are *likely* to be fulfilled."[7] In other words, he is asking for some justification of the inference that the sun is *likely* to rise tomorrow from the fact that it has done so, not of the sun's being *certain* to rise. The task of justifying an inference that something is likely is a more modest one than that of justifying the inference that it is certain. But if both inferences are felt to be in genuine need of justification, then the doubt directed against the weaker inference must be more drastic than that directed against the stronger. Obviously the doubt whether the repetition of concomitances or sequences of events makes a similar concomitance or sequence *probable* is of a more radical kind than the doubt whether it makes this certain. One might feel hesitant, for example, about claiming it was certain that aspirin would stop the present headache on the grounds that it had always provided relief, and not feel at all hesitant about claiming that these grounds made it at least probable.

Such assurance, however, does not for long preserve immunity against the progressive infectiousness of doubt. It is part of the natural history of doubt to spread. Hume raised doubts concerning our certainty of any inductive conclusion p. These can be, and in fact have been, extended to conclusions of the form "p is probable." The same sort of considerations which historically gave rise to the suspicion that even our most assured inductive conclusions are uncertain give rise equally to uneasiness whether *any* evidence could even make them probable. We see this in the progress of philosophers to the more extreme doubt, that brought against the legitimacy, in general, of conclusions of the form "p is probable." In this paper I shall be concerned with doubts of this kind.

It will be useful here briefly to indicate the sources of these in doubts originally raised as to the legitimacy of any inductive conclusion of the form "*p.*" The main sources are two in number: (1) the doubt whether any number of cases of a conjunction of characteristics could make certain any proposition about its continued occurrence; (2) the doubt, even though some number could make it certain, whether one could ever know the number of cases had was sufficient. The first, stated explicitly by Hume, eventuated in the claim that evidence in the form of observations of which we are perfectly certain leaves the inductive conclusion uncertain, the reason being that they are not sufficient for its *deduction.* The fact that two characteristics ϕ and ψ have always been associated is not sufficient to deduce that they always are nor even that they will be in the next instance. To quote Hume:

> There can be no demonstrative arguments to prove, that those instances, of which we have had no experience, resemble those, of which we have had experience. We can at least conceive of a change in the course of nature; which sufficiently proves, that such a change is not absolutely impossible.[8] . . . We have no reason to draw any inference concerning any object beyond those of which we have had experience.[9]

These comments apply equally to inferences that something is probable and are explicitly extended to them by Broad when he says, "Now it is quite certain that, if my *only* premise is, 'I have observed N ϕ's, and 100% of them are ψ,' there is no valid form of argument by which I can either prove or render probable the conjecture that 100% of the ϕ's in nature are ψ."[10] Thus the doubt whether any number of cases are adequate evidence for the truth of a conclusion p has grown into a doubt whether they are ever adequate even to render it probable.

And even though some number of cases could make it probable, we can still be uncertain that it is probable, since our source of uncertainty shifts to a doubt very similar to (2) above: the doubt whether any particular number of cases observed is sufficient. If one can doubt whether N cases make p certain, one can obviously doubt whether they make it probable. For example, do five cases of illness after sweet wine make it probable that the next instance of wine drinking will have such a sequel? Or does one need more cases to assure this? Suppose ten more cases were not so followed. Then we should be inclined to say our first five cases were insufficient to infer a probability. But if after our first five, fifty more cases were so followed, we should not know exactly what to say about our previous limited evidence. And no matter what number we mentioned, a question could be raised to throw the inference in doubt. Can we ever know that our evidence is sufficient to warrant "it is probable that p"?

One further uncertainty about the conclusions of inductive arguments, which infects those of ordinary deductions as well, I wish to mention briefly but without elaboration, since it can be interpreted as an uncertainty about a special sort of inductive inference and its special features are not relevant in this paper. This uncertainty concerns, on the face of it, not the validity of inferring a conclusion from premises, but the premises themselves. According to Reichenbach, no premises about physical objects or events could be certain, and hence nothing inferred from them could be. Only propositions of logic or about one's immediate experience are beyond doubt true. It is never absolutely certain, for example, that there is a die before me when I see it, feel it, bet upon it.[11] Sensory observations is subject to all sorts of error, and for that matter we may not even be sure that what our senses reveal is other than the material of dreams or hallucinations. Error lies, not in any judgment recording one's immediate experience, but in the inference one makes from it to the existence of a counterpart in the real world. Thus the evidential premise of an ordinary induction is in the position of an inductive conclusion from immediate experience. Any doubt about it will therefore be but a special case of doubt about inductive conclusions in general. Clearly Broad's skeptical doubt could be rephrased, as follows, so as to apply to inferences from immediate experience: Can one's immediate experiences, any number of them, ever make an evidential premise probable? This question has special features which give it an even more academic character than the similar question about inductions made from premises about physical objects and events. In fact one would not in ordinary circumstances raise the question whether it was *ever* certain a die was before one, let alone the question whether this was probable. The first kind of question I tried to deal with in my paper in *The Philosophy of G. E. Moore,*[12] treating it along lines developed by John Wisdom and Morris Lazerowitz. In this paper I shall ignore the special features of skepticism with respect to the senses and confine consideration to the general question: Given that we *know* premises which we take as evidence, can they or *any conceivable* premises make our conclusion probable?

This is but a variation on the old problem, "Can inductive inference be justified?" It is not, however, my intention here to attempt a solution of this problem in the form of a detailed philosophical theory to the effect that probable inference can, or cannot, be justified. The questions I should like to answer are quite different, questions which might properly be characterized as "metaphilosophical": Why is there the philosophical problem of justifying such inferences? Is there any genuine problem? The latter question is of fundamental importance. In practice the necessity of justifying every inference, no matter how assured, never presents itself as a problem. Actuaries of insurance companies, after settling the question whether the statistical evidence warrants their probability judgment, would be shocked at the question whether any statistical information could ever justify any such judgment. In calling attention to such a fact, it is not merely that I want to suggest that inductive inference needs no justification, as I think it does not—for this is simply to contradict those who feel it does—but that I want to see if the philosophical problem will disappear when one sees how those who have attempted to solve it have conceived it. In what follows I shall take it that attempted justifications of inductive inference, even though in fact directed toward securing that the inference of p be legitimate, are equally relevant to securing the legitimacy of the inference "p is probable." I have already indicated how doubts about the one can be or have been extended to the other, and I shall therefore treat attempts made so far to eliminate these doubts as directed toward securing a probability rather than a certainty.

As one looks through various attempts at justifying inductive inference in general, say those of Mill, Russell, Broad, it becomes clear what it is supposed justification would be like. This is that we should be able to know that p is probable, given that we know such facts as:

    (1) that ϕ and ψ have always been associated

or

    (2) that ϕ and ψ have been associated in a certain proportion of cases.

Quite a number of different kinds of inference have premises answering to these two general descriptions. From premises of type (1) we infer such conclusions as:

It is probable that illness always follows large quantities of drink.

It is probable that illness will follow drink in the next instance.

And from premises of type (2) such conclusions as:

It is probable that continued throws of a penny will maintain for heads the observed proportion ½.

The probability of lipoid pneumonia being fatal in this particular case is 9/10.

In connection with such conclusions philosophers have admitted the force of Hume's criticisms. But then, being convinced that nevertheless they are sometimes justified in drawing inferences of this sort, they have gone on to seek the justification. Attempts they have made indicate that what they seek is some means whereby inductive inferences may be made *logically valid in form,* such that the premises *entail* the conclusion "*p* is probable." This would satisfy the condition that the conclusion be known once the premises are known.

Mill, Russell, and Broad have all, ostensibly, conceived their task to be that of supplying to the inference a premise to be conjoined with the empirical facts about concomitances, from which the conclusion follows. Mill, for example, writes: ". . . every induction is a syllogism with the major premise suppressed; or (as I prefer expressing it) every induction may be thrown into the form of a syllogism by supplying a major premise."[13] What is to be supplied, he says, "is an assumption involved in every case of induction," and this is "our warrant for all inferences from experience."[14] Russell holds that "All arguments which, on the basis of experience, argue as to the future or the unexperienced parts of the past or present assume the inductive principle. If the principle is unsound, we have no reason to expect the sun to rise tomorrow, to expect bread to be more nourishing than a stone, or to expect that if we throw ourselves off the roof we shall fall. All our conduct is based upon associations which have worked in the past, and which we therefore regard as likely to work in the future; and this likelihood is dependent for its validity upon the inductive principle."[15] Broad, although he is unable to say precisely what premise conjoined with "I have observed N ϕ's and 100% of them are ψ" would justify him in conjecturing that 100% of the ϕ's in nature are ψ, is in agreement that there must be some premise which does this.

The premise which Russell adjoins to the observational evidence, and which as regards unexamined cases he says "alone can justify any inference from what has been examined to what has not yet been examined,"[16] is as follows:

(a) The greater the number of cases in which a thing of the sort A has been found associated with a thing of the sort B, the more probable it is (if no cases of failure of association are known) that A is always associated with B.

(b) Under the same circumstances a sufficient number of cases of the association of A with B will make it nearly certain that A is always associated with B.[17]

This is the so-called "inductive principle," as it applies to the probability of a general law. As I understand Russell, he takes this principle to play the role of a premise in every induction we make about universal concomitances. In order to exhibit this I set out the following inference, in which I make explicit every premise supposedly used in arriving at the conclusion "p is probable." For this purpose I need only part (b) of the inductive principle, and in particular a weakened form of it which I shall designate as (α):

(α) Under similar circumstances a sufficient number of cases of B accompanying A will make it probable that B always accompanies A.

(β) Under similar circumstances a sufficient number of cases of dry leaves burning when lit will make it probable that they always burn when lit.

(γ) In the past dry leaves when lit have burned a hundred times without exception.

(δ) A hundred cases with no exceptions are sufficient to make it probable that dry leaves when lit always burn.

Therefore, it is probable that dry leaves when lit always burn.

In practice when we infer such a conclusion as this we pass directly to it from (γ). But it will be admitted that (δ), to the effect that we have enough cases to render our conclusion probable, is implicit in this passage. Russell seemingly wants to hold that without (β)'s being true we could not assert (δ). That is, unless there is such a thing as a number of similar cases being sufficient to make it probable that dry leaves burn, no number mentioned would tend in the slightest to do this. (α), as we see, is simply the *form* of this general premise (β), and we must have it if we are ever to have a general premise for any other argument than this one.

As this example indicates, I have taken it that according to Russell finding a justification for an inductive inference consists in finding the premises necessary to make it logically valid, that is, in supplying enough premises to throw it into the form of a deduction. Among these are the inductive principle, and its special instance (β). It will be recalled that those who suppose inductive inference requires justification demand it shall be such that one can *know* the conclusion "p is probable." A simple step to securing this is to exhibit it as the conclusion of premises which are such that if they are certain the conclusion is also. Any deduction satisfies this condition. But this is not sufficient. If the conclusion is to be known, then the premises must be also. And, curiously enough, this according to Russell is precisely what is impossible. The inductive principle, premise (α), he says is "incapable of being proved by an appeal to experience"; "we can never use experience to prove the inductive principle without begging the question."[18] Hence we must simply accept it "or forgo all justification of our expectations about the future."[19] Now it is clear that if a particular inductive conclusion is in doubt *only because* it is doubtful whether any number of cases renders any proposition probable, then one does not justify the conclusion by *assuming* that they do. Nothing is gained by using as a premise what is in doubt. For if one is to establish the conclusion one must know the premises are true. Expressing an inductive argument in the form of a deductive one by supplying the requisite premises thus provides a spurious kind of comfort.

Further, a closer examination of the sequence of propositions, (α), (β), (γ), (δ), makes it very puzzling what function Russell expected (α), or (β), to serve in establishing the conclusion "p is probable." For this conclusion follows from (γ) and (δ) without the help of anything further. In addition (α), and its special case (β), appear to be singularly empty tautologies. (β), for example, states that a sufficient number of cases of dry leaves burning when lit will make it probable they always do. The natural question is "sufficient for what?" and the natural answer is given in the following paraphrase of (β):

> If the number of cases of dry leaves burning when lit is sufficient to *make it probable* that they always burn, then it is probable that they do.

(α) permits of a similar paraphrase. It is clear that the addition of these necessary propositions to (γ) and (δ) will in no way help to deduce the conclusion. In fact as the use of truth-tables shows, the conjunction of a necessary proposition p with any contingent proposition q, or set of such, will have no more deductive fertility than the contingent proposition alone: $p.q. = .q$. So giving our inductive argument a deductive form can not in this case be described as consisting in the addition of premises ((α) and (β)) without which the conclusion could not be inferred. On the basis of this account, the relevance, let alone the importance, of the inductive principle in a particular inference is very doubtful.

I think some account of this principle remains to be given.[20] I have pointed out that neither (α) nor (β) is a proposition with the help of which the conclusion is deduced. That is, their role is not like that of the general premise of a syllogism, *e.g.*, "All men are mortal," without which the conclusion "Socrates is mortal," can not be inferred. Suppose now for purposes of comparison with our inductive inference we conjoin to the familiar syllogism the proposition

(θ) If all men are mortal and Socrates is a man, then Socrates is mortal

and that to this we add

(ω) If all a is b and x is a, then x is b.

The adjunction of (θ) and (ω) to the premises of the syllogism is of no help in deducing "Socrates is mortal"; the premises alone are sufficient for this. (θ) and (ω) are both necessary, and hence could not help establish an empirical conclusion. However, the fact that (θ) is necessary is the same as the fact that "Socrates is mortal" may be deduced from the two given premises. And the fact that (ω) is necessary is what is meant by saying this syllogistic argument is valid in virtue of its form. (θ) and (ω) are not premises, but *rules* according to which deductions are made, (ω) being the general rule of which (θ) is the special instance.

Now there is some analogy between the role of (ω) and the role of (α), the inductive principle. If we put (α) in the form

If for some specified number N, N cases of association of A and B occur and if these are sufficient, then it is probable that A and B are always associated,

it appears, not as a premise, but as giving the *form* of the inference

(γ) Dry leaves when lit have burned one hundred times without exception.

(δ) One hundred cases are sufficient.

Therefore, it is probable dry leaves always burn when lit.

A similar thing was pointed out by Whiteley in his paper in *Analysis*,[21] where he maintained that the inductive principle expresses the form common to particular inductive arguments. Unless the form is valid, the particular inductive argument cannot be. The same, of course, characterizes (ω), the form of the syllogistic argument cited. The difference is that whereas everyone would grant that (ω) is the rule according to which "Socrates is mortal" is validly deduced from its premises, it is not as clear, and philosophers such as Broad are ready to challenge, whether (α) is the rule according to which inductive conclusions are inferred. For one thing, the hypothesis of (α), "If for some number N, N cases . . . are sufficient, implies the possibility of *some* number of cases being sufficient, by itself, to render a proposition probable." And this is what Broad denies.

Of course (α), as stated, is undeniable: If some number N of cases occur and are sufficient to make p probable, then p is probable. It can, however, be restated so as to free it of its trivial appearance. In the following form (α) does not look as certainly, nor as trivially, tautologous:

A *sufficient number* of cases of association of A and B make it probable A and B are always associated.

"A sufficient number" seems to denote any of a sequence of numbers having a lower limit, so that (α) might be replaced by:

Some number of cases of association of A and B makes it probable they are always associated.

Here we have the proposition which Broad claims is certainly false, since according to him it is insufficient for making any proposition probable *merely* that there should be N cases of association without exception. Yet one feels inclined to agree with Lewy that in accordance with the English usage of the word "probable" this is a necessary proposition, so that to assert the observational premises of certain inductions and deny that the conclusions is probable is a self-contradiction.[22] "Some number of cases makes p probable" looks to be strictly analogous to the necessary proposition, "Some number multiplied by 2 equals 14." These two propositions can be instructively compared. The function on which the latter is constructed, namely, "$x \times 2 = 14$," is such that it has a necessarily true value, "$7 \times 2 = 14$." Is it similarly the case for the function "x cases make p probable"? If it is, and if in the inductive inference we have used as an example, 100 is a value rendering it tautologous, then our premise (δ), that one hundred cases are sufficient to make it probable that dry leaves always burn when lit, plays no role in deducing the conclusion. This can be deduced from (γ) alone, that dry leaves when lit have been found to burn one hundred times without exception. "One hundred cases make it probable that dry leaves always burn" would not be needed for passing from (γ) to the conclusion any more than "All squares are four-sided" is needed in passing from "This is a square" to "This is four-sided." A necessary proposition, to reiterate what was said before, can never be a *premise* with the help of which an empirical conclusion is deduced. But of course if a given proposition of the form "x cases make p probable" is necessary, then the conclusion "p is probable" follows necessarily from the empirical evidence. And our necessary proposition functions as a rule according to which we deduce it.

Now it is quite obvious that whatever the analogy between "Some number of cases makes p probable" and "Some number multiplied by 2 equals 14," the lack of analogy is equally obvious, and it is this which vitiates Lewy's contention against Broad. The function "$x \times 2 = 14$" has but one tautologous value, whereas "x cases make p probable," if it has any tautologous values, will have many—all those from some number N on. And the difficulty is that we do not know at precisely what point the function becomes tautologous, if it does so. This is merely another way of putting the uncertainty expressed in the question, "How can one know the number of observed cases is sufficient?" One knows by inspection precisely when one has found the value which makes "$x \times 2 = 14$" necessary. But one does not know by inspection whether the empirical evidence entails "it is probable that p."

It is doubtless this fact which is responsible for the feeling that inductive inference needs justifying. Usually this justification has been conceived as a matter of supplying, not a validating rule, but some general empirical premise. At least there is some problem about induction which supplying this is supposed to solve. This problem is, I believe, not "How can any number of cases render anything probable?" but some other problem which, even though solved, would leave the question about cases unanswered. I shall try to support this claim in what follows, for this is not the accepted view about what is gained by supplying a general premise about the constitution of nature. Broad, for example, holds that in order to know a conclusion of the form *"p* is probable" it is necessary that we know some premise of this sort. In general his view is that inductive arguments all involve a premise to the effect that there is in nature constant causal determination and something like "loading" in favor of one alternative rather than another, and that in order for this to be the case nature must answer to the principle of limited variety.[23] Very roughly this principle is that nature is not infinitely complex—that every object and event analyzes into a limited number of elements and hence that a limited amount of variety is possible from combinations of these elements. Again very roughly, what would be secured if the general empirical premise were true is that nature obeys simple causal laws.

Now my thesis is that this concern that nature obey simple casual laws is a concern that it be possible for us to make inductive inferences at all, not that it be possible to *know,* once the conditions for making an inference are satisfied, that any given probable conclusion is validly inferred. That is, there are two questions, "What would justify us in making inductive inferences, *i.e.,* what would make it possible to do this?" and "What would justify, in the sense of 'validate,' the conclusion '*p* is probable'?" Broad has, I think, answered the first question while supposing himself to have answered the second. He makes a premise about nature a requisite for deducing the conclusion, whence we could not know "*p* is probable" without knowing this premise. I want to consider briefly what the consequences are if the premise about nature is false. I am not certain, but I believe that if nature is not of such-and-such a constitution inductive inference would not be possible. And in this case we should have no problem of validating an inductive conclusion. The problem as to what validates an inductive conclusion can arise only if it is possible for inductive inferences to be made.

From a number of statements about nature which have been cited as premises of inductive inference I shall select a few typical ones and see what their falsity entails. Usually, to put it vaguely, it has been held that nature must be uniform, that the law of universal causation must operate. Now, it is not sufficient that the law that every event has a cause and similar causes have similar effects hold. As Russell said, "it is not the reign of law but the reign of *simple* laws which is required."[24] But now for what is it not sufficient, for what is the reign of *simple* laws required? Both Venn and Keynes have provided an answer which supports my contention that the premise about nature which is being sought is one which assures the *possibility* of making inductions. Keynes says[25] that if every configuration of the universe were subject to a separate and independent law and if every difference in bodies led to their obeying different laws—in other words, if it were false that nature is under the reign of simple laws—it would still be the case that nature was uniform and causation sovereign; but prediction would be impossible. If inductions are to be made at all, nature must not be like this. Nor must it be such that though every event is causally determined no causal law has more than one instance in the history of the universe. As Venn points out,[26] induction could not take place in such a world either. Here the reason we should not be justified in inferring "*p* is probable" would simply be that we could not start to make any inference. We should not have any observational premise about repeated concomitances.

The point is clearer if we consider the consequences of falsifying the premise Mill cited as being a warrant for every induction. According to Mill it is a necessary condition for proving any inductive conclusion that nature be uniform. By the uniformity of nature he meant that there are in nature such things as parallel cases —that it is sometimes the case that what is true of one instance of ϕ is true of all instances. In other words, some generalizations hold in nature, or there are uniformities in nature. Let us suppose there are no uniformities in nature, simple or otherwise. In this event two situations are possible: (1) that no characteristic occurs with any other in accordance with any law—that is, that there are no constant conjunctions of any characteristics, but that each occurs with absolutely any other; (2) that there are some repeated concomitances and sequences but that their repetition is not universal. In the first case we clearly have a suspension of the principle of limited variety. In such a world the amount of possible variety would be unlimited. In fact there could not even be what Broad has characterized as "natural kinds"—groupings of characters which constitute such recurrent entities as humans, horses, trees, etc. Were a malignant demon to scramble up such a world, it would be one in which no inductions could be made. For one thing, there would not be human beings to make them. In fact it is doubtful whether what is being described here is even a conceivable situation. As Isaiah Berlin points out,[27] in the extreme case where no character ever occurred more than once, we should have no general terms to refer to it, and such a chaos could not even be talked about let alone inferred from.

However, the case is different if there are some repetitions of sequences or characters, even for relatively short periods of time. Suppose that for some centuries there has been that constant conjunction of characters which constitutes mankind, and that other conjunctions of characters are repeated for a couple of generations. Is inductive inference possible? First of all, if we *knew* it to be false that there were any universal conjunctions we should of course never say it was probable that ϕ and ψ were always associated. However, if it were false that there were uniformities, but because there were some repetitions and recurrences it was not *known* to be false, we could and would still make probable inferences. We should have the same kind of evidence which we now have, the sort expressed in premise (γ), namely, in one hundred cases without exception dry leaves when lit have been found to burn. What we do in establishing the probability of a special uniformity is to make an inference from observed repetitions. Of course if our ancestors told us that things had been different in their day we should be uncertain whether it was probable the next instance of ϕ would be ψ or that all future instances of ϕ would be ψ. And if ϕ and ψ were never observed in conjunction again we should not say it was probable ϕ would be associated with ψ in the next instance. In fact after a time we should most likely say it was improbable.

Exactly how much repetition there must be before we draw probable inferences I do not know, but certainly in a world where there was very little we could not draw them. For we should lack the observational premise, *e.g.*, "One thousand cases have been found without exception . . . etc." And we should need this for inference regardless of what other premise might be needed. The point I am trying to make here is that the question as to what nature must be like before we are justified in making any inductions at all, *i.e.*, what it must be like to have proper observational premises, is different from the question whether, given the observational premises, we are justified in drawing a conclusion from them.

I want to return now to this latter question. The fact that philosophers feel that there is a problem here shows some sort of dissatisfaction. To say what this dissatisfaction is, when we in fact do not for a moment feel uncertain that, for example, the sun will rise again and the springtime come, is to answer *our* question, Why is there the philosophical problem of induction? It seems to me this is a question which ought to be asked. For this need of justifying inductive conclusions never is felt in any ordinary circumstances. Our behavior shows this: We are willing to bet that 1, 2, 3, or 4 will come up on a fair die, as against 6. We never become fearful that the laws of nature will be suspended, so that we hesitate to plant a garden on the grounds that the sun may never shine again. And yet, despite this, we feel challenged by the question, "Are you warranted in supposing it probable the sun will shine again?" as we are by the question, "Are you warranted in supposing it probable that virus *A* is responsible for the illness of all these guinea pigs?"

Certain linguistic analogies between questions and doubts philosophers express, and questions and doubts of the scientist or ordinary man are, I think, responsible for our feeling the challenge. Either the questions and doubts give vent to some dissatisfaction or they positively create it. It is clear that the request that a scientist justify a particular inductive conclusion and the request that inductive conclusions in general be justified bear at least a verbal analogy to each other. And the doubt expressed in "She loved you today and yesterday, but have you any good reason to suppose that she will love you tomorrow?" is analogous in the same way to the seeming doubt expressed in "Yesterday, and for many years before that, things which were dropped fell; but have you any good reason to suppose the law of gravitation will continue to operate tomorrow?"

Further, there is close enough analogy between inductive inferences and deductive ones that questions whether an inference is warranted seem to be such as could be settled. In a deduction it is always possible, even though sometimes difficult, to determine whether a conclusion is validly drawn. And when it is, it is a misuse of language, *i.e.,* self-contradictory, to assert the premises and deny the conclusion. The linguistic pattern of inductive arguments is very similar to that of deductive ones, and there are some cases in which it definitely seems a misuse of language to assert that a conjunction has been repeatedly observed and then to deny the probability of its occurring in a fresh instance. One would feel that a person who said "I have known thousands of cases, and no exceptions, of people being burnt when they touched a hot stove, but it is not probable that I shall be burnt the next time I do it," or "The penny has come up heads a million times straight, and never tails, but it is not probable the penny is unfair," was somehow misusing language—that he didn't know the use of the word "probable," and was saying something self-contradictory.

Now despite all these analogies there are equally obvious lacks of analogy. To ignore these is to fail to see that questions and doubts which the skeptic has about induction are but pantomimes of questions and doubts which are genuine. For example, to ask of a scientist whether his evidence is sufficient to warrant a particular inductive conclusion is to ask a useful question to which certain procedures he commonly engages in are relevant by way of answer. Should he be made unsure by the question, he will reconsider his evidence, and, if satisfied, will reiterate his probability judgment, and, if not, will experiment further. By further tests he could, for example, increase or decrease the probability that a particular virus induced illness in his guinea pigs, or he might even disestablish the probability judgment previously arrived at. But now the question, "Are any empirical facts evidence for any conclusion 'p is probable'?" is not one to which any testing procedure is relevant. Nor is it useful to ask it. For it does not create a doubt which in any way affects our behavior.[28] We don't become uncertain, in virtue of *this* question, of the conclusion of which we were certain.

However, the skeptic's comment, "You must admit that the fact that a law has operated in the past is thin reason for expecting it to continue," manages somehow to be convincing. The main reason for this I believe to be the following: Despite the fact that some inductive arguments closely parallel deductive ones, so very many do not. The skeptic's emphasis on the lack of parallel makes us intellectually uncomfortable even with regard to those inferences we previously felt sure of. For example, we all feel that there would be something peculiar in saying "I have a million favorable cases and no unfavorable ones, but still p is not probable." This seems to be a misuse of language. But even here we are not as sure there is an entailment relation between the observational premise and the conclusion "p is probable" as we are in the case of deductions which are valid in virtue of their form. This uncertainty I believe arises from the fact that we can think of innumerable cases where one doesn't know whether to say the inductive conclusion follows or not. Suppose that one hundred cases of my drinking coffee at night were followed by sleeplessness, and that this did entail the probability of my spending a sleepless night next time, would fifty cases entail it, or twenty-five, or ten? There is no way whatever of deciding this. And the indecision about the special inference spreads to all inference, despite the obvious lack of analogy, already cited, between the genuine question, "Have I sufficient evidence to warrant this inference?" and the question, "Have I ever sufficient evidence to warrant any inference?"

It is one of the features of a philosophic problem that we feel puzzlement and yet not of a kind which in any way alters our behavior. Here we have an instance. In practice we do not doubt that we are in general justified in making inductive inferences—though we all grant that sometimes we are not; and yet certain considerations produce an academic dissatisfaction with inductive inference in general which makes us try to justify it. This justification is conceived as a matter of finding a means whereby, being certain of the observational premise, we can be certain that p is probable. I want to say that the remedy for the dissatisfaction we are made to feel about inductive inference is misconceived. If this can be shown then it will be clear why there is the philosophical problem about inductive inference. I shall begin by tracing the dissatisfaction and the attempt to allay it.[29]

Let us begin by comparing ourselves with an imaginary tribe of beings who are unwilling to call any proposition probable unless supported by a million cases. Such beings would doubtless complain over seldom being able to establish any probability. But would their situation be like our own? Consider the following inference. From this we shall see how dissimilar our situation is, and why the dissatisfaction, which made Broad say no number of cases by itself could make p probable:

> Three cases of drinking coffee at night were followed by sleeplessness.
> Therefore, it is probable that drinking coffee at night is always so accompanied.

Now suppose coffee was drunk at night fifty more times without any unpleasant sequel. This would make us say that our first three cases were insufficient to establish the probability of coffee's causing sleeplessness, that is, that it is false that the observational premise implies the conclusion. It might then be argued that if three cases wouldn't necessitate p's probability, would seven, or eight, or ten? Can one case ever make the difference between the implication's being false and its being necessary? And even though we agreed with Lewy that some number of cases would make the implication necessary, and even agreed on some particular numbers which did this, we should soon find ourselves in the position of being unable to decide, as we diminished the number of cases, the precise point at which the implication became nonnecessary. It is an impressive fact that on substituting consecutive values in the function *"x cases makes p probable"* we derive a numerically ordered sequence of propositions with regard to which there is no reason for saying any one is necessary and its immediate predecessor is not. Apparently Broad is so impressed by this fact that he is willing to deny that any of them is necessary, which is to deny that any number of cases make *p* probable. We are in a much worse position, seemingly, than the people who must find a million supporting cases before they can infer a probability. We do not know exactly how many cases we need. The skeptic makes us feel that we should. In these circumstances it is natural to conceive our task as *finding* either a premise to conjoin with the evidence from which *"p* is probable" would follow, or a rule which inductive inference must conform to if valid. I have tried to argue that what is being sought is a rule or rules, since a premise about nature secures something else.

Now what would such rules do? Clearly what they do in deductions—provide criteria for determining whether the arguments are correct. This means providing exact criteria for the use of the word "probable," *criteria fixed by the number of cases,* such that from a definite number of cases it can be known that *"p* is probable" follows. If such were found we should know which values of *x* in *"x cases make p probable"* yielded something necessary. Whenever the premise involved one of these numerical values we should know it entailed the conclusion just as we know that "this is square" entails "this is four-sided" because we know "all squares are four-sided" is necessary.

Finding such rules would certainly provide us criteria for correct inference. But now where should one look for them? Let us consider what Aristotle did in formulating rules for valid deduction. He examined arguments accepted as correct and derived the rules from them. What is the case with inductive inference? Here, even in those instances when no one doubts that the conclusion is warranted, inspection doesn't yield the rule it conforms to. Now a rule is merely the abstract form of a class of inferences already accepted as correct. But if no rule is found in the inferences themselves, is there a rule? Aren't these our only source for the discovery of rules? If examination yields no rules then our inability to find them is simply due to there not being any. This is, I think, what is not seen by those who demand some justification for induction. They conceive justification as consisting in finding what is hidden, and that if one fails no inference can be known to be valid.

The dissatisfaction with inductive inference which prompts the quest for a hidden principle which justifies it arises from the following commonplace: that instead of certainty that "*p* is probable" follows from the empirical facts, in case after case there is indecision. One does not know whether the evidence is sufficient, nor how to test whether the evidence is sufficient. If we look at the English usage of the word "probable," we see that "Some number of cases makes *p* probable" does give the appropriate context for probability statements; that is, it is a sort of rule for the use of the word "probable." But it does not tell us specifically with *what number* of cases we may use the word. It provides no exact rule, no rule that specifies the precise minimal number of cases from which "it is probable that *p*" *follows*. The complaint is that an inexact rule is no better than no rule at all.

It thus turns out that the apparent dissatisfaction with not being able to find rules is in reality a dissatisfaction with the linguistic fact that there are no exact rules. The philosopher's complaint is quite unlike that of the people who find it difficult to establish a probability because they required for this a million cases. Their language contains a definite rule for saying when a proposition is probable. The philosopher's complaint is that ours does not. We do not know at what precise point a given proposition becomes probable, for in our language this has not been decided. That is, we have no fixed criteria in our language for saying whether an inductive argument is correct. The pair "probable," "not probable" are vague in much the same way "rich" and "poor" are. When a man has only a penny to his name and when he has a million dollars we are certain of the application of the terms "rich" and "poor." But for a whole set of values in between we do not know what to call him. And it is this fact that makes it tempting to argue that no man could be rich since the difference between being rich, poor, or any state in between, could not be in the having or lacking one penny. It seems that there should be some sharp dividing line between these states, some point at which it is proper to apply the one term and not the other. Similarly with the term "probable." For a whole middle range of values of x in "If x cases . . . occur, then p is probable" we do not know whether it follows that p is probable or not. To know this requires knowing which values when substituted in the function yield something necessary, and this has not been decided. Nevertheless it seems that there should be some point at which the function becomes necessary, before which it is not.

There *should* be such a point—that expresses exactly the dissatisfaction about inductive inference. The complaint that we do not in given cases know whether we can validly infer that p is probable appeared to be the complaint that we had *found* no rules to which valid inductive inference conformed. The remedy of this situation would be had when these were found. But this puts the philosopher's dissatisfaction in a misleading way: as though it were over the inability to find rules rather than over the lack of them. The fact is that nothing is hidden. If to justify induction we must look for rules according to which one correctly deduces "p is probable," we are looking for what does not exist. But if the feeling that induction needs justifying is merely the feeling that there *should be* rules of this sort, then the means of remedying the lack is not to be described as finding them, but as making them. To ask that the criteria for the word "probable" be more exact than they are, that there be a sharp line between correct and incorrect inductions as there is amongst deductions—this is a way of urging that exact rules be made up in such a manner that in being certain of the observational statement we can be certain of "probably p." This is, of course, to urge a modification of our language. And to do this is to express a dissatisfaction with it. Here I think we have our answer to the question, "Why is there a problem of justifying inductive inference?"

I cannot here go into whether this urge to modify the language so as to remedy what appear to be its inadequacies is justified. But I will point out that if we try to eradicate the vagueness of the word "probable" we should most likely want hundreds of rules, and all of them would appear quite arbitrarily formulated. For example, we could make it a rule that fifty or more cases of dry leaves burning when lit made it probable they always would burn, and that twenty-five or more cases of sleeplessness following coffee at night made it probable it always would follow. And so on. We should want a rule for each inference. And in no case would there seem to be any special reason for accepting the rule. Why should twenty-four or forty-nine cases be insufficient—why should an inference from these not be necessary while an inference from twenty-five or fifty cases would be? Undoubtedly if such rules were accepted philosophers would find them the source of a new problem. Their complaint would in these circumstances be against the excessive sharpness of the word "probable" instead of its excessive vagueness. The new dissatisfaction would arise from the *arbitrariness* of the rules rather than the lack of them.

It would seem that the word "probable," like the word "rich," is for the purposes of ordinary life as sharply defined as we want it; and even philosophers have shown no real interest in sharpening the criteria for its application else they would have tried to still their dissatisfaction by the only means open to them, namely, by specifying such criteria. All this indicates that present usage is satisfactory, otherwise we should have what we do not now have, precise criteria fixed by the number of cases. Once this is admitted, the need to justify probable inference disappears. At this point we have returned to the common-sense position.

This paper originally appeared in *The Journal of Philosophy*, Vol. XLIV, No. 10 (May 8, 1947) and is reprinted with permission.

1. Bertrand Russell, *Problems of Philosophy*, p. 94.
2. Russell, *op. cit.*, pp. 94–95.
3. *Ibid.*, pp. 98–99.
4. *Ibid.*, p. 96.
5. *Ibid.*, p. 101.
6. *Ibid.*, p. 96.
7. *Ibid.*
8. David Hume, *Selections* (Scribner ed.), p. 35.
9. *Ibid.*, p. 43.
10. C. D. Broad, "Mechanical and Teleological Causation," *Proceedings of the Aristotelian Society*, Supplementary Vol. XIV, p. 89.
11. Hans Reichenbach, *Experience and Prediction*, p. 331.
12. *The Library of Living Philosophers*, Vol. IV.
13. John Stuart Mill, *Logic*, Bk. III, Chap. 3, p. 224.
14. *Ibid.*, p. 223.
15. Russell, *op. cit.*, pp. 106–07.
16. *Ibid.*, p. 106.
17. *Ibid.*, p. 104.
18. *Ibid.*, p. 106.
19. *Ibid.*
20. What follows by way of analysis of it I owe in large part to discussions with M. Lazerowitz.

21. M. Whiteley, "On the Justification of Induction," *Analysis,* Vol. 7 (1940), p. 69.

22. C. Lewy, "The Justification of Induction," *Analysis,* Vol. 6 (1939), pp. 89–90.

23. C. D. Broad, "The Principles of Problematic Induction," *Proceedings of the Aristotelian Society,* Vol. 28, p. 45.

24. Bertrand Russell, *Analysis of Matter,* p. 232.

25. John Maynard Keynes, *A Treatise on Probability,* p. 249.

26. J. Venn, *Empirical Logic,* pp. 96–97.

27. Isaiah Berlin, "Induction and Hypothesis," *Proceedings of the Aristotelian Society,* Supplementary Vol. XVI, p. 99.

28. See M. Lazerowitz, "Moore's Paradox," in *The Philosophy of G. E. Moore,* for a discussion of the academic character of a similar philosophical doubt; also John Wisdom, "Philosophical Perplexity," *Proceedings of the Aristotelian Society,* Vol. XXXVII, pp. 78–79.

29. In this I am indebted to discussions I have had with M. Lazerowitz.

MAX BLACK

Definition, Presupposition and Assertion

1

Whenever I speak of "definition" in this essay, I shall mean an explanation of the uses of some word or expression. In one case to be considered, the definition is a way of teaching somebody how to use the *definiendum;* in another the intention is to give an explicit description or analysis of the meaning of some word or expression with whose uses one is already familiar.

When logicians speak of the definition of a term, they usually have in mind analysis or description of that term's connotation. A characteristic statement is "To define a term is to state its connotation, or to enumerate the attributes it implies. Thus we define a parallelogram as a quadrilateral figure whose sides are parallel."[1] In this type of definition, we are supposed to "state" the connotation by successively dividing an inclusive genus into progressively narrower subspecies. Such a definition provides a necessary and sufficient condition for the application of the term: thus a thing is properly called a parallelogram if and only if that thing is a quadrilateral figure and also has parallel sides. Another way of putting the matter is that the things to which the term applies (*i.e.*, its extension) constitute a sharply delineated class: everything that exists must be either wholly inside the class of parallelograms or wholly outside it. The necessary and sufficient criterion for application of the term "parallelogram" provides a conclusive test for membership in the extension of that term, *i.e.*, for membership in the corresponding class.

It is no accident that favorite examples of this traditional type of definition *per genus et differentiam* are drawn from mathematics. For in a calculus such definitions are often practicable and useful. Because the terms of such a calculus are "uninterpreted," the rules connecting them can be as clear-cut as the rules of chess. But as soon as we pass from "pure" to "applied" mathematics, it is hard to find a single accurate and useful definition of the traditional type. The kind of definition that consists in giving the connotation of a term in the form of a necessary and sufficient condition determining a class, far from being normal or customary, is something exceptional and remarkable.

Consider the problems that arise in defining the meaning of a name for some breed of animal. Suppose we had to explain the meaning of the word "dachshund" to somebody not already acquainted with those agreeable little beasts or with the name applied to them. It is unlikely that a dictionary definition like "one of a German breed of small hounds with a long body and very short legs" would be satisfactory. For a man who had mastered this definition could hardly be expected to recognize a dachshund when he met one. At first sight, a basset hound may resemble a dachshund, and the dictionary definition of the former as "a long-bodied short-legged dog resembling a dachshund but larger and heavier" will not help us much in distinguishing between an oversized dachshund and an undersized basset.

Somebody might be inclined to say that the dictionary definitions are simply poor as definitions and that sufficient ingenuity would provide a satisfactory definition of the traditional type. But if we really wanted to teach the use of the word, a more fruitful procedure would surely be the *exhibition of specimens;* this is how all of us in fact learn to use words like "dachshund," "spaniel," or "bulldog." A successful explanation of this kind will usually require the presentation of a wide range of variation in the specimens, in order to diminish the risk that adventitious common features might be supposed significant. On the other hand, it will be unwise to exhibit abnormal or exceptional specimens; the object is to have an extensive range of variation grouped around some *clear cases*.[2]

The "clear cases" may themselves show considerable variation. The learner may be shown a wire-haired or a smooth dachshund or, again, dachshunds of various colors, all of them being presented as equally good "clear cases."

Part of such a definition of the word "dachshund" might take the following form: "This dog and that one and that one are *clear cases* of a dachshund. This one is very nearly a clear case, but has such and such a deviation. This other one is still further removed from being a perfectly clear case. And this one is a borderline specimen and could be called a dachshund or a basset indifferently." The specimens by means of which the meaning of the label "dachshund" is explained are presented in an *order*, determined by the degree of deviation from one or more specimens that are introduced as typical or "clear cases."

Such exhibition of specimens is usually intended to result in the knowledge of *criteria* for application of the word "dachshund," for otherwise the learner will find it hard to apply the label to new cases.[3] However, the demand for a *necessary* and *sufficient* criterion is too exacting.

All kinds of features are relevant to the claim that a particular dog is a dachshund—its length, weight, the texture and color of its coat, the relative proportion of its legs to the rest of its body, and so on. If *all* these features are within certain ranges of variation, we have a typical dachshund (a "clear case"); if any of them are outside the corresponding range of variation, the animal falls short, in that respect, of complete conformity to the type. No one of these criteria is by itself necessary, nor is any of them sufficient, and the same is true of any simple conjunctive or disjunctive combination of the criteria. The animals we call "dachshunds" have no common "attribute," and there is, strictly speaking, no class of dachshunds. Instead of a sharp boundary between dachshunds and other animals, we have what has been called a "borderline region"—a kind of no-man's land where deviation from typical specimens of the breed is so great that the question whether given animals belong to the breed is no longer determinate. But there is no sharp line between the "borderline region" and the field of clear application.

It is customary to represent the relation of a class of things to the rest of the universe by a circle or some other closed curve. Points inside the circle and on its circumference represent members of the class in question, while points outside the circle represent things excluded from that class. The fact that every point in the diagram is either inside or outside the circle accurately reflects the conception of a class as determined by a strict dichotomy.

For a spatial representation of the mutual relations of the things referred to by a word like "dachshund," we may think of the way in which a mountain range gradually merges into the plains to which it descends. The summits may be taken to correspond to the typical or "clear" cases, while the region where the mountain eventually becomes indistinguishable from the surrounding plains represents the "borderline region." The corresponding geometrical diagram will be a *surface*. Among the many forms which such a surface might take, the case of a "tableland" or "mesa" with precipitous bounding faces will correspond to the special case of a *class term*. I propose to say that the individual dachshunds constitute a *range*, rather than a class, of instances.

It might be thought that the reason there is no necessary and sufficient criterion for the application of the word "dachshund" is its imprecise use by laymen who lack the specialized knowledge needed for the substitution of a more precise word. But the more detailed specifications formulated by breeders reveal essentially the same logical situation. In place of my vague references to length, weight, and so on (which betrayed my own ignorance of the breed in question) we find more detailed instructions concerning the traits and features that must be displayed by a satisfactory specimen of the breed. These criteria, however, are still very numerous, admit of variation in the degree to which they are met, and no simple conjunctive or disjunctive combination[4] of them is both necessary and sufficient. Nor is this due to ineptitude on the part of breeders and dog fanciers. The quest for a definition *per genus et differentiam* would be futile in view of the purposes the definition has to serve. The flexibility of even the technical use of the breed name is demanded by the complexity and variability of the phenomena to be described. Absence of a necessary and sufficient criterion is not a symptom of inadequacy of the language, but accurately reflects the complexity and continuous variability of the subject matter to which the language refers.

The nonexistence of rigidly demarcated classes is not a special and peculiar by-product of canine promiscuity. If we examine instances of the application of any biological term, we shall find ranges, not classes—specimens arranged according to the degree of their variation from certain typical or "clear" cases. And the same is true, so far as I can see, of all the familiar terms of the arts and crafts, of law, politics, education, and aesthetics. Nor are the technical terms of philosophy different in this respect. Variability of joint criteria of application, the existence of ranges, not classes, of instances seems to me to be the rule, not the exception.

According to the account I have been giving, "range definition," as I propose to call it, requires the exhibition or delineation of one or more typical, or "clear" cases. Such cases I propose to call *"paradigms."* The traits or features or properties that vary from instance to instance, and are described in what I have been calling the "criteria" for application of the term, I shall call *"constitutive factors."* I have already proposed that the things to which the term is applied be called a "range"; it will be convenient to say that a word whose instances constitute a range is a *"range word."*

Range words may sometimes be combined to provide what at first sight appears to be a traditional classificatory definition. For a suitable hearer, "bitch" might be simply defined as "female dog." Since both "dog" and "female" are range terms, their combination determines a range also, not a class. The definition tells us, very roughly, how to combine the criteria used in identifying the two ranges, in such a way as to provide criteria for the subrange "bitch." (We notice, however, that if A is a criterion for "dog" and B a criterion for "female," the conjunction AB is not necessarily a criterion—or a criterion with the same "weight"—for "bitch." For the nature and relative importance of the criteria by which sex is determined vary with different species of animals.)

A formal range definition of a word W might take the following form: (a) one or more paradigms, P_1, P_2, P_3, . . . P_m are presented or described, (b) a set of constitutive factors, F_1, F_2, F_3, . . . F_m, all capable of variation and all present in one or other of the paradigms, are indicated or described, (c) rules are formulated for determining how variations in the constitutive factors determine the degree of "distance" from the various paradigms.

This is an idealized description of what would usually be regarded as a satisfactory range definition. In actual practice, we are content with something less precise. Not all the relevant constitutive factors will be explicitly symbolized or described; nor will it usually be possible to give very exact instructions for arranging instances in the order of their distance from the paradigms. In short, the expression "range definition" is itself a range term.[5]

I hope the example of the word "dachshund" will have sufficiently indicated what I would accept as a clear case of a range definition.

2

When we teach a man the meaning of the word "dachshund," we take it for granted that he has a good deal of elementary but relevant knowledge about the behavior of dogs and other animals. For example, we expect him to know that the traits of an animal vary continuously during its lifetime—that leopards do not change their spots, and lions never change into tigers. So far as I can see, no *reference* to such approximate constancy of traits is part of the meaning of the word "dachshund" or other breed names. Yet this fact about the continuity of traits plays an important part in determining the application of the range term "dachshund," as the following considerations will show.

Consider what we should say if a dog that satisfied all the tests for being a clear case of a dachshund were gradually to change until it were indistinguishable from a poodle, and then back again until it looked exactly like a dachshund! Should we feel justified in continuing to call it a dachshund? And should we be speaking correctly if we did? If I am right in thinking that reference to the continuity and constancy of traits is not part of the meaning of "dachshund," we can hardly regard this queer kind of dog as a "borderline case." Our dachshund-poodle or poodle-dachshund still exemplifies in eminent degree all the constitutive factors we have in mind in using the word "dachshund"; and the case is unlike that of a deformed puppy or "sport," deviating so far from the "clear cases" as to fall within the penumbra of vagueness. If we forget its curious history, we have an animal that ought to rank as an excellent specimen of the breed. Nevertheless, I think we should be right to refuse to apply the word "dachshund" in this type of case.[6]

The uses of the word "dachshund" were taught to us on the assumption that the fantastic case I have just been describing never happens. And if such a case were to happen, the correct verdict would be that no provision was made for it in the original process of definition. It would be wrong to say of such an extraordinary freak, "This is a dachshund," and equally wrong to say, "This is *not* a dachshund"—unless the negative statement was used to mean that the word "dachshund" had no application to the situation. (Of course, a man might say, "This *is* a dachshund," in an attempt to enforce a change in the meaning of the word, but I am excluding this type of case.)

The correct judgment would be that such a freak, not having been considered when the definition was framed, falls on that account *outside the jurisdiction* of the definition. The question whether or not such an extraordinary object is a dachshund *does not arise,* because anybody who uses the term "dachshund" according to the usual definition is committed to taking for granted that such extraordinary cases do not occur. (It would be rather odd to say that we normally *believe* in the absence of such aberrant cases, since we very likely have not considered the question. But *if* the question were put, it would be answered unhesitatingly.)

Suppose I bet a dollar that a certain coin will show heads after being flipped into the air, *i.e.,* promise to pay a dollar if it shows tails, in consideration of receiving a dollar if it shows heads. We can imagine that, by some extraordinary chance, the coin in question lands and remains *on edge.* Is either party then obligated to pay any sum? Clearly not. This type of case was not considered in the framing of the conditions regulating the bet. The terms of the wager were framed upon the supposition that the coin would show either heads or tails upon landing. If the coin lands on its edge, or is swallowed by some hungry bird, or explodes in mid-air, or suffers one of the other fantastic and unlikely mischances that were too absurd to have been discussed when we made the bet— why then the bet "is off," as we say. The terms of the wager become null and void, for failure of one of the suppositions whose truth had been taken for granted. It has long been recognized that bets, promises, commands, and other such linguistic acts may depend upon suppositions, in the sense that they become "null and void" if those suppositions prove false. It has not been so clearly recognized that definitions also may become null and void for precisely similar reasons. The example I have given provides a case of this kind, I believe, in which the form of words "This is a dachshund" fails to have a good use, not because it contains a nonsense word like "Snark," and not on account of overt or concealed contradiction, and not, finally, because the instance in question is a borderline specimen. The expression "This is a dachshund" fails to have a predetermined use because the case in question violates one of the conditions determining the kind of case in which either that expression or its logical negation is properly applicable.

The example I have been using was one in which the assumption or supposition upon which the definition was based took the form of a claim about a certain regularity of occurrence in the constitutive factors (the physical traits of a dachshund). The following example illustrates the case of a supposition concerning relations between two or more of the constitutive factors.

In diagnosing a disease, a physician will pay attention both to the observable condition of the patient's body (his temperature, pulse rate, and so on) and to the feelings of pain or discomfort reported by the patient. Features of the conditions of the patient's body and features of his experiences are constitutive factors of such a term as "scarlet fever." Consider now the predicament of a physician who finds a patient exhibiting all the *outward* symptoms of an acute case of scarlet fever, while professing to feel in perfect health. The doctor might be inclined to cry out, incredulously, "This kind of thing just doesn't happen!"—as indeed it does not. And this is one reason why it is a case outside the scope of the name "scarlet fever." It would be wrong to say the patient had scarlet fever, and wrong to say he did not have scarlet fever—just as wrong as to answer the question "Have you stopped beating your mother?" either in the affirmative or in the negative.

Part of the medical definition of scarlet fever might be put in the form: "Scarlet fever is shown by the presence of such and such feelings, and such and such bodily manifestations, *the two occurring together*." Here the words "the two occurring together" express what I have been calling a "supposition" of the definition —the assumption violated in the instance I have conjured up.

Consider, for a last example, the case of a student of theology who believes that there is a Being who is omnipotent *because* he is omniscient. And let us suppose that he gives the name "God" to this Being, so that the definition of that word as he uses it is "the Being who is omnipotent because omniscient." Such a man would believe, I am supposing, that omniscience necessarily confers omnipotence and that omnipotence is impossible without omniscience. He would, therefore, use omniscience or omnipotence indifferently as criteria for application of the word "God." Now let us suppose that further studies led the theologian to revise his original belief by substituting for it the belief that there was a Being who was omniscient but not, however, omnipotent. This discovery might easily appear as a logical contradiction. Qua omniscient, the Being whose existence has now been discovered should be called "God," but qua nonomnipotent he is not "God." However, there is no contradiction. The situation is that a supposition for the use of the name "God" (*viz.*, that a Being who is omniscient will necessarily also be omnipotent) has here been abandoned, and the name no longer has its original use. Whenever a supposition as to the correlation of constitutive factors is falsified, a self-contradiction will seem to result. This appearance is produced by an effort to apply a word in its original meaning to a case outside the scope of that meaning.

Normally, the "suppositions" involved in a range definition are not explicitly stated. When they are accepted by both parties, it is unnecessary to allude to them, and only the new stipulations needed for the definition are stated in so many words. But if the suppositions were explicitly formulated, they would naturally be expressed in a kind of *preamble*. Such an explicit definition would then have the form: "Whereas such and such is the case, therefore the word *W* shall be applied in such and such ways." Here the first clause ("Whereas such and such is the case") is what I have called the preamble.

The proposition expressed by the preamble and any logical consequences of that proposition I propose to call, from now on, *presuppositions* of the word in question. Thus it is a presupposition of the word "dachshund" that breed characters are approximately constant; it is a presupposition of the name "scarlet fever" that the condition of a patient's body is correlated with that patient's feelings; it was a presupposition of the term "God," in the use described, that any Being who was omniscient would be omnipotent. It will be noticed that, according to the above definition, a presupposition of a word is always a proposition, *i.e.*, something that is true or false—and not itself a word.

Of course, the relation expressed by the words "Whereas . . . therefore," is quite different from the relations of material implication or entailment. The words following "Whereas," *i.e.*, the "preamble," express a practical consideration or reason for framing the definition as we do. The definition does not *follow* from the presuppositions of the word defined, nor do the presuppositions follow from the definition.

Though I introduced the foregoing analysis by referring to a case in which a word, "dachshund," was supposed to need explanation for the benefit of somebody unacquainted with its meaning, I have gradually shifted to talking about definitions describing the meaning of a name such as "scarlet fever" or "God" whose use is already known. Indeed, the distinctions proposed will apply just as well to the latter type of case as to the former. In the case of any range word whose use we know, say the word "happiness," we may ask such questions as: "What would be paradigms (or clear cases) of happiness?" By what criteria do we judge the relative degrees of deviation from these paradigms?" How are these criteria related?" "What are the presuppositions of the word *happiness?*" In the case of a word like "happiness," the answers to such questions as these might be said—at any rate by some philosophers—to constitute an analysis rather than a definition. But this distinction is unimportant for the present discussion.

Questions may arise as to the meaning of whole sentences, as well as the words composing such sentences; and some words are of such a character that their meaning can be explained only by reference to the meaning of sentences in which those words can occur. Our account can be easily adapted to apply to sentences, as as well as to words. The "ranges" will now be ranges of situations, rather than things. By the presuppositions of a sentence will be meant a proposition expressed by the "preamble" of an explanation of the meaning of that sentence and all the logical consequences of that proposition. If a presupposition of a word W is falsified, it becomes impossible to say, of the instance falsifying it, either that it is W or that it is not W. Similarly, if a presupposition of a sentence is falsified in a given situation, it becomes impossible in that situation either to say that the sentence expresses a true proposition or that it does not; the question of truth or falsity simply fails to arise.

Some of the presuppositions of a sentence are sometimes shown by explicit symbolic devices. Thus among the presuppositions of the sentence "Napoleon met the Czar of Russia" the propositions *that somebody called "Napoleon" once existed, that there is a country called "Russia," that Russia had one and only one Czar,* and so on. Of these presuppositions, the last is explicitly symbolized by the occurrence of a descriptive phrase of the form "the so and so."[7]

In criticizing a particular philosophical argument, it may be more important to examine the presuppositions of the terms used than to try to refute the considerations advanced in support of the conclusion. Indeed, if the preferred terminology of the author is accepted by the critic, there may remain little scope for radical disagreement about the position in question. Consider, for instance, the difference between arguing about logical topics (a) in terms of "*L*-truth," (b) in terms of "warranted assertibility." Can this be one reason why philosophers so often complain that their critics have failed to understand them?[8]

In order to simplify the discussion, I have sometimes spoken as if the words, expressions, and sentences used for illustration had the same meaning for all their users, so that we might properly speak of "*the* definition" or "*the* analysis" of *the* meaning of the words in question. Of course, the true situation is usually more complicated. Even a relatively unambiguous word like "dachshund" will be used by different speakers at the same time, or by the same speaker at different times, in divergent senses.

When different users of the word succeed in defining a term according to the pattern I have been describing, any divergences in their uses will result in divergences between the various definitions. These may take a number of alternative forms. There may be disagreement about the choice of paradigms, or about the nature of the relevant constitutive factors, or about the rules determining the contribution of the factors to the ordering of specimens with regard to the paradigms, or finally with regard to the choice of presuppositions of the word or sentence in question. In order to have a determinate answer to the question "What is the definition of the word *W*?" we must specify *what usage* of the word *W* we have in mind. Conversely, a range definition is a way of rendering more specific one use among many of the word in question.

3

I want now to use the foregoing theory in trying to become clearer about the notion of "assertion." The word "assertion," and the related and equally troublesome word "proposition," are constantly used by philosophers, but it is not clear what is meant, or intended to be meant, by either word.

The technical term "assert" is connected with the more inclusive layman's word "say." To assert something is to *say* something, in one use of the elusive term "say." I propose, therefore, to begin by making some obvious distinctions in the meaning of the latter word.

When a man says that fish are mammals, he may be doing one of four things:

(i) He may simply be uttering a set of noises which we should recognize as an instance of the sentence, "Fish are mammals," without necessarily even understanding what he is saying. In this sense of "say," a man might say, "Fish are mammals," in his sleep, and a foreigner can say that fish are mammals without knowing the meaning of a single English word. A parrot might say the same thing, and perhaps even a phonograph. (For the sake of simplicity, I shall neglect, throughout this essay, the case of *written* discourse.)

(ii) A man may pronounce the words, "Fish are mammals," as in (i) above and also understand what the words mean (*i.e.*, mean something *by* them) and yet not be using the sentence to make an assertion. If a student has said, in class, "It is my opinion that fish are mammals," the lecturer may echo part of his remark, saying, with the same intonation and expression, "Fish are mammals. Let us consider this." Unlike the student, he is not *claiming* that fish are mammals. Or a man may practice a speech he has promised to make by saying aloud, with the intonation and expression appropriate to an assertion, the words "All men are equal!" Not until he actually makes the speech will he *claim* that all men are equal. An actor in a play understands what he says, but he is not taken by the audience to be claiming that anything is really the case. (All examples in the following discussion will be *declarative* sentences, but parallel distinctions could be made for commands, requests, questions, prayers, and other forms of speech. A man can utter the words "Open the door" without giving a command; he may utter the words "Is Pakistan a sovereign state?" without asking a question.)

(iii) Sometimes a man may utter the sentence "Fish are mammals" while disbelieving what he says, in order to deceive his hearers. He is then making a truth claim, though of course lying. It is customary to say of such a case as this that the speaker *asserts* that fish are mammals, whether he is lying or speaking truthfully.

(iv) Finally, men often make statements seriously, in good faith, knowing or believing what they say, or, at any rate, not disbelieving it. In such a case as this, I shall say the speaker *honestly asserts* that fish are mammals.

In talking about a man "saying" something, we may mean either that he is merely pronouncing a form of words, or uttering them with understanding, or making a truth claim by their means, or finally, making an honest assertion. Here we have four progressively narrower senses of "saying." I want to consider, in more detail, what we mean by an *honest* assertion. And for this purpose I shall begin by describing a paradigm for the application of the sentence, "Tom honestly asserted that it had begun to rain."

The following simple train of events would certainly justify us in saying that Tom had honestly asserted it had begun to rain:

> Mary, sitting with her back to the window, asks Tom, "How is the weather now?" Tom walks over to the window, draws the curtain, sees that rain is falling, and says, "It has begun to rain."

This is as clear and unproblematic a case of honest assertion as we can hope to find. But if we now try to analyze what we *mean* by calling it a case of honest assertion and begin by listing all the factors in the domestic episode that might plausibly be taken to be relevant, we may well be surprised at the number and variety of factors resulting. We shall certainly have to include, besides the mere pronouncing of the words in question, the speaker's linguistic background and knowledge of the particular setting. And these in turn can be broken down into a surprisingly large number of factors.

At the risk of being pedantic, we might obtain some such list as the following:

> (1) Tom pronounced the words, "It has begun to rain," (2) which were words belonging to the English language, (3) making up a complete sentence, (4) indeed a declarative sentence, (5) whose meaning he understood. (6) Those words meant that it had begun to rain, (7) and it had begun to rain. (8) Another person, Mary, was present, (9) who had asked Tom a question, (10) to which his remark was an answer. (11) The speaker, Tom, remembered the question, (12) knew that his hearer, Mary, was in the room, (13) believed that Mary could hear him, (14) intended to use the words "It has begun to rain," (15) intended them to mean what they usually mean, (16) intended to be heard, (17) believed that it had begun to rain, (18) intended his words to be understood, (19) in the sense in which he used them, (20) and intended to be believed.

One might be reluctant to believe that all these listed factors could be relevant to the truth claim we make when we say that

Tom honestly asserted it had begun to rain. For example, some people might say that the prior question addressed to the speaker was merely a cause or reason for his assertion, and no part of what we mean when we say that he made the assertion in question. I am far from wanting to argue that an honest assertion must always be preceded by a question to which it is an answer. But *if* such a question has been asked, it is then relevant to our verdict that a subsequent assertion *has* been made.

Suppose, for example, that after Mary had asked, "How is the weather now?" Tom, walking over to the window as before, says, "Tomorrow is Tuesday." The fact that what he said was *not* an answer to the preceding question would make it appear doubtful that he *was* honestly asserting anything. His hearer would naturally suppose that he could not have heard the question right, or that he was joking or indulging in a piece of silly mystification. Or consider a case in which two men have been walking in the rain for a good hour after the rain has started, and one of them then turns to the other, saying, "It has begun to rain." The hearer would not know what to make of this remark—its inappropriateness to the general context would lead him to question whether anything could have been honestly asserted. He would fail to understand what had been said, in one important sense of "understand," though in another sense of "understand" he would understand perfectly well the meaning of the words used.

I hope enough has been said to indicate, at least in outline, how I would go about trying to show that a great many factors were relevant to the claim that Tom had honestly asserted that it had begun to rain.

So far we have been talking about a single, relatively determinate, situation and the features of the situation that are relevant to the claim that an honest assertion has been made. If, however, we say, "Tom honestly asserted that it had begun to rain," without specifying any particular context of utterance, any one of a wide range of situations would justify our claim. Tom might not have used just those words, "It has begun to rain," but some other sentence; he might have used the single word "Rain!" and not a sentence at all; might have made the corresponding remark in French or some other language; or might simply have used some prearranged signal or gesture. No preceding question need have been asked; the speaker might have made a mistake in supposing somebody was present or that he could have been heard; indeed nobody but the speaker need have been present. The speaker might not have intended to say anything, but found himself blurting out the words; might have been telling the truth while knowing it would inevitably deceive his hearer; and so on, through a whole gamut of variations.

This is how I would try to show that none of the relevant factors *is necessary* for there to be a situation which we should want to describe as one in which Tom honestly asserted that it had begun to rain. However, I do not wish to overemphasize the variety of these situations. My chief contention is that these various, yet related, situations can be organized in terms of their deviation from central cases or "paradigms."

It may be objected that I have not *proved* there is no necessary and sufficient factor present in all cases of honest assertion that it has begun to rain. But if anybody thinks there *is* such an invariable index of honest assertion, he may be challenged to describe it. There is, of course, a certain conventional way of pronouncing a sentence—an "assertive tone of voice," as we might say—which we often use as a reliable sign that something has been asserted. But a man can assert that it has begun to rain without using words at all, and hence without using an assertive tone of voice. On the other hand, one may say, "The boojum is a snark," in an assertive tone of voice and be making no assertion whatever.

The attempt to find a necessary and sufficient factor in a supposed characteristic attitude on the part of the speaker is equally doomed to failure. Suppose somebody said, "To assert that it has begun to rain is to pronounce the words, 'It has begun to rain,' or some sign having the same meaning, in an assertive tone of voice and *with intention*. The speaker has to intend or 'mean' what he says. To assert honestly is to assert while believing what one is asserting." The chief difficulty about this objection to the view I am advocating is that "intending," like all other psychological words, is itself what I have previously called a range word. The word refers not to a class of cases having a common identifiable character, but to a whole spectrum of instances related to one another by gradually shifting criteria.

A clear case of intending to say, "It has begun to rain," would be the following. Our old friends, Tom and Mary, have quarreled so violently that they have not spoken to one another for several days. Now Tom wants to heal the breach and says to himself, "The very first time Mary asks a question, I intend to answer it." Then

Mary asks, "How is the weather now?" and the action proceeds as before.

Here is a clear case of intention, a paradigm. Tom has considered the matter, formulated a prior resolution, and has carried that resolution into effect. But now suppose somebody simply asks me, in a more normal situation, what the weather is. I would probably reply, "It has begun to rain," without taking any particular thought and certainly without needing to screw my resolution to the sticking point. Here there is nothing, over and above my honestly making the assertion, that could properly be called my *intending* to make the assertion. I simply said what I did, and the fact that I did say it in the circumstances in question is a proof that I "intended" to say it, in the peculiar sense of "intended" that is relevant. We do not usually say that a child who alters the position of a chess piece on a chessboard, but knows nothing about the purpose or the rules of the game of chess, has "really" made a move. But when an experienced chess player is playing a game, his making *exactly the same maneuver* as the child counts as a move. There is no reason to believe that each move in a game of chess is accompanied by a specific attitude or intention on the part of the player who makes the move. Similarly, given certain surrounding circumstances, the proof that a man made an assertion may be that he simply pronounced certain words; and whether or not he had any concomitant mental attitude may be irrelevant.

I want to consider now some of the presuppositions governing the usage of the expression "honestly asserts." Examination of the factors relevant to the correct application of the sentence, "Tom asserted that it had begun to rain," would show that these factors could be roughly separated into three groups. In the first group we can put whatever the speaker finally *did, i.e.,* in this case his pronouncing the words in question in an assertive tone of voice. Let us call this his *performance*. In the second group let us put all factors which refer to the speaker's feelings, memories, intentions, at the time of his performance, insofar as they are relevant. Let us call these factors, collectively, the speaker's *mental state*. (This is not a very happy term, but I think its meaning here will be sufficiently understood.) Finally, let us lump together everything else, relevant to the claim that Tom asserted it had begun to rain, by calling the remaining factors, collectively, the *context*. The context of our original paradigm included, *e.g.,*

Tom's having been asked a question, the fact that it was raining, and so on.

Now while the speaker's performance, his mental state, and the context are all relevant to the claim that he honestly made a certain assertion, I think we commonly expect there to be certain causal connections between them. We normally suppose that if a man pronounces the words, "It is raining now," in an assertive tone of voice, and in the context previously described, that is a sufficient sign that he is in the corresponding mental state. It would seem pointless in this familiar type of case to require additional evidence that he has the beliefs, intentions, purposes, and so on, which would be appropriate; his performance in that context is excellent evidence that he is in the requisite mental state. Only in abnormal cases where the performance is very remote from our paradigms, or the context is of a character with which we are unfamiliar, do we find it necessary to inquire into the speaker's mental state. Only in such atypical cases do we find it necessary to ask questions like "What was he trying to say?" "What could he have had in mind?" "What could he have supposed to be the case?" "What was his purpose?"—all directed toward elucidating what I have called the speaker's "state of mind."

One general presupposition of the term "honestly assert" accordingly takes the form, "Given such and such a context, the speaker's performance will signify that he is in such and such a mental state." Accordingly the criteria we use in central and typical cases have reference mainly to performance and context, and not to the mental state that is supposed to be correlated with them.[9]

So far, I have been discussing the meaning of the term *"honestly* assert." I have chosen to do this rather than to begin by considering the term "assert," because I think assertion can easily be explained in terms of honest assertion, while the reverse is not the case. A speaker who asserts, but does not honestly assert, what he says, is lying. He is *pretending* to make an honest assertion in a case in which he disbelieves what he is saying. If we understand what it is to make an honest assertion and what it is to pretend to do something, we can derive a sufficiently clear notion of what it is to make a show of honestly asserting, that is to say, what it is to lie. On the other hand, the expression "honest assertion" does suggest that "honest assertion" stands for a subrange of a wider range of situations called "assertion." If this suggestion were correct, it ought to be possible *first* to describe a range of situations that are what we would want to call assertions (whether honest or dishonest) and then to select from these a subrange to which we give the name "honest assertion." This, however, seems to me to be an inversion of the proper order of definition of the two terms. I cannot see how to describe what we mean when we talk about cases of lying except by saying something like, "Lying occurs when a man tries to give the illusion that he is telling the truth, *i.e.,* that he is honestly asserting something." If this is correct, we need to understand what it is to speak truthfully before we can understand what it is to lie; we must define "honestly assert" before we can define "assert."

We do, in fact, learn to understand language in our infancy because adults begin by telling the truth to us, however much they may afterward use language for deception. A society in which parents constantly lied to their children from the outset, and in unpredictable ways, would be one in which, so far as I could see, it would be logically impossible for the next generation to learn the language. The connection between the words, the environment, and the normal human purposes of the speakers would be destroyed, and for those newcomers to the society who had no previous memories of truthtelling to fall back upon, the words they heard could have no meaning.

From Max Black, *Problems of Analysis* (Ithaca, Cornell University Press, 1954). Reprinted with permission of publisher.

1. J. E. Creighton and H. R. Smart, *An Introductory Logic* (New York, 1932), p. 81.

2. Occasionally it might seem more natural to speak of "normal," "standard," "central," "perfect," or "ideal" specimens. I shall not consider the different varieties of definition that some of these words suggest. I shall use "typical case," throughout, as a synonym for "clear case."

3. By a "criterion" I mean a test which can be used in determining whether the word in question should be rightly applied to a given specimen. Such a test will normally mention some character (or "constitutive factor" as we shall later call it) that the specimen is required to have. Thus, one criterion for the application of the word "dachshund" is that the specimen be within a given size range. In the case of some relatively simple words, however, it would be inappropriate to speak of criteria. It seems impossible to formulate any criterion for the use of the word "mauve" or other color words.

4. It may be that *some* complex truth function of the desired characters will prove roughly adequate. But such a combination of characters will hardly answer to the demands of the traditional classificatory definition, nor will it include any indication of the relative "weight" of the factors.

5. The only previous discussion I have been able to find of something approximating this kind of definition is in J. N. Keynes's *Formal Logic* (Cambridge, 1928): "Men form classes out of vaguely recognized resemblances long before they are able to give an intensive definition of the class-name, and in such a case if they are asked to explain their use of the name, their reply will be to enumerate typical examples of the class. This would no doubt ordinarily be done in an unscientific manner, but it would be possible to work it out scientifically. The extensive definition of a name will take the form: *X is the name of the class of which* Q_1, Q_2, . . . , Q_n *are typical*. This primitive form of definition may also be called *definition by type*" (p. 34). L. S. Stebbing objects to this: "It may, however, be doubted whether the giving of typical examples can be rightly regarded as a process of defining" (*A Modern Introduction to Logic* [London, 1930], p. 422).

Cf. also the following statement: "The conformity of an individual to the type of a particular species depends on the fulfillment of an infinity of correlated peculiarities, structural and functional, many of which, so far as we can see (like keenness of scent and the property of perspiring through the tongue in dogs), have no connection one with another. There may be deviations from the type, to a greater or less degree, in endless directions; and we cannot fix by any hard-and-fast rule the amount of deviation consistent with their being of that species, nor can we enumerate all the points, of function or structure, that in reality enter into the determination of things of a kind. Hence for definition, such as we have it in geometry, we must substitute classification; and for the demonstration of properties, the discovery of laws" (H. W. B. Joseph, *Introduction to Logic* [2d ed.; Oxford, 1925], p. 103).

6. But contrast Locke's discussion of monsters in Bk. III, chap. vi, sec. 27, of the *Essay*. Also Leibniz' *New Essays Concerning the Human Understanding,* Bk. III, chap. vi (*e.g.,* p. 344 of the Open Court edition).

7. *Cf.* P. F. Strawson, "On Referring," *Mind,* Vol. 59 (1950): pp. 320–344, and especially p. 330.

8. It is instructive to read in this connection Royce's article, "On Definitions and Debates" in *Journal of Philosophy,* Vol. 9 (1912), reprinted in *Royce's Logical Essays,* ed. D. S. Robinson (Dubuque, Iowa, 1951). The American Philosophical Association had set up a distinguished "Committee on Definitions" to fix the terms of a general discussion, "The Relation of Consciousness and Object in Sense Perception." Royce argues, in persuasive and sometimes amusing detail, that the definitions chosen all presuppose that a "complex of physical qualities" could be "given in some particular perception." Since Royce, like many other philosophers, could not accept this presupposition, it became impossible for him to participate in the discussion.

9. When this presupposition is violated we get paradoxical utterances, as in the case of a man who says something of the form "*p*, but I don't believe it."

RUDOLF CARNAP

Meaning and Synonymy
in Natural Languages

1. *Meaning Analysis in Pragmatics and Semantics*

The analysis of meanings of expressions occurs in two fundamentally different forms. The first belongs to *pragmatics,* that is, the empirical investigation of historically given *natural languages.* This kind of analysis has long been carried out by linguists and philosophers, especially analytic philosophers. The second form was developed only recently in the field of symbolic logic; this form belongs to *semantics* (here understood in the sense of pure semantics, while descriptive semantics may be regarded as part of pragmatics), that is, the study of constructed *language systems* given by their rules.

The theory of the relations between a language—either a natural language or a language system—and what language is about may be divided into two parts which I call the theory of extension and the theory of intension, respectively.[1] The first deals with concepts like denoting, naming, extension, truth, and related ones. (For example, the word "blau" in German, and likewise the predicate "B" in a symbolic language system if a rule assigns to it the same meaning, denote any object that is blue; its extension is the class of all blue objects; "der Mond" is a name of the moon; the sentence "der Mond ist blau" is true if and only if the moon is blue.) The theory of intension deals with concepts like intension, synonymy, analyticity, and related ones; for our present discussion let us call them *"intension concepts."* (I use "intension" as a technical term for the meaning of an expression or, more specifically, for its designative meaning component; see below. For example, the intension of "blau" in German is the property of being blue; two predicates are synonymous if and only if they have the same intension; a sentence is analytic if it is true by virtue of the intensions of the expressions occurring in it.)

From a systematic point of view, the description of a language may well begin with the theory of intension and then build the theory of extension on its basis. By learning the theory of intension of language, say German, we learn the intensions of the words and phrases and finally of the sentences. Thus the theory of intension of a given language L enables us to understand the sentences of L. On the other hand, we can apply the concepts of the theory of extension of L only if we have, in addition to the knowledge of the theory of intension of L, also sufficient empirical knowledge of the relevant facts. For example, in order to ascertain whether a German word denotes a given object, one must first understand the word, that is, know what is its intension, in other words, know the general condition which an object must fulfill in order to be denoted by this word; and secondly he must investigate the object in question in order to see whether it fulfills the condition or not. On the other hand, if a linguist makes an empirical investigation of a language not previously described, he finds out first that certain objects are denoted by a given word, and later he determines the intension of the word.

Nobody doubts that the pragmatical investigation of natural languages is of greatest importance for an understanding both of the behavior of individuals and of the character and development of whole cultures. On the other hand, I believe with the majority of logicians today that for the special purpose of the development of logic the construction and semantical investigation of language systems is more important. But also for the logician a study of pragmatics may be useful. If he wishes to find out an efficient form for a language system to be used, say, in a branch of empirical science, he might find fruitful suggestions by a study of the natural development of the language of scientists and even of the everyday language. Many of the concepts used today in pure semantics were indeed suggested by corresponding pragmatical concepts which had been used for natural languages by philosophers or linguists, though usually without exact definitions. Those semantical concepts were, in a sense, intended as explicata for the corresponding pragmatical concepts.

In the case of the semantical intension concepts there is an additional motivation for studying the corresponding pragmatical concepts. The reason is that some of the objections raised against these semantical concepts concern, not so much any particular proposed explication, but the question of the very existence of the alleged explicanda. Especially *Quine's* criticism does not concern the formal correctness of the definitions in pure semantics; rather, he doubts whether there are any clear and fruitful corresponding pragmatical concepts which could serve as explicanda. That is the reason why he demands that these pragmatical concepts be shown to be scientifically legitimate by stating empirical, behavioristic criteria for them. If I understand him correctly, he believes that, without this pragmatical substructure, the semantical intension concepts, even if formally correct, are arbitrary and without purpose. I do not think that a semantical concept, in order to be fruitful, must necessarily possess a prior pragmatical counterpart. It is theoretically possible to demonstrate its fruitfulness through its application in the further development of language systems. But this is a slow process. If for a given semantical concept there is already a familiar, though somewhat vague, corresponding pragmatical concept and if we are able to clarify the latter by describing an operational procedure for its application, then this may indeed be a simpler way for refuting the objections and furnish a practical justification at once for both concepts.

The purpose of this paper is to clarify the nature of the pragmatical concept of intension in natural languages and to outline a behavioristic, operational procedure for it. This will give a practical vindication for the semantical intension concepts; ways for defining them, especially analyticity, I have shown in a previous paper.[2] By way of introduction I shall first (in §2) discuss briefly the pragmatical concepts of denotation and extension; it seems to be generally agreed that they are scientifically legitimate.

2. *The Determination of Extensions*

We take as example the German language. We imagine that a linguist who does not know anything about this language sets out to study it by observing the linguistic behavior of German-speaking people. More specifically, he studies the German language as used by a given person Karl at a given time. For simplicity, we restrict the discussion in this paper mainly to predicates applicable to observable things, like "blau" and "Hund." It is generally agreed that, on the basis of spontaneous or elicited utterances of a person, the linguist can ascertain whether or not the person is willing to apply a given predicate to a given thing, in other words, whether the predicate denotes the given thing for the person. By collecting results of this kind, the linguist can determine first, the extension of the predicate "Hund" within a given region for Karl, that is, the class of the things to which Karl is willing to apply the predicate, second, the extension of the contradictory, that is, the class of those things for which Karl denies the application of "Hund," and, third, the intermediate class of those things for which Karl is not willing either to affirm or to deny the predicate. The size of the third class indicates the degree of vagueness of the predicate "Hund," if we disregard for simplicity the effect of Karl's ignorance about relevant facts. For certain predicates, *e.g.,* "Mensch," this third class is relatively very small; the degree of their extensional vagueness is low. On the basis of the determination of the three classes for the predicate "Hund" within the investigated region, the linguist may make a hypothesis concerning the responses of Karl to things outside of that region, and maybe even a hypothesis concerning the total extension in the universe. The latter hypothesis cannot, of course, be completely verified, but every single instance of it can in principle be tested. On the other hand, it is also generally agreed that this determination of extension involves uncertainty and possible error. But since this holds for all concepts of empirical science, nobody regards this fact as a sufficient reason for rejecting the concepts of the theory of extension. The sources of uncertainty are chiefly the following: first, the linguist's acceptance of the result that a given thing is denoted by "Hund" for Karl may be erroneous, *e.g.,* due to a misunderstanding or a factual error of Karl's; and, second, the generalization to things which he has not tested suffers, of course, from the uncertainty of all inductive inference.

3. *The Determination of Intensions*

The purpose of this paper is to defend the thesis that the analysis of intension for a natural language is a scientific procedure, methodologically just as sound as the analysis of extension. To many linguists and philosophers this thesis will appear as a truism. However, some contemporary philosophers, especially Quine[3] and White[4] believe that the pragmatical intention concepts are foggy, mysterious, and not really understandable, and that so far no explications for them have been given. They believe further that, if an explication for one of these concepts is found, it will at best be in the form of a concept of degree. They acknowledge the good scientific status of the pragmatical concepts of the theory of extension. They emphasize that their objection against the intension concepts is based on a point of principle and not on the generally recognized facts of the technical difficulty of linguistic investigations, the inductive uncertainty, and the vagueness of the words of ordinary language. I shall therefore leave aside in my discussion these difficulties, especially the two mentioned at the end of the last section. Thus the question is this: *Granted that the linguist can determine the extension of a given predicate, how can he go beyond this and determine also its intension?*

The technical term "intension," which I use here instead of the ambiguous word "meaning," is meant to apply only to the cognitive or designative meaning component. I shall not try to define this component. It was mentioned earlier that determination of truth presupposes knowledge of meaning (in addition to knowledge of facts); now, cognitive meaning may be roughly characterized as that meaning component which is relevant for the determination of truth. The noncognitive meaning components, although irrelevant for questions of truth and logic, may still be very important for the psychological effect of a sentence on a listener, *e.g.,* by emphasis, emotional associations, motivational effects.

It must certainly be admitted that the pragmatical determination of intensions involves a new step and therefore a new methodological problem. Let us assume that two linguists, investigating the language of Karl, have reached complete agreement in the determination of the extension of a given predicate in a given region. This means that they agree for every thing in this region, whether or not the predicate in question denotes it for Karl or not. As long as only these results are given, no matter how large the region is—you may take it, fictitiously, as the whole world, if you like—it is still possible for the linguists to ascribe to the predicate different intensions. For there are more than one and possibly infinitely many properties whose extension within the given region is just the extension determined for the predicate.

Here we come to the core of the controversy. It concerns the nature of a linguist's assignment of one of these properties to the predicate as its intension. This assignment may be made explicit by an entry in the German-English dictionary, conjoining the German predicate with an English phrase. The linguist declares hereby the German predicate to be synonymous with the English phrase. The *intensionalist thesis* in pragmatics, which I am defending, says that the assignment of an intension is an empirical hypothesis which, like any other hypothesis in linguistics, can be tested by observations of language behavior. On the other hand, *the extensionalist thesis* asserts that the assignment of an intension, on the basis of the previously determined extension is not a question of fact but merely a matter of choice. The thesis holds that the linguist is free to choose any of those properties which fit to the given extension; he may be guided in his choice by a consideration of simplicity, but there is no question of right or wrong. Quine seems to maintain this thesis; he says: "The finished lexicon is a case evidently of *ex pede Herculem*. But there is a difference. In projecting Hercules from the foot we risk error but we may derive comfort from the fact that there is something to be wrong about. In the case of the lexicon, pending some definition of synonymy, we have no stating of the problem; we have nothing for the lexicographer to be right or wrong about." [5]

I shall now plead for the intensionalist thesis. Suppose, for example, that one linguist, after an investigation of Karl's speaking behavior, writes into his dictionary the following:

(1)   *Pferd,* horse,

while another linguist writes:

(2)   *Pferd,* horse or unicorn.

Since there are no unicorns, the two intensions ascribed to the word "Pferd" by the two linguists, although different, have the same extension. If the extensionalist thesis were right, there would be no way for empirically deciding between (1) and (2). Since the extension is the same, no response by Karl, affirmative or negative, with respect to any actual thing can make a difference between (1) and (2). But what else is there to investigate for the linguist beyond Karl's responses concerning the application of the predicate to all the cases that can be found? The answer is, he must take into account not only the actual cases, but also possible cases.[6] The most direct way of doing this would be for the linguist to use, in the German questions directed to Karl, modal expressions corresponding to "possible case" or the like. To be sure, these expressions are usually rather ambiguous; but this difficulty can be overcome by giving suitable explanations and examples. I do not think that there is any objection of principle against the use of modal terms. On the other hand, I think that their use is not necessary. The linguist could simply describe for Karl cases, which he knows to be possible, and leave it open whether there is any-thing satisfying those descriptions or not. He may, for example, describe a unicorn (in German) by something corresponding to the English formulation: "a thing similar to a horse, but having only one horn in the middle of the forehead." Or he may point toward a thing and then describe the intended modification in words, e.g.: "a thing like this one but having one horn in the middle of the forehead." Or, finally, he might just point to a pic-ture representing a unicorn. Then he asks Karl whether he is will-ing to apply the word "Pferd" to a thing of this kind. An affirma-tive or a negative answer will constitute a confirming instance for (2) or (1) respectively. This shows that (1) and (2) are different empirical hypotheses.

All *logically possible* cases come into consideration for the de-termination of intensions. This includes also those cases that are causally impossible, *i.e.*, excluded by the laws of nature holding in our universe, and certainly those that are excluded by laws which Karl believes to hold. Thus, if Karl believes that all P are Q by a law of nature, the linguist will still induce him to consider things that are P but not Q, and ask him whether or not he would apply to them the predicate under investigation (*e.g.*, "Pferd").

The inadequacy of the extensionalist thesis is also shown by the following example. Consider, on the one hand, these customary entries in German-English dictionaries:

(3)   *Einhorn,* unicorn. *Kobold,* goblin,

and, on the other hand, the following unusual entries:

(4)   *Einhorn,* goblin. *Kobold,* unicorn.

Now the two German words (and likewise the two English words) have the same extension, viz., the null class. Therefore, if the extensionalist thesis were correct, there would be no essential, em-pirically testable difference between (3) and (4). The extension-alist is compelled to say that the fact that (3) is generally accepted and (4) generally rejected is merely due to a tradition created by the lexicographers, and that there are no facts of German language behavior which could be regarded as evidence in favor of (3) as against (4). I wonder whether any linguist would be willing to accept (4). Or, to avoid the possibly misguiding influence of the lexicographers' tradition, let us put the question this way: Would a man on the street, who has learned both languages by practical use without lessons or dictionaries, accept as correct a translation made according to (4)?

In general terms, the determination of the intension of a predicate may start from some instances denoted by the predicate. The essential task is then to find out what variations of a given specimen in various respects (*e.g.*, size, shape, color) are admitted within the range of the predicate. The intension of a predicate may be defined as its range, which comprehends those possible kinds of objects for which the predicate holds. In this investigation of intension, the linguist finds a new kind of vagueness, which may be called *intensional vagueness*. As mentioned above, the extensional vagueness of the word "Mensch" is very small, at least in the accessible region. First, the intermediate zone among animals now living on earth is practically empty. Second, if the ancestors of man are considered, it is probably found that Karl cannot easily draw a line; thus there is an intermediate zone, but it is relatively small. However, when the linguist proceeds to the determination of the *intension* of the word "Mensch," the situation is quite different. He has to test Karl's responses to descriptions of strange kinds of animals, say intermediate between man and dog, man and lion, man and hawk, etc. It may be that the linguist and Karl know that these kinds of animals have never lived on earth; they do not know whether or not these kinds will ever occur on earth or on any other planet in any galaxy. At any rate, this knowledge or ignorance is irrelevant for the determination of intension. But Karl's ignorance has the psychological effect that he has seldom if ever thought of these kinds (unless he happens to be a student of mythology or a science-fiction fan) and therefore never felt an urge to make up his mind to which of them to apply the predicate "Mensch." Consequently, the linguist finds in Karl's responses a large intermediate zone for this predicate, in other words, a high intensional vagueness. The fact that Karl has not made such decisions means that the intension of the word "Mensch" for him is not quite clear even to himself, that he does not completely understand his own word. This lack of clarity does not bother him much because it holds only for aspects which have very little practical importance for him.

The extensionalist will perhaps reject as impracticable the described procedure for determining intensions because, he might say, the man on the street is unwilling to say anything about nonexistent objects. If Karl happens to be overrealistic in this way, the linguist could still resort to a lie, reporting, say, his alleged observations of unicorns. But this is by no means necessary. The tests concerning intensions are independent of questions of existence. The man on the street is very well able to understand and to answer questions about assumed situations, where it is left open whether anything of the kind described will ever actually occur or not, and even about nonexisting situations. This is shown in ordinary conversations about alternative plans of action, about the truth of reports, about dreams, legends, and fairy tales.

Although I have given here only a rough indication of the empirical procedure for determining intensions, I believe that it is sufficient to make clear that it would be possible to write along the lines indicated a manual for determining intensions or, more exactly, for testing hypotheses concerning intensions. The kinds of rules in such a manual would not be essentially different from those customarily given for procedures in psychology, linguistics, and anthropology. Therefore the rules could be understood and carried out by any scientist (provided he is not infected by philosophical prejudices).[7]

4. *Intensions in the Language of Science*

The discussions in this paper concern in general a simple, prescientific language, and the predicates considered designate observable properties of material bodies. Let us now briefly take a look at the *language of science*. It is today still mainly a natural language (except for its mathematical part), with only a few explicitly made conventions for some special words or symbols. It is a variant of the prescientific language, caused by special professional needs. The degree of precision is here in general considerably higher (*i.e.*, the degree of vagueness is lower) than in the everyday language, and this degree is continually increasing. It is important to note that this increase holds not only for extensional but also for intensional precision; that is to say that not only the extensional intermediate zones (*i.e.*, those of actual occurrences) but also the intensional ones (*i.e.*, those of possible occurrences) are shrinking.

In consequence of this development, also, the intension concepts become applicable with increasing clarity. In the oldest books on chemistry, for example, there were a great number of statements describing the properties of a given substance, say water or sulphuric acid, including its reactions with other substances. There was no clear indication as to which of these numerous properties were to be taken as essential or definitory for the substance. Therefore, at least on the basis of the book alone, we cannot determine which of the statements made in the book were analytic and which synthetic for its author. The situation was similar with books on zoology, even at a much later time; we find a lot of statements, *e.g.,* on the lion, without a clear separation of the definitory properties. But in chemistry there was an early development from the state described to states of greater and greater intensional precision. On the basis of the theory of chemical elements, slowly with increasing explicitness certain properties were selected as essential. For a compound, the molecular formula (*e.g.,* "H_2O") was taken as definitory, and later the molecular structure diagram. For the elementary substances, first certain experimental properties were more and more clearly selected as definitory, for example the atomic weight, later the position in Mendeleyev's system. Still later, with a differentiation of the various isotopes, the nuclear composition was regarded as definitory, say characterized by the number of protons (atomic number) and the number of neutrons.

We can at the present time observe the advantages already obtained by the explicit conventions which have been made, though only to a very limited extent, in the language of empirical science, and the very great advantages effected by the moderate measure of formalization in the language of mathematics. Let us suppose—as I indeed believe, but that is outside of our present discussion— that this trend toward explicit rules will continue. Then the practical question arises whether rules of extension are sufficient or whether it would be advisable to lay down also rules of intension? In my view, it follows from the previous discussion that rules of intension are required, because otherwise intensional vagueness would remain, and this would prevent clear mutual understanding and effective communication.

5. *The General Concept of the Intension of a Predicate*

We have seen that there is an empirical procedure for testing, by observations of linguistic behavior, a hypothesis concerning the intension of a predicate, say "Pferd," for a speaker, say Karl. Since a procedure of this kind is applicable to any hypothesis of intension, the general concept of the intension of any predicate in any language for any person at any time has a clear, empirically testable sense. This general concept of intension may be characterized roughly as follows, leaving subtleties aside: the intension of a predicate "Q" for a speaker X is the general condition which an object y must fulfill in order for X to be willing to ascribe the predicate "Q" to y. (We omit, for simplicity, the reference to a time t.) [8] Let us try to make this general characterization more explicit. That X is able to use a language L means that X has a certain system of interconnected dispositions for certain linguistic responses. That a predicate "Q" in a language L has the property F as its intension for X, means that among the dispositions of X constituting the language L there is the disposition of ascribing the predicate "Q" to any object y if and only if y has the property F. (F is here always assumed to be an observable property, *i.e.*, either directly observable or explicitly definable in terms of directly observable properties.)   (The given formulation is oversimplified, neglecting vagueness. In order to take vagueness into account, a pair of intensions F_1, F_2 must be stated: X has the disposition of ascribing affirmatively the predicate "Q" to an object y if and only if y has F_1; and the disposition of denying "Q" for y if and only if y has F_2. Thus, if y has neither F_1 nor F_2, X will give neither an affirmative nor a negative response; the property of having neither F_1 nor F_2 constitutes the zone of vagueness, which may possibly be empty.)

The concept of intension has here been characterized only for thing-predicates. The characterization for expressions of other types, including sentences, can be given in an analogous way. The other concepts of the theory of intension can then be defined in the usual way; we shall state only those for "synonymous" and "analytic" in a simple form without claim to exactness.

Two expressions are *synonymous* in the language L for X at time t if they have the same intension in L for X at t.

A sentence is *analytic* in L for X at t if its intension (or range or truth-condition) in L for X at t comprehends all possible cases.

A language L was characterized above as a system of certain dispositions for the use of expressions. I shall now make some remarks on the *methodology of dispositional concepts*. This will help to a clearer understanding of the nature of linguistic concepts in general and of the concept of intension in particular. Let D be the disposition of X to react to a condition C by the characteristic response R. There are in principle, although not always in practice, two ways for ascertaining whether a given thing or person X has the disposition D (at a given time t). The first method may be called *behavioristic* (in a very wide sense); it consists in producing the condition C and then determining whether or not the response R occurs. The second way may be called the *method of structure analysis*. It consists in investigating the state of X (at t) in sufficient detail such that it is possible to derive from the obtained description of the state with the help of relevant general laws (say of physics, physiology, etc.) the responses which X would make to any specified circumstances in the environment. Then it will be possible to predict, in particular, whether under the condition C, X would make the response R or not; if so, X has the disposition D, otherwise not. For example, let X be an automobile and D be the ability for a specified acceleration on a horizontal road at a speed of 10 miles per hour. The hypothesis that the automobile has this ability D may be tested by either of the following two procedures. The behavioristic method consists in driving the car and observing its performance under the specified conditions. The second method consists in studying the internal structure of the cart, especially the motor, and calculating with the help of physical laws the acceleration which would result under the specified conditions. With respect to a psychological disposition and, in particular, a linguistic disposition of a person X, there is first the familiar behavioristic method and second, at least theoretically, the method of a microphysiological investigation of the body of X, especially the central nervous system. At the present state of physiological knowledge of the human organism and especially the central nervous system, the second method is, of course, not practicable.

6. *The Concept of Intension for a Robot*

In order to make the method of structure analysis applicable, let us now consider the pragmatical investigation of the language of a robot rather than that of a human being. In this case we may assume that we possess much more detailed knowledge of the internal structure. The logical nature of the pragmatical concepts remains just the same. Suppose that we have a sufficiently detailed blueprint according to which the robot X was constructed and that X has abilities of observation and of use of language. Let us assume that X has three input organs A, B, and C, and an output organ. A and B are used alternatively, never simultaneously. A is an organ of visual observation of objects presented. B can receive a general description of a kind of object (a predicate expression) in the language L of X, which may consist of written marks or of holes punched in a card. C receives a predicate. These inputs constitute the question whether the object presented at A or any object satisfying the description presented at B is denoted in L for X by the predicate presented at C. The output organ may then supply one of three responses of X, for affirmation, denial, or abstention; the latter response would be given, *e.g.*, if the observation of the object at A or the description at B is not sufficient to determine a definite answer. Just as the linguist investigating Karl begins with pointing to objects, but later, after having determined the interpretation of some words, asks questions formulated by these words, the investigator of X's language L begins with presenting objects at A, but later, on the basis of tentative results concerning the intensions of some signs of L, proceeds to present predicate expressions at B which use only those interpreted signs and not the predicate presented at C.

Instead of using this behavioristic method, the investigator may here use the method of structure analysis. On the basis of the given blueprint of X, he may be able to calculate the responses which X would make to various possible inputs. In particular, he may be able to derive from the given blueprint, with the help of those laws of physics which determine the functioning of the organs of X, the following result with respect to a given predicate "Q" of the language L of X and specified properties F_1 and F_2, (observable for X): If the predicate "Q" is presented at C, then X gives an affirmative response if and only if an object having the property F_2 is presented at A and a negative response if and only if an object with F_1 is presented at A. This result indicates that the boundary of the intension of "Q" is somewhere between the boundary of F_1 and that of F_2. For some predicates the zone of indeterminateness between F_1 and F_2 may be fairly small and hence this preliminary determination of the intension fairly precise. This might be the case, for example, for color predicates if the investigator has a sufficient number of color specimens.

After this preliminary determination of the intensions of some predicates constituting a restricted vocabulary V by calculations concerning input A, the investigator will proceed to making calculations concerning descriptions containing the predicates of V to be presented at B. He may be able to derive from the blueprint the following result: If the predicate "P" is presented at C, and any description D in terms of the vocabulary V is presented at B, X gives an affirmative response if and only if D (as interpreted by the preliminary results) logically implies G_1, and a negative response if and only if D logically implies G_2. This result indicates that the boundary of the intension of "P" is between the boundary of G_1 and that of G_2. In this way more precise determinations for a more comprehensive part of L and finally for the whole of L may be obtained. (Here again we assume that the predicates of L designate observable properties of things.)

It is clear that the method of structure analysis, if applicable, is more powerful than the behavioristic method, because it can supply a general answer and, under favorable circumstances, even a complete answer to the question of the intension of a given predicate.

Note that the procedure described for input A can include empty kinds of objects and the procedure for input B even causally impossible kinds. Thus, for example, though we cannot present a unicorn at A, we can nevertheless calculate which response X would make if a unicorn were presented at A. This calculation is obviously in no way affected by any zoological fact concerning the existence or nonexistence of unicorns. The situation is different for a kind of objects excluded by a law of physics, especially, a law needed in the calculations about the robot. Take the law l_1: "Any iron body at 60° F is solid." The investigator needs this law in his calculation of the functioning of X, in order to ascertain that some iron cogwheels do not melt. If now he were to take as a premise for his derivation the statement "A liquid iron body having the temperature of 60° F is presented at A," then, since the law l_1 belongs also to his premises, he would obtain a contradiction; hence every statement concerning X's response would be derivable, and thus the method would break down. But even for this case the method still works with respect to B. He may take as premise "The description 'liquid iron body with the temperature of 60° F' (that is, the translation of this into L) is presented at B." Then no contradiction arises either in the derivation made by the investigator or in that made by X. *The derivation carried out by the investigator* contains the premise just mentioned, which does not refer to an iron body but to a description, say a card punched in a certain way; thus there is no contradiction, although the law I_1 occurs also as a premise. On the other hand, in *the derivation made by the robot X,* the card presented at B supplies, as it were, a premise of the form "y is a liquid iron body at 60° F"; but here the law I_1 does not occur as a premise, and thus no contradiction occurs. X makes merely logical deductions from the one premise stated and, if the predicate "R" is presented at C, tries to come either to the conclusion "y is R" or "y is not R." Suppose the investigator's calculation leads to the result that X would derive the conclusion "y is R" and hence that X would give an affirmative response. This result would show that the (causally impossible) kind of liquid iron bodies at 60° F is included in the range of the intension of "R" for X.

I have tried to show in this paper that in a pragmatical investigation of a natural language there is not only, as generally agreed, an empirical method for ascertaining which objects are denoted by a given predicate and thus for determining the extension of the predicate, but also a method for testing a hypothesis concerning its intension (designative meaning).[9] The intension of a predicate for a speaker X is, roughly speaking, the general condition which an object must fulfill for X to be willing to apply the predicate to it.[9] For the determination of intension, not only actually given cases must be taken into consideration, but also possible cases, *i.e.,* kinds of objects which can be described without self-contradiction, irrespective of the question whether there are any objects of the kinds described. The intension of a predicate can be determined for a robot just as well as for a human speaker, and even more completely if the internal structure of the robot is sufficiently known to predict how it will function under various conditions. On the basis of the concept of intension, other pragmatical concepts with respect to natural languages can be defined, synonymy, analyticity, and the like. The existence of scientifically sound pragmatical concepts of this kind provides a practical motivation and justification for the introduction of corresponding concepts in pure semantics with respect to constructed language systems.

This paper originally appeared in *Philosophical Studies,* 1955, and was reprinted in R. Carnap, *Meaning and Necessity,* 2nd enlarged ed. (Chicago, 1956).

1. This distinction is closely related to that between radical concepts and L-concepts which I made in *Introduction to Semantics*. The contrast between extension and intension is the basis of the semantical method which I developed in *Meaning and Necessity*. Quine calls the two theories "theory of reference" and "theory of meaning," respectively.

2. R. Carnap, "Meaning Postulates," *Philosophical Studies*, 3:65–73 (1952).

3. W. V. Quine, *From a Logical Point of View: Nine Logico-Philosophical Essays* (1953). For his criticism of intension concepts see especially Essays II ("Two Dogmas of Empiricism," first published in 1951), III, and VII.

4. M. White, "The Analytic and the Synthetic: An Untenable Dualism" in Sidney Hook, ed., *John Dewey: Philosopher of Science and Freedom*, 1950, pp. 316–30.

5. Quine, *op. cit.*, p. 63.

6. Some philosophers have indeed defined the intension of a predicate (or a concept closely related to it) as the class of the possible objects falling under it. For example, C. I. Lewis defines: "The comprehension of a term is the classification of all consistently thinkable things to which the term would correctly apply" ("The Modes of Meaning," *Philosophy and Phenomenological Research*, 4:236–50 (1944)). I prefer to apply modalities like possibility not to objects but only to intensions, especially to propositions or to properties (kinds). (Compare *Meaning and Necessity*, pp. 66 f.) To speak of a possible case means to speak of a kind of objects which is possibly nonempty.

7. After writing the present paper I have become acquainted with a very interesting new book by Arne Naess, *Interpretation and Preciseness: A Contribution to the Theory of Communication* (Skrifter Norske Vid. Akademi, Oslo, II. Hist.-Filos. Klasse, 1953, No. 1). This book describes in detail various procedures for testing hypotheses concerning the synonymity of expressions with the help of questionnaires, and gives examples of statistical results found with these questionnaires. The practical difficulties and sources of possible errors are carefully investigated. The procedures concern the responses of the test persons, not to observed objects as in the present paper, but to pairs of sentences within specified contexts. Therefore the questions are formulated in the metalanguage, *e.g.*, "Do the two given sentences in the given context express the same assertion to you?" Although there may be different opinions concerning some features of the various procedures, it seems to me that the book marks an important progress in the methodology of empirical meaning analysis for natural languages. Some of the questions used refer also to possible kinds of cases, *e.g.*, "Can you imagine circumstances (conditions, situations) in which you would accept the one sentence and reject the other, or vice versa?" (p. 368). The book, both in its methodological discussions and in its reports on experiences with the questionnaires, seems to me to provide abundant evidence in support of the intensionalist thesis (in the sense explained in §3 above).

8. Note added 1956: The following formulation, suggested by Chisholm, would be more adequate: "The intension of a predicate 'Q' for a speaker X is the general condition which X must believe an object y to fulfill in order for X to be willing to ascribe the predicate 'Q' to y." See the notes by Chisholm, pp. 87–89, and Carnap, pp. 89–91, in *Philosophical Studies*, 6 (1955).

9. Y. Bar-Hillel in a recent paper ("Logical Syntax and Semantics," *Language* 30: 230–37 (1954)) defends the concept of meaning against those contemporary linguists who wish to ban it from linguistics. He explains this tend-

ency by the fact that in the first quarter of this century the concept of meaning was indeed in a bad methodological state; the usual explanations of the concept involved psychologistic connotations, which were correctly criticized by Bloomfield and others. Bar-Hillel points out that the semantical theory of meaning developed recently by logicians is free of these drawbacks. He appeals to the linguists to construct in an analogous way the theory of meaning needed in their empirical investigations. The present paper indicates the possibility of such a construction. The fact that the concept of intension can be applied even to a robot shows that it does not have the psychologistic character of the traditional concept of meaning.

NELSON GOODMAN

The Revision of Philosophy

Foreword

My title refers not to the reworking but more literally to the re-vision of philosophy—a new way of looking at philosophy, a new conception of its nature and objectives, and consequently a new appraisal of its methods and results. I am not concerned with the modification of what has been done by able philosophers from Thales on, but rather with a re-vision, in the sense explained, or a new version, of what has been done and is being done.

Let me hasten to say that this "new vision" is not original with me, and that it is not even very new. It has been coming into our consciousness slowly over a long period; and it has, I think, been tacitly adopted for sometime past by those who have contributed most to philosophy. But it is often obscured by what even these same people say when they talk *about* philosophy; and it is almost never understood by those whose participation in philosophy consists solely of controversy. Thus I think it may be well to dust off this rather old new vision and hold it up once more to public view.

Sections 1-6 below constitute a paper written for a forthcoming volume on Carnap.[1] These sections, although cast in the form of a discussion of the significance of Carnap's *Der Logische Aufbau der Welt*,[2] deal almost entirely with the more general questions which must be answered before the significance of such a book can be appraised. Thus I am at the same time implicitly defending the point of view of, for example, my own book *The Structure of Appearance*[3]—which, incidentally, contains an exposition and criticism of a considerable part of the *Aufbau*.

1. *Evil Days for the* AUFBAU

The *Aufbau* is a crystallization of much that is widely regarded as the worst in twentieth century philosophy. It is an anathema to antiempirical metaphysicians and to alogical empiricists, to analytic Oxonians and to antianalytic Bergsonians, to those who would exalt philosophy above the sciences and to those who would abolish philosophy in favor of the sciences. A good part of current polemical writing in philosophical journals is directed against views found in virulent form in the *Aufbau*. The *Aufbau* stands pre-eminent as a horrible example.

My purpose here is to survey and appraise the charges against the *Aufbau,* and to set forth some convictions concerning the significance of the work. This virtually amounts to the unpromising, but welcome, task of defending the *Aufbau* against almost everybody, including Carnap himself—indeed, including a succession of Carnaps who have belittled this early work for different reasons at different times in the twenty-eight years since it was published. But I am more interested in the current atmosphere of opinion concerning the *Aufbau* than in what particular people have said at particular times; and my adversary, except where specifically named, is a composite figure encountered as often in conversation as in the journals.

2. *Phenomenalism and the* AUFBAU

In place of the 'impressions' or 'simple ideas' of 18th century British philosophy, Carnap based his system on total moments of experience—the *elementarerlebnisse*—in order to begin as nearly as possible with what he regards as unanalyzed and unprocessed experience. The system is plainly phenomenalistic, and phenomenalism has been under heavy and incessant attack.

The most popular objection is that phenomenalism is *incom-*

pletable. No full and adequate account of the objective and inter-subjective world of the sciences can be given, it is contended, upon a purely phenomenalistic basis. Carnap's own first disavowal[4] of the *Aufbau* expressed the conviction that a phenomenalistic system, unlike a physicalistic one, could not be all-embracing for science; and perhaps nothing else he has ever written has found such wide-spread agreement.

The arguments commonly adduced to support the charge of the incompletability of phenomenalism cannot, in the nature of the case, be very cogent by themselves; for the thesis they are designed to prove is not precise enough, and there is available no developed body of theory within which a sound proof might be given. Proof that a complete system cannot be constructed on any phenomenal-istic basis prerequires some precise delimitation of the class of phenomenalistic bases, a full statement of admissible methods of construction, and a clear conception of what constitutes complete-ness of the kind in question; and none of these requirements is easy to meet. Thus, for example, the argument that phenomenalism is incompletable because the infinite world of mathematics and the sciences cannot be accounted for upon a finite basis has at first sight the simple force of the statement that an infinite number of things cannot be made out of a finite number. But if we under-stand that the question is rather whether we can interpret in terms of statements about a finite number of entities all indispensable statements that *prima facie* refer to an infinite number of entities, the matter cannot be settled so easily.

On the other hand, the thesis that phenomenalism is incom-pletable hardly needs proof. Surely no complete system will be offered within any foreseeable length of time; and no other means of proving the possibility of completion is in prospect. The task of construction is so formidable, and the tendency to regard it as hopeless is so strong, that the presumption is all against the claim that any phenomenalistic system—or for that matter any system with a very narrow basis—is completable. Even without proof or clarification of the thesis that phenomenalism is incompletable, one is justified in accepting this thesis at least until the opposite is ren-dered more credible.

But if the thesis—proven or unproven—is accepted, what conclu-sion can be drawn from it? Usually phenomenalism is taken to be utterly discredited once its incompletability is acknowledged. It is just this step in the argument—a step commonly passed over as obvious—that I want to challenge. I am ready to maintain that the value of efforts to construct a system on a phenomenalistic or any other narrow basis is very little affected by whether or not the system can be completed. Euclid's geometry is not robbed of value by the fact that the circle cannot be squared by Euclidean means. Indeed, acceptance prior to Euclid of the impossibility of squaring the circle with compass and straightedge would not in the least have diminished the importance of developing Euclidean geometry; and it would not, I think, have been ground for turning attention solely to the discussion of the adequacy of various bases or to the development of geometry on a basis broader than Euclid's. Moreover, propositions affirming the Euclidean insolubility of certain problems could hardly have been precisely formulated or have been capable of proof except against the background of elaborated, even if incompletable, mathematical systems. But my point is not just that it was psychologically necessary or helpful to work in this way. What is accomplished in the incompletable system has permanent value when incorporated into a fuller system. Indeed after a system like Euclid's has been developed as far as possible, questions concerning what can be accomplished with even fewer means (*e.g.* without a straightedge or without a given postulate) often still have interest.

The analogy, I take it, is transparent. Incompletability by itself is no decisive objection against the attempt to build a system on a phenomenalistic basis. Only by positive efforts with severely restricted means can we make any progress in construction; only so can we discern the exact limitations of a basis and the exact supplementation needed. And what we achieve may be retained in an expanded system, and will help solve parallel problems in alternative systems. Carnap's suggestion that his single chosen primitive might be enough for a complete system was indeed rash and untenable. But his mistake here was no worse than that of people who thought Euclid's basis enough for a complete plane geometry. The incompletability of the system of the *Aufbau* or of phenomenalism in general is not a very damaging charge.

Incompletability is not the only count urged against phenomenalism. Sometimes the objection is rather that a phenomenalistic system, whether completable or not, is epistemologically false; that it misrepresents the cognitive process. Phenomenal events or qualities, it is held, are not the original elements of knowledge but are products of an artificial and highly sophisticated analysis, so that a phenomenalistic system gives a highly distorted picture of actual cognition.

Any such view rests on the premise that the question "What are the original elements in knowledge?" is a clear and answerable one. And the assumption remains uncontested so long as we are dominated by the tradition that there is a sharp dichotomy between the given and the interpretation put upon it—so long as we picture the knower as a machine that is fed experience in certain lumps and proceeds to grind these up and reunite them in various ways. But I do not think this view of the matter will stand very close scrutiny. For the question "What are the units in which experience is actually given?" seems to amount to the question "What is the real organization of experience before any cognitive organization takes place?" and this, in turn, seems to ask for a description of cognitively unorganized experience. But any description itself effects, so to speak, a cognitive organization; and apart from a description, it is hard to see what organization can be. The search for the original given is sometimes envisaged as an interrogation in which I am first asked what I just saw. I reply, "I saw the worst criminal alive today," but my questioner complains that I am making too many judgments about what I saw; he wants me to tell him exactly what I could see and nothing more. As he continues to press me, I reply successively; "I saw a man," "I saw a human looking animal," "I saw a moving object," 'I saw such-and-such a configuration of color patches." But if my questioner is consistent and persistent, none of these replies—or any other I can give him—will satisfy him; for all my answers describe my experience in words and so impose on it some organization or interpretation. What he is covertly demanding is that I describe what I saw without describing it. All my answers may be true descriptions of what I saw, but no description can be a satisfactory answer to the question what I *merely* saw;[5] for the question is a bogus one.

But obviously I cannot discuss the whole question of epistemological priority very thoroughly here. And there is no need. For the value and validity of a constructional system do not depend upon the epistemological primacy of the elements it starts from, however one may conceive such primacy to be determined. The old idea that philosophy aims at writing the story of the cognitive process had already been abandoned in the *Aufbau*. Carnap warned that his constructions are intended to preserve only the 'logical value' not the 'epistemological value' of the terms defined, and stated expressly that his system is not to be regarded as a portrayal of the process of acquiring knowledge. Nevertheless, he considered the system to be a 'rational reconstruction' of that process, a demonstration of how the ideas dealt with 'could have been' derived from the original given; and for that reason he bases his system on elements that are as close as possible to what he regards as the given. But it becomes almost immediately obvious that if we do not care whether steps in the system picture corresponding steps in cognition, neither do we care whether the system starts from what is originally given. The function of the system is not to portray the genesis—either actual or hypothetical—of ideas, but to exhibit interconnections between them. The consideration relevant in choosing elements for a system is thus not primacy in the cognitive process but serviceability as a basis for an economical, perspicuous, and integrated system.

I shall have more to say on the nature and purpose of constructional systems as we proceed, especially in the following section; but the brief answer to the charge that phenomenalistic systems are false as pictures of the cognitive process is simply that such systems need not be true in this way. Carnap claims a diluted truth of this sort for his system, as he tentatively claims completability for it; but the system is not to be judged in terms of these needless and misleading claims.

A third and more considered line of attack upon phenomenalism is directed toward showing not that phenomenalistic systems are incompletable or false, but that they are disadvantageous—that the important purposes at hand can be better served by starting from a physicalistic basis. It is pointed out that even the most commonplace objects of daily experience are extraordinarily difficult to construct upon a phenomenalistic basis; that the *elementarerlebnisse* or qualities or appearance-events from which a phenomenalistic system proceeds are unfamiliar units of discourse, elusive if not illusive, difficult to catch and identify; and that a system based upon such elements is an ingrown development of technical philosophy, remote from practical concerns or scientific discourse. In contrast, it is held, a physicalistic system begins with familiar and well-understood elements, is able to deal at once with the world of everyday experience, and much more readily yields the objects of the sciences.

This argument, with its appeal to the familiar, the practical, and the scientific is so overwhelming that those who spend time on phenomenalistic constructions are regarded as stubborn and old-fashioned crackpots who shut their eyes to the facts of life and science. Nevertheless, let us look at the argument more closely.

In the first place, one great advantage claimed for a physicalistic system is that it does not face the difficult and perhaps insoluble problem of constructing physical objects on the basis of phenomena. This is quite true. Likewise, it is true that if you simply use a double compass (a compass with another mounted on one leg) you can trisect any angle. And since a double compass is easy to obtain, and since the goal is to get angles trisected, isn't it impractical and quixotic to deny ourselves use of this instrument? If physical objects are hard to construct in terms of phenomena, why not begin with physical objects? Let's be clear, though, that in both cases we are not solving a problem but evading one. The difference, it will be claimed, is that in the case of geometry the choice is between two equally simple and ordinary bases, while in the shift from a phenomenalistic to a physicalistic system we are dropping an abstruse and elusive basis in favor of a plainly more comprehensible and familiar one. Thus the argument for physicalism here cannot be that it solves a problem that phenomenalism does not, but rather that it begins with a more acceptable basis and frees us of the need for bothering with a difficult and unimportant problem before we come to grips with the realm of everyday life and of science.

The comfortable, homey character of the physicalist's basis lasts only so long as he is arguing for his basis rather than trying to use it. Once he makes any serious beginning toward systematic construction, he quickly finds that ordinary things like tables, desks, and chairs are much too gross, complicated, ill-assorted, and scattered to serve his purpose; and while we are looking the other way, he slips in substitutes. In "Testability and Meaning,"[6] for example, Carnap at first speaks of a 'thing-language' in which atomic sentences consist of observable predicates applied to ordinary things.[7] But a few pages later he is speaking of "observable predicates of the thing-language attributed to perceived things of any kind or to space-time points."[8] This last phrase makes a radical addition. Whether the space-time points in question are those of physics or are minimal perceptible regions, they are by no means the familiar things of everyday experience. What the physicalist and the phenomenalist both do is this: they begin informally with ordinary discourse and indicate in terms of it a set of entities that are quite different from ordinary things but possess a uniformity, simplicity, and joint exhaustiveness that makes them serviceable as elements for a system. The physicalist does not, any more than the phenomenalist, take the usual objects of daily life as the basic elements of his system.

Moreover, there is a good deal of equivocation about the space-time points taken as elements by the physicalist. When he maintains that he is in a better position to construct the objects of science, the supposition is that his elements are the space-time points of mathematics and physics. But this cannot be the case; for he retains 'observable predicates.' Carnap gives as examples of admissible atomic statements: "This space-time point is warm" and "at this space-time point, is a solid object."[9] Obviously no mathematical space-time point is warm, and at no such point is there any object that is solid or red or that has any other observable quality; observable qualities belong to objects of perceptible size. But if the elements called space-time points are perceptible regions, then we are faced with a good many of the problems— for example, the explication of imperceptible differences—that the physicalist sought to avoid. And his claim that his basis is adequate for constructing the objects of science no longer looks so plausible. The problem of deriving the objects of physics from such a basis is hardly less formidable than, and is in many ways not very different from, the problem of constructing ordinary objects from a strictly phenomenal basis; and there is no *prima facie* reason to suppose that the one is soluble if the other is not. The physicalist offers the argument that "For every term in the physical language physicists know how to use it on the basis of their observations. Thus every such term is reducible to observable predicates . . .";[10] but the phenomenalist has characteristically argued in exactly parallel fashion that "for every term that is used at all competently, the user knows how to use it on the basis of what appears to him, and thus every term is reducible to phenomenal predicates." If the former argument is good so is the latter; if the latter is bad so is the former. The serviceability of ordinary thing-language for constructing the realm of physics remains a totally unsupported claim.

If the problem of constructing the entities of physics from observable things is so troublesome, one might expect the physicalist to skip it as inessential—as he has already skipped the problem of constructing ordinary objects from phenomena—and to achieve a language adequate for physics by starting from the particles and predicates of physics itself. This would be consistent with the currently popular idea that the goal of all investigation is the prediction and control of nature;[11] but he never quite takes this step, for to do so would be to drop philosophy for physics. The physicalist and other constructionalists are trying to serve some purpose not served by physics and the other sciences; but they cannot formulate the difference very clearly, and often seem unaware of it.

Here a major and delicate question emerges. A good part of the dispute over the relative merits of different systematic bases arises from confusion as to pertinent standards. The criteria most often appealed to—such as epistemological primacy, and utility for the sciences—are clearly inappropriate; and just what are the requirements upon an acceptable basis for a philosophical system, as distinguished from a system of psychology or phyics, is a neglected, important, and exasperating problem. Luckily, it is beyond the scope of this paper.

In summary, then, the argument that phenomenalism is incompletable has no more weight against the system of the *Aufbau* than the argument that angles cannot be trisected with straightedge and compass has against Euclidean geometry; and the argument that phenomenalism is epistemologically false has no more weight than the argument that Euclid's postulates are not fundamental, self-evident truths. Moreover, the popular arguments for a physicalistic versus a phenomenalistic system involve vacillation as to the physicalistic basis to be used, unsupported claims concerning possible constructions, and tacit appeal to criteria that, applied consistently, would rule out physicalistic as well as phenomenalistic systems and reject all philosophical investigation in favor of the special sciences.

My aim, let me emphasize, is not to advocate phenomenalism as against physicalism, but only to show the weakness of the case against phenomenalism. Systems of both types may well prove to be valuable.

3. Constructionalism and the AUFBAU

So far, I have considered only the opposition to phenomenalism in particular as distinct from the opposition to constructionalism in general. But there is also active opposition to constructionalism (or 'reductionism' as its enemies call it) of all varieties—not just to a certain choice of basis but to the very program of a systematic logical construction from any set of primitives.

The root of such opposition is, of course, the anti-intellectualism that finds forthright expression in Bergson. The complaint against all definition, analysis, and systematic description is that it employs static, abstract, and Procrustean concepts to construct a bloodless caricature of the rich and pulsating world of experience. Conceptualization, abstraction, symbolization, are instruments of excision and dessication. This appears to be an attack less against one kind of philosophy than upon philosophy in general as compared with poetry. Or, since poetry uses words and symbols and selects aspects, perhaps the protest is rather against all verbalization as contrasted with nonverbal living. In this extreme form, the position need not much concern us here; for we are considering the *Aufbau* as compared to other philosophical efforts, not as compared to a moonlight walk or a drunken brawl. Yet the basic anti-intellectualistic complaint that philosophy does not duplicate experience is worth noting; for it underlies many another objection to attempts at precision and systematization in philosophy.

The function of a constructional system is not to recreate experience but rather to map it. Though a map is derived from observations of a territory, the map lacks the contours, colors, sounds, smells, and life of the territory, and in size, shape, weight, temperature and most other respects may be about as much unlike what it maps as can well be imagined. It may even be very little like other equally good maps of the same territory. A map is schematic, selective, conventional, condensed, and uniform. And these characteristics are virtues rather than defects. The map not only summarizes, clarifies, and systematizes, it often discloses facts we could hardly learn immediately from our explorations. We may make larger and more complicated maps or even three-dimensional models in order to record more information; but this is not always to the good. For when our map becomes as large and in all other respects the same as the territory mapped—and indeed long before this stage is reached—the purposes of a map are no longer served. There is no such thing as a completely unabridged map; for abridgment is intrinsic to map making.

This, I think, suggests the answer not only to rampant anti-intellectualism but to many another objection against the abstractness, poverty, artificiality, and general unfaithfulness of constructional systems. Let no one complain that the turnpike is not red like the line on the map, that the dotted state boundaries on the map are not visible in the fields, or that the city we arrive at is not a round black dot. Let no one suppose that if a map made according to one scheme of projection is accurate then maps made according to alternative schemes are wrong. And let no one accuse the cartographer of merciless reductionism if his map fails to turn green in the spring.

The anti-intellectualist confronts us with a spurious dilemma. The choice is not between misrepresentation and meticulous reproduction. The relevant question about a system or a map is whether it is serviceable and accurate in the way intended.

Many contemporary philosophers are opposed not to analysis as such but to the use of logic and artificial terminology and to step-by-step construction. A system of formal definitions, the objection runs, raises irrelevant problems, is too rigid and precise, and is too insensitive to the subtle variations of ordinary use. A philosophic problem is considered to arise from lack of care in the use of ordinary language, and the recommended treatment consists simply of explaining in ordinary language the nature of the misuse or misunderstanding of use. The analyses offered as examples of this method are often much needed and highly illuminating. They are like directions that tell us how to go from the post office to the park without taking a wrong turn at the red barn. In general, we need ask such directions only when we are lost or puzzled, since we do most of our daily traveling quite efficiently without them. And good verbal directions, as compared with a map, have obvious virtues: they are in the vernacular, mention recognizable landmarks, and tell us without waste just what we immediately need to know.

But a map has its advantages, too. It is, indeed, in an artificial language, and has to be read and related to the terrain; but it is consistent, comprehensive, and connected. It may needlessly give us a good deal of information we already have well in mind; but it may also reveal unsuspected routes and lead us to rectify misconceptions that might otherwise have gone unquestioned. It gives an organized overall view that no set of verbal directions and no experience in traveling can provide unaided. Verbal directions may often be useful even when we have a map; they may help us interpret the map or save us the trouble. But they do not supplant the map.

There are dangers in maps, of course. A map may be taken too literally or otherwise misread. But the map is not at fault if the user supposes that the numbering of the lines of longitude reflects a scale of metaphysical priority, or if disputes arise over whether a marking off by square miles or by minutes is more in keeping with reality.

We are still, admittedly, in a rather primitive stage of philosophical map making; and no one is to be blamed for an inclination to trust skilled verbal directions as against new and imperfect maps. Nor is the reputation of cartography improved by elaborate maps drawn too hastily on the basis of too little exploration. Yet the opposition to the principles of constructionalism by the practitioners of verbal analysis has always surprised me; for I think there is no irreconcilable conflict of objectives or even of methods. Verbal analysis is a necessary preliminary and accompaniment to systematic construction, and deals with the same sphere of problems. For example, the verbal analyst may well concern himself with explaining the vague locution we use when we say that several things are 'all alike'; and he may well examine the difference between saying that a color is at a given place at a given time and saying that a color is at a given place *and* at a given time. The constructionalist dealing with qualities and particulars will likewise have to be clear on these points. The analyst, treating these as separate problems, may well miss the intriguing relationship between the two, while a systematic treatment shows them to be two cases of a single logical problem.[12] But verbal analysis and logical construction are complementary rather than incompatible. The constructionalist recognizes the anti-intellectualist as an arch enemy, but looks upon the verbal analyst as a valued and respected, if inexplicably hostile, ally.

Apart from entrenched philosophical positions, the opposition to constructionalism degenerates into greeting each proposed definition of a so-and-so as a such-and-such with the naïve protest that a so-and-so is Not Merely a such-and-such but Something More. This betrays a simple failure to grasp what the constructionalist is doing. In defining a so-and-so as a such-and-such, he is not declaring that a so-and-so is nothing but a such-and-such. Carnap disclaimed any such idea by insisting that his definientia need have only the same extension as his definienda; and as my discussion above suggests, "=df" in a constructional definition is not to be read "is nothing more than" but rather in some such fashion as "is here to be mapped as." But the nature and import of a constructional definition now need to be examined more closely.

4. *Extensionalism, Definition, and the* AUFBAU

Some critics of the *Aufbau* take issue primarily neither with its phenomenalistic orientation nor with constructionalism in general but with the particular conception of constructional method that the *Aufbau* sets forth and exemplifies.

The first such objection is against the extensionalism of the *Aufbau*. The only nonformal requirement there placed upon a constructional definition is that the definiendum and the definiens apply to exactly the same things, so that replacement of the one by the other in admissible contexts preserves truth value.[13] Against this, many critics—including the Carnap of today—argue that since such extensional identity does not guarantee sameness of meaning, some more stringent criterion must be adopted.

Let us grant the premise that extensional identity is not a sufficient condition for synonymy. This alone does not settle the main question. For what is at issue here is not a theory of meaning but a theory of constructional definition; and acceptance of a nonextensional criterion for synonymy does not carry with it adoption of a nonextensional criterion for constructional definition.

From what I have said in the preceding section it will be clear why I sharply disagree with contentions that a stronger requirement than extensional identity should be imposed on constructional definitions. This would mistake and defeat the primary function of a constructional system. That function, as I see it, is to exhibit a network of relationships obtaining in the subject-matter; and what is wanted therefore is simply a certain structural correspondence between the world of the system and the world of presystematic language.

Only in this way, as a "structural description"[14] rather than as a book of synonyms or as a full-color portrait of reality, can we understand a system like that of the *Aufbau*. The extensional criterion for constructional definition, far from being too weak, is too strong. To require that the definientia be extensionally identical with the definienda is in effect to claim a literal and exclusive truth for the chosen definitions; for if a quality is in fact identical with a certain class of *elementarerlebnisse,* then it is not identical with a class of some other experiential elements that might be chosen as basic for a different system. Any such claim of exclusive truth is utterly foreign to the spirit and purpose of construction-alism. If we conscientiously try to elicit the criteria we actually employ in discussing and judging the correctness of particular con-structions, I think we find that the pertinent requirement is not that each definiens be extensionally identical with its definiendum but rather that the entire system of definientia be *isomorphic,* in a certain specifiable way,[15] to the entire system of definienda. This clears away extraneous and unsatisfiable demands, and leaves room for many different but equally valid alternative systems.

The second common objection against the conception of method embodied in the *Aufbau* is almost the opposite of the first. Carnap himself has taken the lead in maintaining that the restriction to definition as the sole method of construction is much too confining. Not only have we small hope of achieving full definition for all the terms we want to introduce, but there is—he argues—another equally legitimate method of introducing new terms into a system. He claims, indeed, that the introduction of terms through what he calls "reduction sentences" has the advantage of reflecting a common actual procedure of the scientist.

The latter argument is quite beside the point; but the chief trouble is that this supposedly new method of introducing terms adds nothing to the means that were already at our disposal. Reduc-tion sentences are merely postulates; and terms introduced through postulates are introduced simply as primitives. The introduction of primitives requires no new method, and there is some danger in concealing it under a new name. For the suggestion that re-duction sentences are fundamentally comparable to definitions ob-scures the fact that each addition of a new and ineliminable primitive (whether by reduction postulate or otherwise) consti-tutes a sacrifice in the economy of basis and the resultant integra-tion of our system. The difference between frankly adopting a term as primitive and introducing it by reduction sentences is the euphemistic differences between a loss of ground and a strategic retreat.

We may indeed have to add new primitives from time to time in building a system, and we may want to use new syntactical or semantical techniques; but the adoption of new primitives in not a new technique.

The standard criticisms of the *Aufbau's* concept of constructional method, then, seems to me wrong in two ways. First, the extensional criteria for constructional definition needs weakening rather than strengthening. Second, the proposed supplementation of the method definition by the so-called method of 'reduction' adds nothing whatever.

5. Faults of Construction

If we set aside all consideration of general principles and examine in detail the actual constructions in the *Aufbau,* we find a great many faults.[16] A number of these are pointed out in the book itself, for Carnap did not profess to offer more than an imperfect sketch of a system. But there are other difficulties, too; and the cumulative effect is that hardly any construction is free of fault. Moreover, not all these defects are minor slips or mere matters of detail still to be worked out. Some of them are so basic and material that nothing short of rather drastic revision of the whole system is likely to correct them.

Nothing that can be said will explain away these faults or make them less serious; but they should be seen in perspective. They are the faults of an honest and early venture in a new direction. Such troubles can always be avoided by attempting nothing or by keeping cautiously vague; the likelihood of error increases with the earnestness and originality of the effort to attain precision. But the making of errors, the discovery of faults, is the first step toward correcting them. Something has already been accomplished when what is being done and what is being attempted have been clarified far enough to make possible a sound accusation of error. If we compare the *Aufbau* not with what we hope for but with what we had before, we may still not condone its errors—but we can appreciate their significance.

Furthermore, some of the most important errors in the *Aufbau* were not invented by Carnap. They had been made repeatedly and unsuspectingly by generations of earlier philosophers, and are still made today. If Carnap did not correct or even notice them all, the rigorous logical articulation he demanded and began brought them much nearer the surface and made their early discovery inevitable. To take just one example, in discussions of the status of qualities it is often assumed that if we take likeness as the relation obtaining between any two things that have a common quality, then we can define a class of things having a common quality as a class of things that are all alike. But if to say that all are alike is to say merely that each two are alike, this does not guarantee that there is a quality common to all; and in fact no sufficient condition can be given solely in terms of the dyadic likeness of things. This difficulty is customarily camouflaged by the easy locution "all alike." Even Russell has fallen into a similar logical trap.[17] But one can hardly study the *Aufbau* intensively without becoming acutely aware of this problem.

What the opponents of the *Aufbau* usually offer us is not something to replace it, but discussions of methods and programs, arguments for one basis as against another, debates over what can and cannot be done. Altogether too much philosophy these days is, like the present article, merely philosophy about philosophy; the characteristic contemporary philosophical refuge is not metaphysics but metaphilosophy. The admission that the *Aufbau* is full of faults has to be coupled with the observation that the player on the field always gets caught in more mistakes than the player on the bench. And concerning many of the constructional errors in the *Aufbau* we may perhaps say, in summary, that they were serious, unoriginal, and worth-while.

6. *The Significance of the* AUFBAU

I am by no means suggesting, however, that the *Aufbau* is valuable only or primarily for its errors. Once misconceptions and groundless objections have been cleared away, the positive significance of the work becomes very evident.

The *Aufbau* brings to philosophy the powerful techniques of modern logic, along with unprecedented standards of explicitness, coherence, and rigor. It applies to basic philosophical problems the new methods and principles that only a few years before had thrown fresh and brilliant light upon mathematics. The potential importance to philosophy is comparable to the importance of the introduction of Euclidean deductive method into geometry. The *Aufbau,* for all its fragmentary character, and for all its defects, is still one of the fullest examples we have of the logical treatment of problems in nonmathematical philosophy. But its significance in the long run will be measured less by how far it goes than by how far it is superseded.

In stressing the novelty of its contribution, we must not be misled into regarding the *Aufbau* as an aboriginal work, unrelated to the course of thought preceding it. It belongs very much in the main tradition of modern philosophy, and carries forward a little the effort of the British Empiricists of the eighteenth century. Although these philosophers thought of themselves as devoted to a "historical, plain method" of dealing with knowledge, their chief contribution is to the geography rather than the history of our ideas. What were ostensibly inquiries into the question how certain ideas (*e.g.* of qualities) are psychologically derived from certain others (*e.g.* of particulars) were more often than not, I think, simply inquiries into the question of how the former ideas may be defined in terms of the latter. And it is just such questions that the *Aufbau* deals with and clarifies. The language may be new but the ancestry of the problems is venerable.

The *Aufbau* cannot yet, however, be relegated to the status of a monument having purely historical interest. Its lessons have not been fully enough learned.

Conclusion

In summary, now, what is the re-vision of philosophy implied in the foregoing discussion? I think its major component is a new and humbler conception of the nature of philosophical truth: a recognition that philosophy aims at describing the world, not at duplicating it, and that analysis, precision, and systematization are thus virtues rather than vices. But along with the permission to be precise, analytic, and systematic goes a heavy responsibility; and the extreme difficulty of achieving these ends, even to a reasonable degree in dealing with even the most limited problems, might well discourage us completely if it were not for another aspect of our new vision of philosophy. And this is simply that we are to apply to philosophy itself the counsel that philosophers are so fond of giving with respect to everything but philosophy: to look upon it *sub specie aeternitatis*.

1. *The Philosophy of Rudolf Carnap,* edited by Paul Schilpp, in preparation. These sections are published here with Professor Schilpp's permission.

2. Rudolf Carnap, *Der Logische Aufbau der Welt* (Berlin, 1928).

3. Nelson Goodman, *The Structure of Appearance* (Harvard University Press, 1951). This book will hereinafter be referred to as *SA*.

4. In "Die physikalische Sprache als Universalsprache der Wissenschaft," *Erkenntnis,* Vol. 2 (1931), pp. 432–465.

5. The snares in the question whether some description describes an experience *just as* it is experienced have been discussed in *SA*, pp. 103–106, and in Wittgenstein's *Philosophical Investigations* (Basil Blackwell, 1953), pp. 193–214.

6. Rudolf Carnap, "Testability and Meaning," in *Philosophy of Science,* Vol. III (1936) pp. 419–471, and Vol. IV (1937) pp. 1–40.

7. *Ibid.,* Vol. III, p. 466.

8. *Ibid.,* Vol. IV, p. 9.

9. *Ibid.*

10. *Ibid.,* Vol. III, p. 467.

11. The recent dominance of this idea seems to me to have blocked any clear understanding of either philosophy or the sciences. But some relief is in sight. Psychologists have lately produced experimental evidence that monkeys will exert more effort out of sheer curiosity than for food. Satisfaction of curiosity may in time become almost as respectable a goal as satisfaction of hunger; and then we shall no longer have to justify astrophysics by what it may eventually do for the wheat crop.

12. For further explanation, see *SA,* pp. 161–169.

13. The avowed extensionalism of so outstanding a monument of phenomenalism and constructionalism as the *Aufbau* would seem to confute Quine's recent charge (*Mind,* Vol. 62 (1953), p. 434) that the notion of analyticity is a "holdover of phenomenalistic reductionism."

14. Carnap's own term (*Strukturbeschreibung*); see Section 12 of the *Aufbau.*

15. See *SA,* Chap. I.

16. For a detailed exposition of many of these, see *SA,* Chap. V.

17. The passages on compresence and complexes in Bertrand Russell's *An Inquiry into Meaning and Truth* (Norton, 1940, pp. 289–290), and *Human Knowledge* (Simon and Schuster 1948, p. 294), suffer from a parallel equivocation concerning the compresence of qualities.

CLARENCE I. LEWIS

Some Suggestions Concerning
Metaphysics of Logic

The suggestions which I should like to present concern small points, each having a bearing on a large topic. But each of them, though small, is too big to be covered adequately in a short compass: as here formulated, they are put forward knowing that you will supply the needed context and in the hope that they may serve as a basis for discussion.

The large question, which my suggestions all concern, is the relation between the conceptual and the existential. And the general thesis which these seem to me to support is that the conceptual and the existential are irreducibly different categories, both required for an adequate *theory of* logic; but that, within logic itself, there are only such truths as are certifiable from conception alone and are independent of existential fact.

Logic is the science which serves the purpose of finding out what can be determined by thinking without looking, and has no business with any fact the assurance of which requires sense experience. All empirical facts belong in the domain of some other and natural science. Logic is concerned with what is deducible from what, and hence with the distinction between suppositions which are self-consistent and those which are not, since Q is deducible from P if and only if the joint statement which asserts P and denies Q is self-contradictory. But it has no concern with the distinction, amongst statements which are both consistently affirmable and consistently deniable, between those which are actually true and those which in fact are false. All that logic can determine, in the case of such contingent statements, is what is deducible from them and what premises are sufficient for them; and these logical relationships of them are unaffected by their truth or falsity.

So much is commonplace. All statements belonging to logic and all statements certifiable by logic are analytic and deducible from any premise, including the premise which denies them. And from premises of logic alone, no contingent truth of existence or non-existence is derivable: they have no consequences save other statements which are likewise analytic. But that leaves it still desirable to identify something by reference to which logical truth expresses a kind of fact and logical falsehood does violence to fact; some ground on which what is logically true is distinguishable from the logically false, and is worth saying.

It is the prevailing practice at present to explain this character of statements of logic by reference to language. That procedure is both apt and economical. But I think that it will prove inadequate for the theory of logic unless certain simple and obvious facts about language are recognized and the implications of them adhered to. A first such fact is that linguistic entities are not physical objects or events but abstract things of which physical existents may be instances. If there are no universals, then there is no such thing as language. As a physical phenomenon, language is identifiable with sounds and marks. But a sound or a mark is not language unless there is a fixed meaning associated with, and expressed by it. Furthermore, it is not the pile of ink on the page, or the noise occurring to 2:15 which is the linguistic entity. The same word or other expression must be able to occur at different times and places in order to be a linguistic entity; even the physical symbol is a universal, identifiable with the recurrent *pattern* of marks or of noises, of which a single physical existent can be an instance.

Second, the meaning associated with a symbol and essential to its being a linguistic entity, must be a psychological or mental entity. I should be glad to avoid the metaphysical question of mind; and I have no full theory of the mental to offer. But we shall all agree that psychological happenings take place in those individuals called conscious, and are not identifiable with marks on pages or with noises a phonograph may emit at certain times unheard by anybody. Whatever the nature of psychological phenomena, they are what is spoken of by common sense by referring to minds. Let me use this common-sense idiom—so far as possible without metaphysical prejudice. A meaning is something which is mind-dependent; no minds, no meanings. We speak of meanings as entertained, and the entertainment of a meaning is an occurrence; an event which is temporal if not spatial. But just as it is essential to a linguistic symbol that it be the same from page to page, and the pile of ink an instance of it only, so the meaning it conveys cannot be identified with the psychological occurrence called the entertainment of it: it must be the same meaning which is entertained when we read the same expression at different times, if the pile of ink is to exercise the function of expressing the same meaning on different occasions. This meaning as characterizing different psychological events, and the same for any occasion of its entertainment, is the concept. And a meaning as relative to such entertainments, I shall speak of as a conceptual meaning.

Third, most meanings, and correlatively most linguistic expressions, have reference to external existents or states of affairs, spoken of as something meant. In relation to such an objective actuality, the meaning entertained or linguistically expressed constitutes the criterion which operates to determine which or what, amongst actualities which may present themselves, are those so meant. And it so operates by determining some recognizable *character* of actualities as essential to their being accepted as what is meant. This character, even if there be no more than one actual entity instancing it, never extends to the whole nature of any individual thing but is, again, an abstract or universal entity; a property or attribute.

This last consideration will, of course, require some comment, lest it should seem to imply that individuals cannot be conceived, and meant by language. I defer such comment to a later point.

Of these three abstract entities; first, the concept as psychologically instanced meaning, second, linguistic meaning as what patterns of sound or of marks convey, and as the meaning of such expressions in terms of other expressions, and third, the character

or property of objective actualities which is essential to their satisfying the condition set by the concept and expressed in language;
of these three, it is the first which is antecedent to the other two.
We do not first have marks and sounds and then invent or try
to discover concepts for them to convey, but devise language to
convey what is conceptually entertained. If there should be any
who announce that there are no such things as meanings, let us
reply that their announcement is meaningless.

Given a meaning, it may be associated with a visual pattern or
pattern of sound by a social convention or by individual declaration of intent. And given a meaning represented by one symbolism,
another symbolism can be stipulated to have the same meaning.
But conventions and stipulations are possible only with respect
to the use of symbols. Given two meanings, the relation of them
can in no wise be affected by any convention of language. Meanings and the relations of them are as they are and could not be
otherwise; and the supposition that meanings arise from or can
be altered by stipulations of language—if anybody should hold that
supposition—would be ludicrous.

I have no intention of saying that concepts or that meanings
exist. (That point we shall return to later.) Nevertheless I would
suggest that they must be granted some manner of being, and that
if any logician were to say, "There are no such things as conceptual meanings," he would be using Occam's razor to cut his own
throat. Existence—I take it—refers to a relation between a conceptual meaning entertained and an actuality, empirically found
or evidenced, which satisfies the intention of that conceptual
entertainment. But in this connection, it is of some importance
to observe that no empirical presentment could determine that
"So and so exists," if the conception of 'so and so' as a meaning
entertained did not function as a condition to be satisfied or not
satisfied by what may be empirically disclosed. This is no more
than to say what is obvious; we must know what we mean by 'so
and so' before we can determine the existence of 'so and so,' since
otherwise we should lack any manner of determining what empirical findings would be pertinent to this question of existence.
The basic relations of empirical knowledge is this relation between
a character mentally entertained as the concept of 'so and so,' and a
perceptual finding of that which evidences this character essential
to being 'so and so.'

Incidentally, perhaps this resolves the puzzle that 'existence is

SOME SUGGESTIONS CONCERNING METAPHYSICS OF LOGIC 97

not a predicate.' In the statement, "So and so exists," this seeming predicate 'exists' does not express any identifiable *character,* distinguishing one thing from another: the relevant character is expressed by 'so and so'; and there is no difference of conceived character between the silver dollar which I cannot find in my pocket and the silver dollar that I do find elsewhere. Strange as it may seem, the subject of "So and so exists" is the conceptually delineated so and so, not the empirically discovered so and so; if it were the latter, then the assertion of existence would be meaningful only when it is true, and we should have the ridiculous consequence that we could not think of or speak of anything which does not exist. What is *predicated* of this conceptually meant 'so and so' is a relation of correspondence of character between it and something empirically findable or evidenced by perception. And again incidentally, this shows that for the being of a *concept* or conceptual meaning, the ontological argument is perfectly good; whatever is mentionable must have this status as conceptual, whether it exists or not.

Empirical knowledge has thus two conditions: the condition of a conceptually entertained meaning and the condition of some relevant perceptual finding. But knowledge, the expression of which would be an analytic statement, has only one condition: the condition of a factual relationship of meanings as conceptually entertained. And this relationship is determined by these concepts themselves.

I have, so far, left the sense of 'meaning' which is here in question unduly vague, and attempted to characterize it principally by reference to its epistemological status and function. When we turn from the epistemological to the linguistic, and seek to delineate that meaning of the word 'meaning' which is here in point as a property of expressions, it becomes evident that conceptual meaning is not denotation or extension but is identifiable with or correlative to connotation or intension.

It is the intensional meaning of an expression which is the criterion of classification and sets a condition to be satisfied; the denotation of the expression is the class of actualities satisfying this antecedent condition. Due to the logically accidental limitations of what exists or is actually the case, a conceptual and intensional meaning is never determinable from, though it may be limited by, the class denoted. And for the same reason, the intensional meaning of an expression does not determine, but only limits, the denotation or extension of it. Denotation or extension is meaning as *ap*plication, coinciding with those actualities which instance the intension which operates as criterion of their selection from amongst things observed or things in general; the intensional meaning which so operates is meaning as *im*plication; as what is entailed and required to be the case *in order that* the expression should apply. Thus the question "What does the expression mean in the sense of denotation?" is the question "What thing or things does it single out as spoken of?" And the question "What does the expression mean in the sense of intension?" is the question "What is said about anything, or implied, by the application or predication of this expression?"

Since I have already done my best with respect to this topic of intensional and extensional meaning in another place, let me merely summarize here.

Linguistically, the intension of an expression, '*A*,' can be identified by the dictum that any other expression, '*B*,' is included in the intension of '*A*' if and only if from the premise that '*A*' applies to *x* it is deducible that '*B*' applies to *x*. Thus in linguistic terms, the intension of '*A*' would be constituted by the and-relation of all the predicates entailed by the predication of '*A*.' Intensional equivalence—reciprocal entailment of two expressions—is the relation of definition (though there are further and psychological or heuristic requirements of a practically satisfactory definition). It should be noted that entailment is not here a truth-value relation, since deducibility is not a truth-value relation.

However, 'linguistic intension,' as I here use that phrase, fails to cover something essential to meaning as condition of the applicability of an expression, because of the farfetched consideration that explicating one expression by means of others will never succeed of its intent unless *some* words used are already understood as rules of discrimination to be followed in applying them. On the side of that to which application is made, what is essential to such correct application is some character. This character or attribute which must be determined as present in determining correctness of the application of an expression, I will speak of as the *signification* of the expression. Thus there are three things here which are correlative; the concept which is the criterion or rule in mind, the character or attribute signified, which is in the *thing*, and the linguistic intension, which is a function exercised by the expression in relating the concept or rule of discrimination to objective entities which satisfy it. This lingustic intension may itself be expressed by reference to other expressions whose applicability is entailed by applicability of the expression in question.

The notions of intension and extension can be applied to propositions in a manner the basis for which is borrowed from my colleague, Professor Henry Sheffer. For every statement 'S,' there is a corresponding expression which 'S' asserts, and which the interrogative sentence, "Is it the case that S?" inquires about, and the postulation, "Let us assume that S," puts forward as an hypothesis. What all three of these modes of entertainment entertain, in their various ways, is the proposition in question. It can be identified, for any given statement 'S,' with the expression '$that$ S,' which 'S' affirms to be the case. (In passing, let us remark that in terms of propositions so expressed, the formulation of their relations of intension never requires quotation marks; and one superficial objection to the logic of intension thereby loses its superficial plausibility.)

When so considered, a proposition turns out to be a kind of term. It expresses a meaning which, as conceptually entertained, stands as the condition to be satisfied if something is to be recognized as being the case; the condition to be met if this propositional term is to apply to the actual. The intension as *linguistic* is the 'and'-relation of all propositions deducible from the one in question. And the signification of this propositional term is that state of affairs which must be found in what is actual if the proposition is to be accepted as true. For propositions, as for other terms, the conceptual meaning as entertained, the linguistic meaning as expressed, and the state of affairs signified, are all correlative; and none of these three is strictly correlative with the extension of it. The denotation or extension of a proposition— the existent to which it applies—is the actual world in case it is true; and is nothing in case it is false. Its extension is thus correlative with its truth-value.

To anticipate points to which I shall revert shortly, the actual world is that unique individual existent identified by the fact that all other individual existents are space-time parts of it. Propositions are, thus, singular terms. But what a proposition signifies is some character or attribute of this individual, and *not* a part of it. The attempt to identify states of affairs with space-time parts of the world must fail—for several reasons, of which I shall mention only one. Whatever is true at some time and false at some other time, is not a proposition but a propositional function. Any proposition which has temporal reference requires, for the full expression of it, that this temporal reference be made explicit; and when that is done, it must be *always* true or else always false.

There are more considerations which cry out for attention than it is possible to discuss here. One of the most important is that there must be a conceptual meaning of the proposition, which is independent of its truth or falsity, because there must be a *criterion* of such truth or falsity—that is, a criterion of applicability of the proposition to what is actual—in order that such actual truth or falsity may be determined. This propositional concept is the same whether the assertion of the proposition—the statement—is true or is false; only on that condition would any truth or falsity be discoverable. Correlatively, the intensional meaning of any expression of the propositional concept entertained, and the signification of it—the state of affairs *supposed*—must remain the same, whether the proposition is actually true or actually false. And again correlatively, logic, which certifies no actual existence and depends on none, has nothing to do with the extensional relations of statements of fact, except hypothetically or—and this is the place to put the emphasis—so far as the extensional relations of propositions are deducible from their relations of intensional meaning. The logic which construes its basic categories as extensional and in terms of truth-values, would seem to be strangely misconceiving itself as one of the natural and empirical sciences. Logic can certify no existential and empirical fact; and no empirical fact or set of such can certify any truth of logic. What logic can certify is the relation of intensional meanings amongst themselves; *e.g.*, that whatever satisfies one condition must also satisfy another condition; that what satisfies one condition must fail to satisfy another condition; that what is requisite to satisfaction of one condition is the same as what is requisite to satisfaction of another; or that two conditions are mutually compatible but have none of the previous relations. None of these relationships can be empirically assured, with the exception of consistency; and consistency is, logically, a negative fact—the negative of a relation of deducibility.

I have so far spoken of individuals, of characters or attributes, of existence, and of an ontological status of conceptual meanings which is not that of existence, with no explanations. Adequacy in an implied metaphysics would take a book; one which I shall not attempt to write. Dogmatically and inadequately: only individuals exist. And I am satisfied to conceive individuals as continuous and bounded parts of the space-time whole. (The space-time whole itself is a Pickwickian individual, not being boundable.) One individual may be wholly contained in another, as the bottom board is included in a box. Two may overlap, as a dog and a hair that it sheds. Individuals having neither of these two relationships are distinct. The space-time attributes of a thing may serve as the 'principle of individuation' but cannot be exhaustive of its individuality; and space-time attributes themselves are specifiable only in relative terms. (In passing, please note that a pile of sand is an individual only if the pieces of air between the grains are parts of this individual pile: the *sand* in the pile is not a continuous boundable entity. This apparently trivial consideration might turn out to be important for clear distinction between individuals and characters.)

A character is an entity which can be instanced, and is the same in all its instances. An instance of a character is an existent individual. Characters themselves do not exist, but they are real or unreal. A character is real if an instance of it exists.

Correlatively, neither concepts nor intensional meanings exist. But a concept is real if there is a psychological instance of its entertainment, or it is logically (and consistently) constructible from element-concepts which are entertained. (The notion of a concept never entertained may seem jejune; but we should remind ourselves that this is the only kind of reality which any but an infinitesimal fraction of the natural numbers have. In this connection also, we should observe the necessity of distinguishing a concept the expression of which would be of the form 'logically constructible from elements such and such by operations so and so' from any concept so constructed.) Similarly, an intensional meaning as a linguistic entity may have the kind of reality characteristic of expressions; that is, it is real if there is some pattern of sounds or of marks having an instance—some noise on some occasion or a pile of ink somewhere—which conveys this conceptually determinate meaning; or if it is consistently constructible by the rules of language from elementary expressions which are instanced.

As between the concept, or the intensional meaning, on the one side, and the corresponding character in an object or objects, on the other, the reality of the concept or the meaning does not entail the reality of the character as instanced in some existent. (It is by this fact that we are able to think of, and speak of, what does not exist. And if we could not so think, we could not act deliberately, since that requires us to choose amongst considered alternatives only one of which will ever be realized.) Also, the reality of the character, as instanced in some individual, does not entail the reality of the concept, or of the intensional meaning as a linguistic entity.

Meanings as concepts, meanings as linguistic intensions, and characters as instanced in existents, are all three of them abstract entities or universals. Concepts and linguistic entities are—I have suggested—mind-dependent. Whether characters or attributes, as abstractable aspects of individual existents, are mind-dependent, is a final question which lies between a metaphysics which is consistent with nominalism and one consistent with conceptualism. I shall attempt merely to indicate the locus of this somewhat tenuous issue. The conceptualist repudiates nominalism, for one reason because it reduces logic to a game played with fictions, having a psychological explanation but no validity. And for another because it reduces the basis of the intelligibility of things to a similar fiction. But he refuses the Platonic reification of abstractions, and he may also repudiate the basic argument of absolute idealism: to be real is to be intelligible, and to be intelligible is to be mind-related; hence no object out of relation to a subject. He may consider the logocentric predicament (Professor Sheffer's phrase) of a rationalizing mind which must think and speak in terms of universals, no better argument for absolute idealism than the egocentric predicament is for personalistic idealism. If so, then he is left with a conception I can only suggest crudely by saying that the conception of a world of individual existents, none of them conscious, is a meaningful supposition; but that, in such a world, there would be no abstract entities; there would be classifiable things but no classes; there would be stars in the heavens but no constellations.

What suggests this manner of conception, and is at once less simple-minded than my crudely put suggestion and more pertinent to logic, is the fact that nothing can be literally apprehended by a mind except some abstractions or universal. Individuals can neither be thought of nor identified except through their inherent characters. The nominalistic conception that individuals are the first knowables and the logically primitive entities, and that individuals are primitively determinable by ostensive reference, is, I think, epistemologically untenable. It is plausible only when a genetic account of psychological origins is substituted for the required epistemological investigation of validities. No one can literally be shown what is meant by means of ostensive indications unless these are supplemented by some manner of empathetic guess-work. In the first place, characters can be pointed to, as well as individuals: it requires that the intention to indicate an individual and not a character should be divined before such an intended identification can be ostensively conveyed. In the second place, whether it be an individual or a character which it is intended to identify as meant, no pointing and no succession of pointings can delimit *precisely* what is meant—this for a number of reasons some of which at least will be obvious. Successive pointings may progressively limit and hence inductively approximate to an intended meaning but—be it noted—such approximation can only be in terms of recognizable characters presented or not presented for observation. And the meaning in question will not be strictly apprehended until the one who observes guesses correctly the *rule of discrimination* which the one who points is using in determining when to point and when not to point. That criterion is the concept.

The intention to identify an individual as meant can, in any case, succeed only on account of the logically accidental limitations of what exists. An individual is apprehendable only as *that which* satisfies certain conditions specifiable in terms of characters it incorporates. The specified characters must be finitely enumerable, but the individual, being subject to the law of the excluded middle, is infinitely specific. I can only suggest and not develop the important features of meaning as denoting or designating which follow from this fact. The mother whose child, now six, was kidnapped at the age of two, passionately intends to refer to just one child. But it is a part of her tragedy that her attempt to identify this child may be mistaken because she is unable to specify sufficiently the characters to be looked for.

I can only suggest and not develop correlative considerations for the logic of singular terms and singular statements. "Zeus is a god" and "Socrates is a man" have the same grammatical form. But they are not of the same form logically. The former means that, for any x, that x is Zeus entails that x is a god. No implication of existence or nonexistence is involved, and the statement is analytic, being certifiable from the definitive meaning of 'Zeus.' "Socrates is a man" would satisfy the same paradigm, but it presumably intends the further implication that a unique individual exists satisfying the condition 'x is Socrates.' Although we know from the meaning of 'Socrates' that no nonhuman individual satisfies this condition, we have inductive assurance only of the existence and uniqueness of an object satisfying it; and the statement "Socrates is a man" is nonanalytic, like every assertion of existence.

One important point of distinction between individuals and characters must at least be mentioned since, without it, the distinction itself could be unclear. For every predicable relation of an individual to a character, there is the converse relation of that character to that individual. Individuals instance just those characters which they do; and conversely, characters are instanced in just those individuals in which they are. The difference is that every character instanced by an individual is essential to that individual's being just the individual that it is. That is implied by the infinite specificity of what is individual. A character, however, is just that character which it is regardless of what individuals exist and are instances of it. In other words, the relation between an individual and a character it instances is essential to the individual; inessential to the character. That is a basic difference between the two categories.

One corollary of this is the fact that any attempt to identify a universal or a character by reference to the class of individuals of which this character is predicable, is doomed to failure. Any given predicate, taken as condition, delimits uniquely a classification of existents (which may be null); but no class of existents determines a unique predicate as that which all its members satisfy. Owing to the logically accidental limitations of what exists, as well as on account of the infinite specificity of each and every individual, there are always, for any given class of existents, at least two predicates (two which are not equivalent in intension) which are common to all and only those individuals which are members of this class. The predicates 'human,' 'featherless biped,' and 'animal that laughs' constitute a familiar though not too good example.

There are, I think, many other implications here involved, the investigation of which would be interesting and logically profitable. But time does not permit even the suggestion of them. In conclusion, let me mention one such consideration only; one with respect to which you may well think I have a prepossession.

The denotation or extension of any expression is always logically accidental: logic can never certify what it denotes or whether it denotes anything, except in those cases in which it is determinable, from its intensional meaning, that it has universal extension or that its extension is null. The statements belonging to any correct logic are those and those only whose truth is certifiable by reference to the intensional meanings of the logical constants of the system (including those conveyed by the syntactic significance of the order of writing). A logic in which the constants are confined to extensional functions symbolizes no element-relation such that whenever it obtains it is logically certifiable. The extensional logic of propositions, for example, instead of symbolizing and asserting that relation which obtains between p and q when and only when q is deducible from p, asserts a relation such that if two sentences be chosen at random from the morning paper, it is certain in advance that this relation will hold between one or other of them as antecedent and the remaining one as consequent. But it asserts this relation *only in those instances* in which the quite different relation which is the converse of 'is deducible from' also obtains. It thus uses tacitly, as criterion of assertion in logic, a relation which is not expressible in the vocabulary it provides; and what it asserts is logically certifiable for that reason only. I think it is desirable in logic that the logical criteria of logical certifiability should be expressed.

Read before the meeting of the Association for Symbolic Logic on December 28, 1949, but not previously published.

ERNEST NAGEL

Mechanistic Explanation
and Organismic Biology

Vitalism of the substantival type sponsored by Driesch and other biologists during the preceding and early part of the present century is now a dead issue in the philosophy of biology—an issue that has become quiescent less, perhaps, because of the methodological and philosophical criticism that has been leveled against the doctrine than because of the infertility of vitalism as a guide in biological research and because of the superior heuristic value of alternative approaches for the investigation of biological phenomena. Nevertheless, the historically influential Cartesian conception of biology as simply a chapter of physics continues to meet resistance; and outstanding biologists who find no merit in vitalism believe there are conclusive reasons for maintaining the irreducibility of biology to physics and for asserting the intrinsic autonomy of biological method. The standpoint from which this thesis is currently advanced commonly carries the label of "organismic biology"; and though the label covers a variety of special biological doctrines that are not all mutually compatible, those who fall under it are united by the common conviction that biological phenomena cannot be understood adequately in terms of theories and explanations which are of the so-called "mechanistic type." It is the aim of the present paper to examine this claim.

It is, however, not always clear what thesis organismic biologists are rejecting when they declare that "mechanistic" explanations are not fully satisfactory in biology. In one familiar sense of "mechanistic," a theory is mechanistic if it employs only such concepts which are distinctive of the science of mechanics. It is doubtful, however, whether any professed mechanist in biology would today explicate his position in this manner. Physicists themselves have long since abandoned the seventeenth-century hope that a universal science of nature would be developed within the framework of the fundamental conceptions of mechanics. And no one today, it is safe to say, subscribes literally to the Cartesian program of reducing all the sciences to the science of mechanics and specifically to the mechanics of contact-action. On the other hand, it is not easy to state precisely what is the identifying mark of a mechanistic explanation if it is not to coincide with an explanation that falls within the science of mechanics. In a preliminary way, and for lack of anything better and clearer, I shall adopt in the present paper the criterion proposed long ago by Jacques Loeb, according to whom a mechanist in biology is one who believes that all living phenomena "can be unequivocally explained in physicochemical terms"—that is, in terms of theories that have been originally developed for domains of inquiry in which the distinction between the living and nonliving plays no role, and that by common consent are classified as belonging to physics and chemistry.

As will presently appear, this brief characterization of the mechanistic thesis in biology does not suffice to distinguish in certain important respects mechanists in biology from those who adopt the organismic standpoint; but the above indication will do for the moment. It does suffice to give point to one further preliminary remark which needs to be made before I turn to the central issue between mechanists and organismic biologists. It is an obvious commonplace, but one that must not be ignored if that issue is to be justly appraised, that there are large sectors of biological study in which physicochemical explanations play no role at present, and that a number of outstanding biological theories have been successfully exploited which are not physicochemical in character. For example, a vast array of important information has been obtained concerning embryological processes, though no explanation of such regularities in physicochemical terms is available; and neither the theory of evolution even in its current form, nor the gene theory of heredity is based on any definite physicochemical assumptions concerning living processes. Accordingly, organismic biologists possess at least some grounds for their skepticism concerning the inevitability of the mechanistic standpoint; and just as a physicist may be warranted in holding that some given branch of physics (*e.g.,* electromagnetic theory) is not reducible to some other branch (*e.g.,* mechanics), so an organismic biologist may be warranted in holding an analogous view with respect to the relation of biology and physicochemistry. If there is a genuine issue between mechanists and organismic biologists, it is not *prima facie* a pseudo question.

However, organismic biologists are not content with making the obviously justified observation that only a relatively small sector of biological phenomena has thus far been explained in physicochemical terms; they also maintain that *in principle* the mode of analysis associated with mechanistic explanations is inapplicable to some of the major problems of biology, and that therefore mechanistic biology cannot be adopted as the ultimate ideal in biological research. What are the grounds for this contention and how solid is the support which organismic biologists claim for their thesis?

The central theme of organismic biology is that living creatures are not assemblages of tissues and organs functioning independently of one another, but are integrated structures of parts. Accordingly, living organisms must be studied as "wholes," and not as the mere "sums" of parts. Each part, it is maintained, has physicochemical properties; but the interrelation of the parts involves a distinctive organization, so that the study of the physicochemical properties of the parts taken in isolation of their membership in the organized whole which is the living body fails to provide an adequate understanding of the facts of biology. In consequence, the continuous adaptation of an organism to its environment and of its parts to one another so as to maintain its characteristic structure and activities, cannot be described in terms of physical and chemical principles. Biology must employ categories and a vocabulary which are foreign to the sciences of the inorganic, and it must recognize modes and laws of behavior which are inexplicable in physicochemical terms.

To cite but one brief quotation from the writings of organismic biologists, I offer the following from E. S. Russell as a typical statement of this point of view:

> Any action of the whole organism would appear to be susceptible of analysis to an indefinite degree—and this is in general the aim of the physiologist, to analyze, to decompose into their elementary processes the broad activities and functions of the organism.
>
> But . . . by such a procedure something is lost, for the action of the whole has a certain unifiedness and completeness which is left out of account in the process of analysis. . . . In our conception of the organism we must . . .take into account the unifiedness and wholeness of its activities [especially since] the activities of the organism all have reference to one or other of three great ends [development, maintenance, and reproduction], and both the past and the future enter into their determination. . . .
>
> . . . It follows that the activities of the organism as a whole are to be regarded as of a different order from physicochemical relations, both in themselves and for the purposes of our understanding. . . .
>
> . . . Biochemistry studies essentially the *conditions* of actions of cells and organisms, while organismal biology attempts to study the actual modes of action of whole organisms, regarded as conditioned by, but irreducible to, the modes of action of lower unities. . . .[1]

Accordingly, while organismic biology rejects every form of substantival vitalism, it also rejects the possibility of physicochemical explanation of vital phenomena. But does it, in point of fact, present a clear alternative to physicochemical theories of living processes, and, if so, what types of explanatory theories does it recommend as worth exploring in biology?

(1) At first blush, the sole issue that seems to be raised by organismic biology is that commonly discussed under the heading of "emergence" in other branches of science, including the physical sciences; and, although other questions are involved in the organismic standpoint, I shall begin with this aspect of the question.

The crux of the doctrine of emergence, as I see it, is the determination of the conditions under which one science can be reduced to some other one—*i.e.*, the formulation of the logical and empirical conditions which must be satisfied if the laws and other statements of one discipline can be subsumed under, or explained by, the theories and principles of a second discipline. Omitting details and refinements, the two conditions which seem to be necessary and sufficient for such a reduction are briefly as follows. Let S_1 be some science or group of sciences such as physics and chemistry, hereafter to be called the "primary discipline," to which a second science, S_2, for example biology, is to be reduced. Then (i) every term which occurs in the statements of S_2 (e.g., terms like "cell," "mytosis," "heredity," etc.) must be either explicitly definable with the help of the vocabulary specific to the primary discipline (e.g., with the help of expressions like "length," "electric charge," "osmosis"); or well-established empirical laws must be available with the help of which it is possible to state the sufficient conditions for the application of all expressions in S_2, exclusively in terms of expressions occurring in the explanatory principles of S_1. For example, it must be possible to state the truth-conditions of a statement of the form "x is a cell" by means of sentences constructed exclusively out of the vocabulary belonging to the physicochemical sciences. Though the label is not entirely appropriate, this first condition will be referred to as the condition of definability. (ii) Every statement in the secondary discipline, S_2, and especially those statements which formulate the laws established in S_2, must be derivable logically from some appropriate class of statements that can be established in the primary science, S_1—such classes of statements will include the fundamental theoretical assumptions of S_1. This second condition will be referred to as the condition of derivability.

It is evident that the second condition cannot be fulfilled unless the first one is, although the realization of the first condition does not entail the satisfaction of the second one. It is also quite beyond dispute that in the sense of reduction specified by these conditions biology has thus far not been reduced to physics and chemistry, since not even the first step in the process of reduction has been completed—for example, we are not yet in the position to specify exhaustively in physicochemical terms the conditions for the occurrence of cellular division.

Accordingly, organismic biologists are on firm ground if what they maintain is that all biological phenomena are not explicable thus far physicochemically, and that no physicochemical theory can possibly explain such phenomena until the descriptive and theoretical terms of biology meet the condition of definability. On the other hand, nothing in the facts surveyed up to this point warrants the conclusion that biology is *in principle* irreducible to physicochemistry. Whether biology is reducible to physicochemistry is a question that only further experimental and logical research can settle; for the supposition that each of the two conditions for the reduction of biology to physicochemistry may some day be satisfied involves no patent contradiction.

(2) There are, however, other related considerations underlying the organismic claim that biology is intrinsically autonomous. A frequent argument used to support this claim is based on the fact that living organisms are hierarchically organized and that, in consequence, modes of behavior characterizing the so-called "higher levels" of organization cannot be explained in terms of the structures and modes of behavior which parts of the organism exhibit on lower levels of the hierarchy.

There can, of course, be no serious dispute over the fact that organisms do exhibit structures of parts that have an obvious hierarchical organization. Living cells are structures of cellular parts (*e.g.*, of the nucleus, cytoplasm, central bodies, etc.), each of which in turn appears to be composed of complex molecules; and, except in the case of unicellular organisms, cells are further organized into tissues, which in turn are elements of various organs that make up the individual organism. Nor is there any question but that parts of an organism which occupy a place at one level of its complex hierarchical organization stand in relations and exhibit activities which parts occupying positions at other levels of organization do not manifest: a cat can stalk and catch mice, but though its heart is involved in these activities, that organ cannot perform these feats; again, the heart can pump blood by contracting and expanding its muscular tissues, but no tissue is able to do this; and no tissue is able to divide by fission, though its constituent cells may have this power; and so on down the line. If such facts are taken in an obvious sense, they undoubtedly support the conclusion that behavior on higher levels of organization is not explained by merely citing the various behaviors of parts on lower levels of the hierarchy. Organismic biologists do not, of course, deny that the higher level behaviors occur only when the component parts of an organism are appropriately organized on the various levels of the hierarchy; but they appear to have reason on their side in maintaining that a knowledge of the behavior of these parts when these latter are not component elements in the structured living organism, does not suffice as a premise for deducing anything about the behavior of the whole organism in which the parts do stand in certain specific and complex relations to one another.

But do these admitted facts establish the organismic thesis that mechanistic explanations are not adequate in biology? This does not appear to be the case, and for several reasons. It should be noted, in the first place, that various forms of hierarchical organization are exhibited by the materials of physics and chemistry, and not only by those of biology. On the basis of current theories of matter, we are compelled to regard atoms as structures of electric charges, molecules as organizations of atoms, solids and liquids as complex systems of molecules; and we must also recognize that the element occupying positions at different levels of the indicated hierarchy generally exhibit traits and modes of activity that their component parts do not possess. Nonetheless, this fact has not stood in the way of establishing comprehensive theories for the more elementary physical particles, in terms of which it has been possible to explain some, if not all, of the physicochemical properties exhibited by things having a more complex organization. We do not, to be sure, possess at the present time a comprehensive and unified theory which is competent to explain the whole range of physicochemical phenomena at all levels of complexity. Whether such a theory will ever be achieved is certainly an open question. But even if such an inclusive theory were never achieved, the mere fact that we can now explain some features of relatively highly organized bodies on the basis of theories formulated in terms of relations between relatively more simply structured elements—for example, the specific heats of solids in terms of quantum theory or the changes in phase of compounds in terms of the thermodynamics of mixtures—should give us pause in accepting the conclusion that the mere fact of the hierarchical organization of biological materials precludes the possibility of a mechanistic explanation.

This observation leads to a second point. Organismic biologists do not deny that biological organisms are complex structures of physicochemical processes, although like everyone else they do not claim to know in minute detail just what these processes are or just how the various physicochemical elements (assumed as the ultimate parts of living creatures) are related to one another in a living organism. They do maintain, however (or appear to maintain), that even if our knowledge in this respect were ideally complete, it would still be impossible to account for the characteristic behavior of biological organisms—their ability to maintain themselves, to develop, and to reproduce—in mechanistic terms. Thus, it has been claimed that even if we were able to describe in full detail in physicochemical terms what is taking place when a fertilized egg segments, we would, nevertheless, be unable to explain mechanistically the fact of segmentation—in the language of E. S. Russell, we would then be able to state the physicochemical *conditions* for the occurrence of segmentation, but we would still be unable to "explain the *course* which development takes." Now this claim seems to me to rest on a misunderstanding, if not on a confusion. It is entirely correct to maintain that a knowledge of the physicochemical composition of a biological organism does not suffice to explain mechanistically its mode of action—any more than an enumeration of the parts of a clock and a knowledge of their distribution and arrangement suffices to explain and predict the mode of behavior of the timepiece. To do the latter, one must *also* assume some theory or set of laws (*e.g.,* the theory of mechanics) which formulates the way in which certain elementary objects behave when they occur in certain initial distributions and arrangements, and with the help of which we can calculate and predict the course of subsequent development of the mechanism. Now it may indeed be the case that our information at a given time may suffice to describe physicochemically the constitution of a biological organism; nevertheless, the established physicochemical theories may not be adequate, even when combined with a physicochemical description of the initial state of the organism, for deducing just what the course of the latter's development will be. To put the point in terms of the distinction previously introduced, the condition of definability may be realized without the condition of derivability being fulfilled. But this fact must not be interpreted to mean that it is possible under any circumstances to give explanations without the use of some theoretical assumptions, or that because one body of physicochemical theory is not competent to explain certain biological phenomena it is *in principle impossible* to construct and establish mechanistic theories which might do so.

(3) I must now examine the consideration which appears to constitute the main reason for the negative attitude of organismic biologists toward mechanistic explanations. Organismic biologists have placed great stress on what they call the "unifiedness," the "unity," the "completeness," or the "wholeness" of organic behavior; and, since they believe that biological organisms are com-

plex systems of mutually determining and interdependent processes to which subordinate organs contribute in various ways, they have maintained that organic behavior cannot be analyzed into a set of independently determinable component behaviors of the parts of an organism, whose "sum" may be equated to the total behavior of the organism. On the other hand, they also maintain that mechanistic philosophies of organic action are "machine theories" of the organism, which assume the "additive point of view" with respect to biological phenomena. What distinguishes mechanistic theories from organismic ones, from this perspective, is that the former do while the latter do not regard an organism as a "machine," whose "parts" are separable and can be studied in isolation from their actual functioning in the whole living organism, so that the latter may then be understood and explained as an aggregate of such independent parts, Accordingly, the fundamental reason for the dissatisfaction which organismic biologists feel toward mechanistic theories is the "additive point of view" that allegedly characterizes the latter. However, whether this argument has any merit can be decided only if the highly ambiguous and metaphorical notion of "sum" receives at least partial clarification; and it is to this phase of the question that I first briefly turn.

(i) As is well known, the word "sum" has a large variety of different uses, a number of which bear to each other certain formal analogies while others are so vague that nothing definite is conveyed by the word. There are well-defined senses of the term in various domains of pure mathematics—e.g., arithmetical sum, algebraic sum, vector sum, and the like; there are also definite uses established for the word in the natural sciences—e.g., sum of weights, sum of forces, sum of velocities, etc. But with notable exceptions, those who have employed it to distinguish wholes which are sums of their parts from wholes which supposedly are not, have not taken the trouble to indicate just what would be the sum of parts of a whole which allegedly is not equal to that whole.

I therefore wish to suggest a sense for the work "sum" which seems to me relevant to the claim of organismic biologists that the total behavior of an organism is not the sum of the behavior of its parts. That is, I wish, to indicate more explicitly than organismic biologists have done—though I hasten to add that the proposed indication is only moderately more precise than is customary—what it is they are asserting when they maintain, for example, that the behavior of the kidneys in an animal body is more than the "sum" of the behaviors of the tissues, blood stream, blood vessels, and the rest of the parts of the body involved in the functioning of the kidneys.

Let me first state the suggestion in schematic, abstract form. Let T be a definite body of theory which is capable of explaining a certain indefinitely large class of statements concerning the simultaneous or successive occurrence of some set of properties, P_1, P_2, . . . P_k. Suppose further that it is possible with the help of the Theory T to explain the behavior of a set of individuals i with respect to their manifesting these properties P when these individuals form a closed system s_1, under circumstances C_1; and that it is also possible with the help of T to explain the behavior of another set of individuals j with respect to their manifesting these properties P when the individuals j form a closed system s_2 under circumstances C_2. Now assume that the two sets of individuals i and j form an enlarged closed system s_3 under circumstances C_3, in which they exhibit certain modes of behavior which are formulated in a set of laws L. Two cases may now be distinguished: (a) It may be possible to deduce the laws L from T conjoined with the relevant initial conditions which obtain in C_3; in this case, the behavior of the system s_3 may be said to be the sum of the behaviors of its parts s_1 and s_2; or (b) the laws L cannot be so deduced, in which case the behavior of the system s_3 may be said *not* to be the sum of the behaviors of its parts.

Two examples may help to make clearer what is here intended. The laws of mechanics enable us to explain the mechanical behaviors of a set of cogwheels when they occur in certain arrangements; those laws also enable us to explain the behavior of freely falling bodies moving against some resisting forces, and also the behavior of compound pendula. But the laws of mechanics also explain the behavior of the system obtained by arranging cogs, weights, and pendulum in certain ways so as to form a clock; and, accordingly, the behavior of a clock can be regarded as the sum of the behavior of its parts. On the other hand, the kinetic theory of matter as developed during the nineteenth century was able to explain certain thermal properties of gases at various temperatures, including the relations between the specific heats of gases; but it was unable to explain the relations between the specific heats of solids—that is, it was unable to account for these relations theoretically when the state of aggregation of molecules is that of a solid rather than a gas. Accordingly, the thermal behavior of solids is not the sum of the behavior of its parts.

Whether the above proposal to interpret the distinction between wholes which are and those which are not the sums of their parts would be acceptable to organismic biologists, I do not know. But, while I am aware that the suggestion requires much elaboration and refinement to be an adequate tool of analysis, in broad outline it represents what seems to me to be the sole intellectual content of what organismic biologists have had to say in this connection. However, if the proposed interpretation of the distinction is accepted as reasonable, then one important consequence needs to be noted. For, on the above proposal, the distinction between wholes which are and those which are not sums of parts is clearly *relative to some assumed body of theory T;* and, accordingly, though a given whole may not be the sum of its parts relative to one theory, it may indeed be such a sum relative to another. Thus, though the thermal behavior of solids is not the sum of the behavior of its parts relative to the classical kinetic theory of matter, it is such a sum relative to modern quantum mechanics. To say, therefore, that the behavior of an organism is not the sum of the behavior of its parts, and that its total behavior cannot be understood adequately in physicochemical terms even though the behavior of each of its parts is explicable mechanistically, can only mean that no body of general theory is now available from which statements about the total behavior of the organism are derivable. The assertion, even if true, does *not* mean that it is *in principle* impossible to explain such total behavior mechanistically, and it supplies no competent evidence for such a claim.

(ii) There is a second point related to the organismic emphasis on the "wholeness" of organic action upon which I wish to comment briefly. It is frequently overlooked, even by those who really know better, that no theory, whether in the physical sciences or elsewhere, can explain the operations of any concrete system, unless various restrictive or boundary conditions are placed on the generality of the theory and unless, also, specific initial conditions, relevantly formulated, are supplied for the application of the theory. For example, electrostatic theory is unable to specify the distribution of electric charges on the surface of a given body unless certain special information, not deducible from the fundamental equation of the theory (Poisson's equation), is supplied.

This information must include statements concerning the shape and size of the body, whether it is a conductor or not, the distribution of other charges (if any) in the environment of the body, and the value of the dialectric constant of the medium in which the body is immersed.

But though this point is elementary, organismic biologists seem to me to neglect it quite often. They sometimes argue that though mechanistic explanations can be given for the behaviors of certain parts of organisms when these parts are studied in abstraction or isolation from the rest of the organism, such explanations are not possible if those parts are functioning conjointly and in mutual dependence as actual constituents of a living organism. This argument seems to me to have no force whatever. What it overlooks is that the initial and boundary conditions which must be supplied in explaining physicochemically the behavior of an organic part acting in isolation are, in general, *not sufficient* for explaining mechanistically the conjoint functioning of such parts. For when these parts are assumed to be acting in mutual dependence, the environment of each part no longer continues to be what it was supposed to be when it was acting in isolation. Accordingly, a necessary requirement for the mechanistic explanation of the unified behavior of organisms is that boundary and initial conditions bearing on the actual relations of parts as parts of living organisms be stated in *physicochemical* terms. Unless, therefore, appropriate data concerning the physicochemical constitution and arrangement of the various parts of organisms are specified, it is not surprising that mechanistic explanations of the total behavior of organisms cannot be given. In point of fact, this requirement has not yet been fulfilled even in the case of the simplest forms of living organisms, for our ignorance concerning the detailed physicochemical constitution of organic parts is profound. Moreover, even if we were to succeed in completing our knowledge in this respect —this would be equivalent to satisfying the condition of definability stated earlier—biological phenomena might still not be all explicable mechanistically: for this further step could be taken only if a comprehensive and independently warranted physicochemical theory were available from which, together with the necessary boundary and initial conditions, the laws and other statements of biology are derivable. We have certainly failed thus far in finding mechanistic explanations for the total range of biological phenomena, and we may never succeed in doing so. But, though we continue to fail, then if this paper is not completely in error, the reasons for such failure are not the *a priori* arguments advanced by organismic biology.

(4) One final critical comment must be added. It is important to distinguish the question whether mechanistic explanations of biological phenomena are possible, from the quite different though related problem whether living organisms can be effectively synthesized in a laboratory out of nonliving materials. Many biologists apparently deny the first possibility because of their skepticism concerning the second, even when their skepticism does not extend to the possibility of an artificial synthesis of every chemical compound that is normally produced by biological organisms. But the two questions are not related in a manner so intimate; and though it may never be possible to create living organisms by artificial means, it does not follow from this assumption that biological phenomena are incapable of being explained mechanistically. We do not possess the power to manufacture nebulae or solar systems, though we do have available physicochemical theories in terms of which the behaviors of nebulae and solar systems are tolerably well understood; and while modern physics and chemistry is beginning to supply explanations for the various properties of metals in terms of the electronic structure of their atoms, there is no compelling reason to suppose that we shall one day be able to manufacture gold by putting together artificially its subatomic constituents. And yet the general tenor, if not the explicit assertions, of some of the literature of organismic biology is that the possibility of mechanistic explanations in biology entails the possibility of taking apart and putting together in overt fashion the various parts of living organisms to reconstitute them as unified creatures. But, in point of fact, the condition for achieving mechanistic explanations is quite different from that necessary for the artficial manufacture of living organisms. The former involves the construction of factually warranted *theories* of physicochemical processes; the latter depends on the availability of certain physicochemical substances and on the invention of effective techniques of control. It is no doubt unlikely that living organisms will ever be synthesized in the laboratory except with the help of mechanistic theories of organic processes—in the absence of such theories, the artificial creation of living things would at best be only a fortunate accident. But, however this may be, these conditions are logically

independent of each other, and either might be realized without the other being satisfied.

(5) The central thesis of this paper is that none of the arguments advanced by organismic biologists establish the inherent impossibility of physicochemical explanations of vital processes. Nevertheless, the stress which organismic biologists have placed on the fact of the hierarchical organization of living things and on the mutual dependence of their parts is not without value. For though organismic biology has not demonstrated what it proposes to prove, it has succeeded in making the heuristically valuable point that the explanation of biological processes in physicochemical terms is not a necessary condition for the fruitful study of such processes. There is, in fact, no more good reason for dissatisfaction with a biological theory (e.g., modern genetics) because it is not explicable mechanistically than there is for dissatisfaction with a physical theory (e.g., electromagnetism) because it is not reducible to some other branch of that discipline (e.g., to mechanics). And a wise strategy of research may, in fact, require that a given discipline be cultivated as an autonomous branch of science, at least during a certain period of its development, rather than as a mere appendage to some other and more inclusive discipline. The protest of organismic biology against the dogmatism frequently associated with mechanistic approaches to biology is salutary.

On the other hand, organismic biologists sometimes write as if any analysis of living processes into the behaviors of distinguishable parts of organisms entails a radical distortion of our understanding of such processes. Thus Wildon Carr, one proponent of the organismic standpoint, proclaimed that "Life is individual; it exists only in living beings, and each living being is indivisible, a whole not constituted of parts." Such pronouncements exhibit a tendency that seems far more dangerous than is the dogmatism of intransigent mechanists. For it is beyond serious question that advances in biology occur only through the use of an abstractive method, which proceeds to study various aspects of organic behavior in relative isolation of other aspects. Organismic biologists proceed in this way, for they have no alternative. For example, in spite of his insistence on the indivisible unity of the organism, J. S. Haldane's work on respiration and the chemistry of the blood did not proceed by considering the body as a whole, but by studying the relations between the behavior of one part of the body (e.g., the quantity of carbon dioxide taken in by the lungs) and the behavior of another part (the chemical action of the red blood cells). Organismic biologists, like everyone else who contributes to the advance of science, must be selective in their procedure and must study the behavior of living organisms under specialized and isolating conditions—on pain of making the free but unenlightening use of expressions like "wholeness" and "unifiedness" substitutes for genuine knowledge.

Reprinted with permission from *Philosophy and Phenomenological Research*, 1951.

1. E. S. Russell, *Interpretation of Development and Heredity*, pp. 171–2, 187–8.

WILLARD V. QUINE

Logical Truth

1

What of the empiricist who would grant certainty to logic, and to the whole of mathematics, and yet would make a clean sweep of other nonempirical theories under the name of metaphysics? The Viennese solution of this nice problem was predicated on language. Metaphysics was meaningless through misuse of language; logic was certain through tautologous use of language.

As an answer to the question "How is logical certainty possible?" this linguistic doctrine of logical truth has its attractions. For there can be no doubt that sheer verbal usage is in general a major determinant of truth. Even so factual a sentence as 'Brutus killed Caesar' owes its truth not only to the killing but equally to our using the component words as we do. Why then should a logically true sentence on the same topic, *e.g.* 'Brutus killed Caesar or did not kill Caesar,' not be said to owe its truth *purely* to the fact that we use our words (in this case 'or' and 'not') as we do?—for it depends not at all for its truth upon the killing.

The suggestion is not, of course, that the logically true sentence is a contingent truth *about* verbal usage; but rather that it is a sentence which, *given* the language, automatically becomes true, whereas 'Brutus killed Caesar,' given the language, becomes true only contingently on the alleged killing.

Further plausibility accrues to the linguistic doctrine of logical truth when we reflect on the question of alternative logics. Suppose someone puts forward and uses a consistent logic the principles of which are contrary to our own. We are then clearly free to say that he is merely using the familiar particles 'and,' 'all,' or whatever, in other than the familiar senses, and hence that no real contrariety is present after all. There may, of course, still be an important failure of intertranslatability, in that the behavior of certain of our logical particles is incapable of being duplicated by paraphrases in his system or vice versa. If translation in this sense is possible, from his system into ours, then we are pretty sure to protest that he was wantonly using the familiar particles 'and' and 'all' (say) where he might unmisleadingly have used such and such other familiar phrasing. This reflection goes to support the view that the truths of logic have no content over and above the meanings they confer on the logical vocabulary.

Much the same point can be brought out by a caricature of a doctrine of Levy-Bruhl, according to which there are prelogical peoples who accept certain simple self-contradictions as true. Oversimplifying, no doubt, let us suppose it claimed that these natives accept as true a certain sentence of the form '*p* and not *p*.' Or— not to oversimplify too much—that they accept as true a certain heathen sentence of the form '*q* ka bu *q*' the English translation of which has the form '*p* and not *p*.' But now just how good a translation is this, and what may the lexicographer's method have been? If any evidence can count against a lexicographer's adoption of 'and' and 'not' as translations of 'ka' and 'bu,' certainly the natives' acceptance of '*q* ka bu *q*' as true counts overwhelmingly. We are left with the meaninglessness of the doctrine of there being prelogical peoples; prelogicality is a trait injected by bad translators. This is one more illustration of the inseparability of the truths of logic from the meanings of the logical vocabulary.

2

Where someone disagrees with us as to the truth of a sentence, it often happens that we can convince him by getting the sentence from other sentences, which he does accept, by a series of steps each of which he accepts. Disagreement which cannot be thus resolved I shall call *deductively irresoluble*. Now if we try to warp the linguistic doctrine of logical truth around into something like an experimental thesis, perhaps a first approximation will run thus: *Deductively irresoluble disagreement as to a logical truth is evidence of deviation in usage (or meanings) of words.* This is not yet experimentally phrased, since one term of the affirmed relationship, *viz.* 'usage' (or 'meanings'), is in dire need of an independent criterion. However, the formulation would seem to be fair enough within its limits; so let us go ahead with it, not seeking more subtlety until need arises.

Elementary logic, as commonly systematized nowadays, comprises truth-function theory, quantification theory, and identity theory. Every truth of elementary logic is obvious (whatever this really means), or can be made so by some series of individually obvious steps.

Now this obviousness (or potential obviousness) of elementary logic can be seen to present an insuperable obstacle to our assigning any experimental meaning to the linguistic doctrine of elementary logical truth. Deductively irresoluble dissent from an elementary logical truth *would* count as evidence of deviation over meanings if anything can, but simply because dissent from a logical truism is as extreme as dissent can get.

The philosopher, like the beginner in algebra, works in danger of finding that his solution-in-progress reduces to '0 = 0.' Such is the threat to the linguistic theory of elementary logical truth. For, that theory now seems to imply nothing that is not already implied by the fact that elementary logic is obvious or can be resolved into obvious steps.

The considerations which were adduced in §1, to show the naturalness of the linguistic doctrine, are likewise seen to be empty when scrutinized in the present spirit. One was the circumstance that alternative logics are inseparable practically from mere change in usage of logical words. Another was that illogical cultures are indistinguishable from ill-translated ones. But both of these circumstances are adequately accounted for by mere obviousness of logical principles, without help of a linguistic doctrine of logical truth. For, there can be no stronger evidence of a change in usage than the repudiation of what had been obvious, and no stronger evidence of bad translation than that it translates earnest affirmations into obvious falsehoods.

Another point in §1 was that true sentences generally depend for their truth on the traits of their language in addition to the traits of their subject matter; and that logical truths then fit neatly in as the limiting case where the dependence on traits of the subject matter is nil. Consider, however, the logical truth 'Everything is self-identical,' or '$(x) (x = x)$.' We *can* say that it depends for its truth on traits of the language (specifically on the usage of '$=$'), and not on traits of its subject matter; but we can also say, alternatively, that it depends on an *obvious* trait, *viz.* self-identity, of its subject matter, *viz.* everything. The tendency of our present reflections is that there is no difference.

I have been using the vaguely psychological word 'obvious' non-technically, assigning it no explanatory value. My suggestion is merely that the linguistic doctrine of elementary logical truth likewise leaves explanation unbegun. I do not suggest that the linguistic doctrine is false and some doctrine of ultimate and inexplicable insight into the obvious traits of reality is true, but only that there is no real difference between these two pseudo doctrines.

3

The linguistic doctrine of logical truth is sometimes expressed by saying that such truths are true by linguistic convention. Now if this be so, certainly the conventions are not in general explicit. Relatively few persons, before the time of Carnap, had ever seen any convention that engendered truths of elementary logic. Nor can this circumstance be ascribed merely to the slipshod ways of our predecessors. For it is impossible in principle, even in an ideal state, to get even the most elementary part of logic exclusively by the explicit application of conventions stated in advance. The difficulty is the vicious regress, familiar from Lewis Carroll,[1] which I have elaborated elsewhere.[2] Briefly, the point is that the logical truths, being infinite in number, must be given by general conventions rather than singly; and logic is needed then to begin with, in the metatheory, in order to apply the general conventions to individual cases.

"In dropping the attributes of deliberateness and explicitness from the notion of linguistic convention," I went on to complain in the aforementioned paper, "we risk depriving the latter of any explanatory force and reducing it to an idle label." It would seem that to call elementary logic true by convention is to add nothing but a metaphor to the linguistic doctrine of logical truth which, as applied to elementary logic, has itself come to seem rather an empty figure.[3]

The case of set theory, however, differs from that of elementary logic. The truths of set theory are not all derivable from obvious beginnings by obvious steps; and in fact convention in quite the ordinary sense seems to be pretty much what goes on. Set theory was straining at the leash of intuition ever since Cantor discovered the higher infinites; and with the added impetus of the paradoxes of set theory the leash was snapped. What we do is develop one or another set theory by obvious reasoning, or elementary logic, from unobvious first principles which are set down, whether for good or for the time being, by something very like convention.

Conventionalism has a serious claim to attention in the philosophy of mathematics, if only because of set theory. Historically, though, conventionalism was encouraged in the philosophy of mathematics rather by the non-Euclidean geometries and abstract algebras, with little good reason. We can contribute to subsequent purposes by surveying this situation. Further talk of set theory is deferred to §4.

In the beginning there was Euclidean geometry, a compendium of truths about form and void; and its truths were not based on convention (except as a conventionalist might, begging the present question, apply this tag to everything mathematical). Its truths were in practice presented by deduction from so-called postulates (including axioms; I shall not distinguish); and the selection of truths for this role of postulate, out of the totality of truths of Euclidean geometry, was indeed a matter of convention. But this is not *truth* by convention. The truths were there, and what was conventional was merely the separation of them into those to be taken as a starting point (for purposes of the exposition at hand) and those to be deduced from them.

The non-Euclidean geometries came of artificial deviations from Euclid's postulates, without thought (to begin with) of true interpretation. These departures were doubly conventional; for Euclid's postulates were a conventional selection from among the truths of geometry, and then the departures were arbitrarily or conventionally devised in turn. But still there was no truth by convention, because there was no truth.

Playing within a non-Euclidean geometry, one might conveniently make believe that his theorems were interpreted and true; but even such conventional make-believe is not truth by convention. For it is not really truth at all; and what is conventionally pretended is that the theorems are true by nonconvention.

Non-Euclidean geometries have, in the fullness of time, received serious interpretations. This means that ways have been found of so construing the hitherto unconstrued terms as to identify the at first conventionally chosen set of nonsentences with some genuine truths, and truths presumably not by convention. The status of an interpreted non-Euclidean geometry differs in no basic way from the original status of Euclidean geometry, noted above.

Uninterpreted systems became quite the fashion after the advent of non-Euclidean geometries. This fashion helped to cause, and was in turn encouraged by, an increasingly formal approach to mathematics. Methods had to become more formal to make up for the unavailability, in uninterpreted systems, of intuition. Conversely, disinterpretation served as a crude but useful device (until Frege's syntactical approach came to be appreciated) for achieving formal rigor uncorrupted by intuition.

The tendency to look upon non-Euclidean geometries as true by convention applied to uninterpreted systems generally, and then carried over from these to mathematical systems generally. A tendency indeed developed to look upon all mathematical systems as, *qua* mathematical, uninterpreted. This tendency can be accounted for by the increase of formality, together with the use of disinterpretation as a heuristic aid to formalization. Finally, in an effort to make some sense of mathematics thus drained of all interpretation, recourse was had to the shocking quibble of identifying mathematics merely with the elementary logic which leads from uninterpreted postulates to uninterpreted theorems.[4] What is shocking about this is that it puts arithmetic *qua* interpreted theory of number, an analysis *qua* interpreted theory of functions, and geometry qua interpreted theory of space, outside mathematics altogether.

The substantive reduction of mathematics to logic by Frege, Whitehead, and Russell is of course quite another thing. It is a reduction not to elementary logic but to set theory; and it is a reduction of genuine interpreted mathematics, from arithmetic onward.

4

Let us then put aside these confusions and get back to set theory. Set theory is pursued as interpreted mathematics, like arithmetic and analysis; indeed, it is to set theory that those further branches are reducible. In set theory we discourse about certain immaterial entities, real or erroneously alleged, *viz.* sets, or classes. And it is in the effort to make up our minds about genuine truth and falsity of sentences about these objects that we find ourselves engaged in something very like convention in an ordinary non-metaphorical sense of the word. We find ourselves making deliberate choices and setting them forth unaccompanied by any attempt at justification other than in terms of elegance and convenience. These adoptions, called postulates, and their logical consequences (via elementary logic) are true until further notice.

So here is a case where postulation can plausibly be looked on as constituting truth by convention. But in §3 we have seen how the philosophy of mathematics can be corrupted by supposing that postulates always play that role. Insofar as we would epistemologize and not just mathematize, we might divide postulation as follows. Uninterpreted postulates may be put aside, as no longer concerning us; and on the interpreted side we may distinguish between *legislative* and *discursive* postulation. Legislative postulation institutes truth by convention, and seems plausibly illustrated in contemporary set theory. On the other hand discursive postulation is mere selection, from a pre-existing body of truths, of certain ones for use as a basis from which to derive others, initially known or unknown. What discursive postulation fixes is not truth, but only some particular ordering of the truths, for purposes perhaps of pedagogy or perhaps of inquiry into logical relationships ("logical" in the sense of elementary logic). All postulation is of course conventional, but only legislative postulation properly hints of *truth* by convention.

It is well to recognize, if only for its distinctness, yet a further way in which convention can enter; *viz.*, in the adoption of new notations for old ones, without, as one tends to say, change of theory. Truths containing the new notation are conventional transcriptions of sentences true apart from the convention in question. They depend for their truth partly on language, but then so did 'Brutus killed Caesar' (cf. §1). They come into being through a conventional adoption of a new sign, and they become true through conventional definition of that sign *together with* whatever made the corresponding sentences in the old notation true.

Definition, in a properly narrow sense of the word, is convention in a properly narrow sense of the word. But the phrase 'true by definition' must be taken cautiously; in its strictest usage it refers to a transcription, by the definition, of a truth of elementary logic. Whether such a sentence is true by convention depends on whether the logical truths themselves be reckoned as true by convention. Even an outright equation or biconditional connecting the definiens and the definiendum is a definitional transcription of a prior logical truth of the form '$x = x$' or '$p \equiv p$.'

Definition commonly so-called is not thus narrowly conceived, and must for present purposes be divided, as postulation was divided, into legislative and discursive. Legislative definition introduces a notation hitherto unused, or used only at variance with the practice proposed, or used also at variance, so that a convention is wanted to settle the ambiguity. Discursive definition, on the other hand, sets forth a pre-existing relation of interchangeability or coextensiveness between notations in already familiar usage. A frequent purpose of this activity is to show how some chosen part of language can be made to serve the purposes of a wider part. Another frequent purpose is language instruction.

It is only legislative definition, and not discursive definition nor discursive postulation, that makes a conventional contribution to the truth of sentences. Legislative postulation, finally, affords truth by convention unalloyed.

Increasingly the word 'definition' connotes the formulas of definition which appear in connection with formal systems, signaled by some extrasystematic sign such as '=df.' Such definitions are best looked upon as correlating two systems, two notations, one of which is prized for its economical lexicon and the other for its brevity or familiarity of expression.[5] Definitions so used can be either legislative or discursive in their inception. But this distinction is in practice left unindicated, and wisely; for it is a distinction only between particular acts of definition, and not germane to the definition as an enduring channel of intertranslation.

The distinction between the legislative and the discursive refers thus to the act, and not to its enduring consequence, in the case of postulation as in the case of definition. This is because we are taking the notion of truth by convention fairly literally and simple-mindedly, for lack of an intelligible alternative. So conceived, conventionality is a passing trait, significant at the moving front of science but useless in classifying the sentences behind the lines. It is a trait of events and not of sentences.

Might we not still project a derivative trait upon the sentences themselves, thus speaking of a sentence as forever true by convention if its first adoption as true was a convention? No; this, if done seriously, involves us in the most unrewarding historical conjecture. Legislative postulation contributes truths which become integral to the corpus of truths; the artificiality of their origin does not linger as a localized quality, but suffuses the corpus. If a subsequent expositor singles out those once legislatively postulated truths again as postulates, that signifies nothing; he is engaged only in discursive postulation. He could as well choose his postulates from elsewhere in the corpus, and will if he thinks this serves his expository ends.

5

We have been at a loss to give substance to the linguistic doctrine, particularly of elementary logical truth, or to the doctrine that the familiar truths of logic are true by convention. We have found some sense in the notion of truth by convention, but only as attaching to a process of adoption, *viz.* legislative postulation, and not as a significant lingering trait of the legislatively postulated sentence. Surveying current events, we note legislative postulation in set theory and, at a more elementary level, in connection with the law of the excluded middle.

And do we not find the same continually in the theoretical hypotheses of natural science itself? What seemed to smack of convention in set theory (§4), at any rate, was "deliberate choice, set forth unaccompanied by any attempt at justification other than in terms of elegance and convenience"; and to what theoretical hypothesis of natural science might not this same character be attributed? For surely the justification of any theoretical hypothesis can, at the time of hypothesis, consist in no more than the elegance or convenience which the hypothesis brings to the containing body of laws and data. How then are we to delimit the category of legislative postulation, short of including under it every new act of scientific hypothesis?

The situation may seem to be saved for ordinary hypotheses in natural science by there being some indirect but eventual confrontation with empirical data. However, this confrontation can be remote, and, conversely, some such remote confrontation with experience may be claimed even for pure mathematics and elementary logic. The semblance of a difference in this respect is largely due to overemphasis of departmental boundaries. For, a self-contained theory which we can check with experience includes, in point of fact, not only its various theoretical hypotheses of so-called natural science but also such portions of logic and mathematics as it makes use of. Hence I do not see how a line is to be drawn between hypotheses which confer truth by convention and hypotheses which do not, short of reckoning *all* hypotheses to the former category save perhaps those actually derivable or refutable by elementary logic from what Carnap used to call protocol sentences. But this version, besides depending to an unwelcome degree on the debatable notion of protocol sentences, is far too inclusive to suit anyone.

6

The notion of logical truth is now counted by Carnap as semantical. This of course does not of itself mean that logical truth is grounded in language; for note that the general notion of truth is also semantical, though truth in general is not grounded purely in language. But the semantical attribute of logical truth, in particular, *is* one which, according to Carnap, is grounded in language: in convention, fiat, meaning. Such support as he hints for this doctrine, aside from ground covered in §§1-5, seems to depend on an analogy with what goes on in the propounding of artificial languages; and I shall now try to show why I think the analogy mistaken.

I may best schematize the point by considering a case, not directly concerned with logical truth, where one might typically produce an artificial language as a step in an argument. This is the imaginary case of a logical positivist, say Ixmann, who is out to defend scientists against the demands of a metaphysician. The metaphysician argues that science presupposes metaphysical principles, or raises metaphysical problems, and that the scientists should therefore show due concern. Ixmann's answer consists in showing in detail how people (on Mars, say) might speak a language quite adequate to all of our science but, unlike our language, incapable of expressing the alleged metaphysical issues. (I applaud this answer, and think it embodies the most telling of Carnap's own antimetaphysical representations; but here I digress.) Now how does our hypothetical Ixmann specify that doubly hypothetical language? By telling us, at least to the extent needed for his argument, what these Martians are to be imagined as uttering and what they are thereby to be understood to mean. Here is Carnap's familiar duality of formation rules and transformation rules (or meaning postulates), as rules of language. But these rules are part only of Ixmann's narrative machinery, not part of what he is portraying. He is not representing his hypothetical Martians themselves as somehow explicit on formation and transformation rules. Nor is he representing there to be any intrinsic difference between those truths which happen to be disclosed to us by his partial specifications (his transformation rules) and those further truths, hypothetically likewise known to the Martians of his parable, which he did not trouble to sketch in.

The threat of fallacy lurks in the fact that Ixmann's rules are indeed arbitrary fiats, as is his whole Martian parable. The fallacy consists in confusing levels, projecting the conventional character of the rules into the story, and so misconstruing Ixmann's parable as attributing truth-legislation to his hypothetical Martians.

The case of a nonhypothetical artificial language is in principle the same. Being a new invention, the language has to be explained; and the explanation will proceed by what may certainly be called formation and transformation rules. These rules will hold by arbitrary fiat, the artifex being boss. But all we can reasonably ask of these rules is that they enable us to find corresponding to each of his sentences a sentence of like truth value in familiar ordinary language. There is no (to me) intelligible additional decree that we can demand of him as to the boundary between analytic and synthetic, logic and fact, among his truths. We may well decide to extend our word 'analytic' or 'logically true' to sentences of his language which he in his explanations has paired off fairly directly with English sentences so classified by us; but this is our decree regarding our word 'analytic' or 'logically true.'

7

Carnap's present position[6] is that one has specified a language quite rigorously only when he has fixed, by dint of so-called meaning postulates, what sentences are to count as analytic. The proponent is supposed to distinguish between those of his declarations which count as meaning postulates, and thus engender analyticity, and those which do not. This he does, presumably, by attaching the label 'meaning postulates.'

But the sense of this label is far less clear to me than four causes of its seeming to be clear. Which of these causes has worked on Carnap, if any, I cannot say; but I have no doubt that all four have worked on his readers. One of these causes is misevaluation of the role of convention in connection with artificial language; thus note the fallacy described in §6. Another is misevaluation of the conventionality of postulates: failure to appreciate that postulates, though they are postulates always by fiat, are not *therefore* true by fiat; *cf.* §§3-4. A third is overestimation of the distinctive nature of postulates, and of definitions, because of conspicuous and peculiar roles which postulates and definitions have played in situations not really relevant to present concerns: postulates in uninterpreted systems (*cf.* §3), and definitions in double systems of notation (*cf.* §4). A fourth is misevaluation of legislative postulation and legislative definition themselves, in two respects: failure to appreciate that this legislative trait is a trait of scientific hypothesis very generally (*cf.* §5), and failure to appreciate that it is a trait of the passing event rather than of the truth which is thereby instituted (*cf.* end of §4).

Suppose a scientist introduces a new term for a certain substance or force. He introduces it by an act either of legislative definition or of legislative postulation. Progressing, he evolves hypotheses regarding further traits of the named substance or force. Suppose now that some such eventual hypothesis, well attested, identifies this substance or force with one named by a complex term built up of other portions of his scientific vocabulary. We all know that this new identity will figure in the ensuing developments quite on a par with the identity which first came of the act of legislative definition, if any, or on a par with the law which first came of the act of legislative postulation. Revisions, in the course of further progress, can touch any of these affirmations equally. Now I urge that scientists, proceeding thus, are not thereby slurring over any meaningful distinction. Legislative acts occur again and again; on the other hand a dichotomy of the resulting truths themselves into analytic and synthetic, truths by meaning postulate and truths by force of nature, has been given no tolerably clear meaning even as a methodological ideal.

One conspicuous consequence of Carnap's belief in this dichotomy may be seen in his attitude toward philosophical issues, *e.g.* as to what there is. It is only by assuming the cleavage between analytic and synthetic truths that he is able *e.g.* to declare the problem of universals to be a matter not of theory but of linguistic decision.[7] Now I am as impressed as Carnap with the vastness of what language contributes to science and to one's whole view of the world; and in particular I grant that one's hypothesis as to what there is, *e.g.* as to there being universals, is at bottom just as arbitrary or pragmatic a matter as one's adoption of a new brand of set theory or even a new system of bookkeeping. Carnap in turn recognizes that such decisions, however conventional, "will nevertheless usually be influenced by theoretical knowledge."[8] But what impresses me more than it does Carnap is how well this whole attitude is suited also to the theoretical hypotheses of natural science itself, and how little basis there is for a distinction.

The lore of our fathers is a fabric of sentences. In our hands it develops and changes, through more or less arbitrary and deliberate revisions and additions of our own, more or less directly occasioned by the continuing stimulation of our sense organs. It is a pale gray lore, black with fact, and white with convention. But I have found no substantial reasons for concluding that there are any quite black threads in it, nor any white ones.

This essay is made up of portions of my essay "Carnap and logical truth," which is appearing in full in *The Philosophy of Rudolf Carnap*, Vol. 10 of the Library of Living Philosophers (New York, Tudor, 1956). Thanks are due the editor of that series, Professor Paul Arthur Schilpp, for permission to make the present use of the material.

1. "What the Tortoise Said to Achilles," *Mind*, Vol. 4 (1895), pp. 278 ff.
2. "Truth by Convention," in O. H. Lee, ed., *Philosophical Essays for A. N. Whitehead* (New York, 1936), pp. 90–124. Reprinted in H. Feigl and W. Sellars, eds., *Readings in Philosophical Analysis* (New York, Appleton, 1949).
3. *Cf.*, §2.
4. Bertrand Russell, *Principles of Mathematics* (Cambridge, England, 1903),

pp. 429 f; Heinrich Behmann, "Sind die mathematischen Urteile analytisch oder synthetisch?" *Erkenntnis*, Vol. 4 (1934), pp. 8 ff; and others.

5. See my *From a Logical Point of View* (Cambridge, Mass., Harvard, 1935), pp. 26 f.

6. See particularly Rudolf Carnap, "Meaning Postulates," *Philosophical Studies*, Vol. 3 (1952), pp. 65–73.

7. See Carnap, "Empiricism, Semantics, and Ontology," *Revue Internationale de Philosophie*, Vol. 4 (1950), pp. 20–40, especially §3, longest footnote. Reprinted in L. Linsky, ed., *Semantics and the Philosophy of Language* (Urbana, 1952).

8. *Op. cit.*, §2, 5th paragraph.

WILFRID SELLARS

Is There a Synthetic A Priori?

1. *Introduction.* A survey of the literature on the problem of the synthetic a priori soon reveals that the term "analytic" is used in a narrower and a broader sense. In the narrower sense, a proposition is analytic if it is either a *truth of logic* or is *logically true.* By saying of a proposition that it is logically true, I mean, roughly, and with an eye on the problem of the relation of logical categories to natural languages, that when defined terms are replaced by their definientia, it becomes a substitution instance of a truth of logic. And a truth of logic can be adequately characterized for present purposes as a proposition which occurs in the body of *Principia Mathematica,* or which would properly occur in a *vermehrte und • verbesserte Auflage* of this already monumental work. If we now agree to extend the convenient phrase "logically true" to cover truths of logic as well as propositions which are logically true in the sense just defined, we can say that an analytic proposition in the narrower sense is a proposition which is logically true.

On the other hand, we find many philosophers using the term "analytic" in the sense of *true by virtue of the meanings of the terms involved.* These philosophers seem, for the most part, to be under the impression that this sense of "analytic" coincides with that defined above. And if "p is logically true" did entail and were entailed by "p is true by virtue of its terms," little damage would result from this ambiguity. Unfortunately, this is not the case, as will be argued in a later section of this paper. Indeed, the more interesting examples given by these philosophers of propositions which are analytic in their sense turn out on examination *not* to be logically true. From which it follows that unless they are mistaken in applying their own criteria, "analytic" in their sense cannot be logically equivalent to "analytic" in the sense defined above. That *true by virtue of the meanings of the terms involved* is indeed a broader sense of "analytic" than *logically true*—broader in that it has a greater denotation—will be a central theme of this paper.

To avoid possible misunderstanding, let me make it clear that I shall use the term "analytic" only in the first or narrower of the two senses distinguished above, and that where I want to refer to the views of philosophers who use the term in the broader sense, I shall make the appropriate translation of "analytic" into "true by virtue of the meanings involved." Accordingly, "synthetic" will be used to mean *neither logically true nor logically false,* and the question under discussion becomes: Are there propositions which are a priori yet not logically true?

To answer this question even provisionally, we must next decide on a meaning for "a priori." Here the going is more difficult, and we shall have to be content with a rather schematic discussion. By and large, philosophers have given (or have believed themselves to give) four different but closely related senses to this phrase. In the first place we have Kant's joint criteria of universality and necessity. The propositions traditionally characterized as a priori, with the possible exception of the proposition "God exists" (in the context of the ontological argument) have been universal propositions—a priori knowledge about individuals presupposing a minor premise of subsumption. Now when he explicates the criterion of universality, Kant makes it clear that it is intended to exclude such universal judgments as are true merely as a matter of fact, so that universality merges with the criterion of necessity. If our knowledge that all A is B is to be a priori, it must be correct to say "All A *must* be B."

But while we should all agree that a person cannot properly be said to know a priori that all A *is* B unless he can also be said to know that all A is *necessarily* B—so that knowing that all A is necessarily B is a *necessary condition* of knowing a priori that all A is B—it does not, at least at first sight, seem to be a sufficient condition. There is no immediate appearance of contradiction in the statement, "It is highly probable that all A is necessarily B," so that there would seem to be no absurdity in speaking of knowing a posteriori that all A *must* be B, though just what account might be given of such knowledge is another, and extremely perplexing, matter to which we shall return at the conclusion of our argument.

This brings us to the second of the four interpretations of apriority. According to this approach, we have a priori knowledge that all A is B, when we *know for certain* that all A is B. If we ask what is meant by "knowing for certain," we are told that this is not a mere matter of feeling confident that all A is B. It must be *reasonable* to assert "All A is B" where this reasonableness is not grounded on knowledge that on such and such evidence *e* is probable that all A is B, nor on an argument of which one of the premises is of this form. Furthermore, not only must it be reasonable to assert "All A is B" but it must in some sense be asserted *because* it is reasonable. In traditional terminology, *knowing for certain* is contrasted with both *probable opinion* and *taking for granted*.

This second approach leads smoothly and easily into the third and fourth explications of apriority. The third arises by scarcely more than a minor reformulation of what we have just said. For to say that the reasonableness of asserting "All A is B" does not rest on knowledge of the form "It is probable on *e* that all X is Y" is but a pedantic way of saying that the reasonableness of asserting "All A is B" does not rest on, or is independent of experience. And according to the third approach, our knowledge that all A is B is a priori, if it is *independent of experience*.

But if the reasonableness of asserting "All A is B" doesn't rest on experience, on what does it rest? The answer to this question brings us to the fourth approach. This reasonableness, we are told, rests solely on a correct understanding of the meanings of the terms involved. In short, a priori truth is truth *ex vi terminorum*.

Now, in sketching these familiar explications of a priori knowledge of universal truths, as knowledge independent of experience, and as knowledge *ex vi terminorum*—I have made it clear that to my way of thinking there is a general confluence of these four criteria, such that each, on reflection, leads to the others. Much more would have to be done before we could claim to have disentangled the various meanings which have traditionally been given to the term "a priori," and we shall have to return to this topic before this paper is complete. But schematic though the above discussion may be, it provides a useful background for a provisional choice of a sense of this term for the interpretation of the question: Is there a synthetic a priori? Accordingly, I shall select the fourth of the above criteria as the defining property of the a priori. Our question thus becomes, "Are there any universal propositions which, though they are not logically true, are true by virtue of the meanings of their terms?"

2. *A Divergent Usage: C. I. Lewis.* It will prove useful to contrast our provisional explication of the original question with what one gets if one adopts the conventions implicit in C. I. Lewis' use of the terms "synthetic" and "a priori." Since he appears to use "analytic" as we are using "a priori" and "a priori" to mean *holding of all possible objects of experience,* in his hands the question "Is there a synthetic a priori?" becomes "Are there any universal propositions which, though they are not true by virtue of the meaning of their terms, hold of all possible objects of experience?" To *this* question Lewis answers "no." That he is correct in doing so becomes clear once it is realized that Lewis picks his meanings for *both* "analytic" and "a priori" from our list of four traditional criteria of a priori knowledge. In other words, if we are justified in speaking of a confluence of these criteria, and given Lewis' interpretation of the terms "synthetic" and "a priori," he is on solid ground in claiming that it is *logically impossible* that there be any propositions which are both synthetic and a priori.

3. *Linguistic Rules and Ordinary Usage.* I shall open the next stage of my argument by pointing out that the phrase "true by virtue of the meaning of its terms" can reasonably be said to have the same sense as "true by definition." This brings us face to face with a sticky issue. Human knowledge is presumably the sort of thing that finds its fitting expression in the *ordinary usage* of expressions in *natural languages.* Have we not therefore reached a point at which the horsehair couch is a more appropriate instrument of philosophical clarification than the neat dichotomies and tidy rule books of the professional logicians? I do not think so. Not, however, because I frown on philosophical therapeutics (on

the contrary!), but because it seems to me that the successes achieved in recent decades by putting ordinary language on the couch were made possible by the brilliant use of tools developed in *Principia Mathematica;* and I believe that recent logical theory has developed new tools which have not yet been put to adequate use in the exploration of philosophical perplexities.

Now I submit that the logician's concepts of *formation rule, transformation rule* and *rule permitting the substitution of one expression for another,* have legitimate application to natural languages. By this I mean not that it is possible for the logician to construct such rules for natural languages, but rather that rules of these types are embedded in natural languages themselves without any help from the logician. That the vague, fluctuating and ambiguous character of ordinary usage extends to these rules is, indeed, granted. But does not the same hold true with respect to the logician's concept of a sentence? or of a predicate? Yet we do not hesitate to discuss natural languages in these terms. I see no reason in the Heraclitean character of ordinary usage to reject what would seem to be the obvious implication of the fact that natural languages can be illuminated by confronting them with artificial languages obeying explicitly formulated rules of transformation and synonymity.

Indeed, can we make sense of critical appraisals of linguistic phenomena as *correct* or *incorrect* by persons uncorrupted by scrutiny of esoteric rule books, without supposing that linguistic rules are embedded in ordinary usage? And the fact that rustics playing a game handed down for generations without benefit of Hoyle would be hard put to it to formulate a set of rules for the game, is surely not incompatible with the idea that when they play the game they do what they do *because of* the very rules they would find it so difficult to formulate! One wonders when philosophers will finally abandon the fiction that rules exist only in public utterance of phonemes or displays of printers ink.

4. *Explicit and Implicit Definition.* The purpose of the preceding section has been to restore some semblance of plausibility to the notion that the concepts *analytic* and *true by definition* can usefully be applied to natural languages. If we have succeeded, we have shown that in the sense in which ordinary usage contains predicates, it may also be said to contain propositions which are analytic and true *ex vi terminorum,* and which can therefore be

said to formulate analytic a priori knowledge. But a synthetic a priori proposition, on our account, is one that is both synthetic and true *ex vi terminorum*. Can there be such a thing?

Now it is at once clear that the "definition," if such it can be called, by virtue of which a synthetic a priori proposition would be true *ex vi terminorum* cannot be *explicit* definition; for the a priori truth to which these give rise is analytic. If anything that has been called definition can serve this purpose, it is what, following Schlick, we shall call *implicit* definition—to an examination of which we now turn.

In rough and ready terms, a number of predicates without explicit definition are said to be implicitly defined if they appear in a set of logically synthetic general propositions which are specified as axioms or primitive sentences by the rules of the language to which they belong. To say that these propositions are axioms or primitive sentences is to say that they are specified to be *unconditionally assertable* by syntactical rules of the language. This account is deliberately skeletal, and is intended to gain flesh from the argument which follows shortly.

If we use the familiar illustration of a geometry, the following points may be noted: (1) Neither the axioms nor the theorems are logically analytic, though the implicative proposition whose antecedent is the conjunction of the axioms, and whose consequent is one of the theorems, *is* logically analytic. (2) If the geometry should be of the Euclidian type, then the theorem "The area of a triangle is ½bh," which is logically synthetic, must not be confused with the proposition "The area of a *Euclidean* triangle is ½bh," which is indeed an analytic proposition, but one which presupposes both the theorem, and an explicit definition of "Euclidean triangle" in terms which specify that an object doesn't belong to this category unless the axioms and therefore all their logical consequences hold of it.[1] Similarly, the axiom "A straight line is the shortest distance between two points," which is logically synthetic, must not be confused with "A *Euclidean* straight line is the shortest distance between two points," which, though analytic, depends on an explicit definition of "Euclidean straight line."

(3) The nonlogical terms of an uninterpreted calculus should not be interpreted as variables. The interpretation of such a calculus by establishing translation rules correlating its nonlogical terms with expressions in actual use must not be confused with the assigning of values to variables. (4) The postulates of a Eu-

clidean geometry do not constitute an implicit definition of its nonlogical terms unless they are specified as unconditionally assertable (and hence as more than generalized material implications, equivalences, etc.) by the syntactical rules of the calculus. (5) A deductive system can gain application either by (a) translating its nonlogical terms into expressions in actual use, or (b) by building it onto language in actual use by establishing rules of inference to take one from sentences in the calculus to sentences in actual use (and vice versa) ; or by a combination of (a) and (b).

But what of expressions which do not belong to a contrived calculus which has gained a use by being co-ordinated with a preexisting language? Does the notion of implicit definition have any application to them? Instead of dealing directly with this question, I shall wait until other dimensions of the problem have been brought into view.

Perhaps the most common complaint against the idea of implicit definition is that a set of terms may be "implicitly defined" and yet have no "real" or extralinguistic meaning.[2] "Implicit definition," it is argued, is a purely syntactical affair, and to expect it to give rise to extralinguistic meanings is as sensible as expecting a number of people to lift each other by their bootstraps.

That this objection calls attention to an essential feature of meaningful language is doubtlessly true. But its force as an argument against the definitional character of implicit definition is somewhat less keenly felt when one realizes that when *explicit* definition is conceived in purely syntactical terms, exactly the same objection can be raised against it. Both explicit and implicit definition are matters of syntax. The difference is that whereas in the case of explicit definition the definiendum and the definientia are distinct, and the "giving extralinguistic meanings"—however this is done—to the definientia fixes the extralinguistic meaning of the definiendum; in the case of implicit definition the extralinguistic meaning must be "given" to all the predicates "simultaneously," as they are all both definienda and definientia rolled into one.

A second objection points out that a set of predicates may be implicitly defined in terms of one another, and yet admit a multiplicity of real meanings.[3] But, as before, the same is true of an explicitly defined term and its definientia. To the set consisting of "man," "rational" and "animal" could belong either the real meanings *man, rational* and *animal,* or the real meanings *brother, male* and *sibling.* It may be granted that to the extent that the definientia themselves are explicitly defined in terms of other predicates, and the definientia of these in turn, and so on, the alternative real meanings capable of belonging to the terms in the chain are increasingly restricted. But it is by no means obvious that the terms in however long a definition chain couldn't possess any one of a number of sets of real meanings. In any event, to the fact that the syntactical structure of a chain of explicit definitions limits the number of alternative real meanings which can be possessed by the predicates in the chain, corresponds the fact that the number of possible "interpretations" of a set of implicitly defined terms can frequently be narrowed by adding a new axiom to the original set. In neither case would the utility of the definition seem to depend on its admitting only one set of real meanings. The purposes of unambiguous communication require only that where one and the same abstract syntactical structure is associated with two different sets of "extralinguistic meanings," this structure be embodied in two sets of visually and audibly different symbols.

But the above is but prelude to the most searching of the objections to the notion of implicit definition. The objection is based on broad philosophical considerations, and takes us to the heart of our problem. Its point of departure is the above familiar distinction between the "linguistic meanings" of an implicitly defined set of predicates, and the "real meanings," the properties and relations, which are correlated with these predicates. As its first step it reminds us that what the implicit definition does is specify that certain sentences containing these predicates are unconditionally assertable. In other words, that we are authorized by the rules of the language to assert these sentences without either deriving them from other sentences, or establishing probability relations between them and observation sentences. But, the objection continues, even though the implicit definition may permit us unconditionally to assert certain sentences involving the predicates "A," "B," "C," etc., the *truth* of what we assert depends solely on the relation of the *real* meanings of these predicates to the world. Thus, even should there be a syntactical rule (implicit definition) authorizing us to assert "All A is B" unconditionally (and therefore to derive "x is B" from "x is A") might there not be an object which conforms to the real meaning of "A" without conforming to the real meaning of "B"? If this were the case, then as far as its real meaning was concerned, "All A is B" would be false, even though the rules of the language blandly authorized us to assert it. There would be a tension between what was authorized by the *linguistic* meanings of "A" and "B," and what was appropriate to their *real* meanings. On the other hand, the objection continues, no such contretemps can arise in the case of explicit definition, for it is not logically possible that something conform to the real meaning of "C" and yet not to the real meaning of "D" where "C" is explicitly defined in terms of "D."

To this the objection adds that even though *as a matter of fact* all items which conform to the real meaning of "A" did conform to the real meaning of "B," we could nevertheless *conceive* of objects conforming to the real meaning of "A" but not that of "B." If, therefore, we were to adopt a syntactical rule authorizing us to derive "x is B" from "x is A," we should be tailoring the verbal clothing of our thought to be shorter than its reach.

The objector grants that it might, in some circumstances, be sensible or convenient to adopt a language in which "x is B" is syntactically derivable from "x is A," even though something might *conceivably* exemplify the real meaning of "A" without exemplifying the real meaning of "B," provided that one were extremely confident on inductive grounds in the truth of the generalization "If anything exemplifies the real meaning of 'A' than it exemplifies the real meaning of 'B.'" But, he continues, it just wouldn't do to say that "All A is B" is true by virtue of the meaning of its terms. Implicit definition, he concludes, is a pale imitation of explicit definition, for it lacks the power to yield statements which are true by definition.

5. *Implicit Definition: A Traditional Defense.* Now the above is only one prong of the attack on implicit definition. But before we develop the other prong, we must take into account the classic counter to this first offensive. For the defenders are ready with an equally venerable reply.

It will have been noticed that lurking in the premises of the above critique was the idea that even should it be true that everything which exemplified the real meaning of "A" also exemplified the real meaning of "B," it would be so *as a matter of fact*. So that it would be *conceivable* that something might conform to that of "A" without conforming to that of "B." If pressed, the critics would give the following reason for this supposition. After all, they would say, since the statement "All A is B" is admittedly *synthetic,* it must be *logically possible* and hence *possible* and hence *conceivable* that something might exemplify the real meaning of "A" without exemplifying that of "B."

It is here that the defense, clothed in the dignity of *philosophia perennis,* quietly adds that for "All A is B" to be synthetic yet true *ex vi terminorum,* it is not sufficient that "x is B" be syntactically derivable from "x is A"; there must also be an *extralinguistic* or *real connection* between the real meaning of "A" and the real meaning of "B." In other words, given real meanings for "A," "B," "C," etc., an implicit definition of these predicates in terms of one another will be adequate only if to the syntactical derivations authorized by the definition, there correspond *synthetic necessary connections* between the properties which are the real meanings of these predicates. Indeed, the defense continues, it will be appropriate to give an implicit definition of these terms only to the extent that one *apprehends* these necessary connections. For only to this extent could we exclude, merely on the basis of what we mean by, say "A" and "B," the possibility that something might conform to the real meaning of "A" but not to that of "B."

6. *Implicit Definition: The Attack Continued.* The opposition to implicit definition now develops the second prong of its offensive, focusing attention on the notion of real or synthetic, necessary connection. It reveals itself to be an "empiricist" opposition, claiming that this notion is incompatible with the most elementary principles of the empiricist tradition.

Historically, the characteristic doctrines of empiricism have been grounded in a theory, or better a type of theory, of concept formation. Theories of this type form a spectrum which at one end touches and is easily confused with a radically different approach (to be developed at the close of our argument) which can also with some justice claim the title "empiricism" though it is committed to few if any of the dogmas associated with this term. Let us begin by reflecting on the consequences for our problem of a characteristic (if somewhat oversimplified) formulation of what we shall call *concept empiricism.* It goes as follows: Concepts of qualities and relations are formed from particulars. We can, indeed, have concepts of qualities and relations of which we have encountered no instances; but only if these concepts "consist" of concepts which have been formed from instances.

Now, from this theory, together with certain appropriate assumptions concerning the composition of concepts, it follows that we can have no concepts of universals which are not satisfied by particulars. "Satisfied by particulars" here means "would be satisfied by particulars if satisfied at all." In this sense the property Centaur is satisfied by particulars, even though it actually has no instances.

The implication of concept empiricism with respect to the concept of real connection is immediate and murderous. There is no such concept. Yet here we must be careful. It is sometimes thought that when Hume and his followers are criticizing rationalistic discourse about necessary connections, their application of concept empiricism consists in pointing out that *they* find no instances of necessary connection among sensibly experienced particulars, and predict that *we* shall find none. If this were the heart of the matter, the obvious comeback would be "You are either looking in the wrong place, or are necessary-connection-blind." The truth, of course, is that if there is such a thing as necessary connection, it is a relation satisfied by *universals* (a relation whose terms are universals), and *not* by particulars. Thus, for the concept empiricist, our failure to have such a concept is not a mere matter of failing to find any particulars which exemplify it; we *couldn't* find particulars which exemplify it.

It should be noted that unqualified concept empiricism equally entails that we have no concept of *logical* necessity, not to mention conjunction, disjunction, negation and class-membership, though concept empiricists have not been quite as assiduous in pointing this out as they have been in scoffing at real connection. And even should the concept empiricist seek to define logical necessity in psychological terms, or, perhaps, give an emotivist analysis of such terms as "necessary" and "must," denying them cognitive meaning, he can scarcely treat such useful terms as "and," "or," "not," and "is a member of" in either of these ways. Sooner or later he is led to distinguish between two types of cognitively meaningful expression: (1) those which "have extralinguistic meaning," *e.g.* "red," and "centaur"; and (2) those which, while they do not "have extralinguistic meaning," have a legitimate (and indeed indispensable) syntactical function in language.

But more of this later. For the moment it is sufficient to note that whatever else he may be committed to, the concept empiricist can have no truck with a relation of real connection between extralinguistic or real meanings. As a result, if he has any use at all for the phrase "implicit definition," it can mean nothing more to him than the building of empirical generalizations of which we are highly confident into the very syntactical structure of our language. The concept empiricist is thus in a position to return to the first prong of the attack on the notion of implicit definition by insisting once again, this time on explicit empiricist grounds, that even should an "implicit definition" authorize us to derive "x is B" from "x is A" at the linguistic level, it nevertheless cannot prevent us from conceiving of something which exemplifies the real meaning of "A" without exemplifying that of "B."

7. *Concept Empiricism: The Conservative Approach.* The moral of the argument to date is that only if concept empiricism is rejected is it possible to hold that there are nonlogically true propositions which are true *ex vi terminorum.*

There are many to whom this would be the end of the matter, as they find some version of concept empiricism to be beyond dispute. Indeed, there was a time, not too long ago, when I myself was a convinced concept empiricist—though I was not as aware of its implications and presuppositions as I should have been. For a number of years, however, I have been a renegade, and in the following pages I shall indicate some of the considerations which led me to abandon concept empiricism, as well as the resulting changes in my interpretation of the synthetic a priori.

In the preceding section it sufficed for our purposes to introduce concept empiricism by means of a studiously vague formulation. We must now call attention to the fact that the phrase denotes two radically different lines of thought which agree, however, in concluding that the basic concepts in terms of which all genuine concepts are defined are concepts of qualities and relations exemplified by particulars in what is called "the given" or "immediate experience."

In its more traditional and conservative form, concept empiricism distinguishes sharply between the intellectual awareness of qualities and relations, and the formulation of this awareness by the use of symbols. In short, it accepts without question a venerable but, at present, unfashionable distinction between thought and its expression in language (or, as it is sometimes put, between "real thinking" and "symbolic thinking") . Thus the concept empiricist of this brand conceives of such symbols as "red" and "between" as acquiring meaning by virtue of becoming associated with such abstract entities as redness and between-ness, the association being mediated by our awareness of these entities. His attention is thus focused on the question, "How, and in what circumstances, do we become aware of abstract entities?"

Now it is characteristic of the concept empiricist to be convinced that an essential role in the process whereby we come to be aware of universals is played by particulars which exemplify these universals. In its more coherent form, the primary ground of this conviction seems to have been a metaphysical conviction to the effect that abstract entities exist only *in rebus,* that is, in particulars, so that only through particulars could mind enter into relations with them. This was usually coupled with the claim that our ability to be aware of even the most complex and recondite universal can be explained on the hypothesis that in the last analysis all awareness of universals is derived from the awareness of instances, together with a more or less crude attempt to fill in the psychological details.

In its classical form, concept empiricism can be dramatized as follows: A mind is about to learn the meaning of the word "red." The abstract entity in question is lurking in the manifold of sense. But so are many others. This one stands out clearly. Here! and here! No, that can't be it! Aha! a splendid specimen. By the methods of Mill! That must be what mother calls "red!"

No one, of course, would recognize a theory of his own in such an absurd picture. Empiricism is notoriously a tough-minded theory, whereas the above is soft-headed. Nevertheless, it is my conviction that although most philosophers who call themselves empiricists would reject it out of hand, they fail to appreciate the extent to which it is part and parcel of the empiricist inheritance, as well as the extent to which some of the most characteristic dogmas of empiricism are expressions of the hold it still has on the empiricist imagination.

This is not the occasion for a detailed discussion of this first main type of concept empiricism. Our present concern is rather with its underlying presupposition of a distinction between the pure awareness of an abstract entity on the one hand, and the linguistic or, in general, symbolic expression of this pure awareness on the other. That I regard this distinction as a mistake will scarcely cause surprise. The proposal to abandon it has lost its revolutionary ring. Once a radical innovation, the notion that thought is a "symbolic process" has become a commonplace, almost a truism. Unfortunately, as is the case with many contentions that have become truisms, its implications are no longer as passionately scrutinized as they were when it was new, and it is often combined with modes of theorizing with which it is radically incompatible. In view of the widespread acceptance of the thesis in question, there is little need to construct one more argument in its defense. Instead, I shall concern myself with certain of its implications which bear on the synthetic a priori.

Let us assume, then, that the situation which obtains when it is true to say that Jones is aware of a quality or relation or possibility or, even, a particular, can (in principle) be exhaustively described in terms of episodes and dispositions relating to the use of linguistic symbols[4] (predicates, sentences, names, descriptions). Indeed, since the tidy, socially stabilized structures we call languages are continuous with more rudimentary conceptual mechanisms, let us assume that the above Jonesean situations can (in principle) be exhaustively described in terms of habits and dispositions relating to the use of symbols. Now, this assumption has an obvious implication of great importance for our problem. If what occurs when we are "aware of a universal" is the use of a symbol, it follows that learning to use a symbol cannot be based on the awareness of universals. In other words, we are committed to the abandonment of what has happily been called the metaphor of the mental eye, which is so deeply rooted in the grand tradition of western philosophy (and is one of the major points on which East Meets West) that its influence crops up where least expected.

If we put this implication in a slightly different way, we immediately establish contact with a characteristic contention of Professor Lewis. All classification of objects, however confident and pre-emptory, is a venture, a venture which at no point finds its justification in a presymbolic vision of generic and specific hearts on the sleeves of the objects of experience. Classification resembles the grasping tentacles of an octopus, now tentative, now confident, rather than a salesman's selection of a suit for a customer after a glance at his build. I am afraid, however, that our agreement with Lewis is more shadow than substance. For while he writes in this manner of the interpretation of the given by means of concepts whose implications transcend the given, he also holds that the sensible appearances of things *do* wear their hearts on their sleeves, and that we do have a cognitive vision of these hearts which is direct, unlearned and incapable of error—though we may make a slip in the expressive language by which these insights are properly formulated. In other words, the assumption to which we are committed requires us to extend to all classificatory consciousness whatever, the striking language in which Lewis describes our consciousness of objects.

8. *Concept Empiricism, Syntactics, Semantics and Pragmatics.* We distinguished above between two radically different lines of thought which lead to the conclusions characteristic of concept empiricism. Of these we have taken a brief look at the first or mental eye variant. Before turning to the second, let me point out that although for analytical purposes we are drawing a sharp distinction between these two approaches, historically they have usually been blended into one confused argument.

The concept empiricism we are now defining arose *pari passu* with the development of association theories of learning in psychology, and has felt as much at home in more recent behavioristic formulations as in the earlier (mentalistic) varieties of this psychological movement. In its traditional form, this second approach, although it agrees verbally with the more conservative form of concept empiricism that such words as "red" acquire meaning by becoming associated with universals (though it tends to stress classes rather than qualities and relations), insists that this association develops, unmediated by awareness of abstract entities, by the joint occurrence of instances of the word and instances of the characteristic in question. In other words, while it is redness that is associated with "red," the mechanism whereby this association is created does not involve awareness of redness, but only the joint occurrence in experience of instances of redness with tokens of "red." In this respect it differs radically from the first approach, for which the formation of the association involves awareness of the universal. In short, the concept empiricism which develops in this context, if it does not entirely escape from the metaphor of the mental eye, at least does not include abstract entities within its visual field.

Now, if we do not limit ourselves to the account thus crudely sketched, but embrace in our view the more sophisticated theories of this general type, there is clearly *something* to them. A philosopher who rejects the mental eye approach and all its implications is indeed committed to the view that it is by the causal interplay of the individual and his physical and social environment, without benefit of a prehension of eternal objects, whether *in re* or *extra rem*, that concepts, meaningful symbols, arise. However, while there is indeed *something* to theories of the above type, they are guilty of a radical confusion, and are in large part responsible for the more implausible features of contemporary empiricism.

Our first comment on the theory sketched above is a restatement and pressing of a point made earlier in this paper. It is simply that unqualified concept empiricism is patently incapable of accounting for many of our most familiar concepts, among others those of logic and mathematics. To remedy this defect, the theory is usually modified by introducing a radical dualism into its account of concepts and concept formation. The theory now recognizes a second mode of concept formation, namely the learning to use symbols in accordance with rules of logical syntax. The concepts of logic and mathematics are held to be symbols which gain meaning in this second way, rather than by association with empirical phenomena.

It is even more important to note that even those terms, such as "red," which are supposed by the theory to gain meaning by association, share in the second mode of concept formation, for only by being used in accordance with rules of logical syntax can they perform the functions by virtue of which a concept is a concept.

Clearly, then, the learning to use symbols in accordance with rules is a pervasive feature of concept formation. Up until now the rules we have considered in this paper have been *syntactical* rules, rules according to which assertable expressions are put together, and properly derived from one another. However, some proponents of the second approach to concept empiricism have been so impressed with the philosophical power of the concept of rule, that they have applied it to the association of a term with an extralinguistic class of objects, which association, as we have seen, is the core of their theory. Thus we find them characterizing the learning to use a language or system of concepts as the learning to use symbols in accordance with two types of rule: (a) rules of syntax, relating symbols to other symbols; (b) semantical rules, whereby basic factual terms acquire extralinguistic meaning. It takes but a moment, however, to show that this widespread manner of speaking involves a radical mistake. A rule is always a rule for *doing* something in some circumstance. And a rule is the sort of thing that one *follows*. But following a rule entails recognizing that a circumstance is one to which the rule applies. If there *were* such a thing as a semantical rule by the adoption of which a descriptive term acquires meaning, it would presumably be of the form "Red objects are to be designated by the word 'red.' " But to recognize the circumstances in which this rule has application, one must already have the concept of red! Those who speak in this sense of semantical rules, therefore, are committed to the view that an awareness of abstract entities is a precondition of learning the intelligent use of symbols.

Now, once the concept empiricist acknowledges the force of these considerations, he is committed to a revision of his theory which, in effect, changes its whole spirit and orientation, and, indeed, deprives it of many of the philosophical implications which are so dear to traditional empiricism. But before developing this point let us briefly review the fundamentals of concept formation as they appear in this new perspective. The learning of a language or conceptual frame involves the following logically (but by no means chronologically) distinguishable phases[5]: (1) The acquisition of habits pertaining to the arranging of sounds and visible marks into patterns and sequences of patterns. The acquisition of these habits can be compared to the setting up that part of the wiring of a calculating machine which takes over once the "problem" has been "punched in."[6] (2) The acquisition of thing-word connections. This can be compared to the setting up of that part of the wiring of a calculating machine which permits the "punching in of information." These connections are a matter of being *conditioned* to respond to kinds of situation with kinds of verbal patterns, *e.g.* to respond to the presentation of a green object with "This is green"; it is *not* a matter of "learning to say '. . .' when one observes that the situation is thus-and-so." Observing that the situation is thus-and-so already involves the use of a conceptual frame.[7]

Let us refer to these two dimensions of (descriptive) concept formation as the learning of *intralinguistic moves* and *language entry transitions*.[8] Now, it might be thought that while a descriptive word like "red" wouldn't be a *word* unless it played the syntactical role of a predicate in intralinguistic moves, its possession of empirical meaning, indeed the fact that it is the word it is, is constituted by its role as a conditioned response to red things. And, indeed, there is a certain plausibility to the idea that to say of the German word *"rot,"* for example, that it means *red,* is to say that this vocable is associated (by Germans) with red things. Certainly, if they did not (tend to) respond to red things with *"rot,"* it could not be true that this German word means *red.* But, as we shall see, to grant the latter point is by no means to concede the former.

Sentences of the form " '*Rot*' means *red*" have had no less a hypnotic and disastrous effect on empiricists engaged in formulating theories of concept formation, than on the most naïve mental oculists. Such sentences, which appear to present meaning as a tête-à-tête relation between a word and a universal, have been misinterpreted as entailing what might well be called a "matrimonial" theory of the meaning of primitive or undefined descriptive predicates according to which the fact that these terms have meaning is constituted by the fact that they are associated with (married to) classes of objects. Yet that these sentences *entail* no such consequences becomes obvious once we reflect that it is just as legitimate and, indeed, true to say "The German word '*und*' means *and*" as it is to say "The German word '*rot*' means *red*"; where it is clear that "*und*" gains its meaning not by a process of association with conjunction or a class of conjoined objects, but rather by coming to be used with other symbols in accordance with familiar syntactical rules.

Let us examine the force of the form " '. . .' means—." Suppose Smith says, "When Schmidt says '*und*' it means *and*." This statement clearly conveys the information that Schmidt has habits with respect to "*und*" which parallel his own (Smith's) with respect to "and." Yet it must not be assumed that if it is the business of a statement to convey information of a certain kind, this information must be asserted by the statement *in the sense that a definitional unpacking of the statement would reveal it.* "Jones *ought to* do A" conveys the information that Jones *can* do A; yet it is a mistake to suppose that a definitional unpacking of the former would reveal a sentence asserting the latter. Thus, Smith is not mentioning his habits, or the habits of English-speaking people generally, with respect to "and." He mentions the German vocable "*und*" but *uses* the English vocable "and." He uses it, however, in a peculiar way, a way which is characteristic of *semantical* discourse. He presents us with an instance of the word itself, not a name of it, and, making use of the fact that we belong to the same language community, indicates to us that we have only to rehearse our use of "and" to appreciate the role of "*und*" on the other side of the Rhine.[9]

Now suppose Smith to say, "When Schmidt says '*rot*' it means *red*." Once again this statement conveys the information, *i.e.* in *some* sense implies, that Schmidt has habits with respect to a German word which parallel his own (Smith's) with respect to an English word. But whereas if one supposes that Smith's statement *mentions* habits, the fact that it mentions *"rot"* but uses "red" is naturally taken to imply that the habits in question are of the word-thing variety, we now see that the statement has no such implication. Smith's statement conveys the information that Schmidt has word-thing habits with respect to *"rot"* only in the course of conveying the *global* information that in *all* relevant respects Schmidt's habits with respect to *"rot"* parallel his own (Smith's) with respect to "red."

Thus, instead of leading us to adopt a matrimonial theory of "the meaning relation between *'rot'* and *red*," the explication of *" 'rot' means red"* makes it clear that this sentence is not a relation sentence at all, or, at least, that it is a relation sentence only in a purely grammatical sense of this term. For its business is not to describe *"rot"* and *red* as standing in a relation, but rather to convey the information characterized above.[10]

Now, the moral of all this is that we need no longer be hypnotized by the facile contrast between the "linguistic meaning" and the "real meaning" of a word. For to say that *"rot"* has real meaning, and, indeed, the real meaning *red,* is merely to convey the information that *"rot"* is the subject (beyond the Rhine) of a full-blooded set of habits sufficient to constitute it a word in actual use, and, indeed, a use which parallels our own use of "red." Consequently, to come to the point, if our use of "red" involves extralogical syntactical rules ("P-rules") as well as "L-rules," it follows that *"rot"* couldn't have the "real meaning" it does unless it, too, were subject to "P-rules" and, indeed, "P-rules" which parallel those obeyed by "red."

I shall suppose, then, that the conceptual status of descriptive predicates can correctly be attributed to the fact that they are governed by rules of usage. These rules of usage include extralogical rules (about which we shall say more in a moment) as well as logical rules in the narrow sense (Carnap's L-rules). Those descriptive predicates which are conditioned responses to situations of the kind they are correctly said to mean, are called *observation predicates*. If a language did not contain observation predicates it would not be *applied*. Descriptive predicates other than observation predicates gain application through rules tying them to observation predicates. However, only if one supposes that for an undefined descriptive predicate to have descriptive meaning is for it to be associated with an extralinguistic class of objects, is one forced to hold that all primitive descriptive predicates are observation predicates. One can, indeed, say that all the other descriptive predicates of language must be "defined" in terms of observation predicates; but it would be a mistake to suppose that in every case these definitions will be *explicit* definitions.

9. *Conceptual Status and Implicit Definition.* The above dialectical examination of concept empiricism has been so designed as to bring me to the position I wish to defend, a position which, as I see it, represents a meeting of extremes, a synthesis of insights belonging to the two major traditions of Western philosophy, "Rationalism" and "Empiricism." Stated summarily, it claims that conceptual status, the conceptual status of descriptive as well as logical —not to mention prescriptive—predicates, is constituted, *completely* constituted, by syntactical rules. Notice that I am *not* saying that " 'rot' means *red*" is true merely by virtue of the intralinguistic moves proper to "*rot*" (in German). For " 'rot' means *red*" can be true only if in addition to conforming to syntactical rules paralleling the syntax of "red," it is *applied* by Germans to red objects, that is, if it has the same *application* as "red." Thus, the "conceptual status" of a predicate does not exhaust its "meaning." The rules on which I wish to focus attention are rules of inference.[11] Of these there are two kinds, *logical* and *extralogical* (or "material"). I can best indicate the difference between them by saying that a logical rule of inference is one which authorizes a logically valid argument, that is to say, an argument in which the set of descriptive terms involved occurs vacuously (to use Quine's happy phrase), in other words, can be replaced by any other set of descriptive terms of appropriate type, to obtain another valid argument. On the other hand, descriptive terms occur essentially in valid arguments authorized by extralogical rules.

Let me now put my thesis by saying that the conceptual meaning of a descriptive term is constituted by what can be inferred from it in accordance with the logical and extralogical rules of inference of the language (conceptual frame) to which it belongs. (A technically more adequate formulation would put this in terms of the inferences that can be drawn from sentences in which the term appears.)

Finally, let me make the same claim in still another way by pointing out that where "x is B" can be validly inferred from "x is A," the proposition "All A is B" is unconditionally assertable on the basis of the rules of the language. Our thesis, then, implies that every primitive descriptive predicate occurs in one or more logically synthetic propositions which are unconditionally assertable—in short, true *ex vi terminorum;* or as it was put at the end of the preceding section, true by implicit definition. But a logically synthetic proposition which is true *ex vi terminorum* is, by the conventions adopted at the opening of the paper, a synthetic a priori proposition.[12]

10. *The Synthetic A Priori: A Terminological Decision.* If I had the courage of my definitions, then, it seems that I should proclaim myself a proponent of the synthetic a priori. Yet I feel uncomfortable. Is the synthetic a priori described above a *real* synthetic a priori? Would those who have fought and suffered for the cause of the synthetic a priori (and one has only to speak to a "believer" to realize that it *is* a cause) welcome me to their ranks? I am afraid that the answer is No; that they would spurn my support and say that if this is all the synthetic a priori amounts to, it is not worth the name, and is probably a peculiar kind of a posteriori.

It does not take long to discover the reasons for their discontent, and the results throw new light on a venerable controversy. At the beginning of the paper we considered four traditional criteria of a priori knowledge: (1) It is knowledge of *necessary* truth; (2) It is *certain* knowledge; (3) It is knowledge *independent of experience;* (4) It is knowledge of truth *ex vi terminorum.* We found it plausible to say that ultimately these four criteria coincide—after which we moved into the detail of our argument. I want now to bring out a certain ambiguity in the second and third of these criteria, and by so doing, make clear that whether or not the position I have sketched is committed to a synthetic a priori is a matter for terminological decision.

Consider, to begin with, the third criterion, namely, *independent of experience.* Let us suppose that in our language "All A is B" is one of the propositions which implicitly define the predicates "A" and "B" so that it is true *ex vi terminorum* that all A's are B. Using, as we do, this language or conceptual structure, we know that all A's *must* be B, that something which is not B cannot be A. This knowledge is independent of experience in the perfectly straightforward sense that it is a function of the very concepts with which we approach the world. As long as we continue to use these words in the same sense, continue, that is, to use the same concepts, we can never find an instance of A which fails to be B.

But though in this sense our knowledge that all A's are B is independent of experience, there is another sense in which it most certainly does depend on experience. After all, the learning of a conceptual frame, the learning to use symbols in accordance with certain logical and extralogical rules is a psychological process essential elements of which are sensory stimuli together with the rewards and punishments which the environment (including the social environment) brings to our motivations. The conceptual frame we have developed is only one of a vast number of alternative frames any one of which we might have been brought to adopt by a more or less radical shift in the course of our environment. The claim that our conceptual frame is only one among many possible conceptual frames, and that our adoption of it is to be explained in terms of learning theory rather than of insight into abstract entities, is what led our true-blue proponent of the synthetic a priori to say that our synthetic a priori is a peculiar kind of a posteriori.

Next, a closely related remark on the second criterion, namely *certainty*. Let us suppose that a person has acquired a firmly embedded conceptual frame. In employing this frame, he will distinguish between those propositions which are *certain,* and those which are *at best merely probable* on the evidence. The former will coincide with propositions which, in his frame, are true *ex vi terminorum*. Notice, however, that when the learning process begins to bring about a modification of his conceptual frame, he will admit to being "uncertain" of even those propositions which, in that frame, are true *ex vi terminorum*. It is clear from this description that *we are dealing with two different senses of the contrast between certainty and uncertainty*. The first may be called the "intraconceptual," the second the "extraconceptual" sense. Thus, it makes good sense to say "I am uncertain about its being certain that all A's are B." Uncertainty in this *second sense* is not something that can be remedied by "paying closer attention to what we mean." It can be overcome (should this be desirable) only by more firmly learning to apply the conceptual system in question to experience, without hesitation or uneasiness.

But is this the goal of wisdom? Not if we are correct in maintaining that to all conceptual structures there are alternatives; and that no conceptual frame carries the imprint "sterling" certifying it to be *the* conceptual frame to which all others, to the extent that they are "coherent," approximate. The essence of scientific wisdom consists in being uncertain$_2$ about what is certain$_1$, in a readiness to move (in circumstances the discussion of which belongs rather to a paper on Induction) from one conceptual frame to another. For not only can we be *caused* to modify our linguistic frame, we can deliberately modify it—teach ourselves new habits—and give reasons for doing so. It is the idea that because (in terms of our present use of "A" and "B") we have *found* all observed A's to be B, it would be reasonable to adopt "All A is B" as an unconditionally assertible sentence, which finds expression in "It is *probable* that all A is necessarily B."[13] Now, the use of a conceptual frame is the awareness of a system of logical and extralogical necessities. The essence of scientific wisdom, therefore, lies in being tentative about what one takes to be extralogically necessary.

In conclusion, if one means by synthetic a priori knowledge, knowledge which is logically synthetic, yet true *ex vi terminorum,* then indeed, there is synthetic a priori knowledge. If one means by it, synthetic knowledge to which there is no significant alternative, then synthetic a priori knowledge is a myth, a snare and a delusion. The question "Is there a synthetic a priori?" calls, therefore, for a decision, before it calls for an answer. What the decision should be, that is, which meaning (if any) should be attached to the term "a priori," it is by no means easy to say. Many factors are involved, by no means the least of which is a sense of belonging to one or other of the two major traditions of Western philosophy. If one's overall loyalty is to Sextus and to Hume, one will be moved to say "There is no synthetic a priori" and, hence, to choose a sense of "a priori" which will make this statement true. If one's heart beats with the rationalists, one will long to say "There is a synthetic a priori," and will make the corresponding terminological decision. If one is tired of philosophical shibboleths, and finds important insights on both sides of the fence, one will content oneself with pointing out that while every conceptual frame involves propositions which, though synthetic, are true *ex vi terminorum,* every conceptual frame is also but one among many which compete for adoption in the market place of experience.

A revision of a paper published in the *Philosophy of Science,* 1953; reprinted with permission of Williams & Wilkins Publishing Co. (The paper has been further revised for inclusion in the present volume.)

1. Unless I am much mistaken, C. I. Lewis thinks of his "categorial principles" as unquestionably analytic, because he thinks of them as analogous to "The area of a *Euclidean* triangle is ½ bh." Now, if he intends this analogy, then his categorial principles are indeed logically true. But then, if the above discussion is sound, must there not be a corresponding set of propositions which are *not* logically true, and which contain a set of predicates which are not explicitly defined in terms of these propositions? predicates which correspond to "triangle" as occurring in Euclidean axioms, rather than to "Euclidean triangle?"

2. Let me make it clear from the beginning that my willingness to use the phrase "real or extralinguistic meaning" in building up the dialectical structure of my argument does not reflect an acceptance on my part of a Platonic or Meinongian metaphysics of meaning. My purpose in this paper is to explore the controversy over the synthetic a priori sympathetically and from within, in the conviction that the truth of the matter lies separated from itself in the opposing camps. Some light will be thrown on the status of "real meanings" by the discussion of " '...' means ---" in section 8 below.

3. See footnote 2 above.

4. It should not be assumed that in calling an event a *symbol* we are describing the event. We are rather serving notice that our discussion of the event will be in semantical terms. (For a more adequate formulation of the idea that *thoughts* are *linguistic* episodes, and are yet *distinguishable from* and *expressed by* overt linguistic episodes, see my essay "Empiricism and the Philosophy of Mind," in *Minnesota Studies in the Philosophy of Science,* Vol. 1, published by the University of Minnesota Press, 1956.)

5. I leave out of account, as a topic too large to be introduced into this discussion, though of equal importance for the understanding of the nature of conceptual systems, the prescriptive or conduct guiding aspect of language. But see footnote 7 below.

6. Note that while the activation of these habits results in verbal behavior which *conforms to* syntactical rules, it cannot be the *following* of syntactical rules unless the subject has learned the prescriptive syntactical metalanguage which permits the formulation of these rules. For an elaboration of this point, see my paper, "Some Reflections on Language Games," *Philosophy of Science,* 1954.

7. Just as an intralinguistic move is not in the full sense an *inference* unless the subject not only conforms to, but follows, syntactical rules (though he may conceive them to be rules justifying the transition not from one *linguistic expression* to another, but from one *thought* to another); so a language entry transition is not in the full sense an *observation* unless the subject not only (in normal circumstances) tokens "This object is green" if and only if a green object is present to his senses, but is able to infer (in a pragmatic metalanguage) from "Jones uttered 'This object is green' (or the thought 'This object is green' occurred to Jones) at time t in place s in circumstances c" to "a green object was present to Jones' senses at t in s." For a more complete analysis of the role of a conceptual framework in seeing that p is the case, and of the relation between *thoughts* and overt linguistic behavior, see the essay referred to in footnote 4.

8. That the acquisition of a conceptual frame also involves *language departure transitions,* and that this notion is the key to the status of prescriptive

discourse is argued in the paper on "language games" referred to in footnote 6.

9. Descriptive discourse, prescriptive discourse and semantical discourse are three different modes of speech. Nevertheless, by virtue of what is presupposed by their correct utterance, statements in one of these modes may convey information properly formulated in another mode.

10. The fact that such a statement as " 'rot' means red" conveys descriptive information about "rot" but does not describe it, undercuts the traditional problem of universals (and abstract entities generally). If one misunderstands the function of such statements, and supposes that " 'rot' means red" describes "rot" as standing in a relation to red, then, if one is anti-Platonist, one will be reluctant to use the semantical mode of speech, and will be particularly unwilling to allow an inference from " 'rot' means red" to "There is a quality which 'rot' means." Statements of the latter kind appear to make bold assertion of the *factual existence* of abstract entities which are suspected to infect the former. The truth of the matter is that the "There is a quality (relation, possibility, particular . . . .) . . ." of the latter is a purely logical device which has no connection with "factual existence." To say, "There is an obligation more stringent than promise keeping," is not to attribute "factual existence" to obligations!

11. A more detailed statement and defense of my thesis will be found in "Inference and Meaning," *Mind*, 1953.

12. Note that, strictly speaking, one can only say that a sentence of L is true *ex vi terminorum*, as one can only say that a sentence of L is true *simpliciter*, if one's own language contains a translation of these sentences, which will not be the case if expressions occurring in these sentences conform to different P-rules from those obeyed by their closest counterparts in one's own language. See "Some Reflections on Language Games," *Philosophy of Science*, Vol. 21, 1954, pp. 224ff.

13. For an account of induction which views it as a matter of having reasons for revising one's conceptual framework, which recognizes that to *have reasons* is to be in a conceptual framework, and which, in the spirit of the above analysis, denies that *any* conceptual framework is *given*, see "Some Reflections on Language Games," *loc. cit.*, pp. 225ff.

CHARLES L. STEVENSON

Persuasive Definitions

1

A "persuasive" definition is one which gives a new conceptual meaning to a familiar word without substantially changing its emotive meaning, and which is used with the conscious or unconscious purpose of changing, by this means, the direction of people's interests.

The object of this paper is to show that persuasive definitions are often used in philosophy, and that the widespread failure to recognize them for what they are—the temptation to consider them as definitions which merely abbreviate, or which analyze, common concepts—has led to important philosophical confusions.

Before considering philosophical examples, however, it will be helpful to consider some simpler ones, which will serve to make clearer what persuasive definitions are.

As an initial example let us take a definition of the word "culture." It will be convenient to invent pure fictions about the linguistic habits of the people to whom the definition is addressed; for this will typify the actual situation in a way that is free from complicating irrelevancies. Let us consider, then, a hypothetical community in which "culture" began by having an almost purely conceptual meaning. Let us sketch the development of its emotive meaning, show why the emotive meaning led certain people to redefine the word, and examine the way in which this redefinition achieved its purpose.

There was once a community in which "cultured" meant *widely read and acquainted with the arts.*

In the course of time these qualities came into high favor. If one man wanted to pay another a compliment, he would dwell at length upon his culture. It became unnatural to use "culture" in any but a laudatory tone of voice. Those who lacked culture used the word with awe, and those who possessed it used the word with self-satisfaction, or perhaps with careful modesty. In this way the word acquired a strong emotive meaning. It awakened feelings not only because of its conceptual meaning, but more directly, in its own right; for it recalled the gestures, smiles, and tone of voice which so habitually accompanied it. A public speaker, for instance, was never introduced as "a man widely read and acquainted with the arts." He was described, rather, as "a man of culture." The latter phrase had no different conceptual meaning than the former, but was more suitable for awakening in the audience a favorable attitude.

As the emotive meaning of the word grew more pronounced, the conceptual meaning grew more vague. This was inevitable, for the emotive meaning made the word suitable for use in metaphors. Men who were not cultured, literally, were often called so, particularly when they were admired for having *some* of the defining qualities of "culture." At first people readily distinguished these metaphorical compliments from literal statements; but as the metaphors grew more frequent, the distinction became less clear. People weren't quite sure whether a person *must* know about the arts in order to be literally cultured. Perhaps some other kind of knowledge would serve as a substitute.

Let us now suppose that one member of the community had no wholehearted regard for mere reading, or mere acquaintance with the arts, but valued them only to the extent that they served to develop imaginative sensitivity. He felt that they were not always a reliable means to that end, and on no account the only means. It was his constant source of regret that such mechanical procedures as reading, or visiting museums, should win instant praise, and that sensitivity should scarcely be noticed. For this reason he proceeded to give "culture" a new meaning. "I know," he insisted, "that so and so is widely read, and acquainted with the arts; but what has that to do with culture? The real meaning of 'culture,' the true meaning of 'culture,' is *imaginative sensitivity.*" He persisted in this statement, in spite of the fact that "culture" had never before been used in exactly this sense.

It will now be obvious that this definition was no mere abbreviation; nor was it intended as an analysis of a common concept. Its purpose, rather, was to redirect people's interests. "Culture" had and would continue to have a laudatory emotive meaning. The definition urged people to stop using the laudatory term to refer to reading and the arts, and to use it, instead, to mean imaginative sensitivity. In this manner it sought to place the former qualities in a poor light, and the latter in a fine one, and thus to redirect people's admiration. When people learn to call something by a name rich in pleasant associations, they more readily admire it; and when they learn not to call it by such a name, they less readily admire it. The definition made use of this fact. It changed interests by changing names.

The past history of "culture" facilitated the change. The emotive meaning of the word, it is true, had grown up because of the old conceptual meaning; but it was now so firmly established that it would persist even though the conceptual meaning was somewhat altered. The old conceptual meaning was easily altered, since it had been made vague by metaphorical usage. The definition could effect a change in conceptual meaning, then, which left the emotive meaning unaltered. Thanks again to vagueness, the change seemed a "natural" one, which, by escaping the attention of the hearers, did not remind them that they were being influenced, and so did not stultify them by making them self-conscious. The effectiveness of the definition lay partly in this, and partly in the fact that it made its results permanent by embedding them in people's very linguistic habits.

The definition may be called "persuasive," then, in a quite conventional sense. Like most persuasive definitions, it was in fact doubly persuasive. It at once dissuaded people from indiscriminately admiring one set of qualities (wide reading and acquaintance with the arts) and induced them to admire another (imaginative sensitivity). The speaker wished to attain both of these ends, and was enabled, by his definition, to work for both at the same time.

There are hundreds of words which, like "culture," have both a vague conceptual meaning and a rich emotive meaning. The conceptual meaning of them all is subject to constant redefinition. The words are prizes which each man seeks to bestow on the qualities of his own choice.

In the nineteenth century, for instance, critics sometimes remarked that Alexander Pope was "not a poet." The foolish reply would be, "It's a mere matter of definition." It is indeed a matter of definition, but not a "mere" one. The word "poet" was used in an extremely narrow sense. This, so far from being idle, had important consequences; it enabled the critics to deny to Pope a laudatory name, and so to induce people to disregard him. A persuasive definition, tacitly employed, was at work in redirecting interests. Those who wish to decide whether Pope was a poet must decide whether they will yield to the critics' influence—whether they will come to dislike Pope enough to allow him to be deprived of an honorary title. This decision will require a knowledge of Pope's works and a knowledge of their own minds. Such are the important matters which lie behind the acceptance of the tacitly proposed, narrow definition of "poet." It is not a matter of "merely arbitrary" definition, then, nor is any persuasive definition "merely arbitrary," if this phrase is taken to imply "suitably decided by the flip of a coin."

Persuasive definitions are often recognizable from the words "real" or "true," employed in a metaphorical sense. The speaker in our first example, for instance, was telling us what "real" culture was, as distinct from the "shell" of culture. The following are additional examples: "Charity," in the true sense of the word, means the giving not merely of gold, but of understanding; true love is the communion between minds alone; "Courage," in the true sense, is strength against adverse public opinion. Each of these statements is a way of redirecting interests, by leaving the emotive meaning of the words unchanged, and wedding it to a new conceptual one. Similarly we may speak of the true meaning of "sportsmanship," "genius," "beauty," and so on. Or we may speak of the true meaning of "selfishness" or "hypocrisy," using persuasive definitions of these derogatory terms to blame, rather than to praise. "True," in such contexts, is obviously not used literally. Since people usually accept what they consider true, "true" comes to have the persuasive force of "to be accepted." This force is utilized in the metaphorical expression "true meaning." The hearer is induced to accept the new meaning which the speaker introduces.

Outside the confinements of philosophical theory the importance of persuasive definitions has often been recognized. In philology they receive occasional stress. Or rather, although little attention is given to persuasive definitions, much is said about the broad heading under which a study of them would fall: the interplay between emotive and conceptual meanings in determining linguistic change, and its correlation with interests.

Leonard Bloomfield[1] presents us with a particularly clear example: "The speculative builder has learned to appeal to every weakness, including the sentimentality, of the prospective buyer; he uses the speech forms whose content will turn the hearer in the right direction. In many locutions 'house' is the colorless, and 'home' the sentimental word. Thus the salesman comes to use the word 'home' for an empty shell that has never been inhabited, and the rest of us follow his style."

Hanns Oertel, having stated that "the emotional element greatly influences the fate of some words," points out that "amica" came to have one sense which was synonymous with "concubina."[2] To be sure there are several reasons for this. "Concubina" had become slightly profane, too strong for delicate ears. And "amica" permitted a convenient ambiguity. Any shocking thoughts could always be ascribed to those who chose to understand the word in its less innocent sense. But a persuasive factor must also have been involved. Tact often required people to refer to concubines without expressing contempt. The word "amica," which retained part of its old laudatory emotive meaning in spite of its new sense, was useful in making concubines appear less contemptible.

Persuasive definitions are too frequently encountered, however, to have been noticed solely by the philologists. An extremely penetrating account, in spite of its cynical turn, is given by Aldous Huxley, in his *Eyeless in Gaza*:

"But if you want to be free, you've got to be a prisoner. It's the condition of freedom—true freedom."

"True freedom!" Anthony repeated in the parody of a clerical voice. "I always love that kind of argument. The contrary of a thing isn't the contrary; oh, dear me, no! It's the thing itself, but as it *truly* is. Ask any die-hard what conservatism is; he'll tell you it's *true* socialism. And the brewer's trade papers; they're full of articles about the beauty of true temperance. Ordinary temperance is just gross refusal to drink; but true temperance, *true* temperance is something much more refined. True temperance is a bottle of claret with each meal and three double whiskies after dinner. . . .

"What's in a name?" Anthony went on. "The answer is, practically everything, if the name's a good one. Freedom's a marvelous name. That's why you're so anxious to make use of it. You think that, if you call imprisonment true freedom, people will be attracted to the prison. And the worst of it is you're quite right."

2

As has been intimated, the study of persuasive definitions falls under a much broader heading: the correlation between terminology and interests. This correlation is highly complicated. A few observations will serve to show that our account of persuasive definitions deals with a severely limited aspect of it.

A change in meaning may be either a cause or an effect of a change in interest; and persuasive definitions figure only when the change in meaning is a cause. When it is an effect, as when our growing disapproval of present conditions in Germany causes us to use "fascist" as an epithet, there is not in this situation itself any element of persuasion; although once the word has acquired its derogatory associations, it may be used in persuasion later on.

Our subject is still more limited in scope than this. We are concerned with *definitions* which change interests. And it is important to note that we are concerned only with *some* of these definitions. Many definitions which redirect interests are not persuasive. Interests tend to be redirected by *any* definition, so long as it at all changes the meaning of a term, or selects some one sense to the exclusion of others. When a scientist introduces a technical term, in no matter how detached a manner, he indicates his interest in what he names—his estimation of the importance of talking about it, or of predicting its occurrence—and he often leads his readers to have a similar interest. It would be quite misleading to call such definitions "persuasive." How, then, are they to be distinguished from persuasive definitions?

The distinction depends upon whether the term defined has a strong emotive meaning, and upon whether the speaker employs the emotively laden word with dynamic purposes—with the predominating *intention* of changing people's interests. Men some-times say, "I do not care what word you use, so long as you make my distinction;" and again, "If you are not interested in my distinc-tion, well and good; I shall confine my remarks to the limited set of people who are." Definitions given in such a spirit are not per-suasive; for although they indicate the speaker's interests, and may happen to influence the hearer's interests, they do not utilize emo-tive meaning in a deliberate effort to sway interests.

Such a distinction is inconveniently stringent, however, and must be slightly qualified. When a definition is given mainly for the pur-poses of distinction or classification, when it is used to guide only those interests which (like *curiosity*) are involved in making the classification understood, and when it in no way suggests that this is *the one* legitimate sort of classification, then the definition will not be called persuasive. (This is not meant to imply that persua-sive definitions are never used in scientific writings, nor that non-persuasive definitions are based on some rock foundation, nor that persuasive definitions are less respectable than others.)

We must now proceed to a further point. Persuasive definitions redirect interests by changing only the conceptual meaning of an emotively laden term, allowing the emotive meaning to remain roughly constant. Clearly, the opposite change is equally important and prevalent: the emotive meaning may be altered, the conceptual meaning remaining constant. This latter device is no less persua-sive. In fact, the same persuasive force can often be obtained either by the one linguistic change or by the other. In our initial example of "culture," for instance, the speaker used a persuasive definition. He might equally well have reiterated statements such as this: "Culture is only fool's gold; the true metal is imaginative sensi-tivity." This procedure would have permitted "culture" to retain its old conceptual meaning, but would have tended to make its emotive meaning derogatory; and it would have added to the laudatory emotive meaning of "imaginative sensitivity." The same purpose would have been served in this way that was served by the persuasive definition. The qualities commonly referred to by "cul-ture" would still be placed in a poor light, and imaginative sensitivity in a fine one; but this would have been effected by a change in emotive meaning, rather than in conceptual meaning.

Cases of this last sort must be excluded from our account of persuasive definitions. Although persuasive, they are not secured through definition, but rather by one's gestures and tone of voice, or by rhetorical devices such as similes and metaphors. It is expedient to restrict the word "definition" to cases where conceptual meaning alone is being determined, or where, at least, this aspect predominates. We must not forget, however, that many statements which change mainly the emotive meaning of words may, in a wider sense, be called "definitions"; and that they, no less than persuasive definitions in our strict sense, may easily be confused with statements that are not persuasive. (For example: "By 'conscience' is meant the voice of destiny.")

The remarks of the last several pages may be summarized as follows: Persuasive definitions, so far from explaining the whole interrelationship between terminology and interests, deal only with the cases where change in terminology *causes* change in interest, where emotive meaning and dynamic usage are involved, and where the terminological change is in conceptual meaning only.

There is one further clarifying remark that deserves mention. The redirection of people's interests obviously depends upon much more than emotive meaning. It depends as well upon dynamic usage; upon the vigor of the speaker, his gestures, his tone of voice, the cadence of his accompanying sentences, his figures of speech, and so on. It is further conditioned by the temperament of the hearers, their respect for the speaker, their susceptibility to suggestion, their latent prejudices and ideals—and indeed, by their factual beliefs, for a sudden change in men's beliefs prepares the way (though often with a "lag") for a redirection of interests. Persuasion is seldom effective unless the hearers are already on the point of changing their interests. A persuasive definition may then be important as a final impetus to the change, and as a mnemonic device, imbedded in language, for keeping the change permanent. In dwelling upon definitions, then, and upon the function of emotive meaning, we have stressed but one aspect of persuasive situations. There are excellent reasons for this stress, however. Emotive meaning is a fairly stable element amid the widely varying set of factors upon which effective persuasion depends, and although a partial factor, is often essential. When a man redefines an emotively laden term, moreover, he is *very* frequently endeavoring to persuade, and takes care that the other factors necessary to successful persuasion are fulfilled. Emotive meaning is a reliable *sign* of persuasion—permits it to be noticed. This is important in the case of definitions, where persuasion, however legitimate and vital in itself, can so easily acquire a spurious appeal by masking itself in the guise of a logical analysis.

3

Having explained what persuasive definitions are, let us now see how they are important to philosophy.

We can readily begin by considering philosophic definitions of the word "philosophy" itself. Ramsey defines it as a system of definitions. Van der Leeuw defines it as an attempt to penetrate behind appearances. Their divergence is no terminological accident. "Philosophy" is a dignified term, and each man reserves it for the inquiry he most wishes to dignify.

Consider the word "Reality." Philosophers often seek not reality, but Reality, or rather, true Reality. But "true Reality," like "true culture," is easily defined in many different ways, with many different persuasive effects. Were the shadows in Plato's cave "real" shadows? Were there "real" shadows of horses and men, as distinct from the imaginary shadows of centaurs? It will not do to express it so. "Real" is too impressive a term to be used in describing shadows and flux; so it must be given a restricted sense which makes it predicable only of the eternal patterns. (When "Reality" is used by the mystics, the effects of a tacit persuasive definition become even more obvious.)

Why did Spinoza, so anxious to free thinking from anthropomorphism, nevertheless tempt his readers to anthropomorphism by using the word "God"? Why did he not speak always of "The One Substance"? One points, of course, to the political and social forces of the times, which made a semblance of orthodoxy imperative. But assuredly this is not all. The word "God" arouses, as if by magic, the very deepest of feelings. By giving the word a new conceptual meaning, Spinoza was enabled to direct its emotional force away from the old anthropomorphic fictions, and center it upon Substance, which he so earnestly thought would be a more rewarding object for all our wonder and humility. Had he said, "There is no God; nothing but Substance and its Modes," he would have spoken what he believed, provided "God" was used in the popular sense. But this would have been poor economy of the emotions. It would have taken away the object of men's wonder and humility, providing no substitute; and so these feelings would have

died, to the great impoverishment of emotional life. The persuasive
definition of a word was needed to preserve emotional vitality.
The change in the meaning of "God" was too abrupt, however, to
escape notice. Spinoza "the atheist" was long in giving place to
Spinoza "the God-intoxicated man"; for the supporters of orthodoxy were not slow to see that his God was God in emotive meaning only.

These remarks are not to be misconstrued as cynical. To point
out persuasion is not necessarily to condemn it, nor to identify all
persuasion with that of a mob-orator. It *is* imperative, however, to
distinguish between persuasion and rational demonstration.

Let us now proceed to a more recent issue. Positivism achieved
its wide appeal before Carnap's "principle of tolerance," and
achieved it largely through the statement, "Metaphysics is without
meaning." But isn't this remark surprisingly like that of the nineteenth-century critics, who said that Pope was "not a poet"? The
Positivists were stating an unquestionable truth, in their sense of
"meaning," just as the nineteenth-century critics were, in their
sense of "poet." The truth of such statements, however, is utterly
beside the point. Controversy hinges on the emotive words that
are used. Shall we define "meaning" narrowly, so that science alone
will receive this laudatory title, and metaphysics the correspondingly derogatory one of "nonsense"? Shall our terminology show
science in a fine light, and metaphysics in a poor one? Shall we,
in short, accept this *persuasive* definition of "meaning"? This is the
question, though well concealed by the dictum that definitions are
"merely arbitrary."

But this conclusion deserves careful qualification. We must remember that the nineteenth-century critics, to return to the analogy,
were not condemning Pope with sheer bombast. They were also
making a distinction. Their narrow sense of "poet" had the
function of stressing, in the reader's attention, certain features
common to most poetry, but lacking in Pope's. Perhaps they meant
to say this: "We have long been blind to fundamental differences
between Pope's work and that of a Shakespeare or Milton. It is
because of this blindness alone that we have been content to give
Pope a laudatory title. Let us note the difference, then, and deprive
him of the title." The contention of the Positivists will easily bear
the same interpretation. Perhaps they meant to say: "We have long
been blind to the fundamental differences between the use of sentences in science and their use in metaphysics. It is because of this

blindness alone that we have been content to dignify metaphysics with such titles as 'meaningful.' Let us define 'meaning,' then, in a way that will at once stress these fundamental differences, and deprive metaphysics of its title." When thus stated, the Positivistic thesis has not only heat, but light, and is not to be scorned. And yet, perhaps there is still too much heat for the amount of light. It is of no little service to stress the ways in which metaphysics has been confused with science; and to the extent that Positivists have done this, their "conquest of metaphysics" has not depended upon exhortation. But do their distinctions take us more than *halfway* to a full rejection of metaphysics? Are we led to go the other half by the word "nonsense," defined so that it may cast its objectionable emotive meaning upon metaphysics, without being predicated of it untruthfully?

The same question arises even when metaphysics is denied "cognitive" meaning only. "Cognitive" is used to mean "empirically verifiable or else analytic," and with exclusive laudatory import. Hence the Positivistic contention reduces to this: "Metaphysical statements are neither empirically verifiable nor analytic; hence they are not respectable." If metaphysicians answer, "Our statements, even though neither empirically verifiable nor analytic, are still respectable," they are scarcely to be led away from their position by mere exhortation.

Metaphysical impulses are too strong for hortatory treatment; they are inhibited by it without being removed. If metaphysics is wholly to give place to science in our esteem, this can come only from a closer scrutiny of both metaphysics and science. Inquiries into verification and syntax make a good beginning, but they are not the only points for study. It would be well to consider how words which suggest graphic images and metaphors are used in the sciences, and contrast their function there with their function in metaphysics; or to examine the psychological needs and specific confusions which lead people to think that metaphysics is necessary. Such inquiries would direct our attitudes toward metaphysics in a more permanent and illuminating fashion; they would shape our attitudes by clarifying and augmenting our beliefs. If an adverse attitude to metaphysics were prepared for in this manner, the word "nonsense," persuasively defined, would be helpful in crystallizing the attitude. Such a program seems more promising than that of the metaphysicians. It is a pity, then, to hide its real complexity by using a persuasive definition prematurely.

4

Let us now turn to ethics, with particular attention to the word "justice," as defined in Plato's *Republic*.

The first book of the *Republic*, it will be remembered, is largely taken up with an argument between Socrates and Thrasymachus. Socrates is the victor, and yet he is not content. "I have gone from one subject to another," he says, "without having discovered what I sought first, the nature of justice. I left that inquiry and turned away to consider whether justice is virtue and wisdom, or evil and folly." (354, Jowett.)

Was this argument about the "virtue or evil" of justice really an unwarranted digression? In the light of our previous discussion, we cannot agree that it was. The argument had the important function of determining whether or not "justice" was to retain its laudatory emotive meaning; and this was essential to the subsequent developments of the dialogue. When a man is about to give a persuasive definition (and we shall see in a moment that Socrates was) he must make sure that the emotive meaning of the term defined is well established. Otherwise a definition which was intended to illuminate a conceptual meaning under a laudatory title will end by obscuring it under a derogatory one. The word "justice," which is a little too stern to be wholly pleasing, is in danger of becoming derogatory, and particularly so when men like Thrasymachus (with a persuasive technique like that mentioned in section 2 above) are using their oratorical ability to *make* the word derogatory. Socrates must praise justice, then, before he defines "justice."

The question about the meaning of "justice" reappears in the fourth book. The two intervening books have redirected our interests by a moving description of the ideal state. These new interests must be rendered permanent. This can be done by dignifying the more significant aspects of the state under laudatory titles. Of the four laudatory terms which Socrates mentions, "wisdom," "courage," "temperance," and "justice," the first three are readily made to serve this purpose, without great change in their conceptual meaning. The remaining term must be reserved for whatever else needs dignity. And so the definition of "justice" is found. "Justice of the state consists of each of the three classes doing the work of its own class." (441) .

The persuasive character of this definition—the fact that it forms a part of a spirited plea for a new class system, a beautiful and inspired kind of aristocratic propaganda—can scarcely be denied. The usual meanings of "justice" must give place to the "true" one, to the meaning which needs the dignity of a laudatory name.

This account would strike Plato as decidedly unfamiliar. Yet he would disagree with it much less fundamentally than may at first appear. Let us follow his own account, stressing such points as bear analogy to the present one.

Plato would have agreed that the usual meaning of "justice" was only a point for departure. We must fashion our definition, not after the common conception of justice, but after justice itself —after the eternal Idea of justice, which we have beheld in a life before birth, and can now know only through careful *recollection*. A definition based on common usage would disclose merely the imperfect recollection of the Idea, as grasped by men bound to the world of opinion.

This point of agreement seems slight, and outweighed by the theory of recollection. But let us look more closely. How did Plato decide whether his recollection was correct? Did he consider it correct when he reached a conception which satisfied his deepest, inmost aspirations? Did the dialectical method serve only to clarify his mind, so that his aspirations could be directed to something articulate? It is difficult to think of any other answer. Plato aspired to the Ideas; but this was not a consequence of some miraculous power of attraction which the Ideas possessed. It was a matter of analytic necessity. Anything which was not an object of his aspirations was not called an Idea. If this is so, then our account is again close to his. If he had consciously been making a persuasive definition, he would still have selected, as the conceptual meaning of "justice," the object of these same aspirations. Nothing else would have been granted the laudatory name. We have retained the factors which led Plato to make his definition, without retaining the poetic realm of the Ideas, whose function, indeed, was only to adorn his procedure, not to alter its outcome.

If Plato's work had been less Utopian, more satirical, he would have had recollections not from one realm of Ideas, but from two. The first realm would have been the dwelling place of the gods, as described in the *Phaedrus;* and the second the dwelling place of the "author of evil" who makes his unexpected appearance in the tenth book of the *Laws.* Just as aspirations would be the criteria for correct recollection from the first realm, so aversions would be the criteria for correct recollection from the second. The theory of definition would then be less closely confined to the laudatory terms. Recollection could function likewise for the derogatory ones. But it would be of vital importance, in defining the derogatory terms, to confine the recollection to the second realm. The most serious philosophical errors would come from a failure to recollect from the "correct" realm, where the correctness of the realm would depend on the emotive meaning of the term defined.

We must return, however, to the definition of "justice." Plato's definition was persuasive; but this is far from being exceptional. Later definitions of "justice," with but few exceptions, are equally persuasive. They exert a different kind of influence, of course. Not all philosophers are aristocrats. But they do exert an influence.

Let us consider Bentham's definition. " 'Justice,' in the only sense which has meaning [!], is an imaginary personage, feigned for the convenience of discourse, whose dictates are the dictates of utility, applied to certain particular cases."[3] More simply stated, "This is a just law" is a hypostatic way of saying, "This law contributes to the greatest happiness of the greatest number." Such a definition may not immediately strike us as being persuasive, since so many of us are willing to be led in its direction. Yet its stress on mere members, its stress on counting the poor man's happiness side by side with the rich man's, clearly marks a plea for greater democracy. The definition propagated the ideals of a great Liberal.

By a "just" wage for laborers, it may be suggested, is meant the wage that anticipates what laborers would get eventually, through operation of the laws of supply and demand, if only there were a perfect market in the economic sense. This definition conceals its persuasion quite well, making it seem to have the detachment of a purely scientific economics. But it is a plea, though slightly compromised, for the operation not of economic laws, but of "natural" economic laws—that is to say, for the operation of economic laws as they *could* be stated *if* the purely competitive, "devil take the hindermost," aspects of industry were guaranteed. So you will find this definition more pleasing to those who thrive under the present industrial conditions than to those who do not.

"Justice" can be defined in a great many ways, always without shocking the lexicographers. An eye for an eye, and a tooth for a tooth? The keeping of contracts, merely? The king's will? The distribution of social wealth in accordance with the amount of *labor* that each man does? We have a wide choice of meanings, and freedom, within wide conventional limits, to invent new ones. Which meaning we choose, however, is no trivial matter; for we shall dignify that meaning by a laudatory title. To choose a meaning is to take sides in a social struggle.

It is curious to note that theorists have all been perturbed by the uncertainty of ethics, and have caught glimpses, even in moments of philosophical calm, of the element of persuasion involved. They sought to avoid this by defining their terms, hoping to give greater rigor and rationality to their inquiries. Yet, ironically enough, these very definitions involved the same persuasion; and in a way that veiled and confused it, by making it appear to be purely intellectual analysis.

5

The examples we have considered, whether from metaphysics, theology, epistemology, or ethics, indicate that persuasive definitions are far from rare in philosophy, and that failure to recognize their persuasive character has been responsible for much confusion. But what, essentially, is the nature of this confusion? Largely this: Blindness to persuasion has fostered a misunderstanding of the *kind of disagreement* that motivates many disputes; and in consequence has led people to support their contentions by far too simple a *method,* or to seek a definitive method of proof where none is possible.

These methodological confusions have so far been evident only by implication, and must now be treated more explicitly. Let us proceed by indicating the *actual* complexity in methodology which persuasive definitions introduce; for the extent to which this complexity has been overlooked will then become obvious, without further mention. It will be convenient to confine our attention to the example of "justice"; but it must be remembered, of course, that the same considerations arise for any case which involves a term that is subject to persuasive definition.

The summary of methodology will be parallel to that given in a previous paper.[4] The pattern of analysis there exemplified by "good," however, is slightly different from the one here exemplified by "justice." The same methodological considerations reappear, but we must recognize them in their new guise, and amid additional complications.

Two men disagree about whether a certain law is just. Let us examine the several forms which their argument may take.

(1) Suppose that both men use "just" with the same conceptual meaning, namely: *leading to consequences A and B*. The argument may then be resolved by use of the empirical method. The disputants have only to see whether the law in question leads to these consequences.

This simple case is seldom found, however. We have seen that "justice" is constantly subject to persuasive definition, with the result that different people come to use it in different senses.

(2) Suppose, then, that the first man uses "just" to refer to A and B, and the second man uses it to refer to B and C. Suppose further that B is the only point of disagreement. In this case the disputants will probably proceed without noticing the discrepancy in their terminology, and will again find the empirical method adequate. The outcome of the argument will depend upon whether the law is or is not found to lead to B.

(3) Let us next make the same supposition as immediately above, save that C, rather than B, is the sole point of disagreement. The discrepancy in terminology will then probably be realized. Yet the argument may proceed, and in *some* cases may be settled empirically. If the second man, who uses "just" to refer to B and C, is the one who denies the justice of the law, his opponent may refute him by showing empirically that the law does lead to C. (B is already agreed upon, by hypothesis.) "You are refuted," the first man will say, "even according to your own faulty conception of justice."

This case raises a point which demands particular attention. The first disputant did not refer to C, in his initial statement, and the second disputant denied the justice of the law on account of C alone. Hence the initial statement of the first man was at no time contradicted by his opponent. Yet the first man will feel, even after the discrepancy in terminology is clearly realized, that he has been opposed from the very beginning. He will feel the need of refuting his opponent's statement, as though this were necessary to support his own. Why is this the case?

This question seems puzzling only because we have attended exclusively to conceptual meaning. We have been tacitly assuming that the disputants were pure scientists, motivated by a detached curiosity. If our example is to be typical of the majority of actual ones, this assumption is wholly unwarranted. The use of "just" and "unjust" clearly indicated that one disputant was *for* the law, and the other *against* it. They argued for this reason, not because they were statistically minded. They were *disagreeing in interest*. Each had a different kind of interest in the law, and neither was content to let the other's interest remain unchanged.[5] This kind of disagreement is evident more from emotive meaning than from conceptual meaning. The fact, then, that the conceptual meaning of the first disputant was not contradicted did not lead him to feel that his position was unchallenged. He wanted his opponent not merely to acknowledge certain consequences of the law, but likewise to praise it; and his opponent would not be praising it if he called it "unjust," no matter what conceptual meaning he assigned to the term.

The disagreement in interest is most easily seen in cases like (3), but a moment's consideration will show that it is equally present in cases (1) and (2). The use of the laudatory term "just" in the earlier cases indicated that they too were concerned with whether or not the law was to be favored. A, B, and C were involved, of course, but no more so than in the third case, and they were relevant for the same reason—relevant because the disagreement in interest, which motivated the argument, was rooted in a disagreement in belief. In other words, the disputants would have the same kind of interest in the law if only they resolved their opposing beliefs about these consequences of it. In the first cases these opposing beliefs were about consequences which *both* disputants referred to conceptually by the word "just." In the third case they were about something which only one referred to by "just." This is the main point of difference between the cases, and it is unimportant. The disagreement was of a sort that would terminate only when both disputants had the same kind of interest in the law. Beliefs were relevant only to the extent that they redirected interests. Which beliefs did so, and whether they were expressed in the initial statements of both opponents, determined merely the complexity of the argument, and not its fundamental character.

These remarks prepare us for a further case:

(4) Suppose, as before, that the first man uses "just" to refer to A and B, and the second man (who denies the justice of the law) uses "just" to refer to B and C. Suppose further that both

have fully established that the law does lead to A and B, and that it does not lead to C. Conceptually speaking, of course, they have as yet located no point of disagreement, nor is there the possibility, as in (3), of one man's refuting the other "even according to the opponent's faulty conception of justice." Yet they may still argue about the justice of the law. The laudatory force of "just," and the derogatory force of "unjust," are still indicative of a disagreement in interest.

With regard to methodology this case is of particular importance. It represents a disagreement which the *empirical method may be wholly incapable of resolving.*

This will be clear if we again consider, at the expense of partial repetition, why the empirical method *was* decisive in the first three cases. In each of the earlier cases the initial judgment of one disputant was false. This was guaranteed either by the law of contradiction or by explicit hypothesis. Each disputant, moreover, would have had a favorable interest in the law only so long as he believed that "just," in his sense, was truthfully predicable of it; for otherwise he would have used the laudatory term in a different conceptual sense. For these reasons the disputants had only to look to the truth of their initial statements, and this would lead them to have the same kind of interest in the law. In short, the disagreement in interest, which was the mainspring of the argument, was rooted in a disagreement in belief—in some belief which at least one of the opponents had falsely expressed in his initial statement. The empirical method, by upsetting this belief, would likewise resolve the disagreement in interest.

In case (4), however, the initial statements of the opponents are both true. The men are disposed, as above, to favor or disfavor the law in accordance with whether "just" and "unjust," in the disparate senses which they employ, are truthfully predicable of it; but an empirical inquiry will serve to *support both* of their statements. Hence the first man will continue to call the law "just," with favor; and the second "unjust," with disfavor. Their disagreement is not rooted in some belief which either is expressing, and may be due solely to their different temperaments. Since the empirical method alters interests only through altering beliefs, how can it be used to resolve this disagreement?

It is immediately clear that the empirical method has not the same direct application, in (4), that it had in the earlier cases.

Yet we shall conclude too hastily if we say that there is no room for it here at all. Let us examine further.

If case (4) continues to be disputed, persuasive definitions, which hitherto have been responsible only for the ambiguity of "just," will come to play a more overt and important role. Each man, in order to influence the other's interests, will insist upon his own definition. They will argue about whether the law is just in the *true* sense of "just." Until they agree upon the sense of the word they will not agree upon their fundamental issue, namely: whether the law is to be described by a name that indicates their praise.

The empirical method, however unavailing it may be in altering the truth of the conceptual predications which the disputants first made, may reappear as a means of supporting their persuasive definitions. The second disputant, for instance, may be led to discover that C, to which he refers by "just," has the further consequences, F, G, and H. If he has an unfavorable interest in these consequences, he may no longer wish to define "just" in terms of C. If he is led to discover that A has the further consequences I, J, and K, in which he has a favorable interest, he may decide to use "just" to refer to A. In other words, he may accept the definition upon which his opponent has been insisting. Both men will then come to agree that the law is just in a mutually accepted sense of "just." This sense will be a product of their wider empirical knowledge, and it will terminate their argument not merely because they both believe that it is truthfully predicable of the law, but because their mutual acceptance of it indicates that they no longer disagree in interest, but both favor the law.

The argument in case (4) *may* be resolved, then, in an empirical fashion; but we must remember that it also may not. Even if the disputants know all the relevant consequences of the law, one of them may still wish to praise it, and the other to condemn it. They will be led to no common conceptual sense of "just," and although neither man need be stating anything false about the law, they will continue to disagree about its justice. The disagreement will be one in interest, not rooted in any sort of disagreement in belief. If resolved at all it will be solved only by exhortation.

It is a general truth that the empirical method can resolve ethical disagreement, or any other kind of disagreement in interest, only when this is rooted in a disagreement in belief. The present outline of methodology has become complicated only with regard to *which* beliefs are at the root of the disagreement in interest—

whether there are any, and if so, to what extent they are expressed in the initial judgments. Such considerations are essential in clarifying the nature of the argument, but they are of no additional importance. This is obvious from the fact that arguments of this sort spring from the emotive meaning of the initial judgments, more than from the conceptual meaning. It is evident from a further consideration: In actual practice "just" is used so vaguely that neither disputant will be sure which consequences are included in the definition of "just," and which psychologically guide him to make this definition.

The present pattern of analysis is conveniently applicable to all of the more specific ethical terms, and likewise to "beautiful." The pattern of analysis exemplified elsewhere by "good"[6] is conveniently applicable only to the more generic ethical terms. (It does not provide any ready means of indicating *differentiae*.) But which of these patterns of analysis we select for any ethical term is largely a matter of technical convenience. "Just" could perhaps be treated after the manner of "good," and distinguished from "good" by the kind of interest involved—though present psychological terminology does not provide a means of making the distinction accurately. "Good" could doubtless be treated after the manner of "just." Moritz Schlick made a beginning of this,[7] but his failure to stress disagreement in interest, and all that it implies, largely vitiates his account. The same may be said, although with several qualifications, of the original account given by Ogden and Richards,[8] and of the account given by C. D. Broad.[9]

The ethical terms are used so vaguely that many different patterns of analysis are relevant to the conventional usage. It is idle to select some one of these as *the* pattern of analysis. All that is required is that the analysis clarify, whether in one way or another, the essential features of ethical arguments. These are emotive meaning, dynamic usage, disagreement in interest, and an important but not definitive role for the empirical method.

Reprinted with permission of the editor from *Mind*, 1938.

1. Leonard Bloomfield, *Language* (New York, Henry Holt, 1933), p. 442.

2. Hanns Oertel, *Lectures on the Study of Language* (New York, Scribner, 1902), pp. 304, 305.

3. Jeremy Bentham, *Principles of Morals and Legislation* (1789), Chap. x, Sect. xl, n. 2.

4. C. L. Stevenson, "The Emotive Meaning of Ethical Terms," *Mind*, Vol. xlvi, N.S., No. 181.

5. Stevenson, *loc. cit.*, p. 27, for a fuller analysis of disagreement in interest.

6. Stevenson, *loc. cit.*

7. M. Schlick, *Fragen der Ethik* (Vienna, J. Springer, 1930), Chap. i.

8. C. Ogden, and I. A. Richards, *The Meaning of Meaning* (Kegan Paul, 1927), p. 149.

9. C. D. Broad, "Is Goodness the Name of a Simple, Non-natural Quality?" *Proceedings of the Aristotelian Society,* 1933–34.

PART TWO

Metaphysics and Theory of Knowledge

BRAND BLANSHARD

The Nature of Mind

By "mind" most people mean consciousness. As examples of the mental, they would take pleasures and pains, loves and hates, purposes, memories, and desires. And consciousness—what is that? They would be unable to say; but they would be untroubled by this, and rightly enough, for there are plenty of things whose meaning is clear and familiar that we cannot define. And whether we can define consciousness or not, we can readily convey what we mean by it to another; for example, it is what makes the difference between being awake and sound asleep. And the natural first question to ask is whether consciousness is what we mean by mind.

I do not think it is. I agree that all consciousness is mental; what is doubtful is whether all that is mental is conscious. Take a case in point. Some time ago I was discussing with a discriminating friend the achievements of the so-called unconscious self. He told me that, being puzzled once as to the demonstration of some theorem in geometry, he went to bed with the problem unsolved. The next morning he found the demonstration written out on the table at his bedside. His memory was clear that he had left the problem unsolved the night before; the writing was unmistakably his own; and there was only one plausible explanation: he had got up in his sleep and written the solution down. This kind of performance, though not perhaps common, has been made familiar to us through Professor D. Lowes' researches on Coleridge, and through such extended inquiries as those of Morton Prince and Freud. Not that in all cases the performance is unconscious; sometimes it occurs in a dream that can be recalled on waking; sometimes there is a process of co-consciousness that is to be recovered, if at all, by technical methods only. But the process does appear on occasion to be genuinely unconscious, Freud thought very frequently so. If and where it is, what are we to say about its being mental? Are we to say of the elaborating of a conclusion or the composing of a lyric that it is not a mental process at all? Of course we can make the word "mental" mean what we wish. But the issue is more than verbal. If we call some processes mental and some not, it is because between them we find a chasm placed by nature. Such activities as inference and artistic invention seem to belong to mind so clearly, whether verifiable as conscious or not, that I prefer to place them there at the outset and make the definition of mind conform, rather than to define mind independently and force our natural classification into line.

If we are willing to start from this natural classification, our question becomes this: Is there any characteristic which is always present, and which *alone* is always present, where mind is recognized? Take some cases at random in which people would generally agree that in some measure or other mind was present and active. A philosopher is philosophizing; a householder is making a budget; a sculptor is carving a block; a poet, asleep or awake, is contriving a poem; an infant is crying for the moon; a dog is sniffing at a hole; a bee is hunting, or apparently hunting, nectar. We should be less sure in the last cases than in the first that mind was at work; but I do not think we should regard any of these cases or levels as simply and totally mindless. Regarding any such series we must ask: Is there anything universally and exclusively present that we can fix on as the common and essential feature of mind?

My own answer is Yes: wherever mind is present, there the pursuit of ends is present. Wherever that pursuit is wholly absent, mind is absent. And when mind is present, it is present precisely in the degree to which ends are in control.

Let us revert to our cases. I should say that in all of them ends are being pursued, but not in the same sense or the same way. Ordinarily when we speak of anyone as engaging in such pursuit, we imply that he takes thought of what he wants and deliberately appoints his means with reference to it. The householder who arranges his budget is aiming at a target in full view, namely, the bringing of his expenses within a limit that is clearly defined. The poet who is writing a sonnet has in mind a poem of a certain length and structure, and the character of this whole presides over his selection of words and images. It is such behavior that we commonly mean when we speak of purposive process—behavior, that, is, in which the controlling purpose is definite and explicit. But is the presence of such purpose typical of behavior that pursues ends? No, it is not. One thinks at once of the lower levels of behavior. Regarding a bird, for example, that gathers materials suitable for building its nest, it seems to me unreasonable to deny that it is pursuing an end at all, and likewise unreasonable to ascribe to it an end that is consciously present. The bird is pursuing an end that is not explicit.

Now we find this kind of behavior, not on the lower levels only, but at every level in the scale of mind. Mental activity is the sort of activity everywhere whose reach exceeds its grasp. So far as is now known, human beings top the scale; but when a man makes a choice—say of one action rather than another as the right one—can he give any adequate account of why he chooses it? Quite possibly he could take a step or two ahead; he wanted to better his business or home or income. But if pressed as to why he wanted *this,* and why he wanted the further end that this in turn subserved, he would soon falter. This does not imply that his choice is unwise, or even that it is not firmly guided; the saint who has the surest sort of practical judgment may cut a very poor figure when he philosophizes on ultimate good. But we may go much further than this. Even in our clearest cases of purposive action, there is a large element of this mysterious kind of end-seeking. When a philosopher philosophizes, he is trying to solve a problem, and he if anyone should know what he is about. Does he? The Greeks had a dilemma for it: If the man who seeks after truth knows what he wants, there is no use seeking, for he has it already; and if doesn't know, he won't recognize it when he finds it. Their answer to this puzzle, of course, was that he may know in general what he wants without knowing in detail, and that this general end is enough to guide his search and check it. The answer is sound so far as it goes. But need even this general end be explicit? And whether it is or not, how can so vague an end exert a control so firm and precise over the course of its realization?

Reflection on such problems would carry us deep, I think, into the nature of mind. To be sure, there may seem at first to be no problem at all. When we are given the premises of a syllogism and required to draw the conclusion, it may be said that we know quite well what the form of the syllogism is, and that with this form or pattern before us, we simply hew to the line. But half the time this is false to fact. Introspection shows that the form or pattern is often absent, and that we hew to the line without it. We see afterward that our thought did conform to the pattern, but the pattern is a later abstraction from the process, not the chart which guided its course. It may be said that such thought is not a case of control by ends at all, but a following of the track of habit. But thought is never mere habit, even on the level of syllogism; and it is obviously more when it breaks new ground.

From the lowest level to the highest, then, in the scale of mind, we find teleology, not the kind of teleology that is found in explicit purpose, but something more generic. Can we say what this is? If we can, we shall have caught the common and distinguishing feature of mental process. We must see what we can do.

The irreducible facts we must start with are, first, that there is a great range of processes whose course is determined with reference to, and in some sense by, an end, and second, that this end is not consciously there to exert control. These facts force us on, I think, to the notion of an immanent end, an implicit end, an end that can lay compulsion on conscious processes without being conscious itself.

Philosophers commonly shy away from this notion. Behavior that is expressly purposive they recognize and in a measure understand; behavior that is mechanical they often think they understand better; but behavior that is purposive without purpose sounds so monstrous that they avert their eyes and withdraw. The psychologists, however, do not. Whether from moral courage or from metaphysical innocence, they dash in with abandon where the philosophers fear to tread, and are soon talking in accents heard by all, except perhaps the philosophers, about unconscious fears, desires, and memories. If a philosopher here or there does take notice, he probably remarks that these things are meaningless. To which the psychologist replies, "It is no more our business to say what these things really are than it is of the physicist to say what a photon is; if he finds that there are x's that behave in a certain way, he has done his job; and so of us. People in fact behave as if unconscious ends controlled them; for us that is enough; whether it makes speculative sense is for you to say, and instead of facing the issue, you avert your eyes and look pained." There is force in this rejoinder. If induction compels us, as I think it does, to say that mind *is* teleological process of the type described, in which there is control by implicit ends, then it is clearly of the utmost importance to make philosophical sense of it.

Now I think that if we are going to make sense of it we must return to a conception of Aristotle which he represents in the *De Anima* as essential to the understanding of mind, and which he stresses again in the *Metaphysics. We must regard mind as a process in which the potential realizes or actualizes itself.* It is the the sort of process in which that which is to be determines, in part, the course of its coming to be. Mind acts as it does because pressing in and through the present is a world that clamors to be born. Is it replied that only the actual can act, and that the notion that what is not yet existent can influence what *is* is nonsense? I answer that this reply rests on a notion of the existent and actual that will not stand. I agree that so far as the actual does act, it does so in virtue of its character. But what is the character possessed at any given moment by a truly developing thing? A shoot appears above the earth, and you ask what sort of plant it is. The answer comes, It is the shoot of a cornstalk or an elm tree. Would you reply that this introduces irrelevance, since the shoot is not yet an elm tree, but only the possibility of one? But so to conceive it is still to conceive it with reference to what it is becoming. Strip off that reference, conceive it not as an incipient elm, but simply as a pattern of cells whose changes are without directive impulse, and would you have a better idea or a worse of what the thing now is? You would have a worse, because, present in the thing that now is, making it what it is, controlling the course of its change, is a special impulsion or drive that cannot be conceived except as a drive toward a special end. This is suggested in our speech; we say, "that is an elm tree shoot," identifying what it is through what it is becoming, and suggesting that if we are to understand its present nature, we must grasp that nature as the imperfectly realized form of something else. This is true always of what develops, and true only of this. A ball of putty can be conceived without reference to anything that, in course of molding, it may become. What develops can not be conceived except as the partial realization of that which, as fully actual, is yet to be.

Now mind, at all of its levels and in all of its manifestations, is a process of this kind. And since this is what I mean by conative process, I can agree with Mr. W. H. Sheldon that mind is essentially conative. May one go further with him and say that mind is secondarily cognitive? Yes, if this means that knowing is a less fundamental, because less universal, mental process than conation is. No, if it implies that cognition and conation are fundamentally different. For in my view mind *is* conation; all mental processes reduce to it.

This obviously needs defense. But it needs defense far more in respect to some processes than to others. Regarding volition, affection, and emotion, one may argue with some plausibility that they are aspects of conation, but to say that cognition in all its forms is a *conatus* toward an end appears less credible. Since I hold that cognition is just this from first to last, it may be well to take some central cognitive process and show that it is unintelligible unless taken as the realizing of an immanent end. I should be willing to rest my case on any process that is clearly cognitive, but let us take one that will not be challenged on that ground and is of great interest in itself, the process of *inference*.

Suppose a crime has occurred and a detective is called in to solve it. What does he do? Normally he begins by gathering evidence through observation and inquiry; on the basis of this evidence he forms one or more hypotheses; these hypotheses he then tests till one of them proves satisfactory. Now none of these steps can be understood unless the movement of thought is taken as under control by an end. The first two steps are those of what James described as sagacity and inference proper. Sagacity consists in seeing what evidence bears on the case, what *is* evidence in the case. If the expert consulted happens to be Watson, he will make a laborious and largely irrelevant catalogue of details; if it is the great Sherlock himself, his selection will be at once narrower and broader, narrower because much of Watson's detail will be for him superfluous baggage, broader because details offer themselves as relevant which Watson would never have noticed. Why is it that Holmes selects the right things for notice, while Watson does not? It is more than a matter of past experience, for a wealth of this without sagacity may fail, while a very little of it with sagacity may succeed. We can only say that working in and through the better observation is a more exacting ideal of relevance. In some instances this is perfectly clear. Perhaps the main contribution of Aristotle to induction was the insight that where, in observation, *nous* or intellect was really active, there was no need for it to wait to pile up instances in order, by association and dissociation, to bare the nerve of a connection; it could seize the connection directly, as when the schoolboy sees that straightness of line in the triangle before him bears on its geometrical properties, while redness and largeness do not. The norm of relevance that is at work in his mind he is no doubt unable to define; it may work less effectively in some minds than in others; in even the best minds it works variably, as when Aristotle thought he saw the same sort of connection between humanity and mortality that he saw between two fives and a ten. But this leaves the result still standing that the selective observation which is normally the base of inference is under the control and guidance of an immanent ideal of relevance.

Now when a certain amount of evidence has been collected, thought leaps to a hypothesis; this is the second step in the process; and it constitutes inference proper. What determines the direction of this leap? According to James's famous chapter, it is similar association; the effective reasoner is the man who is prodigal of analogies, good, bad, and indifferent, between which, once they are laid out before him, he goes on to choose. But surely this is just how a mind in command of its matter does *not* work. If the suggestions turned up by analogy are really random, thought is at sea with no rudder; there is no reasoning at all. If the analogies are in point, the connection that is being sought is present in all of them, and it is more natural to suppose that the presence of this connection within them had something to do with their arising than that, once arisen, they all disclosed it by sheer chance. The working of analogy itself rests on the working of an implicit logic. Hence in favorable cases James's paraphernalia of similars can be dispensed with, and we can go to our result directly. When the conditions of a problem are precisely set out before a mathematician, he does not always need to go groping about for his result through a forest of metaphors; if he can keep hold of the leading-string of logical implication, he may go straight from conditions to conclusion. Nor does this occur only in regions of high abstractness. When an intelligent detective leaps from the evidence given him to the solution of a crime, the movement of inference is as truly under the control of an implicit logic as the thought that deals with numbers or triangles.

It may be replied that logic is a set of timeless relations among concepts timeless themselves, and that it never descends into the flux of events to control or divert the current. It is eternal, and what is eternal does not act. I accept the first statement and reject the second. Just as the form of a sonnet which, abstractly taken, is eternal does, when present in a poet's mind, preside over the work of composition, so logical implication may groove the channel for thought. To me there is something absurd in saying that when you present a man with the premises of a syllogism and his thought leaps on to the conclusion, the fact that the premises implied the conclusion had nothing to do with its appearance. The conclusion appeared precisely because he had succeeded in so surrendering his thought to logic that implication took control. Indeed it is only when we succeed in doing this that true inference occurs.

Both in the selection of evidence, then, and in the leap of inference by which that evidence is completed, there is at work an immanent logical end. It is at work even more clearly in the third step, by which the inferred suggestion is tested. To test anything is to measure it by a standard. Without such a standard, testing would be meaningless. When do we take a problem as solved? When the relation between the solution we offer and the relevant evidence answers to our ideal of proof. Present in the mind of the geometer, whether defined or not, is an ideal of demonstration which forbids rest in any theorem till it is connected systematically with the postulates of his system. Present in the mind of the detective is a standard which tells him when the ring of evidence has snapped shut, which warns him that to stop earlier would be to fail, and that to continue afterward would, for the purpose in hand, be pointless. I say "for the purpose in hand," because it would be untrue to say that when we have satisfied our practical end, or the interest of the law, we have reached the goal of thought. When the law has got its man, there remain a hundred points at which thought, seeking to understand, could still ask Why? And when would thought as such be satisfied? Only when it understood fully. And when would it understand fully? Only when no loose ends were left anywhere in the case—only, that is, when this occurrence, and that, and what led to each, and what led to that, were made intelligible, which means satisfactory to reason, which means in turn logically necessary. When would the end of all this be reached? If I may be allowed to put without argument what elsewhere I have argued at length, only when there are no loose ends anywhere, when all things existent or possible are caught in one web of necessity.

By taking inference as an example of cognitive process and showing that it is under the control of a secret ideal, I have been showing what I conceive mind to be on its intellectual side. A teleological process, I said, must be apprehended through its end. It now appears that mind on the cognitive side is a process of realizing the kind of system in which nothing is omitted and nothing is arbitrary. What has been exhibited of inference, namely, the pressure in and through it of unrealized system, could be shown of any other cognitive process—perception, for example, or the entertaining of an idea, or the passing of a judgment. To think in any form is to have put one's foot on a rung of the ladder that leads to this far-off end; and mind is present precisely in the degree to which such system is embodied. What the end is in detail we can not see. But at every level of thought we can feel its impulse, and our knowledge of what it is and what it asks of us grows clearer with every step of our approach.

But mind is not merely cognition. Besides the pursuit of truth —if we may take a division that is useful, though neither exclusive nor exhaustive—there is the pursuit of beauty and the pursuit of the moral ideal. These are not ways of knowing. But I should deal with them and with any other mental activity in the way I have just dealt with thinking. They cannot be explained by psychology, if this means a natural science of mind, for there is and can be no such science. We have seen that thinking is a teleological process laid under constraint by a logical end, and of the working of this end descriptive psychology knows nothing. If we examined such aesthetic activities as painting, or carving, or composing in notes or verses, we should likewise find that they are attempts to realize an aesthetic end, and are intelligible only by apprehending what Professor Wolfgang Köhler calls "the place of value in a world of facts." So also of practical activity. By such activity I mean, not mere play of arms and legs, but the direction and control of such play. This direction is shown most typically in the act of choice. And what is choice? To see it as one competing pull winning out in a tug of war, or as the resolution of a pencil of forces, is to look at it through distorting similes. Choice is the election of a prospective course because it is conceived to embody an ideal of good more fully than alternative courses. Not that the ideal is clearly defined; that, as we have repeatedly seen, is needless. But choice is meaningless unless the ideal is there. The act thus conforms to our pattern. It evinces mind because it evinces the kind of teleology in which an unexplicit end dominates the course of its own realization.

Mind, then, is not a single process, but a set of processes, a quiverful of arrows of desire. Do the arrows have one target or many? The end of the theoretic impulse does not seem to be the same as that of the aesthetic, or either the same as the moral, or any of these the same as the hedonic. It may be that there is no one goal of mind, that achievement of the moral end might leave the theoretic and aesthetic impulses unsatisfied, that the pursuits might even conflict and that the black and white horses of the soul, to use Plato's figure, might break with each other and tear limb from limb their unhappy charioteer. Mind has a tragic future if this is true. Whether it is true can be found only by following the loadstones of the spirit where they lead, and seeing whether, as functions develop, they will diverge or will support each other. I incline to believe the latter. In the minds of the thinker, poet, and saint, it is not mind in three different senses that is coming to be; it is mind in the same sense, but with emphases temporarily different. If you ask what is the end of mind as such, as distinct from any function within it, I should give an answer which seems to me as inevitable in principle as it is unsatisfactory in its lack of detail; the end is an experience in which the implicit demands of the different sides of our nature are all realized so far as consistency will allow.

To sum up: mind is a set of processes distinguished from others through their control by an immanent end. At its lowest levels and its highest its character is veiled from us. At one extreme it dwindles into mere life, which is incipient mind. At the other extreme it vanishes in the clouds; it does not yet appear what we shall be. Mind as it exists in ourselves is on an intermediate level. It has achieved consciousness, but this consciousness is restlessly transforming itself under the spell of a secret end. What is this end?

Our best clue is gained from studying that function which of all our mental functions has gone farthest toward its goal, the intellectual. To follow that clue is to learn that mind is really mind to the extent that it achieves an experience at once comprehensive and ordered.

Reprinted with permission from *Journal of Philosophy*, 1941.

JAMES COLLINS

God as a Function in Modern Systems of Philosophy

From even a cursory study of the history of modern philosophy, there emerges a salient fact having special significance. Running throughout the entire course of modern speculation is a persistent and central interest in the problem of God. At the very outset, the ferment of Renaissance thought comes in large measure from a preoccupation with the questions of the relationship between God and the world and the extent of man's knowledge of the divine nature. The two extreme answers of Bruno's pantheism and Montaigne's skepticism set the stage for the grand enterprise of the seventeenth-century rationalist systems, in which the role of God is crucially important. And if the empiricists and Kant feel obliged to make a fundamental criticism of rationalism, they are compelled to do so largely because of the difficulties encountered in squaring the rationalist doctrine of God with the deliverances of the scientific method and the implications of the scientific way of knowing the material universe. The proximity of the problem of God to the heart of the modern philosophical development is clearly evident also in the systems of the nineteenth century. We cannot fully understand the basis of the conflict between idealism and positivism, unless we examine their conflicting views about God and about the ability of the human mind to gain knowledge of an infinite and immaterial reality. This same fundamental orientation of philosophy extends into our contemporary age, even when it displays itself only in a semantic interest in the use of the terms "God" and "gods."

There is nothing paradoxical, therefore, in maintaining that the great modern minds have been just as deeply challenged by the question of God's existence, nature and creative activity as were the great medieval minds. Now that the history of modern philosophy is being viewed in multiple dimension, rather than in a narrowly epistemological and methodological way, the bearing of natural theological questions upon the systematic developments in modern philosophy can be clearly discerned. The differences between the medieval theologians and the modern philosophers do not stem from any depreciation of the problem of God, on the part of the moderns. The fact *that* God counts a good deal in determining the nature of one's outlook is universally admitted: oppositions arise in attempting to specify precisely *how* one's view of God is to be integrated with the rest of one's philosophical doctrines. It may be useful, then, to examine briefly a few representative modern approaches to God, in order to discover how this problem does affect in a radical way the spirit and structure of a philosophy.

For this purpose, we will interrogate three leading philosophers from as many centuries: Spinoza from the seventeenth, Kant from the eighteenth, and Hegel from the nineteenth century. In each instance, let us confine our inquiry to some one specific issue which is relevant to our main subject. Of Spinoza we will ask: what relation does God bear toward the starting point of philosophy? The question presented to Kant is this: what difference does one's conception of existence make in the demonstration of God's existence? And finally, Hegel will be invited to state the way in which he envisages the relationship between the God of religion and the Absolute of idealistic philosophy. From the answers which we may be able to extract from these key witnesses, it may be possible to ascertain at least a few of the functions of the doctrine on God in modern philosophical systems. The findings will have more than a purely historical import, however, since at the same time they define the actual speculative situation with which every theistic philosopher today must reckon, if his teaching is to become effective.

1

Our first question is a methodological one, dealing with God's role in the proper starting point of philosophy. This problem was one of the major ways in which seventeenth-century rationalists formulated their doctrine on method.

Descartes had proved God's existence by showing this truth to be a necessary implication of the thinking self. The favorite Cartesian proof was the so-called ontological argument, based on the idea of the infinitely perfect being, an idea which he likened to the workman's stamp upon his product. Spinoza now suggested that the human mind is much more intimately related to the divine substance than the simile of the artisan and his product suggests. For the human mind is an expression of God, in the pregnant sense of being a modal development under the divine attribute of thought. The probative force of the ontological argument derives precisely from viewing the human mind and its ideas as modal expressions of the affirmative power of the unique infinite substance. The specific sense in which the human self "implies" the existence of God was radically redefined by Spinoza. The thinking self is implicated as one finite stage in the pantheistic relationship between God and His modes. Methodology merely requires the philosopher to pattern the order of his ideas after the order of things: this means to begin philosophy with God, who is the purely immanent cause and substantial principle of the finite self.

There is a historical, as well as a doctrinal, sense in which Spinoza regarded the Cartesian order of demonstration as a compromise. To begin philosophy with the existence of the self is to occupy an unstable halfway station between theistic realism and a pantheism of substance. Spinoza recognized three alternate starting points for philosophy: the sensible world, the intelligible finite self, and the infinite substance of God. He looked upon the medieval realists as sensual and deluded minds because they accepted the sensible world as the real starting point of philosophizing, and trusted the senses as indispensable and generally reliable sources of knowledge. In repudiating the sensuous basis of knowledge, Spinoza sided with Descartes against theistic realism. But he felt that the recession from the senses had not been carried through far enough. The thinking finite self is not sufficiently removed from the senses to withstand every skeptical doubt. Above all, the finite existent does not enjoy a sufficiently powerful ontological status, in a theistic outlook, to provide the watershed for a metaphysical deduction of the real. For both these reasons, Spinoza was compelled to expand the Cartesian critique of the senses to include a critique of the finite self, taken as a distinct substantial being. There was nowhere else for Spinoza to make his philosophical beginning than with a pantheistically conceived God.

When Thomists encounter this Spinozistic position, they are reminded sharply of the intellectual sting behind certain remarks in St. Thomas which they may previously have treated as harmless commonplaces. St. Thomas has a clear-cut way of distinguishing between theological wisdom and philosophical wisdom or human philosophy (understanding the latter term simply as the perfection of natural reason, rather than as a counterposition to the Christian doctrine on creation and beatitude). From the standpoint of order, theological wisdom begins with a consideration of God and then proceeds to a study of creatures, insofar as they are related to God and bear the divine likeness. In philosophical wisdom or human philosophy, however, a start is made with sensible created things themselves, which are studied in their own proper causes, and only at the end of the investigation is God reached. St. Thomas' main interest is to show that the theological approach is superior, since it is similar to God's primary inspection of His own essence, in the knowledge of which He knows all other things. Yet St. Thomas adds that there is no basic conflict between these two orders of study, since the principles of both kinds of wisdom are derived from the unity of the divine truth. In our own day, we should not forget this positive Thomistic confidence in human philosophy.

One consequence of the modern rejection of realism was that the Thomistic description of the order of human philosophical wisdom no longer seemed to be indisputable. Descartes asked whether we should begin with sensible finite things or with a purely intelligible finite thing, the thinking self. Spinoza challenged the view that we should start with finite created things at all, whether they be sensible or purely intelligible. What St. Thomas held to be the characteristic order of theological wisdom became, in the Spinozistic perspective, the proper order of philosophical wisdom. Thereafter, this reversal became the watermark of all forms of rationalistic idealism. It was read into the very meaning of a philosophical system, since the idealists aimed to provide a strictly deductive type of speculation. To do so, they were obliged to transfer from sacred to human wisdom the prescription that one must take God as the starting point.

Another cognate distinction of St. Thomas underwent a similar transformation. The entire Aristotelian tradition had wavered between regarding metaphysics as the science of being as such and as the science of the first substance. Aquinas resolved this issue by maintaining that the proper subject of metaphysics is being considered as such or in respect to the act of existing, which is not confined to matter. God is studied by metaphysics or philosophical theology not as the subject of the science but only as the ultimate principle of the subject of this science, *i.e.* insofar as He is the causal source of being and substance, act and potency. But sacred theology does have God as its proper subject, and extends to the various finite realizations of being and substance only in the degree that the latter help us to understand God. Once again, Spinoza unwittingly transferred the traits of Thomistic sacred theology to his own philosophy, in regard to its proper subject as well as its point of departure. He made God the proper subject of metaphysics, and studied the principles of being and the finite world only in reference to God. In order to maintain this conception of metaphysics, however, Spinoza had to provide a naturalistic counterpart for revelation. This he found in the claim that the human mind has an intuitive insight into the divine essence itself. And to back up this claim, in turn, he had to suppose a pantheistic merger of the human mind with the divine intellect, against the background of a monism of substance and its modes.

As a consequence of these fundamental changes, Spinoza claimed a good deal more for metaphysics than did Aquinas. In the Spinozistic metaphysics, there can be an a priori, ontological proof of God's existence, based on our intuitive knowledge of the divine essence. A deductive demonstration of the structure and existence of the finite world is also possible, in virtue of our wholly non-empirical knowledge of the unique divine substance. For Aquinas, on the contrary, the beginning is made with being precisely as grasped by the intellect in the things presented to the senses.

Knowledge that God exists is the result of a posteriori demonstration only, and it leads to no intuition of the divine essence and act of existing in themselves. We are justified in affirming that God exists, only because of the requirements of being and the condition of finite beings of our experience. Only at the end of the metaphysical quest can we conclude that the existence of an infinite, transcendent being is demanded by the experiential world, considered in respect to its principles of being. Metaphysics alone can attain to formal knowledge of the existence of the ultimate source of its proper subject. But this knowledge is terminal and does not serve as the premise for a metaphysical deduction of the finite world. Since the human mind is not a modal expression of the divine substance under the attribute of thought, it cannot construct a deductive and nonempirical metaphysics. But the metaphysical truths which it can indeed establish, respect the integrity of God's transcendent freedom and man's personal subsistence.

2

As a second problem we propose to inquire of Kant how his notion of existence affected his analysis of proofs of God's existence. That there was a definite connection in Kant's mind between these two problems, is clear from his early cosmological writings, where he accepted several current proofs of God's existence. But he soon noticed that even such antithetically related thinkers as Leibniz and Hume agreed upon one thing: the unique significance of existence.

The net result of Kant's consultation of these sources can be summed up in two propositions. (1) From his critical reading of Leibniz and his school, Kant drew the negative conclusion that existence is not a mere predicate or determination of the essence. It cannot be derived solely by analysis of the concept of the essence or logical subject, since even an exhaustive analytic knowledge of the essence leaves us ignorant of whether or not the essence actually exists. Essential analysis remains in the realm of possibility. It does not furnish any real grounds for making the transition to the actuality of the existent things. (2) Hume told Kant that, as far as phenomenalism can ascertain, there is no distinctive real predicate of existence. This did not mean that existence is nothing distinctive but only that it does not have the same status as an essential predicate. Expressed in a more positive way, existence somehow signifies incorporation of the object in the actual order. Existence effects an absolute positing of the essence, along with all its predicates, in the field of actuality. The index of this existential incorporation is the establishment of some real connection between the object in question and the totality of our experience.

Kant recognized at once that these two conclusions had an important bearing upon the question of speculative proofs of God's existence. (1) God is no exception to the rule that analysis of the concept of the essence can never yield the real knowledge of existence. Hence the ontological argument is invalid: it tries to draw out of the concept of the most perfect being something which is not contained therein as an analytic property or predicate. All that the purely a priori approach can do is to invoke the principle of contradiction. This may prove that there is no intrinsic incompatibility between the constituent notes of the essence, but it warrants no assertion about the thing's real existence. The ontological argument remains in the logical order and does not determine anything about God as an existent being.

(2) Having eliminated the a priori approach in the light of his criticism of Leibniz, Kant then employed Hume's view of existence to undermine any a posteriori proof of God's existence. In an a posteriori inference, we must appeal to the principles of experience, in addition to the principle of contradiction. Now, Kant laid down three conditions for determining what is an object of experience or a warranted inference from experience. The presumed experiential object must be subject to temporal process; it must be finite and capable of representation under some pattern of imagination; finally, it must belong to the field of appearances proportioned to our apperceptive consciousness. Clearly enough, the reality signified by the idea of the most perfect being cannot fulfill any of these indispensable conditions. For God is eternal, infinite or beyond imaginative representation, and a thing-in-itself rather than an appearance. Kant concluded that therefore God can neither be a direct object of experience nor be inferred with speculative validity from what does belong to the realm of experience. The a posteriori proof is just as lacking in existential content as is the a priori.

With some aspects of Kant's analysis, a philosophical realist can agree. One major point in common is the doctrinal connection between the problem of existence in general and that of God's existence. An inadequate conception of existence may lead to an invalid argument for God's existence. Furthermore, Kant and Thomistic realism concur in their criticism of the rationalist theory of existence as the culminating predicate in the line of essence itself. This provides a solid reason for rejecting any proof which derives God's existence from some prior affirmation of the power of the divine essence. We cannot import self-causality into the divine essence without simultaneously threatening God's transcendance and freedom in creation. Spinoza's deterministic monism of substance is the pure position toward which every metaphysics based on the strict ontological argument and its presuppositions about existence inevitably gravitates.

Yet Kant's way of saving the divine transcendence and freedom involves the sacrifice of every speculative demonstration of God's existence. His position is not dictated by any direct examination of the realistic a posteriori proofs, however, but by his theory of existence. There are two major characteristics of the Kantian view of existence. First, it is not a doctrine on existence but on the conditions for a certain type of existential *knowledge*. Kant's chief instrument of inquiry is a theory of knowledge which is unregulated by a metaphysics of being in its ultimate act. Accepting Hume's account of the purely phenomenal character of the object of knowledge, he must deny that the human mind can gain any genuine knowledge of things in their own intrinsic principles of being. Hence the paradox that the Kantian doctrine on existence supplies no speculative insight into the act of existing on the part of the existent thing. This accounts for the remarkable divergence between the Thomistic a posteriori way of making the demonstration concerning God's existence and Kant's reformulation of the cosmological argument. Although both Aquinas and Kant agree that the divine essence cannot be the starting point of the argument, they disagree fundamentally concerning the proper starting point in the finite order. Aquinas begins with finite beings, known in their own essence and its distinct act of existing, whereas Kant's only possible point of departure is the contingency of objects of appearance, prescinding entirely from the essential nature and existential act of the thing-in-itself. Kant's criticism holds good only for a proof which accepts his own phenomenalistic starting point.

The second noteworthy feature of the Kantian teaching on existence is its *relational* or systemic basis. Once again, the paramount influence of Hume over Kant is unmistakable. Both men hold that what we know in an existential way is only the coherent and stable connectedness of phenomenal objects in the field of experience. Kant traces this system of phenomenal reality to the necessary and universal structure of consciousness, rather than to Hume's psychological law of association. Nevertheless, Kant continues the Humean tradition of characterizing the knowable existent in terms of something else—its reference to the connected whole of appearances—rather than in terms of its intrinsic principles of being, which remain unknowable. Existential knowledge thus becomes a process of fitting a presumed object of perception into the set of relations constituting the system of possible experience. But such a relational or systemic conception of existence misses the very act in virtue of which a thing can be said to exist. Hence it provides no basis for demonstrative knowledge about God's act of existing. What prevents Kant from achieving this demonstration is not so much the transcendence of God to experience as the thoroughly nonexistential character of the Kantian doctrine on experience and the object of knowledge.

Furthermore, the purely contextual theory of existential knowledge is unavoidably univocal, since the three conditions of experience enumerated previously are themselves univocal, formal aspects of consciousness. Even before he inspects the a posteriori proofs for God's existence, Kant is committed to the position that existential inference can move only within the confines of the finite field of homogeneous appearances. That is why he presents the cosmological argument as though one must abandon the existential terrain entirely and make a purely ideal adjustment of the idea of necessity to the idea of the most perfect being. This procedure is certainly illegitimate, but it is a procedure required only by the relational notion of existential knowledge and its univocal conditions.

The very careful statement which St. Thomas makes about the nature of the demonstration in question serves for critical evaluation of both Leibniz and Kant. What we prove is not precisely God's existence but the truth of our proposition that God exists. The negative part of this statement is relevant for Leibniz, whereas the affirmative part bears upon Hume and Kant. Taken in itself, the divine act of existing is infinite and identical with the divine essence. Hence it transcends the intellect of man, in his temporal condition, so that God in His own being remains in some fashion an unknown God. There can be no question of a demonstration of His existence from a prior knowledge of His essence (or a simultaneous but separate knowledge), both because of the infinite perfection of the divine essence and because its infinite actuality is nothing other than the divine act of existing itself. Outside the imagination of the rationalist systematist, there is no privileged sort of pre-existential power of the divine essence which can be captured and domiciled by the human mind. The ontological argument is not a highway, leading to demonstration *of* God's act of existing, but a byway in which one forgets the majesty of God and the limits of human intelligence.

Nevertheless, we are not left without natural knowledge and even demonstration *concerning* God's existence. The human inquirer can establish the truth of the proposition "God exists," and hence can have demonstrative knowledge that God does exist. In a preliminary way, however, he must make a far more radical renovation of existential inference than Kant made. Kant performed part of the common task by rescuing existential propositions from the dialectic of essences. But he failed to criticize Hume's theory of knowledge and existence with anything approaching the thoroughness of his critique of Leibniz and Wolff on this score. Having determined what existence is not, Kant failed to state its positive perfection. His is an existential epistemology without existence, precisely because of its divorce between the knowable object of experience and the existent thing. When realism reintroduces human intelligence to knowledge of existent beings, it bears a threefold fruit. First, it reincorporates epistemology within metaphysics, since existential knowledge is specified primarily by a grasp of the existent thing as existent. Second, it permits existential inference to ground itself in this grasp of the thing in its ultimate act of being, and thus to regulate itself by the distinctive deliverances and implications of the order of existent finite things. Finally, it enables existential demonstration to terminate in knowledge of the truth of our proposition about God's existence, even though an essential vision of the divine act of existing exceeds our ability here on earth. These three consequences of a realistic theory of existential demonstration render unnecessary the alternative of either inserting a special divine gnosis into philosophy or of relapsing into speculative agnosticism concerning the problem of God's existence.

3

Only the briefest mention can be made of our third main problem. The purpose of inquiring about the relation between God and the Hegelian Absolute is to underline the significance of the word "function," as applied to the modern treatments of God. Modern philosophers have taken a thoroughly functional approach to God, attempting to use the doctrine on God as a means of strengthening their own systems. Thus, Spinoza's God performs the systematic office of guaranteeing the objective truth of ideas, securing the continuity of deductive reasoning, and overcoming the inconveniences of Cartesian dualism. Kant's God has a negative role in the speculative order and a positive role in the practical. The idea of God is the supreme test case, proving the impotence of pure speculative reason to determine existence in a nonempirical way and hence to construct a metaphysics. In the moral sphere, God does not provide the foundation of Kantian obligation but He does render obligation more meaningful, by making the finite, intelligible self free and immortal, and by harmonizing nature and duty. It is in the Hegelian God, however, that the instrumentalist or systematist approach is brought to the climax of subordinating the God of realism and religion to something higher.

Hegel lauded religion for maintaining the universal actuality of the supreme being. But he deplored the fact that the religious apprehension of the supreme being was expressed under the imperfect form of faith and feeling. Relying upon a mere pictorial representation of the relation between man and God, religion prevented the empirical individual from asserting his dialectical identity with the supreme actuality. Hegel's own philosophy intervened at this point to dissolve the illusion that the finite mind and the divine spirit are irreducibly distinct. His philosophy became the final judge of the true import of religious convictions. The God of religious belief and theistic philosophy was sublated into the absolute of Hegel's idealism. Within the philosophy of the absolute, the finite individual was considered valuable only as being a dialectical aspect of the absolute spirit itself. Thus Hegel used the concept of God as a means of demonstrating the unconditioned truth of his doctrine on the absolute and hence the unquestionable primacy of his philosophy over every other philosophical and religious explanation of being.

From the time of Feuerbach onwards, it has been fashionable for naturalistic humanism to protest against "the tyranny of the absolute." This protest is certainly well made, if it is meant as a criticism of Hegel's dialectical monism of the absolute spirit. But it is often expanded to include a rejection of God and theistic religion, in which extended usage the original protest loses its historical bearings. For naturalistic humanism forgets that the Hegelian absolute is itself at odds with the religious view of God as the supreme personal being, who is the free creator of finite persons and respects their integrity of personal being and freedom. The tyranny of the Hegelian absolute is even more intolerable to the theist than to the naturalistic humanist, since it subverts both real terms in the creator-creature relationship. That is why there is an ultimate convergence between religion and theistic metaphysics in the dual affirmation that we can gain some demonstrative knowledge about God's existence and that God's own being is irreducibly distinct from the world. The divine act of existing is reserved from our natural vision and can never properly serve an instrumental function in philosophy.

The negative character of this conclusion may throw some light upon one development in contemporary philosophy. We have seen that each of our representative thinkers misconceived the role of God in philosphy. Spinoza reduced God to a first deductive premise in a monistic determinism. Kant found no way to know God in the speculative order and hence employed Him as a postulate of moral harmony. And Hegel subordinated God to the exigencies of his dialectical absolutism. The unsatisfactory consequences of these typical approaches to God might suggest that the problem of God should be eliminated entirely from philosophy. This is precisely what Heidegger in Germany and Merleau-Ponty in France are now advocating. Their standpoint amounts to a philosophical neutralism, which refrains in principle from making any philosophical pronouncements about God. They claim that both theism and antitheism are nonphilosophical doctrines, belonging solely to the theological sphere (in the sense of a revealed theology). They recognize no properly philosophical way of dealing with the question of God's existence, nature and governance of the universe.

But it does not seem to me that there are sufficient historical grounds for accepting this neutral, methodological "a-theism," which seeks to prescind completely in philosophy from the conflict between theism and antitheism. From the experience of four centuries of modern speculation about God, it can only be concluded that many philosophers have exploited the concept of God unwarrantedly for their own systematic purposes. The trouble does not lie in the fact that they concerned themselves philosophically with the problem of God, but rather in the manner in which they posed this problem and regarded its position within the total system of their philosophy. Hence the historical evidence does not suggest that philosophers should refrain from studying about God but only that they should refrain from making God a mere tool of their own special view of things. More positively expressed, philosophers must come to recognize both that we can demonstrate the truth about God's existence and nature and also that God is the culmination of all our philosophical demonstrations and the goal of our practical strivings. Undoubtedly, this region of inquiry contains more than the average amount of doctrinal pitfalls. But to examine these historical difficulties patiently and illuminate the philosophical route to a sound knowledge of God is surely one of the major responsibilities laid upon those philosophers who are trying to cultivate the resources of St. Thomas within the given context of our age.

Presidential Address, reprinted with permission, *Proceedings of the American Catholic Philosophical Association*, 1955.

C. J. DUCASSE

The Method of Knowledge in Philosophy

Even among philosophers, the part of philosophy called meta-physics enjoys today no great popularity, but rather is the subject of many strictures. Some of its critics allege that its problems are too remote from those of plain men to have any practical impor-tance. Hence they urge philosophers to forget them and to occupy themselves instead with the problems of social and political philoso-phy. Others claim that the agelong failure of metaphysicians to settle their differences is enough to show that any answers proposed to the questions they discuss cannot represent knowledge, but only personal opinions or temperamental preferences. And others yet contend that the problems of metaphysicians are not genuine problems at all and hence cannot be solved, but that they can be eliminated by bringing to light the false assumptions on which they rest.

Since our being assembled here must be reckoned as a long-range effect of the late Professor W. Howison's distinguished lec-tures on metaphysics, I shall assume that most of those present share my own belief that these criticisms of metaphysics are at most but partially justified. I shall therefore not reply to them at any length, but simply indicate at this point in a general way how the matter seems to me really to stand.

I believe, then, that although some of the problems metaphysicians have discussed are indeed pseudo problems, and that some others, although genuine, do not belong to philosophy at all, nevertheless certain others of them are, or contain, genuine problems, which are philosophical and are perfectly capable of solution.

I believe, moreover, that these genuine problems of metaphysics are connected with certain of the plain man's difficulties as intimately and in much the same manner as are, for instance, the problems of theoretical physics with certain others of his difficulties. For the plain man every day passes judgments of approval or disapproval on sundry concrete issues in the fields of morals, of art, of social policy, of religion, of reasoning, and so on; and when the validity of these judgments is challenged and the clash of appraisals does not arise from misinformation as to the concrete facts judged, the plain man finds that he can defend his appraisal of those facts only by appeal to a philosophy of the subject they concern.

The philosophy of it which he improvises at such times may seem to him independent of the more technical problems philosophers discuss. But it is bound to be ambiguous, fragmentary, and inconsistent; and if he were to try to purge it of these defects, he would find that the more careful and thoroughgoing reflections necessary for this would face him sooner or later with the very problems studied in the abstract and theoretical parts of philosophy.

The problems of theoretical physics, it would be granted, have remote but practical implications for the task of putting into the hands of the plain man means to attain the physical ends he chooses to pursue. And the problems of theoretical philosophy have likewise remote yet also practical bearing on something still more important, namely, on the discernment of wisdom from folly in the choices man makes of ends to pursue and of means to reach them. Hence, as Professor G. P. Adams remarked on a certain occasion not long ago, philosophy need not *try* to be practical; it is practical inherently. But it takes already some wisdom to perceive how this is true.

Finally, a word concerning the allegation that one's metaphysics is a matter of one's temperament rather than of truths one has discovered. The fact seems to me to be, as I shall try to show later, that certain metaphysical questions call, and quite properly, for an answer expressing not a hypothesis but a basic choice or ruling interest. On the other hand, the answers called for by certain other metaphysical questions are genuinely hypotheses; and if these are but clear and specific enough, they are as capable of being tested and either confirmed or disproved as are hypotheses in any other field.

I believe, thus, that metaphysics, or, more generally, theoretical inquiry in philosophy, can reach results having title to the name of knowledge. But I also believe that, for this, the modes of investigation used must be purged of the defects which have too often made philosophical inquiry heuristically barren and thus tended to bring it into disrepute. These defects have been such as looseness of inference, ambiguity of terms, confusion of issues, inadequate testing of hypotheses; and they seem to me traceable in the main to two sources.

One of these sources is the assumption, widespread even among philosophers, that in philosophy it is possible to reach knowledge through reasonings carried on in the vague terms of ordinary language without bothering to use a technical apparatus of thought. But the truth is that as soon as inquiry, whether in philosophy or elsewhere, comes to questions more difficult than those which everyday experience or casual reflection is able to answer, a technical terminology becomes a *sine qua non* of fruitful thinking. For a technical term is simply a term whose meaning is known exactly; and hence, not to bother to use technical terms is not to bother to think with precision. One can easily imagine how far chemistry or geometry, for instance, would have progressed if chemists had not bothered to use more exact conceptions of alcohol, of acid, or of ether; or mathematicians, of points, planes, or circles; than the vague conceptions those words stand for in ordinary language. The situation of philosophy is no different. Unpopular as a plea for technical language in philosophy is sure to be today, the fact must be faced that at the point where one ceases to be superficial, there, technical language, far from making for unintelligibility, is on the contrary the only means of being intelligible and of making dependable inferences. This is true in the sciences and equally so in philosophy.

Technical terms, however, must not be confused with jargon

terms. A jargon term is not necessarily precise. It is merely one which is not understood by most persons because it designates things with which only a comparatively few persons occupy themselves. Thus, every trade, art, and craft, as well as every science, has its own jargon. But the jargon terms of the sciences—unlike most of those of the trades or the crafts—get defined exactly; and therefore, in addition to being esoteric like the latter, they become technical.

On the other hand, even terms in common use—such as alcohol, acid, and circle; or, in philosophy, property, truth, substance, proposition, and so on—become technical terms as soon as their meaning is stated exactly.

Philosophers, it is true, have sometimes defined their terms, and sometimes, although more rarely, defined them with some precision. This brings me to the second of the two sources of defective method in philosophy to which I alluded a moment ago. It is that to specify exactly the meaning of a term is not enough to insure that it will be an effective implement for the winning of knowledge. For this, what is needed besides is that its meaning shall not be assigned to it arbitrarily, but shall represent characters which there is reason to believe are possessed by the things the term is used to think about.

Unfortunately, the definitions offered by philosophers have often failed to satisfy this capital requirement, and have then represented mere speculations. Of course, speculation, which is but the making of hypotheses, is just as legitimate and indeed necessary in philosophy as in the natural sciences; but before any conclusions can be based on a speculation, adequate testing of it is as indispensable in philosophy as elsewhere.

Why then have philosophers so often failed to test adequately, or at all, the hypotheses that constituted the definitions they gave of their terms? The chief reason, I believe, has been that they have not realized clearly enough the nature of the facts by which these hypotheses could be tested empirically. Because of this, the testing has too much been limited to a checking of the mutual consistency of the various hypotheses entering into a system—the system as a whole, however, being then left more or less hanging in the air for lack of empirical verification of its hypotheses.

But every genuine problem has data, that is, facts not themselves questioned, about which the problem is and by reference to which any proposed solution of it can be empirically tested. And since in philosophy what these facts are is often not very obvious, one of the basic maxims of knowledge-yielding method in philosophy should be that, when a question is to be investigated, one should not only ask oneself just which facts it is about, but also state them explicitly. Actually, however, they are too often merely alluded to, as if oneself and everybody else already understood quite well what they are.

The procedure I suggest will not only make clear the way to test empirically any hypothesis made about those facts, but will also greatly facilitate compliance with a second, equally important methodological maxim. It is that one should again not be content merely to name or allude to the question which is to be answered about the facts one has listed, but that the question too should be stated as explicitly and unambiguously as possible. Observance of these two maxims will automatically lead one to distinguish, and to treat separately, each of the several questions one's initial vague statement of a problem may unawares have been propounding all at once. This will not only clear away such difficulties as confusions breed, but will also be of positive help in solving the questions one isolates, for a sharply formulated question is one of the most fertile sources of ideas.

These two maxims, however, are not so easy to comply with in philosophy that they need for this only to be accepted. The concrete nature of the method they define, as well as the power this method may possess to solve the problems to which it is applied, can be made fully clear only by an example. In the remainder of my remarks I shall therefore illustrate its use by applying it to the central and most ancient of the problems of metaphysics.

This problem is commonly referred to merely as that of the nature of reality, but it is sometimes formulated more explicitly. A. E. Taylor, for instance, describes metaphysics as "a systematic and impartial inquiry as to what we really mean by the familiar distinction between 'seems' and 'is,' that is to say, a scientific inquiry into the general characteristic by which reality or real being is distinguished from mere appearance, not in one special sphere of study, but universally."[1]

But even this formulation fails to specify the data of the problem. Moreover, it tends to suggest that the data of the problem as to the nature of reality are of the same logical type as would be, for instance, those of a problem as to the nature of chalk, or of rubber; and therefore that to solve it we must compare concrete samples of real being with concrete samples of merely apparent or unreal being, and observe what characteristics differentiate the former from the latter. But that the problem is not of this logical type is perhaps sufficiently shown by the fact that since some philosophers are idealists, some materialists, and others adherents of still other doctrines, samples of real being could not be picked without begging in the very act what the contending philosophers would regard as the question at issue.

To avoid this, the data to which we look as starting point must be of quite a different kind. I submit that they can consist only of concrete examples of the manner or manners in which the word "real" or its cognates, "really" and "reality," are used predicatively. That is, our data will have to consist of *statements* such as that a certain substance, which seems to be paper, is really asbestos; or that mermaids do not really exist; or that trees far away appear blue but in reality are green; and so on. Such concrete instances of the predicative use of the word "real" or its cognates constitute the factual data which a hypothesis as to the meaning of those words must fit and by reference to which its tenability can be empirically tested; for the problem then is as to what those words mean *as applied in the given examples*.

Of course, I take it that what we are interested to analyze is examples which, like those given, illustrate commonly accepted usage; but it is worth noting that if examples of some freak usage of those same words were given instead, then, if it interested us to do so, we could analyze equally well the meaning those words had there. The essential point is that either *no* applications of those words are given us, and then we can make them mean anything we please; or else concrete examples of *some* applicative usage of them are furnished, and then we have data by which to test empirically the soundness of any proposed definition of what they mean in that particular sort of context. A definition of them so reached will be a so-called real or objective definition, as distinguished from an arbitrary, merely verbal definition.

Our second maxim of method, it will be recalled, enjoins us to state explicitly what we are seeking to discover about the data the first maxim requires us to list. In the present case, then, what we wish to discover is the meaning the word "real" or its cognates have in the sample statements we take as data. Any hypothesis as to this will therefore have the form of a definition of the word concerned; and since a definition is good if and only if it is exactly equivalent to the term defined, the test of the adequacy of any definition that occurs to us will consist in the possibility of replacing the term defined by the definition proposed, in any of the sample statements taken as data.

But what will be the test of that possibility itself? It will be, I submit, that this replacement shall not result in making false any of the statements that were true, nor in making true any that were false, nor in altering the truth or the falsity of any other statement implying or implied by the given ones. For this test will be met automatically if a definition expresses a genuine equivalence, and will not be met unless it does.

The nature of the method I propose having now been described in general, let us next apply it in particular to the problem of the nature of reality, and see what it will do for us.

As soon as, in compliance with it, we begin listing statements in which the word "real" or one of its cognates is used predicatively, the suspicion forces itself upon us that the word may mean one thing in some of them, and something else in certain others. We are therefore led to divide our sample statements into several groups and to scrutinize each group separately.

The first may well consist of examples in which the adjective "real" is evidently used in some special, purely technical sense. In law, for instance, real property is contrasted with personal or portable property, and "real" therefore means nonpersonal or immovable. In mathematics, certain numbers are called real numbers and contrasted with imaginary numbers, although both kinds are real enough, in an ordinary sense of the term, to be accurately described and fruitfully employed by mathematicians. Again, in logic real definitions are contrasted with verbal or nominal definitions, although words are just as real, in an ordinary sense, as are things other than words. It is clear that no problem involving the distinction between reality and appearance arises in connection with these or possible other equally technical uses of the word "real." We may therefore dismiss them from consideration.

The group we come to next is much more significant. It consists of statements such as that a certain dog looks or seems or appears ferocious, but is not so really or in reality; or that a certain seemingly valid argument is really fallacious; or that the stone in a certain ring, although it appears to be glass, is a real diamond;

or that a certain substance seems to be paper but is in reality asbestos; and so on. All these, let it be noted, are descriptive statements. That is, in each some entity, for example a substance, is given, and the hypothesis is offered that it is of a certain kind, for example, of the kind called paper. For the sake of generality, let us call E the entity given in any of them, and call K the kind to which it is claimed to belong; and let us note that, whatever the kind K may be, there is always some set of characters, a, b, c, d, such that, if and only if a given entity possesses *all* of them, it is of kind K. This simple analysis puts us in position to describe exactly the occasions which give rise to the question as to whether a given entity E really is, or only appears to be, of a kind K.

They are occasions on which *only some* of the characters of E are manifest to observation, and on which these manifest characters —which constitute the *appearance* of E at the time—happen to be the same characters as would be manifest in the existing circumstances if E should happen to be of kind K.

For example, under present circumstances, the color, shape, texture, and flexibility of the sheet I hold are manifest to observation; they are its present appearance; whereas the combustibility of it, if it be combustible, is not now manifest. But further, the color, flexibility, and other now manifest characters of the sheet, are the *same* characters as would be manifest under present circumstances if the sheet *were* of the kind called paper.

Now, if the things which in our past experience manifested this same color, flexibility, and so on, did later turn out in most cases to possess *also* combustibility and the remaining characters of paper, then what we naturally say in the present case is that this sheet *seems* or *appears* to be paper; that is, its present appearance is the same as that of paper.

Furthermore, if, on applying the proper tests, we find that this sheet does have *also* those remaining characters of paper, then we express this by saying that it not only appears to be paper, but *really* is paper; whereas, if it turns out to lack some of them, what we say is that, although it appears to be paper, it is *not really* so, or is not real paper.

Thus, in terms of an entity E, and of a set of characters a, b, c, d, *all* of which must be possessed by it if it is to be of kind K, but *only some* of which are at the time manifest in it, we have defined exactly the types of situations which govern the use of the notions of appearance and reality in cases where the nature of the thing a descriptive statement describes consists of a complex of characters. When on the contrary a single character is concerned, as when we say that the trees on a distant hillside appear blue but really are green, the analysis of "really" is very different. We shall consider it farther on at the appropriate place.

What now can we conclude is the qualification introduced by the words "real" or "really" in statements of the kind we have been examining? A moment's reflection makes evident that in our example what is qualified as "real" is not in fact the paper itself at all, for paper does not have two species—one called real paper and the other unreal or seeming paper. What is not really paper is not paper at all. Rather, what is qualified is the descriptive proposition, "This is paper," and the effect of inserting the word "really" into it is simply to assert that *that proposition is true:* to say "this is really paper" is exactly the same as to say, "truly, this is paper," or "that this is paper, is true."

Accordingly, the occasions on which we say "this is *really* paper," instead of simply "this is paper," are occasions on which we wish to assert that, notwithstanding some item of evidence to the contrary, it is *true* that this is paper. On the other hand, the occasions on which we say simply "this is paper" are those on which we are answering the question "What is this?" without anything having suggested that it is not paper.

These remarks complete the analysis of the notion of reality as it enters in statements of the type we have been examining. I turn now to examples of a different kind. They consist of existential assertions, that is, of assertions which, instead of answering as before the question "What is this?" answer the question "Are there any so and so's?"

Instances of existential assertions in which the notion of reality enters would be that, in reality, no mermaids exist; that the man called Hamlet by Shakespeare did not really exist; that Utopia is an imaginary country but that Spain is real; that there is really such a psychological state as hypnosis; or that black swans really exist but green swans do not.

In some of these statements, it looks as if "is real" means simply "exists," but in others the notion of reality clearly is additional to that of existence. The examples which are of the latter sort may be dealt with first and briefly, since in them the import of the word "really" or of either of its cognates is essentially the same as in the descriptive statements we have considered. That is, in existential statements too, its import is to assert that the statement in which the word enters is *true* notwithstanding some doubt or item of evidence to the contrary.

For example, the sort of occasion on which one would naturally say "mermaids do not really exist," or "mermaids are not real," instead of simply "no mermaids exist," would be one on which, perhaps, a child had been reading a story about mermaids or had seen a moving picture representing some. For the simplest explanation of such a story or picture would naturally be that there are mermaids, and the story or picture therefore constitutes an item of circumstantial evidence that mermaids exist. The import of the statement that mermaids do not *really* exist would thus be that that evidence is misleading—that, in spite of it, the truth is that mermaids do not exist.

In such examples, realness is thus not a character differentiating one species of existence from another and inferior species called unreal or seeming existence; any more than, in our earlier example, realness differentiated one species of paper from an inferior one called seeming or unreal paper. In both groups of examples alike, what the word "really" or either of its cognates qualifies is the statement itself in which it occurs, and its force is the same as that of the adverbs "truly" or "certainly."

Let us now return to the sort of assertions in which "is real" is used simply as synonymous with "exist." Our task here is then to analyze the meaning of "to exist." This will not only make explicit the meaning of these assertions, but also clarify by contrast that of assertions—such as those just discussed and certain others yet to be considered—in which the notion of reality is added to that of existence.

The question as to what exactly it means, to say that something of a given kind K exists, is best approached by limiting attention at first to cases where what is in view is specifically physical existence, as distinguished from, for example, mathematical or psychological existence.

In all such cases, the assertion that there exists something of a kind K is, I submit, exactly synonymous with the assertion that something of that kind *is somewhere;* that is, occupies some place in space at some time. It is important to notice, however, that an assertion of existence may be more or less determinate.

For example, least determinately, one might assert that there are black swans, or, which is the same thing, that black swans exist; that is, are at *some* place, not specified.

But, somewhat more determinately, the assertion made might be instead that there are black swans *somewhere within a specified region*—for instance, in Australia.

Or thirdly and now quite determinately, the assertion made might be that there is a black swan *here now;* that is, at the specific place to which one is pointing at the time.

These examples make evident that, in the phrases "there is" or "there are," one is using the word "there" not in some idiomatic sense but literally, that is, as indicative of spatial location whether completely indeterminate or partially or wholly determinate. In these phrases, moreover, temporal location also is indicated, likewise more or less determinately, at least by the past, present, or future tense of the verb, and often through specification by date of some period or particular moment also.

Physical existence, thus, is essentially spatiotemporal ubiety; and that which has or lacks ubiety, that is, is or is not present at some place in space at some time, is always some *what* or *kind*—which may be a kind of substance, or of property, or of relation, or of activity, or of change, or of state, and so on.

When existence other than physical is in view—for instance, mathematical existence—the meaning of existence is closely analogous. The difference is only that the place concerned is a place in some order other than the space-time order.

Thus, for example, the assertion that a square root of 9 exists, but no square root of 3, means that the character "being square root of 9" characterizes a certain place in the order of the whole numbers, namely, the determinate place called 3; whereas the character "being square root of 3" characterizes none of the places in the series of whole numbers.

In any assertion of existence, thus, no matter whether it be more particularly one of physical existence, or of mathematical, or psychological, or mythological, or other existence, two components always are essentially involved, namely, a *what* and a *where*. And generically a *where* or place is the sort of thing specifiable in terms of *ordinal* relations; that is, of relations such as between, next to, beyond, among, outside of, and so on.

This analysis, it should be noted, incidentally results in making explicit also the meaning possessed by the word "reality" when it is used not as an abstract term synonymous with "realness," but as a concrete, *denotative* term; as, for example, in such statements as that reality is exclusively material, or exclusively mental, or of both these kinds, or of the nature of will, and so on. When the word "reality" is so used, it means "everything that exists." It is obvious that reality in this sense is not the opposite of appearance, but of nonexistence, or nothing.

At this point, it may be remarked in passing that when the word "reality" is used thus denotatively, then that, *if anything*, which it denotes, is known to us, that is, known to us *to exist*, only if our existential judgments or other existential apprehensions are *true*. Hence, if their truth (or erroneousness) is to be something ascertainable at all, it cannot possibly be defined as correspondence (or noncorrespondence) to reality, that is, to something known at all to exist only if those very apprehensions or judgments of existence happen to be true.

We shall now examine next a use of the word "really" or its cognates radically different from any we have so far considered. An example of it would be the statement that the wood of the table is really a cloud of minute particles at relatively vast distances from one another; and another example, that water is really a compound of oxygen and hydrogen.

When this is asserted about water, the word "really" cannot have the same meaning as when we say that the liquid in a given glass is really water. For the statement that water is really H_2O evidently does not mean that water only seems to be water but in truth is something else; nor does it mean that it only seems to have the familiar properties of liquidity, tastelessness, capacity to quench thirst and fire, and so on, but has *instead* of these the property of being analyzable into oxygen and hydrogen; nor does it mean simply that it is true that the composition of water is H_2O.

What it means, I submit, is that, *for certain purposes*, such as some of those of chemists, the property of being analyzable into and synthesizable out of hydrogen and oxygen is *the important or relevant* property; whereas for such purposes the other, more familiar properties of water are irrelevant.

In statements of this type, then, the definition of realness which, at the time they are made, tacitly governs the use in them of the word "really" is that *to be real is to be relevant to the purposes or interests which rule at the time*. In such cases, the opposite of "to be real" is thus not, as before, to be a deceptive appearance, nor to be nonexistent, but to be irrelevant, unimportant, insignificant, negligible, of no interest or value for the purposes ruling at the time.

Additional examples belonging to this group would be such statements as that the real way to talk to a mob is such and such; that you really must do this or that; that such and such a proposal is not realistic; that nothing is more real than an idea; that such and such a consideration is very real; and so on. The example mentioned earlier, in which we say that the trees on the distant hillside seem blue but really are green, analyzes in a manner slightly different from that in which we say that water is really H_2O; but in it, too, realness consists in relevance to interests or purposes postulated as for the time ruling. For, evidently, that the trees display the color blue when they are observed from far away is exactly as true as that they display the color green when they are observed from a distance of a few feet. The two properties are perfectly compatible, and the trees truly possess both. Which color we say the trees "really" have is therefore a matter only of whether only the near point of observation is relevant to the purposes which rule us at the time (as when they are the ordinary practical or scientific purposes), or of whether on the contrary any point of observation we have chosen is relevant to our then ruling purposes (as when we are landscape painters).

We have studied so far four main types of statements in which the word "really" or one of its cognates figure. The four types differed markedly in certain respects, but they were nevertheless alike in a respect to which attention must now be called, namely, all of them were statements of something or other that had the status of *hypothesis*. That is, what they formulated was in each case something that was either true or false, and was therefore susceptible of being more or less fully verified or confuted.

But now we must notice yet another group of statements in which the notion of reality enters, but which express not hypotheses at all, but something else altogether, to which the categories of truth, falsity, probability, confirmation, proof, or disproof do not apply at all. What they express I shall call *ontological positions*.

Just what an ontological position is, as distinguished from a hypothesis in which the notion of reality figures, will become clear if we return to the tacit major premise which, as we saw, was assumed by the assertion that water really is H_2O. That tacit premise, it will be recalled, was that to be real is to be relevant to certain of the purposes of chemists. Now, to adopt this or any similar major premise for one's activities through a given time is to *take a position* as to what, for the time, one will mean by "being real." And to be governed, even if unawares, by such a major premise at a given time is to be then *occupying a position* as to what it is to be real. That is, the statement of such a major premise is the statement of an ontological position. It is always of the form "to be real is to have such and such a character."

An ontological position, thus, is essentially of the nature of an exclusive or basic interest in the things which have a certain character; it is a rule one adopts as to what things one will regard as alone of interest, or will rank as basic or primary. For example, the ontological position that to be real is to have a certain character C would consist in interest exclusively or basically in things having this character; it would be the rule of admitting to consideration only the things having character C, or at least of positing them as fundamental and absolutely prior in interest or importance.

Now, an ontological position may be consciously embraced, or it may be occupied unawares. It may be occupied by many persons, or by few. It may be congenial to one person, and repugnant to another. It may be occupied at a certain moment, and relinquished the next in favor of a different one. But just because an ontological position is not a contention at all but essentially an interest at the time ruling, an ontological position cannot be true or be false; nor therefore can it be shown more or less probably true than another, or be refuted, or be proved. These possibilities exist only in the case of hypotheses.

The ontological position, for example, which natural scientists, while functioning as such, occupy, is that to be real is to be perceptually public or implicit in what is so. But it is evident that these words do not formulate a hypothesis as to properties empirically discoverable in some concretely given entity called reality; for no empirical facts one might adduce could prove or disprove what those words expressed, or render it probable, doubtful, or improbable. Plainly, they describe no hypothesis at all, but simply the criterion by which the things in which the natural sciences interest themselves are distinguished from the things these sciences ignore.

Truth, falsity, and probability are thus categories logically incongruous to ontological positions—as inapplicable to them as would be the predicates thirsty or bitter to logarithms or to algebraic equations. Ontological positions may only be occupied or not occupied, be embraced or abandoned. This analysis of their nature and logical status, I may say, seems to me in essential agreement with conclusions reached by Professor J. Loewenberg in a penetrating article entitled "The Question of Priority" which he published some years ago;[2] and I therefore look to him hopefully for moral support in a conception of the nature of ontological positions which, I realize, is likely to shock many philosophers.

Additional instances of ontological positions that have been held or might be held would be that to be real is to be introspectively observable or implicit in what is so; that to be real is to be individual; that to be real is to be unique and changeless; that to be real is to be free from contradictions; that to be real is to be a coherent whole; and so on.

There is one ontological position, however, worth special mention here. It is the one occupied by *any* ontologist—and therefore by ourselves here now—at the time he is engaged in an inquiry as to the nature of reality. This position is that to be real is to be relevant to the problem of the nature of reality, appearance, and unreality. Evidently, it is a position different from the idealistic, or materialistic, or other conclusion as to the nature of reality, which an ontologist may believe his reflections on the subject eventually dictate.

But this very remark now leads us to ask whether our inventory of the variety of statements in which the notion of reality figures has been complete. Is there any problem as to the nature of reality which is a genuine, not a pseudo problem, but which we have not yet considered? It might be contended that such metaphysical doctrines as idealism, materialism, voluntarism, and so on, purport to be answers to a question about reality distinct from all those we have examined. An adequate scrutiny of this contention would require more time than I can now dispose of, but I can indicate briefly why I believe it to be mistaken.

The statement, for example, that reality is exclusively mental may be construed in either one of two ways. First, it may be taken as but another way of saying that to be real is to be either a mind or a mind's idea. If so, it is evidently the statement of what we have called an ontological position, not of a hypothesis; and, as pointed out, it is then not the sort of thing which either is true or is false. It only declares the primacy, for the idealist, of minds and their ideas, and his intent to construe everything in terms of them.

But the statement that reality is exclusively mental may be interpreted otherwise. In it, the word "reality" may be taken denotatively, that is, taken to mean "everything that exists." The statement that reality is mental then means that only minds and their ideas exist.

In ordinary usage, however, the words "mental things" denote only such things as feelings, thoughts, volitions, hopes, memory images, and so on, or the minds comprising them; whereas such things as the wood of the table, which, beyond question, also exists, are normally denoted by the words "material things." I submit, therefore, that the statement that reality is exclusively mental, as meaning that everything which exists is minds and ideas—or similarly, that reality is exclusively material—cannot possibly be true unless some meaning at variance with the customary is forced, *ad hoc,* by means of the qualification "really," either on the verb "to exist," or else on the adjective "mental," or "material."

A materialist, for example, might say that what he contends is that nothing which is not material has *real* existence. But then this would be but saying that the realm of material existence is the only one he chooses to acknowledge—the only one of interest to him. Thus, because he would be restricting his assertion to a particular realm of existence, which he elects to rank as alone or supremely interesting to him, he would in fact again not be stating a hypothesis as to the nature of everything that exists, but again only declaring the ontological position he chooses to take.

But instead of using the word "really" to limit arbitrarily the scope of "to exist," one might use it instead to stretch, equally arbitrarily, the denotation of the terms "mental" or "material."

An idealist, for example, might say that what he maintains is that everything which exists is *really* mental, that is *really* consists of minds and their ideas. But then, since, beyond question, the wood of this table can be sawed, scraped, sandpapered, soaked in oil, and so on, it would automatically follow that minds, or their ideas, can in some cases be sandpapered, soaked in oil, used as a table, and so on. But these are the very kind of operations we mean when we speak of material operations.

I submit, therefore, that to assert that the wood on which such operations can be performed is mental would not be to reveal a hitherto unsuspected but verifiable property of the wood. It would only be to reveal that one has arbitrarily elected to employ the word "mental" to denote not only the things it is customarily used to denote, but also those customarily denoted by the word "material." To do this, however, would be exactly the same logically, and just as futile, as proposing to say henceforth that white men are really Negroes, or that Negroes are really white men. This would not be revealing any hitherto hidden fact as to the color of their skins, but only tampering wantonly with language.

But the idealist who asserts that reality is mental, or the materialist who asserts it to be material, usually believes himself to be revealing some generally unrecognized fact about such things as wood, or about such things as thoughts, and thus to be solving a genuine problem. Yet, as I have briefly tried to show, he is in truth doing no such thing, but either stating the ontological position he chooses to take, or else dealing with only a pseudo problem, which evaporates when one distinguishes and analyzes as we have done the different meanings the word "reality" or its cognates have in the several sorts of contexts in which they function in the language.

There is, however, a genuine problem as to mind and matter. But it is not as to whether everything is mental and nothing material, or everything material and nothing mental. For there is no doubt at all that some existing things have and others do not have the properties, such as those I have mentioned, which we mean when we speak of material properties; nor that some existing things have and others do not have the properties we mean to refer to when we speak of mental properties. The datum of the genuine problem as to mind and matter is that certain things, such as wood, in fact are *called* material and not mental, and others, such as thoughts, in fact are *called* mental and not material. And the problem itself is as to what exactly the words "material" and "mental" mean *as so applied and so denied*.

Then, when this has been discovered, the further problem arises as to what, in the light of the discovery, may be the relation between mind and matter. But the remarks which have preceded show that the relation cannot possibly be that of identity.

In concluding, let me say that the analyses I have offered of the several meanings of the word "reality" or its cognates may well have contained mistakes. But the method of inquiry we have used, which has required that the several kinds of contexts in which these words occur be not just alluded to but be unambiguously specified by concrete examples, has thereby furnished the very facts by reference to which the correctness of those analyses can be empirically tested, and the analyses rectified if need be.

I hope, however, that the results we have obtained by that method in our discussion of the ancient problem as to the nature of reality may be judged sufficiently sound and substantial to recommend the use of the same method in dealing with other philosophical problems.

Howison Lecture for 1944. Originally printed in University of California Publications in Philosophy, Vol. 16, No. 7 (1945). Reprinted with permission.

1. A. E. Taylor, *Elements of Metaphysics,* p. 4.
2. J. Loewenberg, University of California Publications in Philosophy, Vol. 13, pp. 37–69.

CHARLES HARTSHORNE

Some Empty Though Important Truths: A Preface to Metaphysics

"Science," defined as inductive study of facts, can scarcely be co-extensive with knowledge; mathematics, for instance, is not inductive. The very principle of induction itself is not obviously a product of induction: at any rate, there is an appearance of circularity in trying to establish it inductively. Speaking vaguely, we may perhaps say that knowledge of the *concrete,* or of *facts,* is inductive; while knowledge of the *abstract principles* of knowledge, or at least, of the *most abstract* principles, is noninductive. The prevailing view today seems to be that such noninductive knowledge is "analytic," "tautologous," or "empty," in that it merely elucidates the import of certain terms occurring in our language. Truths of this empty sort exclude nothing, except nonsense. "Two and two are four" seems to exclude that they are five, or some number other than four, but since, for example, "two and two are five" distorts what we wish to mean by the terms employed, in rejecting it we exclude only a misuse of terms. By contrast, "there are no more than a million men living" excludes "there are more than a million men living," and the one statement is as meaningful and consistent as the other. Factual truth, it is widely agreed, is always exclusive of meaningful alternatives, and in this sense contingent.

Yet this widespread agreement as to the contingency of fact conceals an important possibility of disagreement. For there is a common assumption by which the doctrine of the exclusiveness of factual truths is trivialized. This is the assumption that the excluded alternative can be merely negative. Thus: there are elephants, there might have been no elephants; there is a world, there might have been no world. What the positive fact necessarily excludes, then, is only a privation: in short it may exclude literally *nothing*. But to exclude nothing is not really, I suggest, to exclude. Real transactions are not concerned with nonentity, and exclusion is in some sense a real transaction. If I am just here, I prevent you from being here. If elephants exist, then, in certain portions of the world at a given moment, other large animals cannot exist, for the space they might occupy is otherwise occupied. The nonbeing of wild elephants in North America is a partly *positive* fact, for it means (for one thing) that every portion of the land surface of that continent (outside of "zoos") is covered either by some solid object different from an elephant, or by empty air.

We have arrived at the oft-debated question of negative facts.[1] The partisans of negative facts soundly argue that every positive fact entails negative ones. If X is round, then X is not square. But is it less true that every negative fact entails positive ones? If X is not square, then it has some other shape or character. Negative aspects of fact are one thing, exclusively negative facts would be another.

An example of an allegedly *purely* negative fact is this, "there was not a sound," or "he heard nothing." Is the datum of such a perception simply the absence of sound? Surely we must distinguish between, "he heard nothing," *i.e.,* he observed the fact of silence, and "he did not hear," for example, because he was asleep or unconscious. The perception of silence seems to involve positive characters both in the situation and in the subject's experience. The air particles are arranged otherwise than in the wave patterns which can cause sensations of sound, and the subject's nonauditory experiences have a kind of intensity and coherence which would be somehow disrupted were there the distraction of perceivable sounds. When we detect the absence of food in the ice box, we do not detect the presence of nothing there: the absence of food is implied by positive factors, such as the presence of light waves reflected from the back of the refrigerator at nearly every point. And the absence of food implies that other solid objects than nutrient ones occupy all the space not occupied by air.

But could not the absence of food be a wholly negative fact if it were included in the great negation, "no world, no positive facts, at all"? However, can we really think anything corresponding to such a pure negation? Obviously no conceivable verification of this or any statement could occur on the supposition that nothing at all occurred. Is it not absurd to pretend to conceive a "possibility" whose actualization must thus in principle be entirely beyond experience or confirmation? But perhaps the meaning of "no world at all" is, "God knowing he has not created any world"? This assumes that "God knowing nothing positive other than himself" represents a meaningful idea, which I doubt; but in addition, it does not get rid of the contingent positive side inherent in all fact. For God-knowing-that-he-has-not-created is God knowing something which it is not necessary to his nature to know, namely the fact of noncreation. (For the assumption is that he *might* have created, and then there would have been no fact of noncreation to know.) Thus the nonbeing of the world is still the being of some positive contingent fact—at least the fact that God knows this negative fact. If you deny this, you make the possible nonbeing of the world something in principle beyond all experience or knowledge, and so, I should think, meaningless.

If, then, any possible fact is partly positive, it follows, as I shall now show, that there are two sorts of empty truth, only one of which is "merely linguistic," and in that sense empty. "Two and two are four" cannot be falsified in any possible state of fact; but further, unlike "two apples and two apples are four apples," it could not even fail of positive exemplification, unless in a very odd world or state of fact indeed, namely one so lacking in distinct items that the number four, or the idea of pairs, would have no application to it. It is perhaps dubious if such a state is conceivable. Still less readily conceivable (if possible) is a world totally lacking in order, an existing pure chaos. What, if anything, can we really think corresponding to the sentence, "No real order exists?" Is this an absolutely unconfirmable proposition? Does not the possibility of confirmation imply an order of some sort?

What we thus come to is the idea of analytic truths which are positive. Not only can fact not contradict them, but it must illustrate them. If, then, they are called "empty," we should beware of a radical ambiguity in this term. *All* empty truths are such that nothing can illustrate them negatively (for they exclude only nonsense), but some empty truths (which we may call metaphysical) are such that they are bound to be illustrated positively. How can we recognize truths of this character? The criterion is that positive illustration of the proposition would not exclude anything positive. If, for example, the idea of a world so fluid or continuous that it totally prevents counting of items is really a positive idea, then even "two and two are four" is only negatively a priori in the sense in which "two apples and two apples are four apples" is only negatively a priori. But if, on the other hand, there is nothing positive in such complete "fluidity" (I do not here try to decide this), then arithmetical truth is positively and unconditionally a priori. But the difficulty of deciding as to the positive meaning, or lack of it, of pure "fluidity" warns us that the criterion of positive or metaphysical a priori truth, namely, "can be positive without excluding anything positive," may be incapable of clear and certain application by our cognitive powers. Yet metaphysical truth cannot be unknowable in any absolute sense. For what is common to all possible worlds is included in the actual one, and in any meaningful conception. It is but a matter of abstraction and analysis to find it there.

Ernest Nagel, in his essay, "Logic without Ontology,"[2] argues brilliantly that there need be nothing common to all possible worlds corresponding to logical laws—for instance, to the law of noncontradiction. He seems to me to miss the point, almost "as if by magic." Of course, there is no *fact* common to all possible worlds. But it is a common principle that any possible world will actualize some possibilities and thereby exclude the actualization of certain other possibilities. "You cannot eat your cake and have it too" is a maxim with some valid application in no matter what sphere. This is, if you will, an element of tragedy inherent in all existence. As Goethe said, "Entsagen sollst du, sollst entsagen" (renounce, thou shalt renounce). Things (and good things) are possible disjunctively which are not possible conjunctively; there are incompossible possibilities. This is a principle not merely of language or of true belief, but of action also. It expresses the nature of existence itself as a process of exclusive actualization.

Metaphysics we may now define as the search for necessary and categorical truth—necessary in that, unlike empirical truths or facts, it excludes no positive possibility, and thus imposes no restriction upon the process of actualization, and categorical in that (unlike mathematics interpreted as deduction from unasserted postulates) it applies positively to *any* actuality.

Metaphysical truths may also be described as such that no experience can contradict them, but also such that any experience must illustrate them. Let us take this as an example: "The present is always influenced by the past." Could any experience conflict with this? We surely cannot know that we are uninfluenced by the past, for to know the past is, in one's state of knowledge, to be influenced by it. By the past, we *mean* something which influences the present, and one might very well define "fact" as whatever influences events subsequent to a given date.

What is the use of a metaphysical formula such as: "Every event is influenced by its predecessor"? It is certainly not a prediction in the normal sense. If an expert predicts that the recent unusual weather is going to make for a small wheat crop, astute farmers, politicians, and bankers will take this into account in their plans. They will act in some respects as they would not act if the prediction were for a large crop. But if the metaphysician "predicts" that the future is going to be influenced by what is now going on, people will say, "Of course, but what of it," and turn to their affairs; while if the metaphysician says that the future will be in no way influenced by what is now going on, they will stare at him to see if he be mad, and again turn to their affairs. No practical consequence (except as to his sanity) will be drawn in either case that would otherwise not be drawn, for no matter what anyone says we always expect the future to be influenced by what is now going on. Every animal qualifies its striving with respect to the future by what it is experiencing now. It needs no metaphysician to tell it to do this. Thus if metaphysics has a function, it must be very different from that of science and technology.

What then is this function? The answer, as I see it, has several aspects.

(1) Is it not conceivable that an affirmation which cannot be falsified, or reasonably denied, and is thus perfectly "truistic," may yet be worth making simply to *remind* ourselves of something which is satisfying to contemplate, and not less so because it must always be there, and we have only to think about it to enjoy its value? Take the saying, "Life has a meaning," or "There are real values," or "Some ways of thinking and acting are better than

others." In no case can these affirmations rightfully be denied, for if life itself is never worth-while, then neither is the denial of life's worth-whileness ever worth-while, since this denial itself is a piece of life, an act of a living being. And to say that no way of thinking is better than any other is to say that the way of thinking thus expressed is no better than the contradictory way, and such a manner of talking nullifies itself. But yet the saying, "there are real cases of better and worse," may be significant as a *reminder* that the power to make comparisons of value is a power with a significant use, a power which we share with all men, and in a way with all sentient beings, at least. There is something satisfying in this reminder, something, shall we say, at least slightly inspiring. Now I hold that all metaphysical truisms have this inspiring character. Here is the argument.

Contemplation, like every life function, must always achieve some value. But with matters of fact, part of the value may be the realization that what has occurred could, and should, have been prevented. This realization has positive pragmatic value. In matters of fact, there are reasons for being "realistic," for facing things as they are no matter how much we may wish they were otherwise. But in truths that *could* not have been otherwise, necessary truths, it means nothing to say, "Oh, that they had been otherwise!" Therefore it means nothing to say that they are evil. Evil is that which, in each particular case, should have been, and could have been, unrealized. Now it might appear that good must similarly be defined as that which ought to be, or to have been, realized, and this appears to imply that its nonrealization was possible. Of concrete goods, properly correlative to concrete evils, this is quite correct. Both are contingent in the same sense. But there is this difference between the ideas of good and of evil: that whereas the contemplation of good things is itself a good thing, and in so far needs no further justification, the contemplation of evil things is itself, at least in part, an evil, and hence is in need of further justification. With contingent evils, such justification can be given; with necessary evils it could not be. Either, then, they *could* not be contemplated, which implies that reference to them is nonsensical, or they must be intrinsically rewarding to contemplate, and since contemplation is the only possible act in regard to the necessary, they are then by definition good in whatever sense they could be either good or evil. Necessary goods are not indeed good in the sense that they could be positive goals of practical volition; but the act of thinking about them can nevertheless have a positive reward, the enjoyment of something satisfying to contemplate. This is the most general definition of beauty. Metaphysics seeks "intellectual beauty" in the purest sense of this phrase. Can any inquiry be illegitimate if it discloses such beauty?

Moreover, is it not possible that when something like the totality of truistic affirmations has been made explicit, or when all or most aspects of the necessary element in reality have been disclosed, the mildly satisfying or beautiful character of these aspects, taken singly, will be greatly enhanced by the interrelations which will then appear among them? The *total* truistic picture, as it were, may be much more exciting or beautiful than elements of it isolated by abstraction.

(2) Although the denial of truistic affirmations is not meaningful, nevertheless through confusion, people often indulge in such denials. And there is no sharp line to be drawn between destructive emotions of despair and the utterance of absurdities like, "Nothing matters," or "Life is a tale told by an idiot, signifying nothing." Hence it may be worth pointing out that the denials of these cries of despair are truistically true.

(3) To be vividly conscious of the full truistic meaning of value of existence as such is to have a better chance of noting well and steadily the nontruistic or contingent meanings or values. For despair is deadening; lack of hope leads to neglect of opportunities; also, a one-sided, deficient consciousness of what all life essentially is tends to induce one-sidedness in the observation of the particular values of particular experiences. Thus if a man takes it as a truism that every creature must, or even can, be actuated by sheer self-interest, then he will tend more or less systematically to inhibit other-regarding motivations (which inevitably will be present in fact, since the correct truism is that every creature is social, "self-interest" being possible merely as a special, sometimes morbidly emphasized, form of sociality, a sympathetic interest in past or future states in the same personal series). Thus a principle which in its literal absoluteness could not possibly be applicable, may become, relatively speaking, only too true by virtue of being supposed absolute. To determine what self-regarding, and what other-regarding, motives are actually present is a factual task; but the task is the better performed by one who realizes that the zero value of either sort of motivation is a mere limit of

thought. He will not have to waste his energy on such pseudo-factual statements as that all motivation is entirely selfish.

(4) Metaphysical truisms, though not factual, may nevertheless include the principle that there must be *some* contingent facts or other on a level above that of ordinary, imperfect experiences such as ours. I have sought elsewhere to show that a kind of perfection is conceivable which *inevitably* or infallibly actualizes itself in appropriate contingent states of consciousness.[3] Each particular such state, being contingent, can be known only by empirical intuition, and it must be known as matter of fact, *i.e.*, as something to which there were meaningful alternatives. But it does not follow that to the *nonemptiness of the class* of perfect states of consciousness there was any meaningful alternative. (Every metaphysical truth can be stated as the necessary nonemptiness of a class, or as the necessary emptiness of certain pseudo classes, such as "worlds without order," or "worlds without disorder." The principle here is akin to that expressed in the formula, "That accidents happen, some accidents or other, is not itself an accident, but is necessary, inevitable." Similarly, that the Perfect should be embodied in some accidental state or other may turn out to be necessary, and this necessity may be metaphysically knowable. Such knowledge will encourage us to consider what light our factual experiences can shed upon the question, Which among possible accidental states of the perfect nature is in fact actual? No doubt we can never know clearly anything remotely like the full answer to this question, for to do so would amount to achieving perfect consciousness ourselves. But some very limited approach in the right direction may yet be possible, and the more so if our metaphysics has told us that there is such a direction to look for.

Presupposed in the foregoing is a view of deity as on both sides of the contrast, necessary-contingent. Were God merely on one side, he would not be the supreme reality. For the contingent is also real, and hence so is the totality inclusive of the necessary and the contingent. God must be this totality, rather than (the sole alternative) a mere constituent of it. Besides, as we have seen, his knowledge that the contingent exists must itself be contingent (had the contingent things not existed, he had not known them as existent, for his knowledge cannot err). Nevertheless, merely that God exists cannot be a contingent or factual proposition. Factual existence is always alternative, *this or that instead*. But "God or X instead" is not a valid alternative. There is no "instead" in this

case. There is no "place" which, if God does not occupy it, something else could. A person may worship an idol instead of God,
but the alternative here is in respect to states of mind existing
in the person, not in respect to the existence or nonexistence of
God. There may also (there must also) be divine acts or decisions
which exclude otherwise positive possibilities of fact; but these
can only be free, factual decisions, not inherent in the mere existence of God.

You can, of course, argue as follows: the existence of God means
a divinely ordered world; the nonexistence of God means either
no world or a poorly ordered world. But this line of thought presupposes that a particular sort of order follows logically from the
bare conception of God. This is plausible, perhaps, if one holds a
metaphysics in which the idea of freedom, taken to mean creative
choice, is not held to be a basic requirement of creaturely existence.
For then it seems reasonable to infer that the world, as divinely
created, ought to be a *perfect* order in which every item is exactly
in its place. But on the view, which I should oppose to this, that
any possible world must consist of more or less free individuals
(otherwise they would not even be individuals), the ordering of
these individuals can only consist in setting limits to their exercise
of freedom, that is, in the partial restricting of the chaotic aspect
inherent in individuality. Accordingly, the divine ordering does
not exclude elements of conflict, evil, and disorder; hence no
world ordered enough to make knowledge possible could contradict the statement, "There is a divine orderer." And a world
which could not be known is irrelevant or meaningless.

I once knew a young man who said, "I want to believe in a
man's world, not one coddled by a deity." He was supposing
that the divine existence would exclude something positive. But
if he meant a world in which much depends on human efforts,
and in which we are not told all the answers to our questions but
are permitted, and indeed more or less compelled, to think for
ourselves, then only an arbitrarily defined deity excludes this. God
might perhaps *choose* to coddle us, but his mere existence would
not *require* that he do so. And if coddling is bad, and God is
conceived as wise and good, then God would, it seems, be required
by his nature to avoid coddling man.

My suggestion, then, is that the mere existence of deity interferes with nothing whatever that is positively conceivable.[4] What
follows? Some would say that it follows that the statement, "Deity

exists," is meaningless. But then the statement, "Something exists," is also meaningless, for it too interferes with nothing that is positively conceivable! And so far from being meaningless, "Something exists" is obviously true. Accordingly, "There is a reality which is divine," although it excludes nothing particular, is not *for that reason* without meaning. Its proper status is not that of a fact, but of a claimant to metaphysically necessary truth. The alternative to accepting the claim is indeed the contention that it is meaningless or contradictory. That this is the issue was Anselm's great discovery.

It is strange how few have remarked that the statement, "There is one who infallibly knows all facts, and who, if other facts had obtained, would have known these instead," cannot itself stand for a fact. It affirms, rather, a *universal correlate* of fact, implying this: to be a fact, and to be known to one who also knows all other facts, are but two aspects of the same thing. The inevitability of the divine knowing means the inevitability of facts being known. To be is to be known to God. (Better: to be is to feel one's value as appreciated by God.[5]) Since God is conceived as having self-knowledge, he also *is,* but not solely in the same factual sense. For whatever the facts, God knows his own existence. His knowledge that He exists is not one of the factual alternatives, but the common feature of them all that, if actual, they are known to Him who inevitably is self-known. Thus the existence of an all-knowing or divine being is affirmed in a statement factually empty, telling us not a single one of the facts which the all-knowing being knows. But although empty the statement is not insignificant. For it provides a correlate to every factual statement which enables us to be conscious of its deeper meaning. Such and such is fact, then, means, such and such is known to one who knows also all other things. If the fact is tragic, then we do not face this tragedy alone. If there is need that this tragedy be taken account of in the ordering of the world, then superior wisdom will respond to this need with some suitable action. We cannot know what this will be, for our notion of what in particular is suitable is not binding in the case, we not being supremely wise concerning the particular situation. But we can take legitimate comfort in the sense that what ought to be done for the world will be done, and that what ought to be left to creaturely freedom will be left to it. Is this comfort empty? In a sense, yes. For it says no more than what every animal, in its fashion, affirms by the very act of living. To live, and to accept that in the universe which is not open to any creature's control, is one and the same action. But man, alone among the animals, is able to confuse himself with ratiocinations, and to *imagine* that he can quarrel with the essential character of the universe while still living in it. Theistic faith lifts the unity of life with its essential environment to the level of consciousness. On that level this unity has a new value, a new beauty. Yet it is not the beauty of any fact, but of fact as such, neutral to factual alternatives. This is a pure, unsullied, never-failing beauty. It is not the supreme beauty, for that is the harmony of all things, both necessary and contingent, a harmony which is itself, I hold, contingent—a superior fact which is only vaguely accessible to us in our factual experience. Metaphysics gives us no fact, ordinary or superior, but it gives us the key to fact, on both levels, the clue or ideal by which factual experience is to be interpreted. It gives us a sense of what a German theologian has called the accompanying melody, *Begleitmelodie,* of all existence. The import of the word "God" is no mere special meaning in our language, but the soul of meaningfulness in general, for it refers to the Life in and for which all things live.

Revision of a paper read as the Presidential Address at the sixth annual meeting of The Metaphysical Society of America, Chicago, March 25, 1955; subsequently published in *The Review of Metaphysics,* Vol. VIII (1955), pp. 553–68. Reprinted by permission.

1. See, *e.g.,* Richard Taylor, "Ayer's Analysis of Negation," in *Philosophical Studies,* Vol. 4 (1953), pp. 49–55, and my comment in *The Philosophical Review,* Vol. 63 (1954), p. 488, n. 5.

2. Ernest Nagel, "Logic without Ontology," in *Naturalism and the Human Spirit* (New York, 1944), pp. 210–41.

3. In my *The Divine Relativity* (New Haven, 1948), pp. 19–22, 41–42, 80, 87, 89, 157 f; and in Charles Hartshorne and William Reese's *Philosophers Speak of God* (Chicago, 1953), pp. 10–11, 404, 504–08; also my *Reality as Social Process* (Boston, 1953), pp. 114 fn., 169 f., 204–06.

4. The most plausible exception is the relativity of simultaneity asserted by physics. I cannot explain here why I do not regard this as a real exception.

5. See *The Divine Relativity,* p. 141; and my article, "Ideal Knowledge Defines Reality: What Was True in Idealism," *Journal of Philosophy,* Vol. 43 (1946), pp. 573–82; also "The Synthesis of Idealism and Realism," *Theoria,* Vol. 15 (1949), pp. 90–107.

SIDNEY HOOK

Naturalism and First Principles

In this paper I propose to raise and discuss what I regard as the most fundamental problem in the intellectual enterprise which goes by the name of philosophy, *viz.*, what it means for human behavior to be reasonable or rational. Some philosophers have referred to it as the nature of intelligibility. I have been led to this question primarily because of some recent criticisms of naturalism which charge that this philosophy arbitrarily imposes its own canons of rationality or intelligibility on existence and therefore denies certain important truths about the world and human experience on a priori grounds.

A similar question has also been raised by some fashionable sociological views of knowledge according to which there are irreducibly different modes of knowing illustrated in different cultures so that there is no such thing as a universally, objective valid method of determining rationality or intelligibility, independent of time or society or class, or even of party. On this latter view it is sometimes argued that moral, social and political conflicts are the results of conflicting logics of inquiry. Sometimes the converse is argued, *i.e.*, irreducible social conflicts give rise to irreducibly different criteria of truth. In either case no one method can claim universal and exclusive validity. Indeed, to claim that any one method of establishing truths is better than another is to be guilty of philosophical imperialism almost in the same way that the claim of superiority for the institutions of modern western, democratic society evinces cultural imperialism.

My argument will make—I do not say establish—the following points: (1) that despite all the basic conflicts over first principles of thinking or evidence, there are working truths on the level of practical living which are everywhere recognized and which everywhere determine the pattern of reasonable conduct in secular affairs, *viz.*, the effective use of means to achieve ends. Rationality on this level is not merely as Charles Peirce suggests "being governed by final causes" but so using the means and materials of the situation in which final causes are pursued as to achieve a maximum of functional adaptation between means and ends. (2) Second, this conception of rationality is not limited to our culture and to our time but is supported by the available anthropological evidence. The mind of primitive man, medieval man, communist man, for all the claims that have been made about their differences, is no different from our own. This is not incompatible with believing that in respect to discovering new truth one or another group of men, in virtue of *historical,* perhaps genetic reasons, at a given time may be in possession of superior powers. (3) Third, scientific method is the refinement of the canons of rationality and intelligibility exhibited by the techniques of behavior and habits of inference involved in the arts and crafts of men; its pattern is everywhere discernable even when overlaid with myth and ritual. (4) Fourth, the systematization of what is involved in the scientific method of inquiry is what we mean by naturalism, and the characteristic doctrines of naturalism like the denial of disembodied spirits generalize the cumulative evidence won by the use of this method. (5) Fifth, that the criticisms of naturalism from which the paper takes its point of departure can be met by showing that although the assumptions of naturalism are not necessarily true they are more reasonable than their alternatives. (6) Sixth, "Every reasoning itself holds out some expectation" (Peirce). Ultimately the rules of logic are instruments of discourse which enable us to avoid the shocks and surprises, the disasters and disappointments in attempting to understand the nature of the world and our own intentions and purposes. One method of reasoning is more valid than another because its use enables us to make the knowledge we have today more coherent, and more easily facilitates adding new knowledge to it.

This is the ground plan of the essay. Space permits the development here of only the first five points.

1

That first principles must be justified before we can achieve assured knowledge is a view seemingly held by some philosophers but rarely by anyone else. Scientists, for example, have satisfactorily solved problem after problem without feeling called upon to solve the problem of justifying their first principles. Not only scientists but people of ordinary affairs generally know when something is truer than something else without knowing, or even claiming to know, what is *absolutely* true. To say that we do not have to know what is ultimately or absolutely true or good in order to know what is truer or better, sounds dialectically impossible. But I submit that this is actually the way common sense and science operate. Even the most rationalist of philosophers in their nonprofessional capacity make effective use of everyday knowledge long before they reach their uncertain conclusions about the validity of first principles. It isn't necessary to assert that we know what is absolutely true about the cause of tuberculosis to know that a certain germ has more to do with it than climate. Similarly, few people know what their ultimate values are, and yet almost everyone will claim to know that it is better for human beings to do productive labor for a living than to be recipients of charity. Deny propositions of this sort and insist that declarations of the truer or better must wait upon knowledge of *the* true or *the* good, and the whole of human inquiry anywhere would come to a halt.

This is not to assert that there is no problem concerning the justification of first principles or of those rules of procedure which we follow when we reach the knowledge about which there is a maximum of agreement among human beings. What I am asserting is that the justification of rules of procedure is not of a different logical order, possessing so to speak another or higher type of necessity than the actions of which they are the rule. More specifically what I am asserting is that there is no such thing as strictly logical justification of first principles in science or common sense since proof by definition involves the reduction of all statements to indefinable terms and undemonstrable propositions or to propositions themselves so reducible. And secondly, what I am further asserting is that in the sense in which justification of first principles is an intelligible question—as when someone asks me why I regard naturalism as a truer or more adequate doctrine than its rivals—the answer will take the same *general* form of the answers given by those who do the world's work—the cobblers, the carpenters and gardeners—when they are asked to justify one set of procedures rather than alternative ones.

In other words I am saying somewhat differently what William James observed in *The Problems of Philosophy* although it is alleged he sometimes sinned against the meaning of his own words. "Philosophy," he there says, "taken as something distinct from science or human affairs, follows no method peculiar to itself. All our thinking today has evolved gradually out of primitive human thought, and the only really important changes that have come over its manner (as distinguished from the matters in which it believes) are a *greater* hesitancy in asserting its convictions, and the *habit* of seeking verification for them when it can." [my italics]

Such an approach, as I understand it, is the only one that can consistently be advanced by naturalists in justifying their first principles. This has provoked the retort that it is stupendously question-begging, that since the methods and categories of common day activity and science—upon which naturalism relies—are designed to take note only of the existence of certain things, the existence of other things like immaterial entities, cosmic purposes, Gods, and disembodied souls are ruled out *a priori*. The assertion of their existence on the naturalist's view must therefore be assumed to be not merely false but meaningless or contradictory. Since we are concerned here with questions of existential fact, the naturalist who naïvely believes himself to be imbued with a spirit of natural piety for a world he has not created, is taxed with the ironic charge of legislating for all existence.

Before evaluating the charge of circularity it is important to realize that if valid, it holds for *every* philosophical position. We cannot break out of this circularity by invoking only the law of contradiction, unless we are prepared to hold that all knowledge is analytic and that the differences between nature and history, with all their contingency, and mathematics and logic disappear. Certainly, whatever falls outside the scope of the basic explanatory categories of any philosophical position cannot be recognized. This is a tautology. That these categories are restrictive follows from their claim to be meaningful since a necessary condition of a meaningful statement is that it should be incompatible with its opposite. The only legitimate question here is whether they are narrowly restrictive, whether there are matters of knowledge in common experience which they exclude or whose existence they make unintelligible.

Since every philosophic position must start somewhere and make some preliminary or initial assumptions that can be challenged at least verbally by other philosophers, it is always possible to level the charge of circularity. But what shall we therefore conclude? That these assumptions are mere stipulations or arbitrary postulations which express nothing but the *resolutions* of philosophers. This would be voluntarism gone mad. Philosophers might just as well close up shop insofar as they claim for their position some objective validity in reporting or interpreting the facts of experience. For even voluntarism could not sustain itself against the charge of circularity.

The naturalist does not despair because he cannot demonstrate what is by definition indemonstrable. Nor can he rely upon intuitions or revealed dogmas because of their irreducible plurality. He believes he can show that although not demonstrable, his assumptions can be made reasonable to "reasonable" men. And the mark of a "reasonable" man is his willingness to take responsibility for his actions, to explain why he proceeds to do one thing rather than another, and to recognize that it is his conduct, insofar as it is voluntary, which commits him to a principle or belief rather than any form of words where the two seem at odds with each other. The naturalist does not speak, as one of its critics does, in large terms of "justifying philosophical categories as rationally and comprehensively as possible," and then fail to tell us in what specific ways philosophical rationality and comprehensiveness differ from scientific rationality and comprehensiveness. Are the laws of logic and the canons of evidence and relevance any different in philosophy from what they are in science and common sense?

To every critic of naturalism who has charged it with circularity I propose the following. Consider someone who comes to you and proclaims on the basis of some special personal experience that an all-pervasive R substance exists. It is neither physical nor psychical nor social, neither natural nor divine, nor can it be identified by, defined in, or reduced, in any sense of reduction, to any physical, psychical, or social terms. It is subject, so you are told, to no material conditions of determination whatsoever. The very request that these conditions be indicated is brushed aside as revealing a constitutional incapacity or blindness to grasp this unique entity to which all sorts of edifying qualities are attributed in an analogical sense, including a triune gender. It is granted by the believer in R that its existence cannot be logically inferred from whatever *else* is experienced, but he is quick to add that its existence cannot be logically *disproved* without assuming a question-begging philosophical position which rules out the possibility of this unique cosmic process. The next day he reports personal contact with another presence which he calls the analogical father, and the day after, the analogical grandfather, and so on, until even the most fervent supernaturalist finds himself confronted with an embarrassment of supernatural riches.

Embroider the fancy as you will. It is obvious that he can repeat almost word for word the points in the indictment of those who charge naturalists with circular reasoning.

Even if all philosophical positions are *au fond* question begging, there would still remain the task, pursued by all philosophers of determining which of all question-begging positions is more adequate to the facts of experience. Every philosopher who seriously attempts an answer does assume *in fact* that there is some common method of determining when a position is adequate to the facts of experience and when not. The contention of the naturalist is that this common method is in principle continuous with the method which we ordinarily use to hold individuals to responsible utterance about the existence of things in the world—a method which is pre-eminently illustrated in the ways in which men everywhere solve the problem of adaptation of material means to ends.

2

The procedures which are the matrix of reasonable conduct everywhere seem to me to be clearly involved in what broadly speaking we may call the technological aspect of human culture. It is not necessary to maintain that tool using is the only characteristic which differentiates human society from animal societies to recognize that whereas only some nonhuman animals occasionally use natural objects as tools, all human animals, wherever they are found, *make* their own tools. What distinguishes modern society from primitive society is not the presence of inventions but the organization of inventiveness.

Anthropological evidence leaves no doubt that primitive man wherever found solved tremendous problems of adjustment and survival. With a little imagination we can appreciate that starting from scratch such things as the invention of fire and the wheel, the cultivation of plants, domestication of cattle, and the smelting of metal represent inventive feats of a high order. There is an obvious continuity between our own technology and that of our primitive ancestors. "The sapling," says A. A. Goldenweiser, "bent out of its natural position to provide the dynamic factor in a primitive trap, is the remote forerunner of a spring which runs untold millions of watches and performs numerous other tasks in modern technology. The achievement of Alexander the Great in cutting the Gordian knot, though dramatic, did not equal that other achievement—the tying of the first knot. And this knot, in the midst of an ever-growing family of knots, is still with us."[1]

One can multiply illustrations indefinitely of the ingenious ways in which primitive man everywhere chooses between alternate means to achieve the particular end, improves upon these means and tests them by their relative efficacy in achieving determinate results. What stands out in my mind particularly is the impressive functional economy of the Eskimo's composite harpoon, that marvelous contrivance by which he spears seal, walrus, and whale, and especially the way in which the precious point is recovered. Hundreds of decisions must have been made and tested by their consequences before the instrument finally took shape.

The pattern of rationality does not extend of course to all aspects of primitive life any more than it does to our own life, but it points to a universal pattern of intelligibility understood by everyone who grasps the problem which the tool or technical process is designed to solve. Where religion or myth does not influence technology, the indefinite perfectability, so to speak, of the particular instrument is recognized or another one is substituted which gives more reliable results. Thus, for example, the Eskimo will abandon his ingenious harpoon for a gun when he can procure one.

The contention of Levy-Bruhl that primitive man thinks prelogically, that he denies the law of contradiction, that he is unable to isolate and distinguish logically unrelated things or ideas, that he understands by a kind of "participation" is not borne out by a study of primitive technology. Levy-Bruhl's observations are valid enough for the religious beliefs and social customs of the primitives, for their "collective representations" but not for the individual behavior of the primitive in war or hunt or in the field. One might add that Levy-Bruhl's observations can be extended to much of the religious beliefs and social customs of modern society, too. Even if all of Levy-Bruhl's claims are granted they do not invalidate Franz Boas' plausibly argued conclusion that the mental processes of primitive man in respect to inhibition of impulses, power of attention, logical thinking, and inventiveness seem essentially like our own.[2]

Despite their differences on other questions there is fundamental agreement among Levy-Bruhl, Boas, Goldenweiser and Malinowski concerning the universality of the experimental, commonsensical, practical approach to the environmental challenge. Malinowski points out that the realms of the profane or secular, and the realms of the religious or supernatural are not confused even when their respective activities are conjoined. The native plants his sweet potato with the most exacting care for the conditions of soil, moisture, and other elements which affect its growth: but in addition, he goes through some religious ritual, supported by a myth, before he believes he has a right to expect a successful crop.

"Can we regard primitive knowledge," asks Malinowski, "which, as we found is both empirical and rational, as a rudimentary stage of science, or is it not at all related to it? If by science be understood a body of rules and conceptions, based on experience and derived from it by logical inference, embodied in material achievements and in a fixed form of tradition and carried on by some sort of social organization—then there is no doubt that even the lowest savage communities have the beginnings of science, however rudimentary."[3]

Similarly, Goldenweiser:

"Technique on the one hand, and religion and magic, on the other, present from one angle the opposite poles of the primitive attitude. Industry stands for common sense, knowledge, skill, objective matter of fact achievment. Religion stands for mysticism, a subjective translation of experience, a substitution of mental states for external realities and a reification of such states into presumed existences in a realm which in part is 'another' world but in part also belongs to 'this' world insofar as the two worlds interpenetrate."[4]

What all modern anthropologists seem to agree on, as I interpret them, is that the religious or mystical elements in primitive experience, with their myths and religious rites, arise not in competition with the secular knowledge of technology or as a substitute for such knowledge but as a "complement" in situations in which all the available technical means and know-how are not adequate to a desired end, or where events do not clearly or always prosper when the proper instrumentalities are employed. In a world full of dangers and surprises, in a world of time, pain and contingencies, it is not hard to understand the psychological place of religion. It is a safe generalization to say that the depth of the religious sense is inversely proportionate to the degree of reliable control man exercises over his environment and culture. In this sense religion is a form of faith, emotion, not knowledge: when it is something more than this and competes with science or technology it becomes superstition.

We may restate this a little differently. Science or technology and religion represent two different attitudes toward the mysterious: one tries to solve mysteries, the other worships them. The first believes that mysteries may be made less mysterious even when they are not cleared up, and admits that there will always be mysteries. The second believes that some specific mysteries are final.

This relation between technology and religion is not restricted to primitive societies. Somewhere in the Talmud it is written that if a man's son is ill, the correct thing for him to do is not merely to call a doctor or merely to pray to God but to call a doctor *and* pray to God. And in our own culture this seems to be the function of nonsuperstitious religion. The theology comes as an afterthought. Even those who do not believe in God often look around for Him to thank or to blame somewhat like the atheist in the well-known story who when asked why he nailed a horseshoe over his door replied, "I really don't believe in it but I've heard it brings luck even if you don't."

In modern societies our attitudes are more complex. There is religion and religion. If you pray to God expecting rain or a baby boy, that is one thing. It is bad science, although if Rhine establishes the existence of psychokinesis (the PK effect), a power which some subjects allegedly have to influence the way dice will fall by wishing or willing, this kind of praying may not be bad science. If you pray in order to relieve your mind that is another thing. It is good psychology although there may be better psychology. If you pray without any purpose at all but out of a sense of relief, gratitude, awe or fear—that is not science at all but pure religion or art. "If scientific statements are to be called truths, religious statements should be called something else—comforts, perhaps."[5]

<h1 style="text-align:center">3</h1>

I turn now to a brief consideration of the nature of technology and technological behavior. All technological behavior is purposive behavior; the purpose provides a test of relevance, and the achievement of purpose, a test of the adequacy of alternative means suggested. Its every feature takes note of the compulsions of the environment as well as the much more limited powers of man over the environment. Its knowledge is a form of *ack*nowledgment—an acknowledgment of the nature of materials, the effect of motor action on the redistribution of materials, the importance of sequential order and spatial configuration. It is obviously reconstructive in intent, and makes of a natural order one that is also reasonable. It discounts the immediate qualities of use and enjoyment for the sake of anticipated consequences. Wherever we have a tool or technique, it refers not to a unique situation but a class of situations so that it has a kind of implicit universal import not separable from ultimate individual applications. The better instrument recommends itself to us to the extent that it enables us to make a more reliable prediction of *observable* effects that bear on the purpose in hand—the resolution of the problem. Learning from these simple inductions of experience is usually the first manifestation of intelligence. The violation, or rather the attempted violation of established inductions, like walking off a roof or out of a window, is sometimes the first evidence of insanity.

Technological behavior may be overlaid with all sorts of propitiatory rites but it is usually possible to distinguish between the functional and ritualistic aspects of the use of instruments. In its purely functional aspect every feature of the technique can be justified by its normal fruits or consequences. In time the process of adaptation tends to give us structures that are as simple and beautiful in their economy as the axhandle and oar, turbine and jet plane.

An analysis of the implicit logic of technology and the common-sense operations it involves, reveals that no hard and fast line of separation can be drawn between the general pattern of scientific method and reasonable procedures in the primary knowledge-getting activities of men struggling to control their environment. With the development of new instruments of discovery and measurement, and the use of mathematical notation, science becomes more abstract, more systematic, more precise, more complex. But wherever a man has had an idea sufficiently clear to enable him to draw a valid inference from it, the truth of which he sought to test by some controlled observation or experiment, he was proceeding—no matter how primitively—in a scientific way. The continuity between reasonable procedures in reaching conclusions about matters of fact of everyday concern and the procedures by which we make the most esoteric discoveries in the advanced sciences cannot be breached without making the whole enterprise of science a mystery, for every science starts from, and returns to, some of these reasonable procedures. If the common-sense world is radically unreliable or illusory, every theoretical construction which is based upon it or which it tests, is no more credible.

What we might call the first order facts of science are drawn directly from the world of common-sense experience—*e.g.* that a sponge holds more water than a cloth, that a polished surface is a better reflector than an opaque one, that white clothing is cooler than black—all of which were once discoveries. In the development of science no matter what the succession of theories, these first order facts are the last to be challenged. Whether the wave theory or corpuscular theory or any other theory of light is defended, the law which states the inequality of the angles of incidence and refraction when a ray of light passes from one medium to another is not questioned. For the class of phenomena it characterizes must be accounted for irrespective of what other predictions are made. From this point of view the laws of nature may be plausibly interpreted as instrumental devices to bring within the largest explanatory scheme our empirical knowledge of first order facts and successfully to predict future experiences which then become first order facts for all other theories.

Science differs from technology in two important respects. First in generality, and second in purpose. Technology is restricted in its practical reference to useful results; whereas the practical purpose of science, if we choose to use this language, is "the advancement of knowing apart from concern with other practical affairs," *i.e.*, the building up of a systematic body of knowledge.[6]

4

If there is no break in the continuity between life sustaining technological and vocational activities anywhere, and developed scientific activities, there is still less to be said for the view that science is so intimately tied up with culture that we must in Spenglerian fashion speak of Apollonian science, Magian science, and Faustian science with irreducibly different criteria of scientific validity. This is carried to extreme lengths by the current dialectical materialistic interpretation of science which denies its classless, international character and asserts that all sciences, social as well as physical, are class sciences and party sciences. More is meant here than the obvious view that social and political circumstances, interests and ideas have influenced the kind of scientific problems considered, and the direction of their application. The actual content of science is allegedly dependent upon a class or party approach, and the philosophy of dialectical materialism is recommended because by following its lead, problems within science can be presumably solved which defy solution on the basis of other philosophies. It would follow from this, to paraphrase Mannheim, that different classes think differently about everything, or at least everything important, which is manifestly false. There are no "national truths" in science, and Pierre Duhem is obviously right in his claim that it is only by its deficiencies that a science can become the science of one nation rather than another. The belief that there are "class truths" or "party truths" in science rests upon the elementary confusion between the objective evidence for a theory, which if warranted, is universally valid, with the uses, good, bad, or indifferent that are made of it.

Much more worthy of notice is the claim made that what constitutes "objective evidence for a theory" is an historical conception. The history of science reveals that the conditions which a scientific theory must fulfill to be accepted have been more rigorous at some times than at others. It becomes pointless to speak, then, of scientific method *überhaupt;* there are only scientific methods.

This is a very difficult and interesting question which I can treat only briefly and with the appearance of a dogmatism I do not feel. As a possible solution of this problem I venture the following: At any given time scientists accept as working truths hypotheses of varying degrees of generality and strength. They are more firmly convinced of the genetic theory of heredity than of the theory of organic evolution. They would be less surprised if the general theory of relativity were abandoned than the special theory. The degree of confirmation which a theory must pass muster at any time seems to be a function of the fruitfulness of previous theories in the field with similar degrees of confirmatory strength in extending our knowledge of the unknown. In addition the strength of an hypothesis is a function of the number of alternative hypotheses that are available as explanations. As a rule the more numerous the confirming instances the stronger the hypothesis. But if there are no alternative hypotheses present, we may be satisfied with far fewer confirming instances than where alternative hypotheses are present.[7] Further, the bearing of an hypothesis upon the direction of inquiry, the leads it opens up to new ways of experiment, must be taken into account.

To use a distinction of Peirce, in science a *valid* reason for believing a theory may not be a conclusive reason or even a strong reason. My contention is that what makes any reason in science a *valid* reason for believing an hypothesis is not historical, but invariant for all historical periods in the growth of science. But whether a reason is a strong reason for believing an hypothesis varies with the presence or absence of other leads and the evidence for them. This is an historical matter since no one can predict how many creative, competing insights will be current when an hypothesis presents its credentials for confirmation. I therefore do not believe that the variations in the degree of confirmatory completeness which scientific hypotheses have had to meet at different times relativizes in any way the logic of scientific method.

In passing it should be noticed that even in the history of mathematics standards of rigor seem to have varied, and for centuries mathematicians believed propositions which were only conclusively proved in the nineteenth and twentieth centuries. No one would infer from this that the notion of mathematical validity is historically conditioned, for despite the variations in rigor they progressively illustrate one underlying logical pattern of proof to which no alternative has ever been formulated.

If the foregoing is sound then I think it constitutes some reason for believing that there is only one reliable method of reaching the truth about the nature of things anywhere and at any time, that this reliable method comes to full fruition in the methods of science, and that a man's normal behavior in adapting means to ends belies his words whenever he denies it. Naturalism as a philosophy not only accepts this method but also the broad generalizations which are established by the use of it; *viz*, that the occurrence of all qualities or events depends upon the organization of a material system in space-time, and that their emergence, development and disappearance are determined by changes in such organization.

Common sense takes the word "material" as loosely equivalent to the *materials* with which men deal as they go from problem to problem; naturalism as a philosophy takes it to refer to the subject matter of the physical sciences. Neither the one nor the other asserts that only what can be observed exists, for many things may be legitimately inferred to exist (electrons, the expanding universe, the past, the other side of the moon) from what is observed; but both hold that there is no evidence for the assertion of the existence of anything which does not rest upon some observed effects.

The objections that have recently been urged against naturalism sometimes proceed from the notion that a philosophical position must justify its general assumption in some absolutely unique way. This is, as we have seen, a blind alley. Naturalism makes no assumptions over and above those that have been made every time the borders of our knowledge have been pushed back. It therefore has the cumulative weight of the historic achievements of common sense and science behind it. *If* we want to acquire new knowledge, the naturalist asserts, we should follow the basic pattern of inquiry —recognize the problem, state the hypotheses, draw the inferences, perform the experiment, and make the observation. There is no logical necessity or guarantee that we will achieve new knowledge this way but it is reasonable to act on the assumption. If one chooses to call this faith, it is certainly of a different order from the faith that new knowledge will suddenly be won in some other way—as different as the faith that "if I sow, reap, mill and bake the wheat, I shall get bread" is from the faith that "manna will fall from heaven." This difference would remain even if men decided not to reach for new knowledge, and depressed by Hiroshima, were to cry "Sufficient unto the day is the knowledge thereof." The connection between the method that one *could* follow and the conclusions that depend upon its being followed, remains unaffected by what one wants or does not want.

It is all the more surprising therefore to hear from one critic that "the most fundamental objection to the naturalist's procedure is that in Peirce's words it 'blocks the path of inquiry' in that it seeks to settle by stipulation the very issue that we need to be reasonable about if we can." Why? Because, he answers, "having committed themselves in advance to a position which identifies reasonable procedure with that which does not differ 'sharply' from that of the more developed sciences, they (the naturalists) will limit the scope of reasonable inquiry to what can be settled by the methods these sciences employ."[8]

This charge rests upon a double confusion—one of interpretation and one of observation. It is not reasonable procedure—what Dewey calls the basic pattern of inquiry—of which the naturalist says that it does not differ sharply from the more developed sciences. It is the techniques and body of knowledge which enable us to control everyday affairs of which he says that they do not differ sharply from the techniques and body of knowledge that the sciences have developed. For some of the techniques and parts of the body of knowledge of the former are always incorporated in the latter. The reasonable procedure—which according to naturalists is emphatically *not* a special technique of any special science—is *identical* in every formal aspect in every field in which we can lay claim to tested and universally agreed on knowledge about the world. How, then, can it serve as an obstacle to further inquiry, unless it is held that some disciplines have a basic pattern of inquiry quite different from that employed by critical common sense and science. What are these disciplines? What is this pattern? And what tested and universally agreed upon knowledge about this world or any other has been won by it? We are not told.

The error of observation derives from the failure to note that the driving motivation of modern naturalism has been not to block but to open up the paths of inquiry into whole fields which until now have not been investigated scientifically—especially the social disciplines. If this criticism of the danger threatened by naturalism were just, we should expect to find naturalists opposing attempts to employ scientific method in anthropology, history and economics on the ground that the methods and techniques of mathematical physics—"the more fully developed sciences"—were not applicable to them. But it is precisely the naturalists who by distinguishing between the basic pattern of inquiry and the special techniques applicable to different subject matters have been trying to banish methodological purism.

It is true that there have been occasions in the past when those concerned with the logic of scientific method have seemed to show excessive caution in evaluating the first efforts of scientific theories struggling to be born. Before the theory of evolution was buttressed by the findings of experimental genetics some biologists regarded its claims as too speculative. Today many scientific psychologists are very dubious about the validity of psychoanalytic theories which are somewhat in the same state as theories of magnetism at the time of Oersted and Oken. But all of these doubts, including those that follow from a too rigorously formulated canon of verifiability, far from obstructing inquiry are a challenge to it, and melt away as fruitful results are achieved and systematized. Such hypercritical doubts about evidence usually lead to suspension of *judgment* not of inquiry; they do not establish or enforce nontrespass signs. The dogmatism of a Comte who ruled out the possibility of our ever learning anything about the internal constitution of the stars, derided the undulatory theory of light, and professed skepticism about the results of microscopic investigation is as rare as it is inconsistent, and was repudiated by his scientific colleagues as soon as his views were made known.

If we take a long view of the history of scientific inquiry, the evidence is overwhelming that it has not been the naturalists who have obstructed investigation into new fields by insisting that the methods of the more advanced sciences be taken as paradigmatic for all inquiry, so much as those who have contested the validity of the naturalist position, particularly in the study of the human body and mind. The deliverances a few years ago by high church dignitaries against psychoanalysis follow a precedent established by a long line of more distinguished predecessors. An interesting chapter remains to be written on the distortion produced in other fields of science by those who took mathematics as the *model* of all knowledge. But the mathematical ideal for all human knowledge was held by comparatively few naturalists. Those thinkers who took it seriously tended to regard scientific knowledge as mere opinion lost in the welter of appearances and unable to grasp reality.

The most powerful opposition to naturalism comes not from those who feel that it obstructs the path of inquiry and closes the gates to new knowledge but from those who fear that it arbitrarily excludes from the realm of existence and knowledge something which we actually have good reason to believe in, *viz.,* God and man's immortal soul. Naturalism *arbitrarily* excludes the existence of God and man's immortal soul, it is alleged, because its first principles and categories of explanation are such as to make the very assertion of their existence meaningless. If true, this charge would be serious indeed, for the naturalist professes to be open-minded about the possibilities of existence in a world in which his greatest efforts seem so modest in the cosmic scale.

There are many conceptions of God and the soul which are unintelligible because they involve the attribution of contradictory qualities to Him; and there are other conceptions which are so vague and indeterminate in meaning, that nothing significant can be affirmed or denied of them. But it is not difficult to find conceptions that are sufficiently meaningful to make the contention of the *impossibility* of their existence arrant dogmatism. Are naturalists guilty of this kind of dogmatism?

I do not believe this to be the case. For one thing this would remove the sting from naturalism. Its criticisms of the belief in Deity have not been based on semantic considerations but on what it presumed to be the weight of scientific discovery. Some theologians and even some Catholic scientists like Duhem have sought to bolster the beliefs in God precisely on the ground that in relation to the categories of naturalistic science, the affirmation as well as the denial of God's existence would be meaningless. Such a view of naturalism is more devastating to atheism than to theism because the atheist does not profess to have any other categories at the disposal of his understanding while the theist emphatically does.

Secondly, wherever declared naturalists assert that the existence of God is impossible, it will usually be found they are using the term impossible not in the logical or mathematical sense but in the physical or medical sense in which we say that it is impossible for anything to burn or for a man to breathe without oxygen, Neither Professor Ducasse in his recent discussions of immortality nor Professor Ewing in his discussions of the body and its mental attributes have established anything more than what a sophisticated naturalist is prepared to grant them *to begin* with, *viz.*, that God's existence and personal survival are synthetic propositions and that therefore their denial cannot be contradictory or a matter for logic alone to settle. G. E. Moore once observed that the fact that one needs one's eyes for seeing is an empirical discovery, and this is obviously true for more recondite matters like the role of the brain in thinking and of the nerves in feeling. To see without eyes is physiologically impossible but every believer in immortality known to me is convinced that in his disembodied state he will see at least as well as he sees now. The two assertions are not *logically* incompatible for obviously the believer in immortality expects the laws of physiology to be suspended in the hereafter. This is not logically impossible but the absence of a logical impossibility does not constitute a scintilla of evidence against the usual validity of physiological law as we know it. Every reasonable person in his behavior denies the assumption "that we have no right to disbelieve in anything which cannot be logically disproved."[9]

The history of naturalism, it seems to me, has been marked by two main tendencies. The first has interpreted God in the same way as the great historical religions; *viz.*, as an omnipotent personal power who guides the destinies of the world He has created—and concluded that the evidence does not warrant belief in the existence of anything corresponding to this conception. The second has reinterpreted the conception of God and used the term "God" to signify a principle of order in the universe, the totality of all things, the possibility of good in the world, or the object of human allegiance. Karl Marx once observed that even the profession of belief in deism on the part of scientists was motivated by a desire to win freedom to continue scientific inquiry and to escape molestation from those whom we would today call religious fundamentalists. But in most cases the attribution of such motives seems to be entirely gratuitous even though a greater freedom from interference by revealed religion may have been among the effects of the profession of deism.

Whatever the historical facts, the charge of dogmatism against naturalism on the ground that it rules out by definition the possible existence of God and the soul has often been made. Recently it has been renewed and fortified by quoting from an essay by Mr. Dennes some ambiguous passages which are interpreted to mean that all things in the world *must* ultimately be described and explained in terms of the categories of quality, relation, and event. One critic then asks, "How do we know that the world consists of events, qualities and relations, and nothing more? We know that we must so describe it if we are committed to basic categories of a naturalistic philosophy. . . . But would the nature of a spiritual substance be so determinable?"[10] Another critic referring to the same point writes, "If everything has to be an event, the idea of a timeless God is excluded from the outset and without argument. The writer asserts that his list of categories makes no demand upon the metaphysical commitment of the reader, as though giving up one's belief in God were nothing."[11]

These questions seem to me to misconceive both the meaning of the text criticized as well as the position of naturalism. I shall, however, discuss only the latter.

(1) Naturalism is not committed to any theory concerning which categorial *terms* are irreducible or basic in explanation. Naturalists differ among themselves about this in the same way that scientists may differ among themselves as to what terms in the language of science should be taken as primary. What all naturalists agree on is "the irreducibility" of a certain method by which new knowledge is achieved and tested. The analysis of this method may be made in terms of categories like thing, structure, function, power, act, cause, relation, quantity and event. The choice of which categories to take as basic in describing a method depends upon the degree to which they render coherent and fruitful what we learn by the use of the method. Historically, and up to very recently, the most widely used category among naturalistic philosophers has been matter or substance. It is a complete nonsequitur to assume that because one asserts that the fundamental categories of description are X and Y and Z, and that they hold universally, he is therefore asserting that the world cannot be significantly described *except* in terms of X, Y, and Z, or as so many critics assume that the world consists of "nothing but" X and Y and Z. One may use categorial terms A and B and C that are not fundamental and maintain either—what most naturalists do *not*—that they are logically definable in terms of X, Y, and Z or—what most naturalists do—that the conditions under which any existing thing is significantly describable in terms of A, B, and C are such that they are always describable in terms of X, Y, and Z.

This gives us two possibilities in respect to a term like substance. It might be defined as a constellation of events instead of a substratum in which predicates inhere, and all statements about substances translated without loss of meaning into statements about organized sets of events or processes. Or second, an attempt might be made to show that whatever else a substance is, its manifestations or appearances can always be described in terms of activities or operating powers, themselves definable as events or powers. This does not require that substances whether material or spiritual have to be directly observed, but it does require that their presumed manifestations or effects must be observable in our experience, else we can populate the world at will with the creatures of our fancy.

Whether the existence of the identifiable "effects" of an allegedly spiritual substance justifies our belief in the existence of a separable and immortal soul rather than our belief that they are "effects" of a highly organized body in a given culture is something which the naturalist proposes to solve, either (i) by proceeding in the same way and with the same logic that he makes inferences from the presence of certain observable occurrences to the presence of other unobserved occurrences, or (ii) by examining the experimental evidence for the survival of the soul or personality after the death of the body, which brings us into the field of parapsychology and psychical research.

That the choice of which categorial terms to use in description is a problem independent of determining what actually exists in heaven or earth may be clear if we bear in mind that even if we were to conclude that man has an immortal soul, that would not by itself answer the question whether it was to be described as a spiritual substance or an organized set of spiritual functions. Conversely, Whitehead denies the explanatory primacy of the category of substance, and using the categories of event, quality and relation reaches altogether different conclusions from naturalism.

(2) Nor does naturalism exclude the very idea of a "timeless" God at the outset and without argument, as Mr. Demos alleges. Otherwise, as I have already indicated, it could not deny his existence or be denounced for its atheism. Naturalists use the term "timeless" to designate traits and qualities in existence which either do not change or to which the predication of temporal quality is irrelevant. Circular things exist in time but their circularity is timeless. Before we can assert that there are timeless "entities" in existence which do not change, we should need some experience of them in time in order to distinguish them from what lacks changeless character. The point is not whether timeless nonexistential entities can be conceived without contradiction. Assume that they can. But Mr. Demos is talking not of a purely conceptual or logic construction from whose meaning we can deduce existence. He is talking about a timeless entity whose existence must be inferred, as in orthodox theology (*e.g.* the Aquinate proofs of the existence of God) from a series of temporal and contingent events. And he must meet the naturalist contention that there is neither empirical nor logical warrant for the leap from what we can observe in our experience in time to a creature outside of time. That

there must be some disclosure in time of what is presumed to be outside of time as a starting point of the argument, Mr. Demos must admit, else the whole concept of God is useless for the purposes for which Mr. Demos and orthodox theology invoke him.

(3) If God and man's immortal soul are so conceived that they have no empirical effects, then there is nothing to prevent anyone from imputing any set of logically consistent attributes to them. They would then take their place with other imaginary creatures in the realm of mythology. I can very well understand the refusal of historical religions to take such conceptions of God and the soul seriously, since it makes them completely otiose in understanding the world, superfluous entities that can be shaved away with a flick of Occam's razor.

It is of course true that in modern philosophy the term "God" has stood for many different ideas—natural structure, the order of cause and consequence, the principle of concretion or logical limitation, the experience of value and righteousness. Avowed atheists, like Morris R. Cohen, have described their dedication to truth, and not only out of piety to the memory of Spinoza, as "the intellectual love of God." Naturalists are under no more compulsion to observe terminological taboos than other philosophers although one would expect them to be more careful of the context of familiar terms used to convey new meanings. If anyone gets particular satisfaction out of the use of the term God, then fortunately or unfortunately, he can find it in the writings of most naturalist philosophers. Naturalism, as a philosophy, however, has nothing to do with such linguistic matters important as they may be in other respects. Naturalism as a philosophy is concerned only with those assertions about existence from which something empirically observable in the world follows that would not be the case if existence were denied. And it proposes to treat assertions about God's existence in the same generic way that it treats assertions about the existence of invisible stars or hidden motives or afterimages or extrasensory perception. Critics of naturalism who regard this as dogmatic might put their charge to the test by furnishing the reasons or evidence which *they* hold warrant belief in the existence of God or gods, cosmic purpose or personal survival after death.

Some beliefs are reasonable even if we cannot finally confirm or disconfirm them. But if we take technological and practical behavior as the matrix of the reasonable, then beliefs in the existence of supernatural entities are not reasonable. They are not warranted even if they turn out to be true, just as a guess is not warranted knowledge even when it turns out to be true. Santayana somewhere suggests that the reason most people believe in immortality is that they cannot imagine themselves dead. This raises an interesting methodological point since only if we are immortal can we prove it, while the naturalists who deny the immortality of the soul will never have the satisfaction of saying, "We were right." "Wouldn't naturalists be surprised," a critic of the position once observed, "if after they died they woke up in the presence of God." They certainly would be surprised. The degree of their surprise would be the measure of the unreasonableness of the belief. Unreasonable behavior or conduct may sometimes turn out right —*e.g.,* if I gave six to one odds on the toss of a well made coin— but it is no less unreasonable for all that. And what is true for conduct is true for belief. Consequently, in respect to the available evidence in our possession, the naturalist is reasonable in his belief even if it turns out he is wrong about God and survival, while the supernaturalist in respect to the same data is unreasonable even if it turns out he is right. "Faith in the supernatural," says Santayana, "is a desperate wager made by man at the lowest ebb of his fortune." The scientist who predicts that life will disappear because of the second law of thermodynamics will never be around when the last flicker of life dims. The logic of the argument is no different in the case of immortality.

In conclusion, the naturalist believes that his assumptions are reasonable because they express, in a more general way, no more than what is expressed by any nonphilosopher as well as by all philosophers, whatever their school, in their successful working practice on solving problems concerning the nature of things. And by successful is meant here something independent of the categorial terms of naturalism or any other philosophy, something as simple, naïve, and indefeasible as discovering a substance that on friction will burst into flame, building a house that will withstand an earthquake, producing a seed that will yield a better harvest. Naturalism, as a philosophy, is a systematic reflection upon, and elaboration of, the procedures man employs in the successful resolution of the problems and difficulties of human experience. To use a phrase of Peirce, without giving it necessarily his special interpretation, it is "critical commonsensism." But it is more than this. It is a proposal. It is a proposal to continue to follow this general pattern of procedure in all fields of inquiry where it has enabled us to build up a body of knowledge, and to extend it to fields where we have not satisfactorily settled questions *of fact* of any kind. As a proposal it seems hardly less reasonable to the naturalist to follow than, when thirsty, under normal circumstances, to look for some liquid to quench one's thirst. Could any other procedure be more reasonable or as reasonable? Or must we solve *the* problem of induction first? But to raise the problem of induction no less than to solve it assumes that we are already in possession of undisputed knowledge. And to facilitate the transition from the problematic to the undisputed in human affairs has been one of the underlying purposes of all historical forms of naturalism.

This paper, not previously published, was read before a meeting of the Philosophy Club of New York at the Men's Faculty Club of Columbia University, May, 1950.

1. A. A. Goldenweiser, *Anthropology*, N. Y., 1937, p. 134.
2. F. Boas, *Mind of Primitive Man*, N. Y., 2nd edition, p. 131.
3. B. Malinowski, *Science, Religion and Reality*, N. Y., 1929, p. 35.
4. Goldenweiser, *op. cit.*, pp. 420–21.
5. W. Crawshaw-Williams, "True Truth: or the Higher the Deeper," *Rationalist Annual* (London), 1948, p. 28.
6. J. Dewey, in *Journal of Philosophy*, 1945, p. 206.
7. C. Peirce, *Collected Works*, Vol. II, Par. 2, p. 780.
8. Arthur Murphy, in *Journal of Philosophy*, Vol. XLII, p. 413.
9. Crawshaw-Williams, *loc. cit.*
10. A. E. Murphy, in *Journal of Philosophy*, Vol. XLII, pp. 411, 412.
11. R. Demos, in *Philosophy and Phenominological Research*, Vol. VII, p. 271.

STEPHEN C. PEPPER

Metaphysical Method

There are definitions of metaphysics to the effect that it is a theory of the nature of all things, or a theory of how all facts fit together. Though these are not quite equivalent, I wish to accept their common intent and to suggest that the most accurate way of expressing this is to identify metaphysics with unrestricted hypotheses. Then any unrestricted hypothesis will by definition be a metaphysical theory.

Most hypotheses are explicitly or implicitly restricted. They are hypotheses about this or that field of fact or cognition. So with all physical, biological, psychological, sociological, mathematical theories. These adjectives qualify the range and limits of these theories. It is always possible in these qualified or restricted theories to answer certain types of objections on the ground that the data or the considerations brought up lie outside the field of the application of the theory. So, objections to relativity or quantum theory in physics on the ground that the conceptions of space and matter developed there conflict with common sense or with immediate perceptions, can be properly rejected by physicists on the ground that these latter are not physical data. And objections to mathematical conceptions such as the geometrical point or the null class on the ground that all physical points have some size and all physical classes have some members, can similarly be rejected on the ground that these are not mathematical considerations and fall outside the mathematical field. So with all restricted fields and restricted hypotheses. And the great bulk of human knowledge proceeds along such restricted and specialized channels.

But a metaphysical theory, as above defined, cannot reject considerations of this kind in this way. It cannot excuse itself from taking any fact, comment, or criticism into consideration on the ground that these lie outside its field, or its scope of inquiry, for the simple reason that by the definition of its enterprise, there is no outside of its field. Or, in words more commonly heard, though not often fully understood, metaphysics is general theory in contrast to specialized theory, somewhat as a general practice in medicine is contrasted with a specialized practice.

This analogy incidentally suggests the social importance of metaphysics. Just as a specialist in medicine sometimes misses a diagnosis because of his restricted attention to his special field, so with specialists in cognition in general. There is need of the general practitioner in cognition, a specialist in nonspecialization, to keep a proportion and balance among specialized fields, to diagnose ambiguous cases, to have his eye out for undeveloped fields, to direct problematic cases into the proper special fields where these exist, and to institute these fields if they do not already exist.

But this medical analogy is not quite correct, for there is nothing in the practice of a general practitioner corresponding with the unique task of metaphysics in drawing up an unrestricted theory. It is frequently asked, Is there any difference between a scientific and a metaphysical theory? I should reply, None except the difference between restrictedness and unrestrictedness. Metaphysics has no special or private realm of data, except as the restricted theories may have failed to cover certain kinds of data. It has no special methods except as the restricted theories may have failed to use some. Unquestionably, there is a greater variety among metaphysical theories than among scientific theories. But this would be expected in the nature of the enterprise, for clearly the body of unrestricted theories would include all the discrepancies that these exhibited among themselves, together with whatever discrepancies of method existed among the restricted theories. Cognition is after all cognition, and the sum of the successes of the restricted fields of cognition does not justify the uncritical extension of those restrictions into unrestricted cognition. For instance, the successes of the physical sciences do not justify the uncritical extension of the data and methods of the physical sciences over all cognition. The only way to find out whether the methods and data of the physical sciences can be indefinitely extended is to try them out unrestrictedly. We get an interesting metaphysical theory when we do that. But there is not sufficient evidence yet to justify us in rejecting other metaphysical theories developed on other bases. Moreover, when the methods of science are given unrestricted extension, it becomes unclear just what is "scientific method," so that we see incidentally that without dictating to science, metaphysics automatically becomes a critique of science. In general, there is no difference between a scientific and a metaphysical hypothesis, except that the former is restricted and the latter is not.

Now it might be said that the very conception of an unrestricted hypothesis is fantastic. For is there not an infinite number of facts and an infinite number of possible methods? Perhaps, but the history of philosophy indicates that the human mind has been undismayed. We find a certain uniformity of method in spite of countless variations in the enterprise of constructing unrestricted hypotheses.

First, there is a general fund of material which philosophers recognize as critical material to be handled in any serious unrestricted theory. This fund has grown somewhat in the course of cognitive history, but it is not strikingly larger now than it was among the Greeks, even though the mass of detail that has sprouted from many of the items has grown prodigiously. I am going to be rash enough to make a list of the main items in this fund, dividing them into methodological and evidential items. They will be recognized as a typical table of contents for any extensive work on metaphysics.

Methodological Items
1. Infallible Authority.
2. Certainty, the *a priori*, self-evidence, immediacy, intuition.
3. Corroboration
   a. Multiplicative: numerical induction, etc.
   b. Structural: hypothesis and verification.

Evidential Items
{
1. Mystic experience.
2. Self.
3. Consciousness.
4. Sensations, sensa, impressions, etc. as analytical elements.
5. Will, volition, purpose.
6. Feelings, satisfactions, desires, interests.
7. Meanings, referential connections, internal relations, Gestalten.
8. Similarity, repetition, regularity, laws, universals, qualities, abstract relations.
9. Space.
10. Time.
11. Things, objects (such as trees, houses, dogs).
12. Physical matter, atoms, electromagnetic fields, etc.
13. Life.
14. Social structures.
15. Spirits, ghosts, gods, etc.
16. Efficient causality.
17. Chance, indeterminism, probability, etc.
18. Change, becoming.
19. Basic or ultimate substance or God.
}

The next step in the construction of an unrestricted hypothesis is to select among these items for what I shall call the "base" of the world theory. The selection of this base predetermines the structure of the unrestricted hypothesis. Naturally, I do not mean to say that this is the way the metaphysicians of the past brought forth their theories. They brought them forth in struggle and pain, in disappointment and with the joys of illumination. But looking back calmly over their results, and examining the cognitive significance of what they did, I find that they made selections among alternative possible methods, and among alternative possible materials.

Their selection among the methodological alternatives—infallible authority, certainty, or corroboration—was in one respect decisive; in another, of no material importance whatever. The way in which the selection of a method was decisive is that, if a metaphysician chose either the method of infallible authority or that of certainty, then whatever constructive items he selected by either of those methods became frozen and incapable of further scrutiny or criticism. A man who feels he has divine authority for the ultimacy of any item—say, self, will, space, efficient causality, or indeterminism—is not prepared to suffer these to be mauled by doubts and criticisms, except for the pleasure of refuting the objections. The same with the method of certainty—though it has lately become a fad of some philosophers to seek a reputation for ingenuousness by admitting that they were once quite certain of certain things but that now they have become quite certain of quite other things. This was not the way of the classical philosophers who espoused the method of certainty. Having once become really certain of any constructive items, these men stood by their convictions. For "certainly" the one consistent conclusion to draw from an error in certainty is that certainty is subject to error. For myself, I regard the testimony of the past in the history of philosophy as decisive in exhibiting the high probability of the unreliability and consequently the unprofitableness and illegitmacy of the methods of infallible authority and certainty. Their sole effect is to freeze philosophical discussion within the limits they have set. In this effect, the action of these methods is decisive.

Beyond this freezing effect, however, the choice of one of these methods has remarkably little influence on the structure of a metaphysical theory. That is, there is very little ground for arguing that any of the evidential items entail any of the methodological items or vice versa. It might be maintained that the mystic experience implied certainty. But this is precisely the philosophical issue in mysticism, and therefore cannot be regarded as certain. Certainty, of course, does not imply mysticism. One may apply the criterion of certainty to the list of evidential items, item by item, and see for himself that the addition of certainty to the item involves nothing at all, except, as we said before, a restriction against disbelieving that item. To say, "Consciousness exists," and to say "It is certain that consciousness exists," have no difference in meaning except that the latter closes (or tries to close) further investigation into the evidence for the statement.

The method of infallible authority is not quite so vacuous in its effects. It can be truly said that this method (which as a metaphysical method must, it would seem, refer to divine authority) implies a God as a source for that authority. This entails an interpretation of God as a self (2), a will (5), an efficient cause (16), a spirit (15), or a basic or ultimate substance (19), or some combination of these. But beyond this array of choices an authoritarian metaphysician may with the grace of God and within the accidents of theological creed select any constructive items he pleases. The variety of metaphysical systems developed under theological authority in European and Oriental culture suggests that the method of authority is almost as empty as that of certainty. It is, of course, open to criticism by both the other methods. But for this present discussion, all I wish to show is that the method of authority and the method of certainty have had very little effect in the long run on the structure of metaphysical theories, little more than to seal the selections philosophers had made among the evidential items.

The main work of building up metaphysical theories has always been done by the method of corroboration, which is nothing more than the method of gathering and organizing evidence. The very fact that philosophers have always argued and reasoned with one another is implicit recognition of the fact that they have been constructing theories, hypotheses, and not creeds, manifestos, ukases, or dictatorial commands. That philosophers should frequently have tried to slip into their evidence tags of authoritarian compulsion was only human and sometimes was inevitable under the cultural pressure of their time. Just at this moment in America it is still unnecessary to consider anything but the weight of evidence in the construction of hypotheses.

We shall consider a metaphysical hypothesis, then, as based entirely on its evidence. It follows that the variations among world theories depend primarily upon the selection of basic evidence. The variations depend upon what I called the base of the hypothesis.

Two pertinent questions will be asked at this point. First, do not the variations depend equally on the constructive processes following the selection of a base? Second, why is it necessary to select a base? Why is not all evidence the base of an unrestricted hypothesis? Isn't it a self-contradiction to speak of a restricted selection of evidence for an unrestricted hypothesis?

The answer to the first question is that the processes of construction (what is often called the "logic" of a world theory) constitute part of the evidence selected as a base, or, what amounts to the same thing, follow directly from the selection of a base. This point is most strikingly exhibited in the traditional organistic theories of the Hegelian type. The concrete universal selected as basic empirical evidence carried with it the constructive principles for the development of the whole system. The same I believe is true, though not quite so obviously, with all other types of world theory set up on other bases.

It follows from this situation, as the vigilant critic will already have noticed, that different world theories have different "logics" (in the sense of modes of rational construction). I do not say that there are as many "logics" as there are basic types of world hypotheses. But clearly there are many "logics" (in this sense) and it would be unlikely that different bases of world hypotheses would lead to exactly identical modes of construction for the hypotheses generated.

These remarks, of course, have no effect upon the validity of the specialized work done by professional logicians. The point is simply that the sort of work done by logicians as specialists is just as much subject to criticism and interpretation within the framework of unrestricted hypothesis as the work of mathematicians and physicists. To make further claims for specialized logic would amount to lifting this logic out of the sphere of criticism and appealing to the method of certainty. It would amount to claiming an *a priori* status for specialized logic. Not that a metaphysician in his capacity as a metaphysician would be likely to question the validity of a logical proof certified by a consensus of specialists in logic, but he is sure to look for the relation of such a proof to all the other things he finds in the world. It is, of course, merely a matter of historical record that some metaphysicians have given the principles of formal logic (or of its successors, mathematical and symbolic logic) a place of ultimacy in their systems and others have given them a derivative place. In other words, in some unrestricted theories, these principles are included in the base of the hypothesis and in some not. They are, of course, included in all relatively adequate unrestricted hypotheses either as basic or derivative, for otherwise the hypothesis would be restricted by the exclusion of them.

Whether to call the basic procedures for the construction of an unrestricted hypothesis a "logic," when these are not the procedures of Aristotelian formal logic or its modern developments in symbolic logic, is a matter of mere definition, as they say—that is a mere matter of agreeing in the designation of a word. Logic as a specialized discipline refers to a body of material such as that in *Principia Mathematica*. The term logic is sometimes equated with this specialized discipline. But logic has also been traditionally used to designate any rational method for handling evidence. I personally prefer the wider usage. On this wider usage, it is clear that the selection of the base of a world theory carries with it a logic for the extension of that base to unrestricted proportions, and that the expectancy is for the logic to vary with the variations of the base.

To the first question we raised following our assertion that the differences among unrestricted hypotheses depended upon the selection of a base—the question, namely, whether these do not also depend upon the procedures employed in expanding from that base, our answer is that the procedures are themselves included or entailed in the selection of the base.

This brings us to the second question we raised: Why make any selection? How can one honestly choose among facts—accept these facts and reject those—in the construction of an unrestricted hypothesis? Is not a fact a fact? So practically every philosopher has asserted. But the difficulty, the awareness of which also furnishes our answer to our second question, is that each philosopher (or rather school of philosophers) indicates a *different* selection of items as the facts that are *the* facts. The doctrine of the self-certification of fact is a myth. For those who require to be persuaded of this statement, the few paragraphs in which I could present some evidence in this paper would scarcely suffice. All I can do here is to explain the lines of argument I should employ. Essentially there are two lines. First, the exhibition of contradictions and incompatibilities in the offerings of ultimate facts and truths by different philosophers of generally acknowledged integrity. Mistakes have, to the best of man's judgment, been made in the assignment of factuality, or of ultimate truth, to items of experience. On the evidence of these mistakes, I submit that the act of judging items of experience as ultimate, in any of the various ways with which we philosophers are familiar, is subject to error. That is my direct line of approach to the issue.

My second line is to examine the grounds offered by philosophers or schools of philosophers in assigning ultimacy of fact or truth to any item. These always resolve into some form of infallible authority or incorrigible certainty. These methods, as methods of philosophical procedure, can be shown to have frequently led to error or uncertainty. Accordingly, as methods they are unreliable; and if, moreover, they are supported by corroborative evidence, they are superfluous. This is an indirect line of approach to the issue.

To the objection that past errors never imply a present error, and that accordingly any present candidate for ultimacy on the grounds of infallibility, certainty, or what you will, may well be a genuine instance of ultimacy, I reply, "Yes, the new present candidate always *may* be an ultimate, but how can we know that it is, if the ground or method for believing that it is, is one that we have frequently found in error?" Once more I urge that corroboration is our only security against error.

To the objection that the method of corroboration leads to an infinite regress unless supported by the certainty of ultimate fact somewhere, I reply that the objection is irrelevant. I am not asserting that there are no ultimate facts, but only that no infallible method has yet been suggested for finding them, and that the method of corroboration (admittedly fallible) is the only fruitful and reliable method that the history of cognition has so far presented. I urge that we make the most of it and do not waste our time upon methods that have frequently proved deceptive.

It needs only to be noted that the method of corroboration does not imply that any items of experience are either corrigible or incorrigible. There might be items which never failed to be corroborated. From various restricted points of view many such items could be mentioned. But from an unrestricted point of view— at least as a methodological practice in the construction of unrestricted theories—I do not see how one can assume that any item is incorrigible. All we have to do is to consider the convictions of the metaphysical mystic who denies the reality, which means in part at least the incorrigibility, of all experienced items except the immediacy of his mystic experience, to see that for at least one school of philosophers there is nothing in the world that can be corroborated by his experience except other identical mystical experiences. Likewise the idealistic philosophers who hold the view that the internality of relations is incorrigible imply a sweeping corrigibility of all other items. To a lesser degree the exponents of other world theories follow the same procedure. I conclude that as a general maxim in the construction of unrestricted hypotheses, we must not assume the incorrigibility of any item; or conversely that we must assume all items are subject to review (that is, to the tests of corroboration) in the light of all other items.

Now it might have been that all suggested candidates for factuality or truth should have mutually corroborated one another either positively by adding active evidential support for one another, or negatively in the sense of not indicating any grounds of evidential conflict. Actually, however, a cursory glance at the list of evidential items which I gave earlier, and which various philosophers and schools of philosophy have accepted as basic facts or truths, shows that mutual corroboration either in a positive or in a negative sense fails to appear among these items. The more experienced the philosopher in the issues involved in these items, the more aware he is of the conflicts that have appeared. The only way of handling these items in the construction of unrestricted hypotheses is to make a selection among them of certain items that will be accepted as basic, and to make adjustments or what we generally call interpretations of the rest. Such a selection is what I call the base of an unrestricted hypothesis.

Once we reject the methods of infallible authority, and of certainty, and note the evidential conflicts resident among the evidential items, no alternative is open to us in the cognitive enterprise of building up an unrestricted hypothesis other than that of selecting a base and proceeding to make adjustments among the remaining items in the search for a maximum of corroboration. This, I believe, has actually been the philosophic enterprise from the beginning. This enterprise has frequently been diverted from the direct line by cultural and authoritarian pressures coming from religious and political sources, so that there is some justification for the view that a metaphysical theory is simply the reflection or the systematization of the convictions of a contemporary culture. Even so, a base of selected items for the metaphysical theory is implicitly admitted. The cognitive strength of the theory still depends on its corroborative powers. What the philosopher wanted was cognitive support for his cultural convictions, religious or otherwise. It is always possible for other philosophers to consider how successfully he got it. And once more, barring the futile type of criticism which consists in putting one dogma face to face with another, with nothing but brute force or vociferation to settle an issue (in the manner of the methods of infallible authority and certainty), the only criteria of cognitive success available, and the criteria regularly employed, are those for the marshalling of evidence, or corroboration.

We, therefore, return to our original thesis that the method of constructing an unrestricted hypothesis consists in selecting a base and seeking the maximum corroboration of all available evidence. A philosophically adequate base is one that leads to a large amount of corroboration in the handling of the totality of evidence; an inadequate base, one that fails to do this.

It follows that in characterizing a metaphysics the most illuminating procedure is to reveal its base. If this is difficult to do, we have a serious criticism of the theory at once. It becomes probable that the man is merely verbalizing and has no clear conception of the relation of evidence to his words. I am not referring to the kind of difficult philosophy where a new vocabulary must be learned, or where a man has uncovered a new phase or body of evidence for which no well understood vocabulary has been developed. I am referring to the difficulty not of mastering words and concepts (which any philosopher may demand of another) but of finding evidential significance for the words. For instance, I would never, or at least very rarely, accuse Whitehead of verbalizing, but I suspect many Whiteheadians of having lost all contact with an evidential base.

Now the base may be very wide, or quite narrow. It might seem that the best results would occur in taking a very wide base: that is, in accepting a large number of items at whatever we may consider their face value, and then noting their independence of one another or tracing out their positive corroborative connections. Many, perhaps most, philosophers think that this is their method, and that they have taken no liberties with what other philosophers regard as the face values of evidential items and have performed no interpretations or reductions of proffered evidence. They think they are just describing the evidence in the common-sense way. Even Berkeley with all his paradoxes apparently had this illusion. But the illusion becomes manifest when you notice what one group of ingenuous philosophers says about the descriptions of items made by another group of ingenuous philosophers. Unless I am much mistaken, most of the notable philosophers show a tendency to seek a very narrow base.

The reason for this, I believe, is the search for precision of corroboration. One way in which corroboration may break down is the discovery of a number of mutually incompatible conclusions all equally compatible with some given interpretation of an item of evidence. This failure of corroboration can generally be corrected by greater precision in the original interpretation. There is thus a strong cognitive drive toward a maximum of precision in basic evidence for the sake of maximum corroboration. For a precise intensive interpretation of one or a few items of evidence ordinarily leads to a compatible precision in the interpretation of many other items of evidence, and in general these interpretations do not correspond with common-sense ideas nor with certain other precise interpretations.

Such an intensive analysis of a rather narrow base for the purpose of extensive corroboration I have called a "root metaphor." It might seem as though an indefinite number of root metaphors would develop, and that there would be very little to choose among them. Actually, I believe they are not many. Since the purpose of a root metaphor is to bring about a maximum of mutual corroboration, the method turns out to be highly controlled.

The procedure is strictly bounded on two sides. On the one side an unrestricted hypothesis cannot totally ignore or exclude any proposed item. Philosophers frequently try to do this by calling recalcitrant items "unreal," so that an appeal to unreality is an excellent symptom of inadequacy in an unrestricted theory. It signifies inadequacy of scope. It means that in terms of that root metaphor and its detailed modes of corroboration, the unreal items cannot be fitted in either as independent or as connected facts within that hypothesis. On the other side, an unrestricted hypothesis must give an unequivocal description of any item offered (or, at least, show how such a description could be theoretically obtained if further evidence were available). Failure in this respect signifies inadequacy of precision; and means that the method of corroboration employed lacks sufficient refinement to give definite answers to cognitive questions. Answers that are mutually contradictory or incompatible appear.

This demand, however, for precision in an unrestricted hypothesis does not, of course, imply that indeterminism, vaguenesses, fusions, etc., are unacceptable items within an hypothesis. Every world hypothesis must be able to handle them, since in some sense or other we frequently come across them. They may be handled as ultimate, or they may be analyzed into components. But whatever is done with these items must be decisively done, otherwise they cannot be corroborated. There is nothing illegitimate in the demand that a philosopher describe an indeterminate or vague event with precision, and one way to do it is to designate the event as irreducibly indeterminate or vague.

These two demands for adequacy of scope and adequacy of precision in an unrestricted hypothesis thus control the corroborative procedure within narrow limits and keep the number of root metaphors that have yielded a relatively high degree of adequacy to a very few. I should say that up to the present, philosophy has yielded only four relatively adequate unrestricted hypotheses, which may be called formism, mechanism, contextualism, and organicism.

Risking some exaggeration for the sake of simple illustration one could say that each one of these world theories takes as its base just one item out of the list I gave earlier. But the intensive analysis of that item made by the theory that employs it as its base, renders the item often somewhat unfamiliar to people who have taken it rather casually. Formism takes #8, similarity; mechanism #9, space; contextualism #18, change; organicism #7, meanings with a particular emphasis on internal relations. These have proved fertile bases for corroborative extension.

Before following any one of these through, however, let me point out some other items that have been used as bases without the same degree of success. #1, the mystic experience, is obviously the base of mysticism. This furnishes the outstanding illustration of a base that forces the exponent of its developed theory to deny the reality of all other evidential items. It is the supreme example of an unrestricted theory lacking in scope. #15, spirit, is the base of animism, and a supreme example of inadequacy of precision. #4, sensation, etc., is the base of phenomenalism, which is plausible and which some philosophers still esteem rather highly. In extending its interpretations, however, it runs into difficulties with the evidences for what we roughly call the public world. In order to take care of this evidence, it finds itself driven either into organicism or into mechanism. In other words, it has not by itself the corroborative power that it has if amalgamated with either of these more adequate views. Historically, it arose out of mechanistic concepts and problems (if we may take Berkeley as its progenitor), and I should under pressure regard item #4, sensation, etc., as one of the included items in the base of mechanism. The point is that if space is taken as a basic category, then sensation must be accepted as a basic category too, in order to provide a means of describing all that we call mental. #5, will, is the base of voluntarism. But this view, like phenomenalism, is rather unstable and in seeking corroborative extension tends to resolve itself into organicism. #12, matter, etc., is the base of materialism. But this lacks scope in its treatment of at least half the evidential items listed. Moreover, it is very easily absorbed into mechanism, and is usually regarded as part of its base. #13, life, is the base of vitalism, but, so far as I know, this has never been seriously put forward as an unrestricted theory (unless one wished so to classify Bergsonianism). So far as we see, it would not acquire much scope. Consciousness, #1, is another evidential item that every unrestricted hypothesis has to cope with, but which never itself expands as the fertile base of a theory.

These examples are sufficient to show that the evidential items listed are by no means on a par in their capacity to generate unrestricted hypotheses. The examples also show that there is no foundation for the fears some men express that, in giving up claims of certainty for these items, we may be giving up the control of facts over cognition. Evidence still guides theory along corroborative channels, and from some sources extensive corroboration flows and from others none at all. Indeed, only when evidence is freed from the trammels of claims to certainty and infallibility does it show us clearly the way it goes.

Now to return to the relatively adequate theories and their root metaphors. In forcing these theories to a single item as their base, we were, as we intimated, distorting their corroborative action. The base of these theories is really much wider, and includes a number of items. What I mean is that there are a number of items which these theories find they can take at what we might call practically their face value, items with regard to which there is a minimum of interpretation. For instance, with space, #9, as a primary base, a complete mechanism, I believe, accepts sensations (#4), satisfactions (#6), time (#10), and matter (#12). I am referring here to the type of mechanism which accepts as its categories a spatiotemporal field within which atomic or distinguishable field structures are differentiated in some sense and built up into more and more complex structures, molecules, living cells, etc., which are regarded as atomically analyzable, and with which at a certain level of complexity are correlated mental states which are themselves analyzable into sensory and affective elements, the latter being equated with value in terms of a hedonistic or interest ethics.

In these terms typical interpretations are made of the other evidential items listed. It may be useful to suggest how. The mystic experience (#1) is interpreted as a psychopathic state in terms of mechanistic analytical psychology, and its noetic element of cosmic certainty is described as a neurotic illusion. The self

(#2) is described as a complex psychophysiological structure. Consciousness (#3) regarded as a distinct datum may be either accepted or rejected. It acquires little corroboration in terms of the indispensable items in the base of the theory and is likely to be questioned. But it may be accepted as virtually an independent item in the base. Volition (#5) is likely to be described in terms of sensations and satisfactions, though volition may be atomized into activities regarded as irreducible mental elements parallel with sensations and affections. Meanings (#7) are ordinarily interpreted in associational terms and so reduced to sensory and physiological elements. Similarity (#8) is nominalistically interpreted so far as possible, and for the rest referred to the descriptive laws of the spatiotemporal-material field. Things (#11) are described as perceptual objects and reduced to associations of sensations, their reliability as cues to action depending upon their psychophysical relations. Life (#13) is described as a complex chemical structure, though an independent element of life may be accepted in the same questionable way that an independent element of consciousness may be. Social structures (#14) are interpreted on the biological side as interacting aggregates of individual organisms, and on the psychological side as sentiments analyzable in affective-volitional terms. Efficient causality (#16) as an alleged intuitive certainty is interpreted as a psychological illusion. Physical causation is basically equated with spatiotemporal-material field structures. Spirits (#15) are fictions derived from dreams, hallucinations, etc. Indeterminism and probability (#17) may get either a subjective or an objective interpretation, though the tendency is to seek a determinate base in the spatiotemporal field and thence seek a cosmic determinism. Change (#18) is ultimately analyzed into motion. As for substance (#19), this must probably be denied, since there is no single entity, not even the spatiotemporal field, which absorbs all others without residue. Yet Spinoza, who can plausibly be interpreted as a mechanist, ingeniously provides for substance through his concept of modes and attributes.

I have used mechanism simply as an illustration—and the conception of mechanism I have in mind may strike some persons as something less than the most adequate that could be given. If so, there is nothing, we note—no claims of certainty or infallibility— to restrain any persons from presenting their interpretations for comparison in terms of corroborative power. But one important point may have been gained by this brief detailed treatment. We can see what may be desired of such a theory, how flexible and yet resistant and resilient evidence is, and how men are able to meet one another without an *impasse* over issues involving unrestricted evidence. Our common aim is to get as large a mass of corroborative evidence as we can. When evidence that is organized on a chosen base appears recalcitrant to corroboration in either the positive or the negative sense, then we may either seek readjustments within the framework of that structure of evidence to take care of the difficulty; or we may seek for fresh evidence of a kind expected to clear up the difficulty; or, the most radical alternative, we may see, as a result of an analysis of the structure of the theory on the chosen base, that the difficulty lies in the basic categories of the theory, and so be willing and anxious to discover what may be done in organizing corroborative masses of evidence on other bases—that is, by means of other categories.

In most of this paper I have been speaking of types of unrestricted hypotheses rather than of particular philosophers. If the principal aim is to seek the organization, the structure, or the possible orders, of the world's evidence, particular philosophers soon come to be regarded as so many experimenters in this enterprise. We become interested less in what such a man historically said or intended to say than in what he contributed to the organization or to the store of the world's evidence.

But for a judgment of a philosopher's contribution, and (still more important) for our own ability to perceive and profit from his contribution, there is no better way, I believe, than to seek out as quickly as possible the base on which his theory is constructed. We are then probing into the vital joints of his thought. Stripped of all authoritarianism, verbalism, and dogmatism, what, we ask, is the evidence for what he says, and, having found the evidence, how, we ask, does it hold or stand together.

When we approach individual philosophers in this way, their personalities, their language, and their cultural settings drift to the periphery; but the central movement of philosophy, its persistent drive for the facts and the truth of the world, comes clearly out to the focus.

I will conclude with a comment on eclecticism. This will serve as a summary of my main theses in the preceding discussion of metaphysical method. An eclectic, in terms of the preceding analysis, is one who tries to build up an unrestricted hypothesis simultaneously from two or more incompatible bases; and consequently, as we indicated, tries to work simultaneously with two or more incompatible corroborative procedures.

It follows that an eclectic by his method unnecessarily reduces the corroborative range of his evidence, and, consequently, the strength of his hypothesis. For by mixing incompatible corroborative procedures in one unrestricted hypothesis, he fails (in direct proportion to the relative adequacy of the bases mixed) to get any corroboration at all, since both bases furnish alternative and in general incompatible descriptions for their complete corroborative range. Even if the eclectic does not himself carry the alternative descriptions from the different bases through (and, of course, he does not, for if he did he would see his difficulty), some other philosopher following out the structural lines of the two bases is bound to do so. The only way an eclectic can put a stop to this following out of alternative descriptions entailed by the selection of incompatible bases, is to asseverate the certainty, indubitability, self-evidence, infallibility, what you will, of the particular descriptions he happens to pick. Eclecticism is thus a tempting invitation to dogmatism, and would scarcely exist without it.

The eclectic's hypothesis is thus not even as adequate as an hypothesis which consistently carries through one corroborative procedure derived from one fruitful base. With the consistent hypotheses, we see at least without confusion the way the evidence builds up on its base, however biased the world view on that base may be. But this is not our suggested alternative to eclecticism—not the choice between one clear hypothesis consistently biased in its procedure, and one confused hypothesis confusedly unbiased in its procedure. Our alternative to the single confusedly unbiased hypothesis is the whole unbiased array of clear relatively adequate hypotheses, from which the eclectic has arbitrarily chipped a piece here and a piece there. The relatively adequate hypotheses are, to be sure, as wholes mutually incompatible. But the difference between incompatibilities within an eclectic theory, and incompatibilities among relatively adequate clear theories, is that among the latter the grounds for the incompatibilities are clearly visible and not confused or hidden. The array of relatively adequate unrestricted hypotheses amounts to a summary of our human experience with corroborations. The corroborative procedures are themselves thus clearly exhibited as part of the world's total fund of evidence. I am even tempted to suggest that these corroborative procedures constitute our best contemporary answer to the problem of induction. They are the means by which we thread our way through evidence and make rational judgments regarding the extension of evidence.

Reprinted with permission of the editors from *The Philosophical Review*, May, 1943.

HERBERT W. SCHNEIDER

To Be and Not to Be

Hamlet knew perfectly clearly the difference between being and not being; to distinguish between them was not his question, for he had a practical decision to make which involved knowing which of the two "were better" for him. And yet the deliberations of Hamlet as he tried to decide are among the many evidences to be found in human experience and reflection which show that the distinction is not easy to make, and that a clear and distinct definition of being which will show precisely how it differs from nonbeing may be impossible. Thus we have a question before us of a very elementary sort, which we ought to explore in terms of what we know today about being and not being and which we ought to be able to analyze without dragging it laboriously through its long historical career and its metaphysical, philosophical, and poetic associations. In what follows I shall not ignore the history of the question, but I shall refer to the classical literature of the subject only in so far as it is convenient in the course of a factual examination.

It is a common practice among scientists to observe how the

things they are trying to explain come into being. Following this practice, I shall begin with the question of the *generation* of beings: What does it mean to become? I must, therefore, put aside those beings which to all appearances do not come into being, whose origins are obscure, or which have no temporal dimension. It would be extremely dogmatic to dismiss nontemporal, unchanging beings, as if there were none such. My excuse for beginning with beings that come into being is simply that they are easier to observe. Poverty, for example, we have with us always, but when one becomes poor then one knows distinctly that something has happened, that a kind of being has been generated; something is which was not and which may, we hope, pass as it came. Thus, the process of generation is an obvious, practical point of departure for an exploration of being, of becoming, and of passing out of being. Passing out is a somewhat more complicated process, for reasons which may become clearer as we proceed.

From an observer's point of view, that is, in the order of discovery or empirical disclosure, there is a good reason for beginning the analysis with events rather than with things, for an event is a concrete example of generation. It is not the *presence* of the given which is primary; it is not *Dasein* which first suggests the difference between being and not being; it is coming and going, happening, which makes being problematical. In a changeless Now there would be no meaning in trying to distinguish being from not being. The changes among things make "being" and "non-being" meaningful. A universe at rest, that is, without *relative* motion, in which nothing is generated, could be as extended as space may permit, could contain discrete bodies, could even be a pure milky way, but nothing would *be* in it, and its own being, if we grant it one, would be meaningless. There would be no individuals; there are no things where there is nothing doing. A temporal perspective is necessary for a spatial world to give it significant being. Things stand out as distinct individuals not because bodies are separated but because they change position. Hence the changes or events that "take place," as we say, are the measure of the existence of things. An exploration which centers its attention on facts of passage is, therefore, in possession of a genuine *principium individuationis*. Not matter, not substance, not body is the principle of individuality. Matter, substances, bodies *become* things or individuals in so far as their relative movements create changes in their relations to each other. What bodies *endure* not only measures their *duration* but constitutes their individuality. Things *be* what they are in virtue of their *pathé,* in virtue of their modifying each other. This is the first discovery of so-called process philosophy, and the discovery was made clearly in ancient times.

But how shall processes be conceived so as to bring out their power to generate individuality? Let me begin by commenting on three current, radical attempts to make processes intelligible in terms of entities that are supposed to be more empirical or "real" than processes themselves.

(1) Some say that there must be *unit events* or atoms of duration. Whitehead and Russell were tempted by this idea because atomism had been for centuries regarded as the most intelligible theory of individuality, and because "units" are elementary in mathematics, or were elementary until recently. Atomic logic seemed to be ideal logic, for it could unify the elements of sense and the elements of mechanism. Physical occasions and sense experiences were conceived as compounds of unit-events, which might be either "subjective simples" or objective atoms. Whitehead went furthest in developing a two-dimensional temporal atomism: the dimension of "presentational immediacy" was explained as a succession of data, and the dimension of "causal efficacy" as a string of events. In either case, relations are "external," which is another way of saying that unit events are atomic. The intelligibility of this system rests on the notion that genuine individuals are literally atomic, indivisible. This notion, that individuality implies indivisibility, has a very long, respectable tradition behind it, and has maintained itself until recently despite the effective criticism of Zeno. But it is now evidently unnecessary to engage in a refutation of this idea, for even if it be difficult to refute, it is no longer useful in physical science and definitely discarded in psychology. If logic wishes to cling to it, so much the worse for logic. In ordinary usage as well as in scientific terminology an individual need not be regarded as literally indivisible, nor need a continuous line or function be defined as literally a succession of points. This whole method of analysis, whatever may be its mathematical value, is now futile in ontological analysis, for it is not true that discontinuity is more intelligible or elementary than continuity, nor abstractions more evidently individual than concrete events.

(2) This leads me to comment on a second theory, the theory that events or processes are individual in virtue of their being

"qualified." What happens, they maintain, does not really enter the realm of being until it is blessed with an "ingression" from above; an essence must descend upon an existence before it can claim to be; to be implies to be somewhat. This theory, I suppose, is a heritage from the notion that a soul must be baptized before it has status. To be sure, an event will not get into a dictionary or a system of knowledge without some sort of verbal tag and conceptualization, but it is evidently generated before it is interpreted. To be sure, an understood process is transformed to an even greater extent than a baptized soul, but it is certainly a serious confusion to identify the process of conceptualization with the process of becoming, or to think that nothing is particular until it is given a proper name. There is an opaqueness in temporal being which usually makes it impossible to determine the meaning of an event immediately, and because of this opaqueness idealists have tried to dismiss time as unreal. But an observer of facts must find some better way of doing justice to the fact of temporal obscurity. Darkness comes before light; God said "let there be light" only after he had made sure that there was something to be seen. Events are powers before they acquire an essence. For essences are the generation of processes of interpretation, and these cognitive processes are intelligible only in so far as they themselves find a place among the multifarious events or happenings or temporal powers. "An event . . . is the presence of an operative power,"[1] says Ushenko. Very well, let this pass as a *definition* of an event. Here we have its essence. It is a presence; but not a presence which announces its arrival by showing its "ingression" passport as a presence. It comes as a power. (An operative power, if I understand the terminology correctly, is a power which has come into being; for even powers must wait their turn to act in the waiting room of potentialities.) Powers are not existentially distinct from the events which make them "present"; they do not ingress into events. The event *is* the act of generation or the power in action. Here we must be on our guard against the temptation of interpreting events as substitutes for bodies or things or energies or powers. Happenings are certainly not intelligible without a world of bodies in relative motion. This world is being, according to what I said above, in so far as it is eventful; to attribute being to it in any other sense robs "being" of its "-ing." Now, it may be that there are worlds in which the "-ing" is not necessary; but in the world of happenings being must itself be understood in the context of processes, and processes in terms of relative motion among bodies or energies or powers or quanta, as the case may be. Events individualize the world of powers; but there is no reason to suppose that events are created *ex nihilo*. Events are not generated, they are generations.

(3) A third theory, notably George H. Mead's theory, puts the whole burden of process philosophy on the theory of *presence*. Despite his attempt to escape the fallacies of atomism and of assuming artificial discontinuities, Mead is in danger of interpreting *the* present (which I shall signify by *Dasein*) as a collective term for individual perspectives or *presents*. A correlation of presences may not differ very much from a construction of private spaces. But what makes Mead's theory more realistic than Russell's is his doctrine that though a present is the principle of individuality, these presences or presents operate in a public domain or "area of manipulation." This area of manipulation is really the domain of "facts of passage" or processes, which receive individuality in a given perspective or interpretation, but which constitute an "objective" relational field (a realm of *Dasein*) in which presentational relativity and the course of events combine to form the historial context of experience. The difficulty may be largely verbal, but I have difficulty in following Mead as he shifts from *a* present to *the* present. It seems to me that there is a danger here of making *Dasein* rather than *passage* the basic fact of individuality and of being. And I wish to make my own position quite unambiguous, by regarding the processes and not their presentation as the facts of individuality. At the same time, I wish like Mead to interpret events as facts of passage in a world of "doings" or "goings on" without reducing them either to atomic or unit events or to phases of a single world process. Accordingly, I conceive the primary problem of analysis to be the recognition of distinctive "categorial" types of happenings or processes. I wish to distinguish different types of being among processes. In other words, even admitting that events or changes are the *principium individuationis* and as such a basic aspect of coming into being, an ontological science cannot stop at this starting point, but must observe qualitative differences among these temporal individuals. To have a *principium individuationis* is a mere beginning for descriptive or analytical ontology.

I shall not attempt here an exhaustive exploration of the various categorial processes, but be content to call attention to three types of processes which are important for any theory of being, and which will enable me to make some observations on historical being and historical processes. Each of these processes creates distinct types of individuality and has its characteristic structure. The ancient Greek names for them are still useful, since Greek has now become a technical language, but I must try to translate these technical concepts into the familiar distinctions of men who are not accustomed to philosophical analysis, for the processes themselves, to which I call attention, are indeed very ordinary beings. They are: *physis, poésis,* and *noésis;* or, in Latinesque English; generation, creation, and cognition; in German, I suppose one might say: *Entstehen, Wirken, und Verstehen.*

The first process, generation, in order to make its English name roughly equivalent to the Greek, we might better call "natural production" including "growth." Such generation involves the natural changes through which bodies or energies are transformed. Composing this process are such events or subprocesses as collision, combustion, decay, assimilation, erosion, birth, death, etc. Though each such event or subprocess is an individual, when taken out of its "natural," its generating context, it loses itself to some extent in the production of culminating individuals. These culminations of cumulative changes also have their being *in process,* but they mark endings of particular processes of generation. For a process is by definition individualized. Thus, a physical individual is a generated being; such individuality characterizes both the things called happenings or events or occasions and the things traditionally known as "substances." Beings such as mountains, clouds, trees, galaxies, animals are the same kind of beings as fires, collisions, growths, respirations; they all become "in the course of events," endure a while, then pass out through transformation into other individuals. The various attempts to conceive this course of events and successive existence of things, this vast array of natural production, as phases of a single process of "evolution," or "natural history," or cosmic development which culminates in some single great end product, are mythologies that feed the imagination, but they cannot be taken seriously as hypotheses to explain the supposed unity of natural processes. The need for a postulate of unity in nature, which is still being asserted, may at best represent a kind of faith or trust in natural being and may be felt as a moral need, but it is certainly not an intellectual need. On the contrary, the first need in factual ontology is not to exaggerate the unity or continuity in nature; the continuities and discontinuities in observed fact and in systematic explanation must both be respected. Unless and until nature becomes intelligible as a whole and the natural sciences are thoroughly integrated, the natural world should be regarded pluralistically as a complex of more or less related processes of generation. "Nature" is strictly a collective term, and any theory of natural individuality is limited by a diversity of observable processes, which have different structures and many beginnings and endings.

The second type of process, *poésis* or making, includes the various modes of *construction*. Constructions are more purposive processes than natural generations, more unified teleologically: the contributing events and materials lose themselves more completely in the culminating individual or end product. The subprocesses are *merely* parts or means toward an individual creation. A constructive process is *intentional* and *progressive* as well as cumulative. It need not be consciously designed, but its structure is a design, or a perspective. Thus a living organism may have been generated naturally, but the functioning of its organs is a process which must be interpreted as a construction, it is a *working* together of parts. The constructional functioning of a creation is the culmination of the creative art and the test of the success of the intention. Intentionality, creativity, constructiveness, perspectivity and the like are not necessarily descriptive of motivation or of a conscious viewpoint, though consciousness is itself a culminating creation of such processes. They are primarily or ontologically descriptive of dynamic structure. I am here suggesting that mechanical perfection and artistic success are extreme illustrations of the same categorial type of process. Here integration and perspectivity are essential, for a creative process necessarily involves the co-operation of events in a single, individual design or functioning. In most philosophies the term "act" is reserved for this kind of systematic, intentional action. But the kind of action which is a genuine working, a constructive motion, a *Wirken,* is a special kind of organization of energies and events. To it the name of "actuality" or "Wirklichkeit" may appropriately be applied.

The third type of process, cognitive activity, understanding, *Verstehen,* is a very special form of creative or constructive activity, whose central feature is conceptualized consciousness or *systematized experience*. In this process a type of individuality is created known as a *self*. A self or person is a being which *possesses* experience, that is, which has appropriated other processes through memory and conceptual construction. These other processes can now serve as *motivation*. Here Socrates' contrast is instructive—the contrast between the artist who creates but fails to understand what he has created and how he has done it, and the philosopher who understands beauty and art, though he creates neither. Understanding is necessarily the work of a self or person, but this fact does not imply that the self precedes the process. The self is the fulfillment of the experiencing process, not a prior being.

Having distinguished these three familiar types of process, I am now prepared to interpret what is called "the historical process." I believe that history, in the categorial sense, is no process at all, but the field of human experience out of which histories can be taken. There are careers and stories, some historical others not. These stories and careers are finite, individual processes; in each there is a beginning, middle, and end. Whether the end be an abrupt terminus or, as it should be in a "good" story, a culmination of a career, a story is an attempt to understand a career. It unites with the process of understanding either a natural career of generation and destruction (as, for example, of a river valley) or a construction (as, for example, of an empire). There is individuality both in the career and in the telling of it. But when we speak of *the* historical process and regard it as a special ontological problem, we are faced with an entirely different subject matter. For history in this comprehensive sense is not a story but the matrix of all true or false stories. It is the field of human experience, which is no one's experience. There is in it no inherent perspective, no organized structure such as a story has or as is embodied in any particular "course of events." It is temporal, but not itself a course of events. It's beginnings and end are lost in darkness; it cannot be grasped as a whole. Past and future, the essential categories of history, are relative to a shifting present. All events happen in the present, unless they are historically irrelevant, uneventful. To take a trivial example: you know as well as I do that between my birth and death there has been taking place a long physical process of heartbeats, respirations, and digestions. Very few of these heartbeats took place in any present whatsoever; a somewhat larger number of my respirations entered into my presence, that of my physician, or that of my acquaintances; and a still larger number of my digestions, the poorer ones, were present. But on the whole all this is an unhistorical process, a chain of events that is neither meaningless nor unintelligible, but that is insignificant, endured but not experienced, lived but not recalled. The present is an ontological field, by no means specious; it is the locus of human experiencing, the gathering of meanings. The various interests which it generates furnish the perspective for all histories, and the being of *the* past. For *the* past is not the sum total of events that have happened, nor even the sum total of events that once were present; it is the past of a present subject to the changes which the present works upon it. However, though history begins in the present, it is not true that all histories are histories of the present. A history is not even *merely* of the past, for in throwing the past into perspective with the present, it also generates a prospection. It anticipates a future. Though memory be the primary, positive pole of history, there is always an implicit reference to prophecy, to the negative pole of history. For without a past, no one has a future. What was and what may be are the beings that make of the present a duration, and without duration the present would not be.

For these reasons I cannot agree with Donald Williams who regards history as an "ordinary" temporal structure, based simply on the four-dimensional continuum. To him the "perfect or complete history" would be the complete record of human events, possibly nonhuman events, too. This is a fantastic conception of the historical idea. God's "mind" has sometimes been pictured as such a perfect storehouse for all events, but I am sure that even God records only human "deeds," and deeds are already a highly selected set of events, revealing God's interests. History is not chronology nor a hall of records. The whole story of human learning by experience, if it be a story at all, is a very difficult process to conceive and is continually retold. Historians may be tempted, as all men are, to see in it a linear progress, or a series of cycles, or a growth of reason, freedom or what not. I need not recall the history of philosophies of history. But I need to call attention to the fact that there is among ontologists, even more than among historiographers, a serious effort to understand historical being, and to the fact that this effort meets with serious obstacles.

It is not difficult to understand why human beings should regard their historical being as the most important dimension of their being. But it is paradoxical that their search for importance brings with it a sense of insecurity, an understanding of the central importance of an ever-shifting, contingent present. In their attempt to anchor the present and to master the future, men must take account of all three types of process of which I have been telling. But though all three play their roles in history, they do not play together. Historical being is not a synthesis or harmony of processes; it is a confusion, not a fusion. It seems to be a storehouse for an endless number of histories; to understand the structure of the whole remains an elusive task.

The fact that the past will not stay put is good evidence that it has not passed out of being. Some events pass out and are lost in the irrecoverable void; others get re-presented. What was, may again be in some process or other. And its recoverability proves that it did not become nonbeing when it left the present. As memory grows, as the storehouse enlarges, historical understanding becomes increasingly complicated. The growing past means a more problematic present, and it puts a greater responsibility on the historian. For a historian is not free to create the past; he must disclose or discover it in the resources of the present. He must keep a double perspective in view: on the one hand, he must know what was, and on the other, he must know what past is relevant. No history without evaluation, and no evaluation without an *actual*, present perspective. Thus historical understanding is far more complicated than physical science of temporal being. It takes the imagination close to that dangerous, adventurous land of nonbeing. It leads to the "once upon a time" and to the "utopia." To these no man's lands human beings are not strangers, but in them they lose their understanding. Bringing these nonbeings into the present is one of man's favorite processes of construction. But this field of imaginary being, a most attractive field, is not the historian's concern; and I, too, shall leave it for another essay.

1. A. P. Ushenko, *Power and Events* (Princeton, Princeton University Press, 1949), p. 197.

WALTER T. STACE

Time and Eternity

The critic of [our] conceptions may argue in the following manner.
It is supposed, he will say, that there exists in mystical intuition
a kind of experience which is inherently incapable of being conceptualized. But this is, in the first place, impossible. And in
the second place, even if it were possible, it would imply that that
experience is so completely cut off from the rest of human experience that the two will stand in no relation at all. This in turn
will imply that God is so "utterly other" that there is no relation
whatever between God and the world. Further unacceptable implications will also be involved, for instance, that there cannot be
any relation of similarity between the experience of one mystic
and that of another, nor even between two mystical experiences of
the same person. All this is not only unacceptable, but strictly
unthinkable, inconceivable, and therefore impossible.

We must examine these contentions with great care. We shall
find that they lead us to the conception of two distinct dimensions
or orders of being, the order of time and the order of eternity.

Why, first of all, is it supposed that there could not be an experience which is inherently incapable of being enmeshed in concepts? The reason given will be that if there be any experience, datum, or thing of any kind whatever before the mind, it must be related in some way to the other experiences of the same mind. It must at least be either like or unlike those experiences, that is, it must bear to them the relations of similarity or dissimiliarity. It must also be distinguishable from them, that is, it must bear to them the relation of difference. But whatever has relations is conceptualizable, since to know a thing's relations is to know its concept. More precisely, to have a concept of anything means no more than to know to what other things it bears the relation of similarity. The concept of a triangle is formed by noting the points in which all triangles resemble one another, namely in being bounded by three straight lines. Thus if the mystic knows the resemblances between the various occasions on which he has the mystic experience, and their differences from his ordinary experiences of daily life, he has already in this knowledge a concept of them. This is reflected in the very fact that he uses such words as "mystical," "numinous," and even "experience" of them. These are all concepts. They all connote resemblances and differences between his mystical and his other experiences. Indeed even to say that his experience is unconceptualizable is to apply a concept to it, since it connotes a resemblance between different occasions of the experience, and a difference between it and other experiences. If a man could have one set of experiences without any relation to his other experiences, this would mean that the two sets of experiences could not be within the unity of the same mind. Moreover, if there were a being or existence out of all relation to the other beings and existences of the world, then it could not be part of the universe, since the universe simply *is* the totality of all interrelated and interconnected things.

We shall have to point out later that God is not a *part* of the universe, one thing among other things and standing in relations with them. For this would involve His otherness to them and would accordingly destroy His infinity. For the moment we may make a partial answer to the above criticism by pointing out that it relies on a use of the word "experience" which is inapplicable to the case in hand. By an experience we ordinarily mean something which is before the mind or present to it. This involves a distinction between the mind and its experience or object. Thus the color or smell is "there," and I, who cognize it, am different from it. Moreover one color is like another, and is unlike a smell. In all such experiences, therefore, the concept comes into play. But the mystic experience is not of this kind. For there is in it no division of mind from its object, nor any other distinction between this and that. It is a flawless indivisible unity, which gives no foothold for the concept. This is what it is *in itself.* It is true that, if it is looked at *from the outside,* as for example it is by the mystic himself when he returns to the level of his everyday or temporal experience, then it will be different from that ordinary experience, and will be conceptually distinguished as the mystical from the nonmystical. In short, conceptualization implies the distinction between subject and object as well as other distinctions, and the religious experience is nonconceptualizable because no such distinctions exist in it.

But it will be said that all this implies a God who stands in no relation to the world at all, and for obvious reasons this is impossible. We have therefore to discuss the problem of the relation of God to the world. Now it follows from all that has been said that when we speak of God having some relation to the world our language must be symbolic only. "God is related to the world" is a proposition about God, and is therefore false if it is taken in a literal sense. That no predicates apply to God is a statement which must be understood as including relations among predicates. To see that this must be so we have only to see that the attribution of relations to God leads to the same sort of contradictions and absurdities as does the attribution of qualities. It is inconsistent, for example, with God's infinity. For a relation implies at least two terms between which the relation holds. In this case the two terms would be God and the world. But if the world is other than God, then God is limited by the world, and is not infinite. He is not "that than which there is no other."

We may look at the various attempts which have been made in different religions to state or conceive the relations between God and the world. We shall find that, if taken literally, they are all impossible and absurd. Space relations, time relations, and causal relations have been those which have been most commonly implied in these conceptions. Men began perhaps with spatial relations. God was above the sky, above the stars, or outside the spherical universe. It would be generally recognized today that any such conception could be only symbolical. To this succeeded the notion that God is "omnipresent." This was taken quite literally by Newton who thought that space was God's "sensorium," that God is spread all through it, so that the planets are actually moving through the space occupied by God's mind. No doubt the metaphor of omnipresence has a meaning, but it can hardly be anything so crude as this. We should hold that it is a metaphor for God's infinity, according to which conception space cannot be outside of God—that is, other to God—nor can any part of it be outside Him. Evidently we cannot conceive the relation between God and the world as a spatial one.

A time relation between God and the world finds expression in the phrase that God is "before all the worlds," and is also implied by the common conception that God created the world at some moment in time. However we conceive it, a temporal relation of God to the world puts God in the time-stream, makes Him part of the natural order, a temporal being. According to some theologians, the conclusion that God is in the time-stream is not to be drawn, because the creation of time was part of the creation of the world. God created time, along with the world which exists in it. But this obviously involves contradictions. If the creation was a temporal act at all—and so it must be conceived if we are to take any of these ideas literally—then there was a moment *in* time at which the world came into being, and before that there was a time when it was not in being.

A causal relation between God and the world has been, on the whole, the most common conception. It is implied by the doctrine of creation. God is the cause, the world is the effect. Since a causal relation means a succession of cause and effect in time, this involves the same difficulties as those set out in the last paragraph. It either places God in the time-stream, or it involves contradictions in its concept of time. It also destroys the infinity of God, since in any causal relation the effect is other than the cause.[1] And if it be said that God's causality is to be understood differently from the ordinary causality which we find in the created world, as for example the causing of ice by cold, this is to admit our point, namely that none of these relations, temporal, spatial, or causal, as applied to God's relation to the world, can be taken literally, but that all such language is symbolical in character.

In Hinduism, God's relation to the world is not conceived as creation, but as manifestation. This, however, can be understood only by the use of some metaphor. God is not then "before" the world, but "behind" it. He is that which is behind the veil of

Maya, though possibly He shines through the veil as a lamp shines through the lamp shade which hides it. But "behind" is a spatial metaphor just as "before" is a temporal one. Sometimes, indeed, the notion of manifestation is conceived by means of the ideas conveyed by the words "form" or "aspect." Brahman takes on the form or aspect of being the world, as carbon takes on the form of diamond, or as energy takes on the forms of light, heat, or electricity. Plainly all such ideas are metaphorical. If taken literally, they contradict the infinity of Brahman. Brahman is "the One without a second." Therefore the world cannot be other than God, even in the sense in which a form of something is other than the thing when it is not in that form. The world, in Hinduism, *is* Brahman. But also the world is *not* Brahman, because the appearance, the illusion, is not the reality, because the world is in time and space, while Brahman is "above time, above space," and because the world is marked by manyness and division of one thing from another, whereas there is no division in the being of Brahman. Thus the contradiction involved in the conception of manifestation, if taken in any literal way, is explicit.

Thus all conceptions of the relation between God and the world, which have been commonly affirmed by the religious consciousness, must be taken as no more than metaphors, since to take them literally leads to contradictions. And the conclusion is that the very idea of relation, as holding between God and the world, is metaphorical. It might perhaps be said that God may have some relation to the world other than those which we have just examined, or even some relation of which the human mind is incapable of conceiving. What we are striving to show, however, is that to assert any kind of relation at all between God and the world, known or unknown, conceivable or inconceivable, is of necessity to use language which cannot be literal but must be metaphorical only. For any relation whatever, in as much as it would imply that the world is other than God, would destroy His infinity. It would also conflict with that intuition of God's relationlessness which is a part and parcel of the religious consciousness everywhere. The same conclusion is implied by the conception of the negative divine, which, as we have seen, is an essential element of the religious consciousness. For according to that conception, no predicates, and therefore no relational predicates, can be applied to the Ultimate.

The conclusion is that any proposition asserting any relation between God and the world is a symbolic proposition and not a literal truth. If the word relation be taken in a literal sense, then God has no relation to the world. And this is what, on other grounds, we ought to have expected. For if God were related to the things in the world, then He would Himself be one among other things. He would be a part of the universe, a part of the natural order. He would be a natural, not a supernatural, being. For the natural order is to be defined as the totality of things— whether these things be minds or material things—which are linked into a single system by relations. Yet though we may say that the word relation, as used of God, is a metaphor, we are bound— unless we are to be charged with the fault of using "mere" metaphor—to say what this metaphor means in terms of the actual religious experience. What do the metaphors of creation, manifestation, being before the world, or behind it, mean? And the answers to these questions have still to be found.

But in order to develop our conceptions we will continue for the moment to speak in metaphorical language. We will take our metaphor from the lines of T. S. Eliot:

> "To apprehend
> The point of intersection of the timeless
> With time is an occupation for the saint."[2]

There are two orders, the natural order, which is the order of time, and the divine order, which is the order of eternity. In the moment of mystic illumination the two orders intersect, so that that moment belongs to both orders. The image of the intersecting straight lines breaks down in one respect. Two physical straight lines intersect at only one point, and then diverge. But we have to suppose that, in some way, every moment of time is an intersection of the divine order with the natural order. But if every moment of time is thus in fact traversed by the line of the divine dimension, it is only in the rare moment of illumination in the life of the saint that this is clearly apprehended and fully realized.

Within that single moment of time are enclosed all eternity and all infinity. This is the meaning of Blake's words:

> "To see the world in a grain of sand,
> And a heaven in a wild flower,
> Hold infinity in the palm of your hand,
> And eternity in an hour."[3]

It is a commonplace that eternity is not an endless prolongation of time, has nothing to do with time. Eternity is a characteristic of the mystical experience. The word eternity doubtless meant originally endlessness of time, which must count, therefore, as its literal meaning. But in its religious and metaphysical use it is a metaphor for the characteristic of the experience. For in that experience time drops away and is no more seen. The same is true of infinity. This does not mean the endlessness of a series. The mystic illumination is infinite in itself because there is nothing outside it, because there is within it no this or that, no limiting otherness. And the word infinity, originally and literally meaning the endlessness of a series, is now used as a metaphor for this. And that the experience is eternal, that is to say timeless, also follows from the fact that there are in it no divisions or relations. For there cannot be time where there are no divisions and relations of "before" and "after." We have spoken of the infinity and eternity of the divine moment in the experience of the saint. But we may also speak in the same terms of the infinity and eternity of God. For these two are identical.

The eternal moment, being a point of intersection, can be looked at either from within or from without. Since it belongs to both orders, it is both temporal and eternal. Looked at internally—that is as the mystic himself sees it in that moment—it is infinite and eternal. Looked at from the outside—as it is seen, not only by all of us in our normal consciousness, but by the mystic himself when he has passed out of it into the time-order, and looks back upon it in memory—looked at thus externally it is a moment in time. From within it is God. For it is not a consciousness of God, a divided consciousness wherein the mystic as subject stands over against Deity as object. It is the immanence of God Himself in the soul. But, as it is looked at from the outside, its content is merely a passing state of the mind of the mystic.

Naturalism is the philosophy which asserts the sole reality of the natural order, and denies the reality of the divine order. That is, it looks at the divine moment only externally. The content, the inner filling, of the moment is then for it illusion. Not that it denies that the moment occurs as a fact in time. Not that it denies that the saint has the experience which he says he has. But the experience is seen as merely subjective, that is, illusory. God is then an illusion.

But there is also necessarily an opposite kind of illusionism. For if we take our stand within the moment itself, it is then the world, the natural order, which is illusion. For the content of the moment is the infinite, and outside the infinite there is nothing. The world is therefore nothing. The content of the moment is also eternity, and there is therefore outside it no time. Hence arises that acosmism, that denial of the reality of the world, which is associated with mysticism and with those systems of metaphysics which have their origin in mysticism. Acosmism reaches its highest point in the religious philosophies of India with their doctrine of the world as maya. In the West it appears in philosophies like that of Bradley. Bradley is only dimly aware of the mystical character of his own philosophy, and supposes himself to be in general a rationalist. But his remark in the introduction to his book *Appearance and Reality* that philosophy is "a satisfaction of what may be called the mystical side of our nature," reveals the secret sources of his thought. For him time and space and the world are only "appearance," not reality. Appearance is a word which is not so extreme as illusion. Yet it is only a lesser degree of the same denial of the reality of the world. All philosophies which declare that time, space, and the world, are unreal, or half real, or phenomenal, or appearances, or illusion, have their roots in mysticism. For the proposition "the world is unreal" is a mystical proposition, not a factual proposition. It derives from the mystical vision of the eternal and infinite moment outside which there is no other and therefore no world, no space, no time. But, for the majority of so-called and self-styled rationalistic philosophers, the divine moment is so deeply buried in their subconscious that they are only dimly aware of it and suppose that their conclusions are the result of logical argument. In them the mystical wells up from the depths to the surface consciousness, where it is then rationalized.

The mystic lives in both orders, that of eternity and that of time. He passes from one to the other. This is also true of other men in the degree in which the mystic consciousness is developed in them. But this dual existence gives rise to confusion of the one order with the other. For the pure mystic consciousness there is no world at all. It is pure illusion. For the pure natural consciousness there is no God and no divine. They are entirely illusory. But because men live in both orders the two extremes of illusionism, atheism and acosmism, are rarely met with—though of course atheism is much the commoner. When the great mystic passes back from the order of eternity into the order of time, the world which has been, in that pure moment, a total illusion, reappears and forces itself upon him. It again asserts its reality. Yet the memory and influence of that tremendous moment are still upon him, and cause him to attribute to the world a shadowy half-reality. Hence arises the notion of *degrees* of reality, which is so common in philosophies like those of the Vedanta, Bradley, and Hegel, and which is so puzzling to the naturalistically minded man. According to this conception, one thing can be more real than another. Only the Ultimate—which is the content of the pure mystic moment— is absolutely real. Other things are more or less real according as they are nearer or further away from the divine order.

Since there are two orders of being, there are therefore two solutions of every metaphysical problem, the naturalistic solution and the mystical solution. Each is, in its own right, absolute and final. They seem to contradict one another, but this contradiction occurs only as a result of the confusion between the two orders. If the divine order is, in the minds of men, as it almost always is, brought down into the natural order and *supposed to be a part of it,* then a contradiction arises. God is thought to be one being among other beings, though He may be the cause of these other beings. His existence then becomes a superstition against which the scientist, the naturalist, or the philosopher has to fight. This being cannot be found anywhere among other beings either by telescopes or by rational arguments or inferences from the other beings. This confusion, this taking of the eternal order for a part of the natural order, is the source of all skepticism, and of the whole conflict between science, or scientific naturalism, and religion. For as soon as the divine is thus put within the natural order it is seen that it cannot be found there, that it does not exist there; and so its reality is denied. All efforts to compromise between science (or philosophy) and religion are puerile attempts to divide the world of existence, the natural order, into areas, of which one is to be assigned to science, the other to religion. The true way to resolve the conflict is to realize the difference of the two orders. It is then possible to give to each the *whole* of what it claims and not merely some ungenerously clipped off portion.

In this conception of the intersection of the divine and natural there is a point which is at present obscure. We cannot hold that the divine intersects the natural only at that one point which is the consciousness of the saint. We must surely believe that the divine interpenetrates the natural everywhere. The divine order must intersect the temporal order at every moment of time and at every point of space. For this is demanded by the intuition of the "omnipresence" of God. We cannot at present see how this is possible. We see how the intersection occurs in the moment of human mystical illumination, and since this moment is not only present in the great mystic, but in all men, we may say that we see—at least dimly—how it occurs throughout that area of the natural world which is the human mind. But what is to be said of animals and plants? And what of inanimate objects, such as rocks and metals? Mr. Gandhi is reported to have said "God is in the stone." This is, of course, religious language, and is therefore symbolical. (To suppose that it is literally true would mean that God is in the stone in the same sense as silica or feldspar are in the stone.) But if it is not to be mere metaphor, some symbolized meaning must be given to it. And the question is, what meaning? Of how God is in the human heart we know something from our own inner experience. But how is God in the stone? How does the eternal order intersect the natural order at the space-time point where the stone is?

It may be said that God's being in the stone is a pantheistic doctrine, not acceptable to Christianity. But this would be a mistake. Pantheism is the error that God is *only* in the world, and that He is not transcendent of it. And if we reject pantheism it should not be on the ground that we deny God's immanence everywhere and in everything, but rather on the ground that although God is immanent everywhere, at every point of space and moment of time—which is the meaning of His omnipresence—He is also transcendent. And, in the conception of a divine intersection of the natural order, the immanence of God is represented by the assertion that the intersection takes place at every point, while His transcendence is represented by the fact that the divine and eternal is a wholly different order or dimension from the natural.

Hence we still have the question how God can be in the stone. We do not, I believe, know enough to give any sort of confident answer. I will give the answer which I believe to be true, while admitting its speculative character. It seems probable that, as the panpsychistic philosophy of Whitehead has suggested, there is no distinction, except one of degree, between the organic and inorganic, or between life and mind. Alexander's doctrine of emergent evolution supposed the following levels of emergence—space-time, inorganic matter, life (found without consciousness in plants) , and mind or consciousness. This may well be correct, but Alexander supposed an absolute break between each of the levels. The organic philosophy of Whitehead would suppose, on the contrary, that there is no such break. There is continuity. The common thread running throughout the series is life. All things are living. Even an electron is a very low-grade organism, a living being. The essence of its being, as of every being, is feeling or experience, although in the preanimal levels the feelings and experiences are blind and unconscious. This is supported by many analogies, and also by some "scientific" considerations. For instance, it makes possible an explanation of how life appeared on the earth out of previous "inorganic" existences. There is also the fact that in the virus we have a being which exhibits some of the characteristics of the organic and some of the characteristics of the inorganic, suggesting that it is not possible to draw a sharp line between the two. We may then well suppose that what we call the deadness of inorganic existences is but a deep hypnotic sleep of their consciousness.

If we combine this suggestion with another, which has already been made in these pages, we can perhaps obtain some light on our problem. This other suggestion was that, in those men who are not what are commonly called mystics, the divine moment lies in the subconscious, far down in some, nearer to the surface in others. In the great mystic it has emerged into the full light of conscious mentality. In common men it exists not far from the surface, so that it stirs the surface and appears there as dim religious feeling, which can be evoked and enhanced—that is, drawn nearer to the surface—by the symbolic language of religion and especially by the language of the mystic. Experiments in hypnosis plainly show not only that there are the conscious and the unconscious, but that there are also levels of unconsciousness. We easily accept the fact that there are degrees of consciousness. A man's mind may be alertly conscious or only dimly aware of things. A state of dreamy or drowsy awareness passes by degrees into sleep. But we are apt to suppose that unconsciousness is without degrees, that it is simply a total absence of consciousness. But even the common fact that one sleep may be deeper than another should dissipate this belief. And the facts of hypnosis make it certain that it is false. There are deeper and deeper levels of hypnosis, greater and lesser darknesses, darkness below darkness. It may well be that what we call the life of the plant is but a level of the hypnotic sleep of consciousness lower than is ever found in the animal, and that in the metal and the rock the darkness is deeper still, but that, even there, a blind unconscious mentality exists. Perhaps, then, in the plant and the metal the divine moment exists, utterly submerged. The point of intersection is there, buried in the blackness of the night of that metallic consciousness, or that plant consciousness, which we can only dimly apprehend as akin to hypnotic or sleep states in ourselves. And there, too, perhaps the eternal moment awaits that evolutionary liberation from the darkness, that passage into the light, which has already come in some degree to man, and, in a supreme degree, to mystic man.

We may now try to answer some of the questions which, as we saw, were pressing upon us. What is the meaning of the metaphor of intersection? This intersection means precisely what the eternal moment is experienced to be. It is one and the same human consciousness which experiences both the temporal or natural world and that eternal and infinite order which is disclosed in mystical illumination. Thus this identity of eternity with a temporal moment is an actual experienced fact, and this fact is what is metaphorically represented by the image of intersection.

What relation does one eternal moment bear to another— whether the two which we compare belong to the mind-stream of the same man, or to the mind-streams of two different men? To this, as to all religious or metaphysical questions, there are two different answers, according as we take our stand within the moment or outside it. From the outside, we shall say that one such moment bears to another the relation of resemblance, and also no doubt some relations of nonresemblance. Thus what one mystic reports resembles what another reports in most ways, but there may be some differences. This result seems to lead to embarrassment, because it introduces relations into what purports to be relationless, and thereby renders the mystic experience a proper subject matter for concepts and predicates. For to say that experience A is like experience B is to assert a common element as between them and therefore the possibility of a concept. And it is in this way that in fact we get such concepts as "mystical" and "numinous."

But obviously if we thus start our inquiry from the naturalistic standpoint we come out with a naturalistic conclusion. The eternal moment is then a point in the line of time, and so must be related to other such points. But looked at from within the point, these questions do not arise. Since the point is the infinite and eternal, there is no *other* point to which it can bear a relation. But, it will be said, even the mystic cannot deny that there are other mystics, or that he himself at other times has had, or may have, other mystical experiences, and that there must be relations of likeness or unlikeness between his own different experiences, and between the experiences of different mystics. This is quite true. But it is true because the mystic is himself a thing among other things, a person among other persons, an occupant of the time-order, traveling along with other persons and things in the stream of time. He belongs—as of course all men do and, in some sense, all things —to both orders. And his experience is, from this external standpoint, a point in time for him as well as for us. But if we persist in asking whether, if we take our stand within the eternal moment itself, all this must not still remain true, the answer is, no; because in that experience there is no subject and no object, and as the mystic is therein identical with God, so he is therein identical with all other mystics, and his mystic experience is identical with all other mystic experiences, whether of himself or another, and this moment of time is identical with all other moments of time. And hence there is, from within, no relation at all between one mystic experience and another, and therefore no likeness or unlikeness, and therefore no concept. The time-order is a line, and we have thought of the religious moment under the image of its intersection with another line. But the image fails, as all images do. For it is only from the external standpoint that there is a multiplicity of religious moments represented by the multiplicity of points in the line. In itself the eternal moment is single. For it is the one God. It is one self-identical point; but it is a point which is everywhere, coextensive with the universe.

We may now return to the question of God's relation to the world. Since God and the eternal moment are one, whatever may be said of the relation of the eternal moment to the world may be said of the relation of God to the world. In the intersection of the two orders God is the eternal, the infinite, the divine order. God as He is in Himself, as transcendent, is that order taken alone. God as He is in the world, as immanent, is the intersection of the two orders. The world as it is in itself is the time-order taken alone. And as at a point of intersection there are two coincident points, belonging each to one of the intersecting lines, which are nevertheless one point, so God and the world are both two and one, distinct and identical. We find this identity in difference of God and the world in all those philosophies which have their source in mysticism. In Bradley's metaphysics the Absolute, being infinite, has nothing outside it. The world therefore cannot fall outside it. The world is the Absolute. Nevertheless the Absolute is different from the world, for in it there is no space, no time, no relation, no division, these being attributable only to the world. In the Vedanta also Brahman both is, and is not, the world. In the philosophy of Spinoza the attributes, which are the world, *constitute* the Substance. And yet Substance is something other than the attributes.

We may say also that, from the standpoint of time, God is in relation to the world. He is omnipresent in it. But from the standpoint of the eternal, which is the inner view of the divine moment, God has no relations either within Himself or with other beings, or with the world.

From Walter T. Stace, *Time and Eternity* (Princeton, Princeton University Press, 1955), pp. 69–85; reprinted with permission.

1. It is true that there are identity theories of causation, according to which cause and effect are identical. But they are patently absurd. They are compelled to maintain that cause and effect are different "forms" or "aspects" of the same identical thing. But then the difference between cause and effect reappears as a difference of form or aspect. There may be some intelligible sense in which charcoal and diamond are two forms of carbon, but that charcoal is not the same thing as diamond will be discovered if you try to sell it to a jeweler.

2. T. S. Eliot, *The Dry Salvages.*

3. William Blake.

PAUL WEISS

The New Outlook

This is a book in philosophy. As a philosophic work should, it attempts to articulate a vision of the whole of things. This means it must run counter to the temper not only of critics of philosophy, but of many contemporary philosophers as well. Every one of us, in these last decades, has often heard the complaint that the world of knowledge has grown enormously, and that it is now too big for any one to envisage. Too many of us have too quickly said that it is futile to hope that the meaning of the whole, or even of man's place within it, can be grasped by anyone. We must be content, it has been supposed, to master limited branches of knowledge, to try to learn exactly what is the case here or there, and should give up the attempt to say something more. There seemed to be no real fear that such self-restraint might turn us into partial men. Encyclopedias and staff conferences, surveys and texts, it was felt, could bring all together, and in harmony. We were confident that we needed nothing more than co-operation, interchange and communication to help us produce our well-made parts one with the other, and interrelate them to give us a clearer, more lasting, a better articulated account of the whole. As a consequence, many today are somewhat content to be community thinkers, union men, who know how to work in tandem.

It seems safe to say that the advances made in recent years in medicine and war, in psychology and sociology are in good part traceable to the fact that we have specialized together. But it is equally safe to say that the achievements depended in part on our refusal to use our critical powers to the full. A world of experts, each concerned with asserting only what he really knows, is a world of men who must accept without cavil what the other experts offer to them as data, method and outcome or it is a world of separated items, cut off from all else. Such experts practice what none is willing to preach. Each naïvely accepts what other experts affirm of their different specialties. On the one side they accept nothing but what they can themselves certify, and on the other embrace, with equal confidence, that which they confessedly could not possibly certify. But this is to abandon the right to ask if others are wrong in result, method and value, to wonder if their frames are wide enough, their methods sound enough, their values rich enough for the world in which we all live. By putting the actual failure or inadequacy of other disciplines outside the reach of real questioning, he denies himself the opportunity of knowing whether or not they are really sound, and whether or not they will ever betray us. To know this much we must know something other than what they report of themselves.

It is fairly safe to say that the successes of our modern ways of thought depend in good part on the chance that the methods and outcomes of the different specialized inquiries happen for the time to fit together; when parts are dealt with in independence of one another, discords sooner or later, and almost inevitably, arise among them. Even now they are sometimes found to conflict, and surely do not now form a single whole. The realms of specialized knowledge are not yet integrated. There are methods and results in almost every vigorous science which no one has made cohere with the rest. Nor has anyone ever related the achievements and methods of all the sciences to one another, or brought the sciences into harmony with history, law and sociology; and what has been discerned by the poets, the mystics, the philosophers is still far from being united with what has been learned elsewhere.

But, it will perhaps be said, this is as it should be. Every living enterprise is incomplete; its problems are its nerve ends, its growth tips. It would be foolhardy to force the different disciplines into harmony now, to try to get rid of the gaps in and between them at once. The critical powers, of course, should not be suspended; nor should they be allowed to destroy the tolerance on which co-operative inquiry depends. We should be patient. The occasional breaks and disharmonies in and between the different disciplines will soon, and surely must eventually be overcome. Knowledge is accumulative and grows in cohesiveness as it grows in magnitude. Ignorance, and ignorance alone, is what keeps honest inquiring men apart.

There is force in this reply. We have a right to expect, as we progress in our mastery of the world and of ourselves, that what we know will form a more solid block than it now does. Yet, what might, even at the end of an inquiry, have the status of knowledge in that inquiry, may not have that status when outside it or when made part of a different inquiry. There are certainties in some disciplines and only probabilities in others; some cherish local truths while others specialize in cosmic ones. Their different claims must be assigned different weights; account must be taken of their different methods and ranges. What we call knowledge in physics is not exactly what we call knowledge in history or philosophy or perhaps even biology. The items in the one discipline are obtained along a different route and must meet criteria and be certified in ways not relevant to the items in other disciplines. It makes no difference whether or not we take one of the disciplines as the model for the others; or whether or not we look outside them all for some standard in terms of which we can determine what is and what is not knowledge. In either case we are forced to evaluate and perhaps modify or qualify the claims which each, even at the end of its road, takes to be reliable and true. Some, and perhaps even all of a given discipline's certified truths might have to be altered if they are to be brought into harmony with the certified truths of other inquiries. Unless we can somehow stand outside all disciplines, unless we can somehow use common principles, categories, values, we cannot hope to adjudicate authoritatively the claims which each discipline makes within its own framework; we can therefore have no surety that its results will ever form an harmonious single body of knowledge.

It seemed for a time as if this challenge would be accepted in a most promising way. A group of well-trained, meticulous, energetic "analytic" philosophers seemed willing to take as their task the discovery of criteria and principles by means of which the efforts and outcomes of the different disciplines would be evaluated and harmonized. Bold, perhaps even a little arrogant and contemptuous of older ways, these thinkers were nevertheless at once modest and cautious. They did not take themselves to be superior to other investigators. Yet rather rapidly they turned themselves into another race of specialists having the restricted task of clarifying the intent or methodology or usages of other specialists. They became the masters of a new discipline resulting from a fresh union of modern logic, linguistics and methodology, to be used to promote or clarify other inquiries. The gathering of data they left to others; it was not their task they thought to try to add more facts to those which the empirical sciences provided. They sought only to occupy themselves with a study of the structures, procedures, implications, grammar that are inevitably exhibited in every sound inquiry, claiming that nothing was sensible or legitimate unless it was so certifiable by the methods sound inquiries endorsed.

These men accomplished much. But they could not do all that needs be done if knowledge is to make one exhaustive, coherent whole. For that, their specialty would have to be all-encompassing. Not only the methods, assertions, structures, but the values and the results of the various disciplines, need evaluation. Ends as well as means must be critically examined. One must know not only how sound procedures are, but what place the results can have within a comprehensive whole. But then something must be known of the nature of that whole. One must no longer be content to be one among many inquiries; one must also be a one for them, over against them, including them and much else besides.

No one of course knows everything. No one even knows one limited field exhaustively. Yet if we did not somehow grasp the nature of all there is, we would not be able to have specialties, nor could we deal adequately with their different claims and contributions. Only if we know what it is to be a man can we engage in co-ordinate investigations into his nature; only if we know what it is to be a man can we estimate the rival claims of doctors, biologists, psychologists, anthropologists and the rest. Only if we know what it is to be, to inquire, to know, can we recognize that we are dealing with different phases of the same object, and can know how to bring together the different results that were obtained along different routes of investigation. Before, while, and after we specialize we have, and must have, a grasp of the whole, vague, blurred, even incoherent though it may be. To ignore that whole is to ignore our roots, to misunderstand our aims, to lose our basic tests. It is to forget that we engaged in limited inquiries in order to understand the whole of things from many independent and we trust convergent sides. It is to adopt the prejudice that only the limited and piecemeal is significant and intelligible, and that without any guidance it will inevitably form one seamless unity. It is to be so impatient to get down to work that no time is left to ask what it is that is being sought, and why. If we are to engage in limited enterprises, if we are to know what they diversely seek and express, if we are to understand what contribution they can make to the enterprise of life and learning, we must somehow take account of all there is and can be known. Whether we wish it or not, we must, we do think cosmically. Our choice is only to do it uncritically, precipitately moving to the body of some limited enterprise and vainly trying to remain there always, or critically, by taking some thought of where we start and ought to end, and in a sense always are.

No matter how much this last observation be softened, it can I fear never be entirely freed from the smell of paradox and dogmatism, presumption and foolhardiness and of decayed and discarded systems of the past. There is something repugnant in the temper of the grand philosophers, the system builders, the wholesale thinkers. They sound like gods and yet are only men. Even the best of them contradict themselves and one another, omit much that should have been included, and at crucial points are most unclear and unreliable. Their errors are fabulous—but so is their vision. They leave us with no alternative but to try ourselves to understand the real world in a way they could not. This is possible for they taught us by their achievements and by their failures something of what we ought to say and what we ought to avoid. And also we have at our disposal, as they unfortunately did not, such excellent guides and instruments as the history of later thought, modern science, poetry, music, painting, analysis and logic.

There are today, I think, signs of a renewed interest in fundamental questions on part of many thinkers. There is a new spirit just beginning to stir, transforming the world of ideas. Occupied primarily in getting a firm grip on reality, it has so far ignored the question of how to judge and adjudicate the various specialized inquiries. These must eventually look to it, and it to them. But first it must come to clearer and more systematic expression. What now seems certain is that a re-examination of fundamentals will force us to entertain a view of ourselves and of the world which is quite different from that entertained in the past.

It is time for the new spirit to pervade our lives. We must become at once more bold and humble, more catholic and cautious, freer and more disciplined than before. For too long a time prejudice has been allowed to narrow our perspectives; for too long a time impatience has made us receptive to ideals and values inappropriate to our full being and the world. We need a new viable systematic philosophy, which unlike those of the past, is alert to the advances in modern logic and science, metaphysics and theology, history and the arts, and thus can be more abreast of the world in which we live.

One of the objectives of the present work is to outline the nature of this new philosophy. Unfortunately I did not myself discern even its main features until quite late, and then only after I had struggled through the writing of three books. Reflections on the implications of the first of these drove me on to the second, and this in turn led to the third. The present book in a way continues the progress. An independent venture, it systematizes while it purges, moves beyond while it takes advantage of the insights and achievements of the previous works.

The first of those books, *Reality,* presented a systematic account of what I took to be the essential features of both knowledge and nature. It maintained that knowledge and nature presupposed one another, making the philosophic enterprise a circle, but one large enough to encompass all forms of thought and existence. Every item of knowledge and being was seen to be incomplete, since there was something beyond it, real and obstinate, which it needed and sought. The book made an effort also to work, not as Russell does with a minimum vocabulary, or as others do, with a minimum number of acceptable ideas or beliefs, but with a minimum number of presuppositions. It tried in fact to avoid taking for granted anything outside the system, except of course the world which that system portrayed. The world it knew was not philosophy; but philosophy, it also knew, had to omit nothing of the essence of the world.

It is sound, I still think, to hold that philosophy is a circle, that every item in thought and in being is incomplete, and that a good philosophic account presupposes nothing beyond its capacity to encompass conceptually. It is sound too, I think, to maintain, as was done in *Reality,* that each thing necessarily points to all the others, as the object of its needs, what it must master or take account of in order to be complete. The rest of the world is its final cause, what must be considered if we are to understand the things nature does and why it acts as it does. But the point needs supplementation. Alone it cannot stand, since it fails to do justice to what seems now to me to be a rather obvious truth.

If, as *Reality* maintains, each thing is directed toward, and acts in terms of all the rest, no two of them would have exactly the same objections. No two would point in exactly the same direction. They would have different final causes. Each would have a different objective and thus a different prospective future from that which concerns others. Since the existence of each would be spent in the area defined by its distant objective, there would be no assurance that any of them, contemporaries at one moment, will be contemporaries at the next. Each will look out at the world from its own perspective. It will have its own private time in which it lives. That time will have its own rhythm, its own divisions, its own pace. There will be no reason to suppose that it will be intermeshed with the times characteristic of others, that there could be a single time and thus a single cosmos in which they all dwell together. Each is occupied with a future peculiar to it, it will endeavor to make it present in its own way and at its own pace. The different futures of course share a number of features, making it possible to treat the things as members of various classes. But the things do not act in terms of those common features. The features exert no controlling power. They are abstractable from a set of disconnected singular objectives; they cannot possibly keep the contemporary beings in temporal accord.

This is a serious difficulty and not peculiar to the system explored in *Reality.* It faces Aristotle's philosophy, and Whitehead's too. Aristotle's contemporary objects move together in time not on their own account but because they are confined within a single spatial whole whose rhythms and pace limit the rhythms and pace of the subordinate realities within it. Whitehead's contemporary objects keep abreast in time not because they must intrinsically do so but because the diverse final causes which govern them are under the supervision of an interested God. Whitehead here reminds one of Leibniz with his doctrine of a divinely pre-established harmony which guarantees that the independent adventures of things are in accord with one another. Aristotle here reminds one of Kant and his attempt to treat time as having two sides, the one private or ideal, the other public or actual which, though quite different in purport and in experienced content, are though somehow to have the same divisions and rate of passage. The one overcomes the difficulty by a special and cosmological assumption; the other does it by a theological one. But these are exteriorly imposed devices. In principle, these thinkers allow that things may move in time independently of one another and therefore may, if contemporary today, not be contemporary tomorrow. Yet no matter whether beings are sluggish or quick, asleep or awake, lost in privacies or engaged in public work, all, while living at their own pace, live together in a common time.

There are contemporary beings. Otherwise there would be nothing to interact with us, nothing with which we could be together, nothing which could limit us and thus define us as incomplete. And some beings, contemporary now, are contemporary later. All move to the next moment together, some altering in nature or position, others remaining unchanged or unmoved. One can imagine all of them in the grip of some single cosmic being, some dialectical force, some all-encompassing power which both drives them forward and keeps them in accord. But this idea compromises the basic fact that it is individuals who act, and act in their own ways and at their own rates. The time through which I live is my own; if there be another time or temporal power keeping me abreast of others, it is more powerful than I and they, and wise beyond belief. There must of course be something common to us all which limits and even controls us somewhat, so as to enable us, despite our independent existence and independent adventures in time, to be co-ordinate now, and later. To avoid supposing something like a cosmic agent who runs alongside or overhead and keeps the individual things adjusted one to the other, or some all-embracing time or being out of which the individual times are conjointly precipitated—suppositions which reverse an obvious state of affairs, since they overlook the irreducible ultimacy of individuals in the world, and the fact that it is they who spend energy, and dictate what the common pattern of the world will be—we need attend only to the fact that things are members of various groups, not because they happen to share some character, but because they all have the same objective. Despite their individuality, all spatiotemporal things form a single contemporaneous set, the group of actualities, because each inevitably points toward the very prospect pointed toward by the rest. A number of them may further specify that common prospect in common ways and thereby reveal themselves to be members of some more limited group as well. Whether they do or not, each and every one of them acts as a distinct being, and thus brings the common objective to realization in an individual way.

It is desirable to show that there is and must be one objective, subtending whatever limited objectives individuals or groups of them may be directed toward. And it is important to know the nature of that common objective. *Nature and Man,* my next book, was written in part to satisfy these reasonable and therefore imperious demands. The book stresses the fact that the common objective is essential, that it is inseparable from the very being of individual things. Nothing existed, it saw, solely in the present; each being was partly in the future and was governed in part by that common objective in which it essentially terminated. This defined its direction, and when specialized as a limited objective, defined the range of the things a being could do.

The discovery that all beings inevitably point to the same common future objective made it possible to show how they could exist together in time even though they acted independently, and sometimes even came into conflict. And an awareness that the common objective was itself indeterminate in nature made it possible to understand why it needed realization and could be realized—questions which were unanswerable by Plato and others who like him recognize that there is a common objective to which all beings are inevitably directed, but who mistakenly suppose that it is itself perfect, complete, wholly determinate.

If one avoids the Platonic supposition that the idea of perfection is itself perfect, that the idea of the good is itself the best of beings, one could safely agree with Plato to call the common inevitable objective of all beings by the grandest of titles, The Good. A recognition of the nature and needs of that good makes it possible to offer new ways of understanding the nature of causation, inference, action—all change in fact. Every occurrence, it could then be shown, is at once predictable in the abstract and unpredictable in the concrete, at once limited and free, occurring in the present but within bounds determined by what was future. The separation of theories of artistic creation and logical deduction, of history and physics, which had ruined so many philosophies, could at last be avoided. Every act and thought, *Nature and Man* saw, was present, concrete, transitory, unpredictable in principle because produced only then and there, and thus incapable of being known in advance. Every act and thought it also saw was in addition abstract, future, fixed, and as such predictable because entailed by present actualities. Art and history, logic and physics have both an unpredictable and a predictable side, the first two stressing the one, the second two the other. Although they have different starting points, media, objectives and go through different processes, they exhibit the selfsame fundamental principles.

Nature and Man affirmed, even more vigorously than did *Reality*, that man was not only an integral part of nature, but a product of evolution. It tried to show that the advance which began with the inanimate, moved through the animate and ended with man was the consequence of an occasional successful strategy by frustrated beings. These, to overcome grave obstacles, to avoid defeat and annihilation, changed their directions, pointed to new objectives, thereby becoming transformed in nature and in promise. It concluded that man was, while different in degree, distinct in kind from all other beings. He alone, it said, possessed a persistent self. That self stood out over against the body and the rest of the world because it alone was persistently occupied with the realization of a single, all-inclusive objective, the Good. Because of his self, man had self-identity, and was capable of self-discipline and self-criticism, privileges which were outside the reach of any other being in nature.

The position explored in *Nature and Man* does not, I think, have to be changed in any fundamental respect. But it has important implications which it did not pursue. It was one of the tasks of *Man's Freedom* to note these implications and to complete the account. The book stressed the fact that the good was focused on and striven for by man, for the most part without consciousness, but with a freedom peculiar to him. That freedom was exhibited primarily in three more and more effective and inclusive forms, as preference, choice and will. These were man's primary agencies by which he freely adopted and tried to realize the all-inclusive good.

Man does and man ought to try to bring the good to its most complete realization. It is his task to do good, and nothing but good, to every being whatsoever. But he is finite, feeble, ignorant;

he must inevitably fail to do what he ought. Man is the guilty animal. But this is paradox. That paradox cannot be overcome by narrowing the range of man's obligations. No area of responsibility is so small as to be within the power of man to fill completely. No one ever does all that ought to be done even to only one other being. No one does or can do all he ought, even to himself. A man has too little knowledge, too little strength, too unstable a constitution to be able to do full justice to the rights of any being. Nor can his knowledge, strength and constitution be so improved that he will eventually do all he ought. Finite always, he will always fall short of his full obligations.

I find the paradox intolerable. My struggle with it led me to see my previous speculations as part of a much wider four-dimensional whole. Suggestions of the nature of those four dimensions can be found in *Reality* and in other places, but they became clear to me only when I turned to the study of ethics and saw the full force of the paradox that a man had obligations which he could not himself fulfill. As long as I worked with anything less than a four-pronged view I found that the paradox could not be resolved. One had to distinguish and assume in turn the perspectives of four distinct realities—actuality, the good, existence, and God. All four—one had to affirm—were final, irreducible, with their own integrity and careers. The universe they together exhausted requires for its understanding a system in which each is as basic and as explanatory, and as incomplete, as the others.

It is the task of this work to lay bare the nature of these four realities and to grasp something of the way they affect one another. Before engaging in it, it is desirable I think, to know why it is necessary for anyone—not only I—to consider these four; it is desirable too to get some idea of their diverse natures and roles.

Actualities are finite beings in space and time. To complete themselves they strive to realize relevant, essential objectives which, in diverse ways, specify a single common future good. Since only man focuses on the good in its unspecified form, only he can hope to embody that good in himself and in others. He cannot, as an individual, do full justice to that good. That can be done only through the conjoint effort of all that there is. A man can hope to do all he ought only if he can accept as his own all the work that the world can do. We would, with this observation, reach an end to our system were it not that we had presupposed existence as an energizing field in which actualities act, and which terminates in the good, and that we had presupposed God as the unity in which both actualities and the good can be together, and in which existence finds the unitary essence it needs in order to be intelligible. Both existence and God, of course, are presupposed by a system which begins with the good, for these sustain it in different but necessary ways.

And we ought also to make a beginning with the good. It has a nature of its own, as is evident from the fact that it is striven for. Indeed it has power enough to attract a man and make him concerned with its fulfillment. A correlate of actualities, it is an Ideal possibility which acts to master them by turning them into types, meanings, representatives of one another and of itself. From the standpoint of the Ideal all that ought to be done is done if whatever there be is idealized, turned into a part of the Ideal. This action of the Ideal on the actual is the reciprocal of that by which the actual acts on it. And, like the actual, the good presupposes material to work upon. Just as the actual presupposes the Ideal, the Ideal presupposes the actual, and both of them presuppose existence and God as regions in which they can be together.

The Ideal is incomplete, indeterminate. It needs completeness, and achieves this by fractionating itself into more and more determinate and limited forms of itself. It demands, not specific activities by actualities, but the prevision of opportunities so that it can transform those actualities from what is external to it into what is subordinate. By offering the actualities attractive objectives, desirable goals, commanding choices, obligating goods, restraining laws and finally a compelling destiny, it turns the actualities into purposive, preferring, choosing, willing kinds of beings, into citizens of a state and finally into beings who fulfill themselves while enabling all other actualities to be idealized. From the perspective of the good, men are required to adopt roles, to become public and representative beings. So far as they achieve this status the good becomes determinate, not by virtue of the introduction of alien material, but by the good's adoption of what is nothing more than diverse, fragmentary, harmonious parts of itself. Man's task from the standpoint of the good is the making of this fractionization easy, complete and concordant, just as it is the task of the good from the standpoint of man to be receptive of their efforts to make it concrete. The good ennobles, universalizes actualities when and as they sustain it, just as actualities enrich the good, make it concrete when and as it lures and guides them.

An ethical man fulfills his obligations by accepting as his own the effective, concordant activities of the rest of the world; so far as he is one with the totality of actualities, he does all that needs to be done in order that the good be realized. A public man, in contrast, attains completeness by functioning as a representative of others and as an instance of the good, becoming thereby part of the very good that ought to be.

The actual and the Ideal, even when made one by mastery and fractionization, have each their own integrity, enjoy an independent status. But they are still correlatives. An examination of them separately and in relation to one another enables us to encompass most of what is—but not all. God and existence are also essential, inescapable dimensions of the universe, illuminating what is left dark by the joint use of the perspective of actuality and ideality.

Actualities and the Ideal both change. The series of changes must somehow be brought together in a unity if there is to be a single interconnected set of epochs in time. God is that being who, among other things, makes a unity out of what otherwise would be a detached set of occurrences. He sees to it that the Ideal is fulfilled in actualities, and conversely. This means that men should recognize that they inevitably submit themselves and their acts to God, as the being who alone can make them adequate to the demands of the good. Since men, their acts and their aspirations are part of a realm of existence, where alone they can be vital and present, no account of God can be complete which forgets that existence is His counterweight, the locus of the data He supports and interrelates.

Existence is a restless force at once ingredient in and overflowing the borders of actualities, connecting each with every other, and coming to a focus in the good at which all actualities are directed. Men are able to exist properly within this world just so far as they accept the surging onrush of the world as containing within it all that is of substance and importance. On this view actualities and the Ideal are subject to a single, cosmic flux, itself identical in reach with the living immanent God. It is a view which should be supplemented with accounts where God, the Ideal and actualities are recognized to have independent natures and functions, since without them there would be no unified world of values, no focused and uniting futures, and no distinct loci of action.

We are confronted, evidently, with a vast and complex set of ideas. It is desirable to bring them within a small compass, so that they can be readily grasped in themselves and in their bearing on one another. The warming flesh of rhetoric must be cut away, and the somewhat ugly, naked musculature of a systematic account exposed. This I must now try to do.

Paul Weiss, *Nodes of Being* (in preparation); from Chap. 1.

DONALD C. WILLIAMS

The Myth of Passage

At every moment each of us finds himself the apparent center of the world, enjoying a little lit foreground of the here and now, while around him there looms thing beyond thing, event beyond event, the plethora of a universe. Linking the furniture of the foreground are sets of relations which he supposes also to bind the things beyond and to bind the foreground with the rest. Noteworthy among them are those queerly obvious relations, peculiarly external to their terms, which compose the systems of space and time, modes of connection exhaustively specifiable in a scheme of four dimensions at right angles to one another. Within this manifold, for all that it is so firmly integrated, we are immediately struck by a disparity between the three-dimensional spread of space and the one dimension of time. The spatial dimensions are in a literal and precise sense perpendicular to one another, and the submanifold which they compose is isotropic, the same in all directions. The one dimension of time, on the other hand, although it has the same formal properties as each of the other three, is at least sensuously different from them as they are not from

one another, and the total manifold is apparently not isotropic
Whereas an object can preserve the same shape while it is so
shifted that its height becomes its breadth, we cannot easily con
ceive how it could do so while being shifted so that its breadth
becomes its duration.

The theory of the manifold, I think, is the one model on which
we can describe and explain the foreground of experience, or
can intelligibly and credibly construct our account of the rest of
the world, and this is so because in fact the universe is spread
out in those dimensions. There may be Platonic entities which
are foreign to both space and time; there may be Cartesian spirits
which are foreign to space; but the homely realm of natural
existence, the total of world history, is a spatiotemporal volume
of somewhat uncertain magnitude, chockablock with things and
events. Logic, with its law of excluded middle and its tenseless
operators, and natural science, with its secular world charts, concur inexorably with the vision of metaphysics and high religion
that truth and fact are thus eternal.

I believe that the universe consists, without residue, of the spread
of events in space-time, and that if we thus accept realistically
the four-dimensional fabric of juxtaposed actualities we can dis-
pense with all those dim nonfactual categories which have so
bedeviled our race: the potential, the subsistential, and the influential, the noumenal, the numinous, and the nonnatural. But I am
arguing here, not that there is nothing outside the natural world
of events, but that the theory of the manifold is anyhow literally
true and adequate to that world: true, in that the world contains
no less than the manifold; adequate, in that it contains no more.

Since I think that this philosophy offers correct and coherent
answers to real questions, I must think that metaphysical difficulties raised against it are genuine too. There are facts, logical and
empirical, which can be described and explained only by the concept of the manifold; there are facts which some honest men deem
irreconcilable with it. Few issues can better deserve adjudication.
The difficulties which we need not take seriously are those made
by primitive minds, and by new deliberate primitivists, who tra-
duce metaphysics in general, and recommend specifically, with
respect to time, that we follow out the Augustinian clue, as
Augustine did not, that the man who best feels he understands
time is he who refuses to think about it.

Among philosophical complainants against the manifold, some

few raise difficulties about space—there are subjectivistic epistemolo-
gists, for example, who grant more reality to their own past and
future than to things spatially beyond themselves. The temporal
dimension of the manifold, however, bears the principal brunt.
Sir James Jeans regretted that time is mathematically attached to
space by so "weird" a function as the square root of minus one,[1]
and the very word "weird," being cognate with *"werden,"* to become, is a monument to the uncanniness of our fourth dimension.
Maintaining that time is in its essence something wholly unique,
a flow or passage, the "time snobs" (as Wyndham Lewis called
them) either deny that the temporal spread is a reality at all, or
think it only a very abstract phase of real time. Far from disparag-
ing time itself, they conceive themselves thus to be "taking time
seriously" in a profounder sense than our party who are content
with the vasty reaches of what is, was, and will be.

The more radical opposition to the manifold takes time with
such Spartan seriousness that almost none of it is left—only the
pulse of the present, born virginally from nothing and devouring
itself as soon as born, so that whatever past and future there be
are strictly only the memory and anticipation of them in this Now.[2]
One set of motives for this view is in the general romantic polemic
against logic and the competence of concepts. The theory of the
manifold is the logical account of events *par excellence,* the teeth
by which the jaws of the intellect grip the flesh of occurrence.
The Bergsonian, who thinks that concepts cannot convey the
reality of time because they are "static," the Marxist who thinks
that process defies the cadres of two-valued logic, and the Heidegger who thinks that temporality, history, and existence are leagued
outside the categories of the intellect, thus have incentives for
denying, in effect, all the temporal universe beyond what is immanent in the present flare and urge. To counter their attack,
it is a nice and tempting question whether and how concepts are
"static," whether and how, in any case, a true concept must be
similar to its object, and whether and how history and existence
are any more temporal than spatial. But we cannot here undertake
the whole defense of the intellect against its most violent critics.
We shall rather notice such doubters as trust and use conceptual
analysis and still think there are cogent arguments against the
manifold. One argument to that effect is an extreme sharpening
of the positivistic argument from the egocentric predicament. For
if it is impossible for my concepts to transcend experience in gen-

eral, it may well be impossible for them to transcend the momentary experience in which they are entertained. Conversely, however, anybody who rejects the arguments for instantaneous solipsism, as most people do, must reject this argument for diminishing the manifold. The chief mode of argument is rather the finding of an intolerable anomaly in the statement that what was but has ceased, or what will be but has not begun, nevertheless *is*. This reflection has been used against the reality of the future, in particular, by philosophers as miscellaneous as Aristotle and neo-Scholastics, C. D. Broad, and Professors Weiss and Hartshorne. In so far as it is an argument from logic, charging the manifold with self-contradiction, it would be as valid against the past as against the future; but, I have argued elsewhere, it is by no means valid.[3] Since to deny the reality of past and future is to reject the law of excluded middle—or still worse, to think that *p-or-not-p* can be true though *p* is not true and *not-p* is not true—the theory of the manifold can hardly wound logic worse than the denial of the manifold; but the theory of the manifold does not wound it at all. The statement that a sea fight not present in time nevertheless exists, is no more contradictory than that one not present in space nevertheless exists. If it seems so, this is only because there happens to be a temporal reference (tense) built into our verbs rather than a spatial reference (as in some Indian languages) or than no locative reference (as in canonical symbolic transcriptions into logic).

I am not to contend now for the reality of the manifold, however, but against the extra *weirdness* alleged for time both by some champions who reject the manifold out of hand and by some who contend anyhow that it is not the whole story, both parties agreeing that the temporal dimension is not "real time," not "the genuine creative flux." If our temporalist means by this that the theory of temporal extension, along with the spatial models provided by calendars, kymographs, and statistical time charts, is in the last analysis fictitious, corresponding to nothing in the facts, he is reverting, under a thin cloak of dissimulation, to the mere rejection which we have agreed to leave aside. If he means, at the other extreme, no more than that the theory and the models themselves are not identical, either numerically or qualitatively, with the actual temporal succession which they represent, he is uttering a triviality which is true of every theory or representation. If he means that the temporal spread, though real and formally similar to a spatial spread, is qualitatively or intuitively very different from it, or lies in a palpably and absolutely unique direction, he says something plausible and important but not at all incompatible with the philosophy of the manifold. He is most likely to mean, however, another proposition which is never more than vaguely expressed: that over and above the sheer spread of events, with their several qualities, along the time axis, which is analogous enough to the spread of space, there is something extra, something active and dynamic, which is often and perhaps best described as "passage." This something extra, I am going to plead, is a myth: not one of those myths which foreshadow a difficult truth in a metaphorical way, but altogether a false start, deceiving us about the facts, and blocking our understanding of them.

The literature of "passage" is immense, but it is naturally not very exact and lucid, and we cannot be sure of distinguishing in it between mere harmless allegorical phenomenology and the special metaphysical declaration which I criticize. But "passage," it would seem, is a character supposed to inhabit and glorify the present, "the passing present,"[4] "the moving present,"[5] the "traveling now."[6] It is "the passage of time as actual . . . given now with the jerky or whooshy quality of transience."[7] It is James' "passing moment."[8] It is what Broad calls "the transitory aspect" of time, in contrast with the "extensive."[9] It is Bergson's living felt duration. It is Heidegger's *Zeitlichkeit*. It is Tillich's "moment that is creation and fate."[10] It is "the act of becoming," the mode of potency and generation, which Hugh King finds properly appreciated only by Aristotle and Whitehead.[11] It is Eddington's "ongoing" and "the formality of taking place,"[12] and Dennes' "surge of process."[13] It is the dynamic essence which Professor Ushenko believes that Einstein omits from the world.[14] It is the mainspring of McTaggart's "A-series" which puts movement in time,[15] and it is Broad's pure becoming.[16] Withal it is the flow and go of very existence, nearer to us than breathing, closer than hands and feet.

So far as one can interpret these expressions into a theory, they have the same purport as all the immemorial turns of speech by which we describe time as *moving*, with respect to the present or with respect to our minds. Time flows or flies or marches, years roll, hours pass. More explicitly we may speak as if the perceiving mind were stationary while time flows by like a river, with the flotsam of events upon it; or as if presentness were a fixed pointer under which the tape of happenings slides; or as if the time sequence were a moving-picture film, unwinding from the dark reel of the future, projected briefly on the screen of the present, and rewound into the dark can of the past. Sometimes, again, we speak as if the time sequence were a stationary plain or ocean on which we voyage, or a variegated river gorge down which we drift; or, in Broad's analogy, as if it were a row of house fronts along which the spotlight of the present plays. "The essence of nowness," Santayana says, "runs like fire along the fuse of time."[17] Augustine pictures the present passing into the past, where the modern pictures the present as invading the future,[18] but these do not conflict, for Augustine means that the *events* which were present become past, while the modern means that *presentness* encroaches on what was previously the future. Sometimes the surge of presentness is conceived as a mere moving illumination by consciousness, sometimes as a sort of vivification and heightening, like an ocean wave heaving along beneath a stagnant expanse of floating seaweed, sometimes as no less than the boon of existence itself, reifying minute by minute a limbo of unthings.

The doctrine of the moving present has some startling applications, notably in the idea of a time machine. The theory of the four-dimensional manifold seemed already an invitation to the notion of time travel, and the additional idea that we move with respect to time confirms it. For if I normally voyage through time in a single direction at a fixed rate, I can hope to make a machine which will enable me to voyage slower or faster or backward.

Now, the most remarkable feature of all this is that while the modes of speech and thought which enshrine the idea of passage are universal and perhaps ineradicable, the instant one thinks about them one feels uneasy, and the most laborious effort cannot construct an intelligible theory which admits the literal truth of any of them. McTaggart was driven to deny the reality of time because he believed that while time must combine the dimensional spread with the fact of passage, the B-series with the A-series, every attempt to reconcile the two ended in absurdity. Broad can only cling to the hope that a better reconciliation may yet be found. My present thesis would resolve the antinomy by rejecting the extra idea of passage as spurious altogether.

The obvious and notorious fault of the idea, as we have now localized it, is this. Motion is already defined and explained in the dimensional manifold as consisting of the presence of the same individual in different places at different times. It consists of bends or quirks in the world lines, or the space-time worm, which is the four-dimensioned totality of the individual's existence. This is motion in space, if you like; but we can readily define a corresponding "motion in time." It comes out as nothing more dramatic than an exact equivalent: "motion in time" consists of being at different times in different places. True motion then is motion at once in time and space. Nothing can "move" in time alone any more than in space alone, and time itself cannot "move" any more than space itself. "Does this road go anywhere?" asks the city tourist. "No, it stays right along here," replies the country-man. Time "flows" only in the sense in which a line flows or a landscape "recedes into the west." That is, it is an ordered exten-sion. And each of us proceeds through time only as a fence pro-ceeds across a farm: that is, parts of our being, and the fence's, occupy successive instants and points, respectively. There is passage, but it is nothing extra. It is the mere happening of things, their strung-along-ness in the manifold. The term "the present" is the conventional way of designating the cross section of events which are simultaneous with the uttering of the phrase, and "the present moves" only in that when similar words occur at successively dif-ferent moments, they denote, by a twist of language, different cross sections of the manifold. Time travel, *prima facie,* then, is analyz-able either as the banality that at each different moment we occupy a different moment from the one we occupied before, or the con-tradiction that at each different moment we occupy a different moment from the one which we are then occupying—that five minutes from now, for example, I may be a hundred years from now.[19]

The tragedy then of the extra idea of passage or absolute be-coming, as a philosophical principle, is that it incomprehensibly doubles its world by reintroducing terms like "moving" and "be-coming" in a sense which both requires and forbids interpretation in the preceding ways. For as soon as we say that time or the present or we move in the odd extra way which the doctrine of passage requires, we have no recourse but to suppose that this movement in turn takes time of a special sort: $time_1$ moves at a certain rate in $time_2$, perhaps one $second_1$ per one $second_2$, perhaps slower, perhaps faster. Or, conversely, the moving present slides over so many seconds of $time_1$ in so many seconds of $time_2$. The history of the new moving present, in time$_2$, then composes a new and higher time dimension again, which cries to be vitalized by a new level of passage, and so on forever.

We hardly needed to point out the unhappy regress to which the idea of time's motion commits us, for any candid philosopher, as soon as he looks hard at the idea, must *see* that it is preposterous. "Taking place" is not a formality to which an event incidentally submits—it is the event's very being. World history consists of actual concrete happenings in a temporal sequence; it is not necessary or possible that happening should happen to them all over again. The system of the manifold is thus "complete" in something like the technical logical sense, and any attempted addition to it is bound to be either contradictory or supererogatory.

Bergson, Broad, and some of the followers of Whitehead[20] have tried to soften the paradoxes of passage by supposing that the present does not move across the total time level, but that it is the very fountain where the river of time gushes out of nothingness (or out of the power of God). The past, then, having swum into being and floated away, is eternally real, but the future has no existence at all. This may be a more appealing figure, but logically it involves the same anomalies of metahappening and metatime which we observed in the other version.

What, then, we must ask, were the motives which drove men to the staggering philosophy of passage? One of them, I believe, we can dispose of at once. It is the innocent vertigo which inevitably besets a creature whose thinking is strung out in time, as soon as he tries to think of the time dimension itself. He finds it easiest to conceive and understand purely geometrical structures. Motion is more difficult, and generally remains vague, while time *per se* is very difficult indeed, but being now identified as the principle which imports motion into space, it is put down as a kind of quintessential motion itself. The process is helped by the fact that the mere further-along-ness of successive segments, either of a spatial or of a temporal stretch, can quite logically be conceived as a degenerate sort of change, as when we speak of the flow of a line or say that the scenery changes along the Union Pacific.

A rather more serious excuse for the idea of passage is that it is supposed necessary and sufficient for adding to the temporal dimension that intrinsic *sense,* from earlier to later, in which time is supposed to differ radically from any dimension of space.[21] A meridian of longitude has only a direction, but a river has a "sense," and time is in this like the river. It is, as the saying goes, irreversible and irrevocable. It has a "directed tension."[22] The mere dimension of time, on the other hand, would seem to be symmetrical. The principle of absolute passage is bidden to rectify this symmetry with what Eddington called "time's arrow."

It might be replied that science does not supply an arrow for time because it has no need of it. But I think it plain that time does have a sense, from early to late. I only think that it can be taken care of on much less draconian principles than absolute passage. There is nothing in the dimensional view of time to preclude its being generated by a uniquely asymmetrical relation, and experience suggests powerfully that it is so generated. But the fact is that every real series has a "sense" anyhow. This is provided, if by nothing else, then by the sheer numerical identity and diversity of terms. In the line of individual things or events, *a, b, c . . . z*, whether in space or in time, the "sense" from *a* to *z* is *ipso facto* other than the "sense" from *z* to *a*. Only because there is a difference between the ordered couple *a; z* and the couple *z; a* can we define the difference between a symmetrical and an asymmetrical relation. Only because there are already two distinguishable "ways" on a street, determined by its individual ends, can we decide to permit traffic to move one way and prohibit it the other. But a sufficient difference of sense, finally, would appear to be constituted, if nothing else offered, by the inevitably asymmetrical distribution of properties along the temporal line (or any other). Eddington has been only one of many scientists who think the arrow is provided for the cosmos by the principle of entropy, and entropy has been only one principle thus advocated.[23] In so far as what men mean by "the irrevocability of the past" is the causal circumstance that we can affect the future in a way we cannot affect the past, it is just a trait of the physicist's arrow. They often mean by it, however, only the inexorability of fact, that what is the case is the case, past, present, or future; or the triviality that the particular events of 1902, let us say, cannot also be the events of 1952. Very similar events might be so, however, and if very few of them are, this is the fault of the concrete nature of things and not of any grudge on the part of time.[24]

The final motive for the attempt to consummate or supplant the fourth dimension of the manifold with the special perfection, the grace and whiz, of passage is the vaguest but the most substantial and incorrigible. It is simply that we *find* passage, that we are immediately and poignantly involved in the whoosh of process, the felt flow of one moment into the next. Here is the focus of being. Here is the shore whence the youngster watches the golden mornings swing toward him like serried bright breakers from the ocean of the future. Here is the flood on which the oldster wakes in the night to shudder at its swollen black torrent cascading him into the abyss.

It would be futile to try to deny these experiences, but their correct description is another matter. If they are in fact consistent with our theory, they are no evidence against it; and if they are entailed by it, they are evidence in its favor. Since the theory was originally constructed to take account of them, it would be odd if they were inconsistent with it or even irrelevant to it. I believe that in fact they are neither, and that the theory of the manifold provides the true and literal description of what the enthusiastic metaphors of passage have deceptively garbled.

The principal reason why we are troubled to accommodate our experience of time to the intellectual theory of time goes very deep in the philosophy of philosophy. It is that we must here scrutinize the undoctored fact of perception, on the one hand, and must imagine our way into a conceptual scheme, and envisage the true intrinsic being of its objects, on the other hand, and then pronounce on the numerical identity of the first with the second. This is a very rare requirement. Even such apt ideas as those of space and of physical objects, as soon as we contemplate them realistically, begin to embarrass us, so that we slip into the assumption that the real objects of the conceptions, if they exist at all, exist on a different plane or in a different realm from the sensuous spread and lumpiness of experience. The ideas of time and of the mind, however, do not permit of such evasion. Those beings are given in their own right and person, filling the foreground. Here for once we must fit the fact directly into the intellectual form, without benefit of precedent or accustomed criteria. First off, then, comparing the calm conceptual scheme with the turbid event itself, we may be repelled by the former, not because it is not true to the latter, but because it *is* not the latter. When we see that this kind of diversity is inevitable to every concept and its object, and hence is irrelevant to the validity of any, we demur because the conceptual scheme is indifferently flat and third-personal, like a map, while the experienced reality is centripetal and perspectival, piled up and palpitating where we are, gray and retiring elsewhere.

But this, of course, affecting the spread of time no more than that of space, is only because every occasion on which we compare the world map with experience has itself a single specific location, confronting part of the world, remote from the rest. The perspectivity of the view is exactly predictable from the map. The deception with respect to time is worse than with respect to space because our memories and desires run timewise and not spacewise. The jerk and whoosh of this moment, which are simply the real occurrence of one particular batch of events, are no different from the whoosh and being of any other patch of events up and down the eternal time-stretch. Remembering some of the latter, however, and anticipating more, and bearing in mind that while they happen they are all called "the present," we mistakenly hypostatize *the* Present as a single surge of bigness which rolls along the time axis. There is in fact no more a single rolling Now than there is a single rolling Here along a spatial line—a standing line of soldiers, for example, though each of them has the vivid presentment of his own Here.

Let us hug to us as closely as we like that there is real succession, that rivers flow and winds blow, that things burn and burst, that men strive and guess and die. All this is the concrete stuff of the manifold, the reality of serial happening, one event after another, in exactly the time spread which we have been at pains to diagram. What does the theory allege except what we find, and what do we find that is not accepted and asserted by the theory? Suppose a pure intelligence, bred outside of time, instructed in the nature of the manifold and the design of the human space-time worm, with its mnemic organization and the strands of world history which flank it, and suppose him incarnated among us: what could he have expected the temporal experience to be like except just about what he actually discovers it to be? How, in brief, could processes which endure and succeed each other along the time line appear as anything other than enduring and successive processes?

The theory of the manifold leaves abundant room for the sensitive observer to record any describable difference he may find, in intrinsic quality, relational texture, or absolute direction, between the temporal dimension and the spatial ones. He is welcome to mark it so on the map. The very singleness of the time dimension, over against the amalgamated three dimensions of space, may be an idiosyncrasy with momentous effects; its *fourthness,* so to speak, so oddly and immensely multiplying the degrees of freedom embodied in the familiar spatial complex, was bound to seem momentous too. The theory has generally conceded or emphasized that time is unique in these and other respects, and I have been assuming that it was right to do so. In the working out of this thesis, however, and in considering the very lame demurrals which oppose it, I have come a little uneasily to the surmise that the idea of an absolute or intrinsic difference of texture or orientation is superfluous, and that the four dimensions of the manifold compose a perfectly homogeneous scheme of location relations, the same in all directions, and that the oddity of temporal distances is altogether a function of features which occupy them—a function of *de facto* patter like the shape of an arrow, like the difference between the way in and the way out of a flytrap, and like the terrestrial difference between up and down.

Even a person who believes that temporal distances are a categorially peculiar mode of relation, intrinsically different from spatial distance, regardless of how they are filled, must grant that they nevertheless *are* filled differently: things, persons, and events, as a matter of natural fact, are strung along with respect to the time axis in rhythms and designs notably different from those in which they are deployed spacewise. Entropy and the other scientific criteria for the "sense" from past to future distinguish no less the whole temporal direction from the spatial ones. The very concept of "things" or "individual substances" derives from a peculiar kind of coherence and elongation of clumps of events in the time direction. Living bodies in particular have a special organized trend timewise, a *conatus esse conservandi,* which nothing has in spatial section. Characteristic themes of causation run in the same direction, and paralleling all these, and accounting for their importance and obviousness to us, is the pattern of mental events, the stream of consciousness, with its mnemic cumulation and that sad anxiety to *keep going* futureward which contrasts strangely with our comparative indifference to our spatial girth. The same fact of the grain and configuration of events which, if it does not constitute, certainly accompanies and underlines the "senses" of space and time, has other virtues which help to naturalize experience in the manifold. It accounts for the apparent *rate* of happening, for example; for the span of the specious present; and for the way in which the future is comparatively malleable to our present efforts and correspondingly dark to our present knowledge. An easy interpretation would be that the world content is uniquely organized in the time direction because the time direction itself is aboriginally unique. Modern philosophical wisdom, however, consists mostly of tying the cart before the horse, and I find myself more than half convinced by the oddly repellent hypothesis that the peculiarity of the time dimension is not thus primitive but is wholly a resultant of those differences in the mere *de facto* run and order of the world's filling.

It is conceivable, then, though doubtless physically impossible, that one four-dimensional area of the manifold be slued around at right angles to the rest, so that the time order of that area, as composed by its interior lines of strain and structure, runs parallel with a spatial order in its environment. It is conceivable, indeed, that a single, whole human life should lie thwartwise of the manifold, with its belly plump in time, its birth at the east and its death in the west, and its conscious stream perhaps running alongside somebody's garden path.[25] It is conceivable too then that a human life be twisted, not 90° but 180°, from the normal temporal grain of the world. F. Scott Fitzgerald tells the story of Benjamin Button who was born in the last stages of senility and got younger all his life till he died a dwindling embryo.[26] Fitzgerald imagined the reversal to be so imperfect that Benjamin's stream of consciousness ran, not backward with his body's gross development, but in the common clockwise manner. We might better conceive a reversal of every cell twitch and electron whirl, and hence suppose that he experienced his own life stages in the same order as we do ours, but that he observed everyone around him moving backward from the grave to the cradle. True time travel, then, is conceivable after all, though we cannot imagine how it could be caused by beings whose lives are extended in the normal way: it would consist of a man's life-pattern, and the pattern of any appliances he employed, running at an abnormal rate or on an abnormal heading across the manifold. I may be overbold, I know, when I unveil these speculations, since to some they will seem a warning of the dangers of any dimensional view. The more reasonable reflection, however, is that if even this extravagant version, a completely isotropic theory of space-time, can be squared pretty well with the experience and idea of passage, there can be no serious doubt of the adequacy of the more moderate theory which neither asserts nor denies that the manifold is isotropic.

As the dimensional theory accommodates what is true in the

motion of passage, that is, the occurrence of events, in contrast with a mythical rearing and charging of time itself, so it accounts for what is true in the notions of "flux," "becoming," "emergence," "creative advance," and the rest. Having learned the trick of mutual translation between theory and experience, we see where the utter misrepresentation lies in the accusation that the dimensional theory denies that time is "real," or that it substitutes a safe and static world, a block universe, a petrified *fait accompli*, a *totum simul*, for the actuality of risk and change. Taking time with the truest seriousness, on the contrary, it calmly diagnoses "novelty" or "becoming," for example, as the occurrence of an entity, or kind of entity, at one time in the world continuum which does not occur at any previous time. No other sort of novelty than this, I earnestly submit, is discoverable or conceivable—or desirable. In practice, the modern sciences of the manifold have depicted it as a veritable caldron of force and action. Although the theory entails that it is true at every time that events occur at other times, it emphatically does not entail that all events happen at the same time or at every time, or at no time. It does not assert, therefore, that future things "already" exist or exist "forever." Emphatically also it does not, as is frequently charged, "make time a dimension of space,"[27] any more than it makes space a dimension of time.

The theory of the manifold, which is thus neutral with respect to the amount of change and permanence in the world, is surprisingly neutral also toward many other topics often broached as though they could be crucial between it and the extra idea of passage. It is neutral, so far, toward whether space and time are absolute and substantival in the Democritean and Newtonian way, or relative and adjectival in Spencer's and Whitehead's way, or further relativistic in Einstein's way. The theory of space does not, as Bergson pretended, have any preference for discontinuity over continuity, and while a time order in which nothing exists but the present would be fatal to any real continuity, the philosophy of the manifold is quite prepared to accept any verdict on whether space or time or both are continuous or discrete, as it is also on whether they are finite or infinite. Instead of "denying history," it preserves it, and is equally hospitable to all philosophies of history except such as themselves deny history by disputing the objectivity and irrevocability of historical truth. It does not care whether events eternally recur, or run along forever on the dead level as Aristotle thought, or enact the ringing brief drama of the Christian episode, or strive into the Faustian boundless. It is similarly neutral toward theories of causation and of knowledge. The world manifold of occurrences, each eternally determi*nate* at its own place and date, may and may not be so determi*ned* in its texture that what occurs at one juncture has its sufficient reason at others. If it does evince such causal connections, these may be either efficient (as apparently they are) or final (as apparently they are not). The core of the causal nexus itself may be, so far as the manifold is concerned, either a real connection of Spinoza's sort, or Whitehead's, or the scholastics', or the mere regular succession admitted by Hume and Russell. It was a mistake for Spinoza to infer, if he did, that the eternal manifold and strict causation entail one another, as it is a worse mistake for Whitehead, the scholastics, and Professors Ushenko and Weiss to infer the opposite (as they seem to), that "real time" and "real causation" entail one another.[28] The theory is similarly noncommittal toward metaphysical accounts of individual substances, which it can allow to be compounds of form and matter or mere sheaves of properties.

The theory of the manifold makes a man at home in the world to the extent that it guarantees that intelligence is not affronted at its first step into reality. Beyond that, the cosmos is as it is. If there is moral responsibility, if the will is free, if there is reasonableness in regret and hope in decision, these must be ascertained by more particular observations and hypotheses than the doctrine of the manifold. It makes no difference to our theory whether we are locked in an ice pack of fate, or whirled in a tornado of chance, or are firm-footed makers of destiny. It will accept benignly either the Christian Creator, or the organic and perfect Absolute, or Hume's sand pile of sensation, or the fluid melee of contextualism, or the structured world process of materialism.

The service which the theory performs with respect to all these problems is other than dictating solutions of them. It is the provision of a lucent frame or arena where they and their solutions can be laid out and clearheadedly appraised in view of their special classes of evidence. Once under this kind of observation, for example, the theories of change which describe becoming as a marriage of being and not-being, or an interpenetration of the present with the future and the past, become repulsive, not because they conflict especially with the philosophy of the manifold, but because if they are not mere incantations they contradict themselves. When we see that the problem how Achilles can overtake the tortoise is essentially the same as the problem how two lines can intersect one another obliquely, we are likely to be content with the simple mathematical intelligibility of both. When we see that the "change" of a leaf's color from day to day is of the same denomination as its "change" from inch to inch of its surface, we are less likely to hope that mysterious formulas about the actualization of the potential and the perdurance of a substratum are of any use in accounting for either of them. If then there is some appearance of didactic self-righteousness in my effort here to save the pure theory of the manifold from being either displaced or amended by what I think is the disastrous myth of passage, this is because I believe that the theory of the manifold is the very paradigm of philosophic understanding. It grasps with a firm logic, so far as I can see, the most intimate and pervasive of facts; it clarifies the obscure and assimilates the apparently diverse. Most of the effect of the prophets of passage, on the other hand, is to melt back into the primitive magma of confusion and plurality the best and sharpest instruments which the mind has forged. Some of those who do this have a deliberate preference for the melting pot of mystery as an end in itself. Others, I suppose, hope eventually to cast from it a finer metal and to forge a sharper point. No hope of that sort is altogether chimerical. But I suggest that if a tithe of the animus and industry invested in that ill-omened enterprise were spent on the refinement and imaginative use of the instrument we have, whatever difficulties still attend it would soon be dissipated.

Originally published in the *Journal of Philosophy*, 1951, and reprinted with the permission of the editors.

1. Sir James Jeans, *The Mysterious Universe* (New York, 1930), p. 118.

2. This I think is a fair description of G. H. Mead's doctrine, *The Philosophy of the Present* (Chicago, 1932). See also, *e.g.*, Schopenhauer, *Die Welt als Wille und Vorstellung*, Bk. 4, Sec. 54.

3. Donald C. Williams, "The Sea Fight Tomorrow," in *Structure, Method, and Meaning: Essays in Honor of Henry M. Sheffer* (New York, 1951).

4. William Dennes, "Time as Datum and as Construction," in *The Problem of Time* (Berkeley, 1935), p. 103.

5. Isabel Stearns, "Time and the Timeless," *Review of Metaphysics*, Vol. 4 (1950), p. 198.

6. George Santayana, *Realms of Being* (New York, 1942), p. 258.

7. Clarence Lewis, *An Analysis of Knowledge and Valuation* (La Salle, 1946), p. 19. This is pretty surely phenomenology, not metaphysics, but it is too good to omit.

8. William James, *A Pluralistic Universe* (New York, 1928), p. 254.

9. C. D. Broad, *Examination of McTaggart's Philosophy* (Cambridge, 1938), Vol. II, Pt. I, p. 271.

10. Paul Tillich, *The Interpretation of History* (New York, 1936), p. 129.

11. Hugh R. King, "Aristotle and the Paradoxes of Zeno," *Journal of Philosophy*, Vol. XLVI (1949), pp. 657–70. This is an exceptionally ingenious, serious, and explicit statement of the philosophy which I am opposing.

12. A. Eddington, *Space, Time, and Gravitation* (1920), p. 51; *The Nature of the Physical World* (1928), p. 68.

13. W. Dennes, "Time as Datum and as Construction," pp. 91, 93.

14. A. P. Ushenko, *Power and Events* (Princeton, 1949), p. 146.

15. J. McTaggart, *The Nature of Existence*, Vol. II, Book v, Chap. 33.

16. C. D. Broad, *Scientific Thought* (1923), p. 67; *Examination of McTaggart's Philosophy*, p. 277.

17. George Santayana, *Realms of Being*, p. 491.

18. Augustine, *Confessions*, Book XI, Chap. 14; cf. E. B. McGilvary, "Time and the Experience of Time," in *An Anthology of Recent Philosophy*, ed. Robinson (New York, 1929).

19. "He may even now—if I may use the phrase—be wandering on some plesiosaurus-haunted oolitic coral reef, or beside the lonely saline seas of the Triassic Age"—H. G. Wells, *The Time Machine*, epilogue. This book, perhaps the best yarn ever written, contains such early and excellent accounts of the theory of the manifold that it has been quoted and requoted by scientific writers.

20. Bergson's theory of the snowball of time may be thus understood: the past abides in the center while ever new presents accrete around it. For Broad, see *Scientific Thought*, p. 66, and on Whitehead see King, *loc. cit.*, esp. p. 663.

21. See, for example, Broad, *Scientific Thought*, p. 57.

22. P. Tillich, *op. cit.*, p. 245.

23. A. Eddington, *The Nature of the Physical World*, Chap. 3. For the present scientific state of the question, see Adolf Grünbaum, "Time and Entropy," *American Scientist*, Vol. 43 (October, 1955), pp. 550–72.

24. Dennes argues thus, *loc. cit.*

25. I should expect the impact of the environment on such a being to be so wildly queer and out of step with the way he is put together, that his mental life must be a dragged-out monstrous delirium. Professor George Burch has suggested to me that it might be the mystic's timeless illumination. Whether these diagnoses are different I shall not attempt to say.

26. "The Curious Case of Benjamin Button," reprinted in *Pause to Wonder*, ed. Fischer and Humphries (New York, 1944), pp. 16–41.

27. See Charles Hartshorne, *Man's Vision of God*, p. 140, and Paul Tillich, *op. cit.*, pp. 132, 248; and remember Bergson's allegation that the principle of the manifold "spatializes" time.

28. See, for example, Alfred Whitehead, *Process and Reality* (New York, p. 363; Paul Weiss, *Nature and Man* (New York), 1947.

PART THREE

Ethics and Social Philosophy

WILLIAM R. DENNES

Conflict

That violence breeds violence is not a new discovery. Even Thucy-
dides was not the first to observe that wars, which sometimes exhaust some oppositions between peoples, are likely also to generate
new antagonisms and severer ones. But must we now count reason
itself as one of the casualties of the hot and cold wars and the
ideological clashes of our generation? Have these joined with genetic psychology and cultural relativism to destroy the faith which
philosophers, from Plato to Dewey, have placed in reason as the
sovereign remedy for human conflicts? Can we no longer hold that
fighting is the attempt to solve problems without understanding
them, while reason attempts to solve the same problems by understanding them; that we resort to force only when we are unwilling to think issues through? For many insist that in their most
thoroughgoing philosophical development the activities ordinarily
called "reason," far from resolving conflicts (theoretical or practical), characteristically generate *conflicting alternatives of explanation or interpretation.*

In order to understand the issues involved in the contemporary distrust of reason it will be useful to distinguish some—I do not pretend they are all—of the kinds of activity we commonly discuss as the work of reason.

I. Science—the exploring of events in the world outside our bodies and inside them, with their qualities and relations; the search for similarities and differences and for correlations between transactions of one kind and transactions of other kinds. Such work prompts us to expect further instances of, or approximations to, the correlations which are often manifested or approached. But nothing in the procedures of science ever allows us to say that we know for certain that such further instances have occurred, are occurring, or will occur. Of our best hypotheses, dignified by the title of laws, we can never say that it is impossible that there are, or will be, exceptions to them—indeed, that from now on there may be nothing else but exceptions and no more confirming instances at all. Yet we have no better justified method for developing and supporting beliefs about unexplored areas of existence—past, present, or future, fine-scale or large-scale—then those procedures of science. For beliefs so developed have betrayed us less often than beliefs developed in any other way, and also the method supplies the fullest possible opportunity for the alteration of beliefs with enlargement of experience and extension of evidence.

Some indeed advise us that history, social studies, the fine arts, require—and also supply us with the basis for—a kind of explanation different from the scientific and even antithetic to it. To be sure, one may best form hypotheses about an historical epoch or transaction, not by manipulating statistics but by immersing oneself in the relevant documents, monuments, literary materials, plays, diaries, conversations, and then formulating one's intuitive and imaginative sense of the structure and quality of what went on, or is going on, or will probably occur. Similarly, one achieves comprehension of a person not merely by listing indexes of reaction-times, thresholds, predominant Gestalten, etc., etc., but largely by living and working and talking with him. But these perfectly familiar facts do not in any way remove us from the orbit of scientific procedure. Natural scientists themselves regularly develop hypotheses intuitively and imaginatively. But once an hypothesis is thus developed, whether in history or in physics or in geology, we have no serious way to confirm it except by examining further materials—documents, rocks, paintings, buildings, pieces of sculpture, traces in cloud chambers, sayings or doings of persons—to see whether these are as they probably would be if our hypothesis were correct. Neither in history nor in physics can a man satisfactorily ground, or confirm, hypotheses by telling us that he has imagined them very vividly, feels the greatest confidence in them, or has a compelling intuition of their truth. People have told us all these things (and with complete sincerity) in support of such hypotheses as that the earth is flat and is absolutely at rest, that heretics should be burned and witches pressed to death, or that they were themselves the master race, charged by destiny with the duty to control and exploit the rest of mankind.

II. Reason in a second sense, as logic and mathematics, does indeed give us a kind of necessary truths, of undeniable (or perhaps we should better say unrejectable) formulations. For—to take the very simplest instance—wherever any symbol means anything more than nothing and less than everything, that is whenever any entity or class of entities functions as a symbol at all, a formal structure of symbolizing is entailed, a structure which we try to intimate (and to guide ourselves in using) by means of rules and systems of mathematics and logic. It is impossible (to illustrate by this simplest of instances) that any entity should belong to the class named by a symbol if it does not have the characteristics connoted by that symbol; and necessary that it should so belong if it does have the character thus meant. But all who so distinguish formal logical (or mathematical) necessity and impossibility from mere factual occurrences and nonoccurences are agreed that logic and mathematics as such can give us no knowledge and no probability with respect to what has gone on in any universe, or is going on, or will go on; although without the analyses and techniques of logic and mathematics, science as now developed would hardly exceed the powers of any men known to us.

III. Such philosophical work as the analysis, and if justified the distinction, of logic and mathematics from scientific explanation, is work different from either logic or science as these are generally understood; though of course there is no theoretical reason (but only the limits of men's time and energy and capacity) to prevent scientists and mathematicians from doing such philosophical work as we may thus designate Reason in sense III; as there is no theoretical reason why geologists and historians should not also be quite as expert mathematicians as any mathematician, and vice versa.

IV. There is still a fourth widely used and important sense of "reason," in which we say that a reasonable man is one who appreciates science and logic and philosophy, and also the arts and techniques by which men may progressively satisfy their basic needs for food and health and love and imaginative play, as well as their curiosity. A man reasonable in this fourth sense will form his opinions upon evidence, or at least alter them as he finds things other than he had supposed—will be open-minded, co-operative, and friendly because otherwise (among other grounds) no headway could be made in the work of Reason in senses I or II or III. When we say that science and logic and philosophy are good—when we approve reasons in these three senses—we are I think expressing such attitudes as make up what is meant by Reason in this fourth sense—and not merely expressing knowledge of facts, or necessities of logic, or theoretic philosophical insights. For two men might be equally masters of science and history and logic—theoretically, each might know all that can be known and harbor not one difference of belief from the other—and yet one might come to hate all these and desire the annihilation of such activities of reason and also the annihilation of his companion and himself, while the other might approve all these works of reason and all the persons who take part in them. For there is, as Spinoza held,[1] nothing whatever which cannot equally be loved or hated, either one—nothing whatever except only that substance or God or nature of which the love is identical with adequate knowledge, and of which *no mode, no person,* but only substance or God or nature itself, can have such adequate knowledge, since that knowledge is absolutely all of God's infinite modifications as they are under the infinite attribute of thought.

My suggestion is the familiar one that so far as we are in earnest with reason in the first three senses just distinguished, or even in the first two senses, conflicts in belief—theoretical oppositions—literally cannot survive. Our Greek spiritual ancestors and the dominant tradition of our philosophy are thus far right, that reason can indeed resolve one immense area of conflict—conflicts in beliefs. But such achievement of theoretical accord cannot be said either strictly to entail, or automatically to carry with it in fact, the disappearance of practical oppositions: of differences and antagonisms of attitude. However, it may do an immense deal—and in many cases it may do quite enough—toward removing such differences. For whenever, for example, human beings are agreed in fundamental attitudes of approving life over death and health over disease for themselves and their children and their friends, their practical differences may reflect nothing but opposed beliefs as to the likeliest means to secure or enhance what they thus approve. And if it can, for example, be shown to be predominantly probable as belief, that a growing co-operation of peoples generally is the surest way to those fundamental (though not absolute) ends, the practical conflicts and tensions of such people as agree in approving these ends should so far approach resolution.

But have we claimed too much? When men differ in beliefs—not merely as thinking about different materials but as holding opinions which are mutually incompatible—is it really satisfactory to say that, whatever else they may be doing they are not doing the work of reason, not thinking scientifically, as logicians or mathematicians, or as philosophers? In particular have we neglected grounds that would justify the belief (fashionable at the present time) that philosophy as such, when prosecuted with vigor and imagination, characteristically develops alternative and conflicting explanatory systems?

Certainly the familiar suggestion of which I have reminded you is confronted immediately by thousands of instances of what seem to be lively theoretical conflicts among the opinions of accomplished scientists, physicians, economists, historians, statesmen and philosophers. Let us examine a few samples.

Many people—psychologists and others—have felt that there is a basic conflict between (on the one hand) the whole enterprise of stimulus-response explanation of human or animal behavior, as against (on the other hand) dynamic-field theories. Yet it is plain that no serious student of stimulus-response patterns is excluded from recognizing the correlations with sorts of stimuli, and the correlations with sorts of responses, of *any* factors whatever, external or internal, which are found in *any way* to influence, or to be significantly related to, varying stimuli and varying responses. And nothing in stimulus-response investigation prevents any student from being prompted to look for such factors by his feel for the direction of complex processes, his sense of dynamic continuities, his intuition, or any other factor that may operate in (or on) the experience of *any* inquirer. Not only is the student of stimulus and response not excluded from finding and reporting, or from supposing, anything that *anybody* can find or suppose about such factors, but one discovers Pavlov himself studying in great detail such interrelations of factors within and without neural processes, and specifying the respects in which the fusion and synthesis of the factors culminate in effects quite different from any simple-minded mechanical repetition.[2] And just how different, and in what ways? Precisely as different as they may be found, or inferred (with support of serious induction) to be; but *not* different as, or because, some prior mechanistic postulate or field postulate entails differences. On the other hand, Köhler in his *Dynamics in Psychology* can say no more in explanation or support of his thesis that "a theory of perception must be a field theory," than that "the neural functions and processes with which the perceptual facts are associated in each case are located in a continuous medium; and the events in one part of this medium influence the events in other regions in a way that depends directly on the properties of both in their relation to each other."[3] We must dare the postulate, "that as a dynamic agent it [the percept] extends into the surrounding tissue."[4] Well, Pavlov had not merely dared a postulate but had actually traced out a few of the ways in which neural processes are influenced by events in their fields; and he thus gave the only kind of serious support relevant to this section of Köhler's field theory. Can we say that Pavlov must therefore have abandoned stimulus-response investigation and become a field theorist? Only if the price of adopting an ism in psychology is to abandon intelligence! And that price Pavlov was evidently not disposed to pay. Why should any thinker imagine he has to pay it?

The discovery of some limited regularities of stimulus and response is not, and could not be, incompatible with the occurrence or with the discovery of variations in both, either (so far as we may know) spontaneous, or fairly regularly correlated with alterations found in other areas of the context, whether neighboring or remote. Conflict can arise only if we abuse reason in senses I and II and assert that a pattern found in one area must necessarily also be the pattern that pervades other areas of existence—and thus we either mistake the nature of hypotheses and of their grounds, or else define some term like "perception," let us say, by a specific stimulus-response pattern (or equally, a specific field-configuration) and then imagine we are making significant descriptive statements when we say that it is impossible that X be an instance of perception and yet fail to exhibit the stimulus-response pattern in question, or fail to be a constituent or an instance of the specified field-configuration.

Where the correlations between stimuli and responses, or between various strands in field-configurations, have remained "highly irregular" even after exploration (as thorough as feasible to date) of further relevant factors in the context, conflicts seem to have arisen between psychologists on the one hand who wish to smooth out the correlations by postulating intervening determinants (such as "cortical sets, traces, residues, synaptic resistances, inhibitory and excitatory substances, inhibitory and excitatory tendencies . . . valences, urges, abilities, instincts, and so on"[5]) , and psychologists on the other hand who prefer to state the complex correlations between observed factors without benefit of such simplification by postulate. However, there is no slightest iota of reason (in any of the four senses) why these latter should deny the possibility of, or should close their minds to the search for, factors in fine-scale physiology, or in environment or conditioning, or anywhere else without limit, which may be found to explain what seems to be arbitrary deviations from correlations which are otherwise fairly regular. And so far as evidence is found supporting the operation, or the probability of the operation, of any of these factors, a man needs no partisan commitment to one side or the other in the above seeming controversy in order to develop, and to use seriously, hypotheses about such factors. To insist, however, irrespective of specific evidence, that some such factors *must* be operating wherever there is deviation from what have been called "smooth correlations" would be on all fours with a physicist's insisting that there can be no jerks, no gaps, no discontinuities in natural processes, and that therefore where there is evidence of quantumlike shifts we can be sure, regardless of evidence, that there *must* be unknown factors regularly operating to produce the quantum discontinuities.

Besides, it is always extremely important to notice how far our talk about smooth or simple correlations is actually a comment on the methods and the capacities of interpreters. For a graph of correlations (to take one example) which on one set of axes is "most irregular" can always be made as straight or smooth or rhythmic as we wish by using another set of axes. And surely today no one would allege that there is a set of axes which is *the* right set, the absolute frame of reference. When we skew or alter axes in order to make a given scrawl smooth or harmonious, there is of course always the possibility that on the new axes the development of the graph required to represent the next set of data will violate the harmonious pattern presently achieved. But there is *always* precisely this same risk when, on *any* set of axes without exception, there is the prospect of developing any line which represents any sort of evidenced correlation in order to take account of further measured values.

If we object to complexity of statement as opposed to simplicity, we may always correct the fault by altering the notation used. But as for the structures meant by our statements, all of them (however various) are intrinsically equally intelligible. There is not one of God's modifications of which we can say that it could not fall under the attribute of cognition, that to add to its being thought, would involve contradiction. Hence when we talk of the degree of intelligibility of the structures dealt with by theories, we are usually changing the subject of discussion from those structures to biography or autobiography, and are talking about the ease or the strain, the long effort or the brief effort, which somebody experiences in dealing with the structures in question. An instance is the familiar fact that some people find Einsteinian formulations in mechanics much simpler than Newtonian, and others the reverse; as some people find a highly logicized (or formalized) geometry much simpler than Euclid, and others the reverse.

But let us examine an instance of what seems to be theoretical conflict in another field of study. There are influential people who insist that we cannot even begin the explanation of social processes unless we bring to the job an interpretive principle, say the Marxist principle that in the last analysis economic factors are always decisive of all social changes. Others urge that we must bring to, and use in, our social studies some other fundamental explanatory principle antithetic to Marx's. But must we not all agree that there is no serious way of determining how influential (or whether exclusively influential) economic factors, or any other kinds of factors, have been or are in historical changes except by examining the evidence from records and other cultural and technological remains, making observations of processes now under way, developing hypotheses (however intuitively or imaginatively or speculatively), and believing one or other of those hypotheses only so far as it is confirmed by the evidence upon which it was based and by further findings? And these findings are *equally* accessible to every inquirer regardless of his postulates as to the influence of the factors in question, or of his want of any such postulates. Hence it appears that commitment to a material interpretive principle is by no means logically required if a man is to enter upon social studies. And it appears further that the commitment of one man to one such principle, and of another to some other such principle, logically entails no conflict between the hypotheses the two may develop; and more than that, the two men thus committed cannot in fact generate conflicting hypotheses unless they support their beliefs by activities other than those who have distinguished as Reason in senses I, II, and III, and hence are not reasonable persons in sense IV.

In the eighties and nineties of the last century, scientifically minded students of social processes began to urge that the "well-known" intellectual inferiority of Negroes to whites should not merely be asserted but should be carefully measured. As Gunnar Myrdal has remarked, "The history of the measurement of the psychic traits of the American Negro began with attempts to quantify what was already 'known' about him. And usually the scientists *found* what they were seeking."[6] Now is this an instance of assumptions determining findings which would not be valid except on the assumptions? Is it an instance of the necessity of altering assumptions if men are to secure other findings? Not, I think, for reasonably careful investigators. For we have no grounds for asserting that the students of the decades down to 1920 could not measure as reliably the performance of Negroes as they did the performance of whites in intelligence tests, but instead could only derive their figures from their assumptions. The real fault was the failure to recognize that evidence is needed to support *all* synthetic propositions; and that such evidence was needed but was largely lacking to support the particular synthetic proposition which asserts, for Negroes *or* for whites, that performance in certain so-called intelligence tests is a simple function of native capacity. The fault lay precisely *in assuming* that this was the case; and the fault would not have been corrected simply by *assuming* that it was not the case. Progress was made, not by veering from one assumption to the other, but by exploring the materials and finding significant correlations between factors of nurture (as well as of native endowment) and performance in tests.

But does the analysis we have sketched depreciate ideas? Does it imply, or even suggest, that investigators can or should approach any subject matter with minds that are *tabulae rasae*? To say that the analysis logically implies this would involve us in strict contradition. And if the analysis has suggested it, then its rhetoric is very deficient. For it is almost a truism—almost a tautology—to say that if a person is to accomplish anything toward explaining any subject matter he must bring curiosity, imagination, patience, the disposition to alter even favorite beliefs so far as the evidence runs against them (and usually also the more previously mastered information he can bring with him the better) : in a word, he must bring intelligence with him to the job. This is almost, but not quite, a truism, since people do develop these virtues in the process of inquiry and explanation. And unless they possess them as Platonic memories from the heaven of Ideas, or their thinking is guaranteed them by Kantian necessary forms of perception and understanding, presumably first steps in developing such interests, habits, and skills do occur sometime after the fertilization of that ovum which is to become a social scientist.

There could hardly be a more impressive instance of the elimination of the appearance of theoretic conflict mainly by the sort of work we have called Reason in sense III (the philosophical analysis of meaning) than the recognition by physicists and mathematicians of the equivalence of Einsteinian and Newtonian formulas about motion, provided sufficient qualifications are introduced systematically into the Newtonian formulas in order to take account of deviations such as those connected with very high velocities (the evidence for which, *nota bene,* is observed equally by Newtonians and relativists). The only differences that remain which might seem to constitute or to support conflicting hypotheses are involved in Newton's words about homogeneous absolute time and the absolute motion, rest, and positions of which it is said to be a function. Although of course a Newtonian may, if he likes, assert that these terms designate for him various felt qualities (as of utter repose), this will not give him hypotheses in conflict with the relativists. What he would need to do, in order to make out his theory as thus in conflict with relativist mechanics, would be to show that there is some difference of theoretic content expressed by describing changing positions by their relations to whatever has the felt quality he calls rest, as against formulations which either exactly reverse that procedure or read off the relations by reference to frames distinct from either.

To move closer to our own bailiwick: Which of us has not—at least in our salad days—been pursued through the watches of the night by the question: *When* should we say we have a finding—a datum upon which to build beliefs and by which to check them? *Which* are acceptable grounds for the belief that the bell tower has a clockface and hands on its south wall? The noting of a configuration of that class which I believe that I, and others, have commonly named by the term "clock"? Yes. But again, no; for the slips of memory and the eccentricities of perception are notorious. Have I, then, more acceptable grounds for my belief when the statement I make in the presence of the tower converges with the statements of a dozen, or a hundred, or the majority of, other observers? That's better. And yet, after all, what should I be doing then but exactly the same *sort* of thing as before, though perhaps more of it, namely *noting* the tower, various persons, their positions, motions, and statements. I have changed, enlarged, the subject of my attention, but I have achieved no different *kind* of finding. Shall I turn pragmatist and say that a finding, to be taken seriously, must be an operation that leads into proliferation and growth of transformative operations? If I do thus turn pragmatist, then on the central question whether this operation or that does so lead, and which of the two is the more fruitful of such growth, I can get no relevant knowledge except by noting operations of the two sorts, and their contexts and sequelae. And, after all, how very odd of me to think that I can note reliably the divergences and convergences of the doings and sayings of a dozen or a hundred people (and note that these go on in the vicinity of the tower), or note the operations these lead into, but cannot note so reliably the clock configuration on the south face of that tower!

But the problem is not so simple as all this. Schlick and Carnap and Russell and Moore (and hundreds of others, including Dewey) would scarcely have veered back and forth from one of these positions to another if they were thus merely changing from the consideration of one area or sort of subject matter to the consideration of some other area or sort. There are indeed very important differences between what we accomplish when we consider merely what is within our field of awareness, when we consider intersubjective communication and what it probably involves, and when we consider what little we can learn of the immense operational contexts of either of these. But so far as we deal with these differences by the procedures labeled Reason I, II, and III above, all semblance of theoretical conflict between them seems to dissolve. Private notings, intersubjective convergences of statements and manipulations, strands of operational context—all of these occur, all are worth studious attention; but we have no serious grounds for defending any of them as if it were the rival or opponent of the others, as evidence for, or support for, our beliefs. For all that any of them is evidence for, is whatever sorts of entity have been found (or inductively inferred by analogy with observed correlations between entities similar in some respect) to be more or less regularly correlated with the privately noted contents, with the intersubjective convergences, or with the operational strands in question. This result ought to cure some species of epistemological insomnia.

To take another instance, we all remember that some people have regarded two-valued and three-valued or (two plus n)-valued logics as somehow mutually incompatible (and not just as different, and like all different things therefore such that if all a man's attention and energy are concentrated upon one of them it is impossible that he should at the same time be dealing with any other of them). Many have interpreted a third value (in addition to truth and falsity) as some kind of function of frequencies of truth (or falsity) values in some sort of set, or else as what is asserted by true statements to the effect that some man ascribes a certain intuitive weight to a proposition of a certain set. Yet there are a few of such interpreters who then surprise us by alleging that relations could be expressed by the formulas of (two plus n)-valued logics which could not be expressed in the formulas of two-valued logics. Of course if any two-valued logic contains, quite apart from its being two-valued, some kind of self-denying ordinance which restricts its development by ruling out certain very commonly treated sorts of functions of true or false propositions, we might well say that the two-valued logic in question was incompatible with some of the analyses carried out in (two plus n)-valued logics if those lacked the self-denying ordinance. But even in this case the incompatibility is not an instance of any theorem in the one system *taken as in that system* being incompatible with any theorem of any other system *taken as in that other system,* but only an instance of some sorts of development in one, being ruled out by a self-denying ordinance from development in the other. But why anybody should introduce such self-denying ordinances, except merely as indications of plans of concentration (which are in no way incompatible with other men's different plans of concentration, or with one's own plans at other times)—that I cannot see. Certainly a logic's being two-valued does not require its author to impose any such restrictive ordinance upon himself or others. And it would seem to be true that we cannot rule out a two-valued rendering of any multivalued logistic system unless some of the many values merge, so that we cannot say of any proposition that it must either have or not value #1 (where of course its failing to have value #1 may consist in its having value #2 or value #3 or value #4 or value #5 and so on). What attracts many empirical scientists to multivalued logics is, I think, their feeling that those logics yield them some sort of support for considering, and also respectable labels to attach to, hypotheses which they do not know to be true and also do not know to be false. However, the distinguishing of any number of attitudes of belief or doubt toward the asserta of propositions is quite compatible with a two-valued logic. Such a logic would be strained only if a man were to say of the statement, "My attitude toward p is one of doubt (or of rejection, or of confident belief, or of interested curiosity, or *whatever*)," that this statement is not true, and yet it is not not-true either.

Again logics of strict implication and of material implication do not seem to be incompatible with one another, although truistically the concentration of *all* of anybody's efforts on the one is incompatible with his developing the other. Nothing in so-called material systems prevents the interpretation of the dominant implications (in the material systems themselves) of theorems by postulates (or by other theorems), as being strict implications in the sense that the denial of the theorems joined with the assertion of the postulates is self-contradictory. And many years ago, our colleague, Clarence Lewis did not merely argue that material logistics could be developed as subsystems of strict logistics, but actually carried out an instance of such development.

Even those who talk of the logic of love or the logic of power or the logic of events or the logic of art or the logic of cookery (as probably more people do than ever talk of logic in any of the senses just mentioned), as if they somehow conflicted with the logics of the logicians, need only to apply the procedures we have distinguished as Reason in senses I and II and III in order to discover (a) that they are talking (so far as they are asserting anything at all) about various causes and effects of love, power, food, poems, or some other sorts of entities, which causes and effects are not entailed, and are not ruled out, by any of the logics of the logicians and also do not entail or rule out any of those logics, and hence are not in conflict with any of them; or (b) that they are expressing approvals, preferences, disapprovals which could of course in no sense be theoretically incompatible with, or be ruled out by, any logic even where the logic itself might be the object of disapproval.

The supposed conflicts between what have sometimes been called different ways of knowing is another case in point. For we are often tempted to contrast knowledge by authority, knowledge by logico-mathematical demonstration, knowledge by utility, and knowledge by mystic intuition, as if they were conflicting alternatives. But if by saying that a proposition is known to be true, one of us actually means only that it is enunciated by authorities, and another of us means that believing it is in some sense useful, and so on, then we would eliminate all semblance of conflict if each of us would simply say what he thus means—that is would substitute wherever appropriate our respective *definientes* for the *definiendum*. Thus we would make clear that what we mean by our apparently conflicting theses is only that propositions affirmed by authorities are affirmed by authorities, whereas propositions belief in which is in some specified way useful are propositions belief in which is thus useful, and so on and on. And these locutions are all perfectly compatible with one another.

But it is plain that serious philosophers have meant nothing so trivial as this. They seem generally to have intended synthetic statements when they have said that opinions affirmed by authorities, or opinions belief in which is useful, or opinions prompted by mystic insight, *aut alia,* are true or pre-eminently probable. Quite generally they seem to have meant, by calling a proposition true, that it asserts such relations and characters of its subject matter as that subject matter actually possesses. One partisan then holds that propositions enunciated by authorities are not merely true in the sense of being enunciated by authorities, but are true in the sense that they assert some entities or other to be qualitied and related as they actually are; and so on of the other partisans. But if this is what is intended, the question of how high the correlation is between the statements of authorities, or the usefulness of beliefs, and the truth or probability of those statements or beliefs, is not a question that can be significantly settled by a definition, or by committing oneself to a postulate that the correlation is highest (or even infallible) in one case or the other. We have no serious way to approach an answer to the question except by gath-

ering evidence as to how often authority X's predictions are confirmed, and so on. And this evidence is intrinsically as accessible
to the partisan of one way of knowing as to the partisan of any
allegedly opposed way of knowing. Otherwise the partisans could
not possibly recognize their opinions as opposed.

From this conclusion there are two ways of escape. One way is
for one partisan to assert that truth really is nothing but what is
affirmed by authorities, another partisan that it is really nothing
but what is useful to believe, and so on. But then we are back
among the trivial tautologies which were just exposed. I do not
think that considerable philosophers have espoused them; and
even if they had, the various tautologies could not stand in theoretic conflict. The other way of escape is for each partisan to say
that what he *really* means is that he is most interested in, or most
hopeful of, the results of believing what is affirmed by authorities,
or of believing what in some specified sense is useful to believe,
aut alia. But here again there can be no conflict between any hypotheses which are supported by Reason in senses I or II or III,
but only manifestations of diverse temperaments and condition-
ings, interesting to psychologists, and also of very *general* and
moral interest if the persons thus expressing their temperamental
differences happen to be influential in some field of theory or of
practice.

In constructing histories of philosophy, nineteenth-century
scholars set up patterns which quickly became traditional and
have persisted with remarkable stubbornness. None of these patterns (or stereotypes) has been more rigid than that of representing
as in dramatic (or even melodramatic) conflict the attempts of so-
called "continental rationalists" to establish truths about nature
and history by logico-mathematical deduction, and the attempts
of so-called "British empiricists" to rely on sensations only, rejecting necessities of reason altogether. Yet every reader of Descartes is impressed—indeed, if he has previously read the available
histories of philosophy he is literally *shocked*—to find Descartes
insisting in the *Regulae* that no deduction from other propositions
could possibly demonstrate the truth of any proposition, although
it might help us toward convenient exposition of them all. If the
proposition called a conclusion is true, it can only be true (Descartes argued) because it is evident to the natural light, and not
because any set or sequence of *other* propositions is thus true. And
in letters to his old friend Mersenne, he complained that he could

make no further progress in his study of vision unless he could get from the abattoirs of Paris a better supply of ox-eyes to dissect. This is the same Descartes, fragments from whose *Le Monde* promised to establish by the procedures of what we have come to call analytical geometry *all* the facts that make up the universe, past, present, and to come.

Again, in Leibniz's account of synthetic propositions as all of them only contingently true (if true at all), and of all necessary truths as analytic, we find a clearer statement than any which Hume gives us of the view that there can be no logically necessary connections between entities of any sorts that are distinguishable from one another.

If, on the other hand, to use general synthetic principles as self-evident without empirical support—as necessary truths—is to be a rationalist, then both Locke and Berkeley in their use of such principles as that of causation were very much more rationalists than was Leibniz. For the full story of this alleged major conflict the work of Spinoza and the work of Hume are especially important; and if anybody ever tells that story faithfully it will be a very long one. But we can say confidently that the widely accepted story of the conflict between able rationalists and able empiricists (as distinguished from the straw men of the textbooks) is very largely mythology.

Such seeming theoretic conflicts in scientific and historical explanation, and in restricted fields of philosophic study, are innumerable and very challenging. The temptation is to go through a great many of them, and in very much fuller detail, in order to determine whether in fact they do yield or do not yield to the application of the sorts of activity distinguished as four phases of the work of reason. But certain other questions press upon us as philosophers, questions which are said to cut under and to expose as superficial all of our present considerations. Have we too glibly and carelessly talked of findings as being evidence for one specific hypothesis or another—and evidence equally for all interpreters? With the question "What is a finding? What is a datum?" we have dealt cursorily; and also with the seeming conflict between immediate notings, interpersonal convergences and agreements of the reports of several observers, and operations which lead into the transformation of other operations. But take any of these, *or anything else,* as findings—for *what* are they evidence? Will not this depend upon one's theory of evidence and of probability and one's basic convictions as to the structures and the kinds of being? And what is a fully developed theory of events, findings, and evidence but a philosophy, or a metaphysic? And are not philosophers and philosophies conspicuous for their sharp oppositions—never, some say, since the medieval controversy over universals, so sharp as they are today? And does not each major philosophical position, for all its differences from rival positions, claim to reject no evidence, to ignore or exclude no findings? If, holding even faintheartedly the ancient faith, we suppose that philosophical thought contributes at least something to the resolution of conflicts, but if also we learn that such thought characteristically develops opposing systems, the problem of the nature of theoretic conflict is indeed pressed home to us students of philosophy, and in aggravated form. For at this level the puzzles seem to grow in number, in complexity, and even in a kind of self-perpetuating if not automatically expanding circularity. But I have good reason to believe that neither twenty pages nor twenty volumes would suffice to formulate—let alone to discuss—the questions which (in this connection) genuine perplexity or ingenuity or the love of debate can construct. I shall make only a few simple suggestions and leave to other occasions—and largely to the philosophic gifts, the special information, and the special quandaries of others—their application and their testing.

Men have, of course, meant many different sorts of activity, and many sorts of structures of concepts or of beliefs, by the word "philosophy." And so far as they are different sorts of activity, these are not in theoretic conflict any more than doing mathematics and doing archeology and singing a song and sailing a boat are in theoretic conflict. But when philosophies are construed as conflicting, they have usually been conceived as very comprehensive theories of the universe, developed with special attention to problems of the method and validity of explanation, to problems of the relation of interpretive activity to materials interpreted, and to problems of value.

Now rival philosophies are often conveniently distinguished by the different sets of basic categories which each characteristically employs. Thus it has been said of Platonists, Aristotelians, Kantians, Christian cosmologists, organicists, materialists, naturalists, that their basic categories are respectively: essense and becoming; form, process and purpose (or, rather crudely, substance and attribute) ; thing-in-itself, forms of organization, and phenomena; God's purposes and God's acts; dynamic organic interrelatedness; matter and motion; event, quality, and relation.

The question whether there exists instances of the kinds of traits or entities meant by any of these terms is not settled (or even in any way affected) by anybody's using the terms (or the kinds of things the terms mean) as basic categories—unless what we mean by saying of anything that it exists is simply that we are using it (or the name of its kind) as a basic category in our explanatory procedures. If we mean something else by existence (and I do not pretend to impose a "right" or "best" definition upon that term) , then we must determine whether instances of the entities meant by our basic categories, whichever they are, do in that sense (whatever it may be) exist, by means of evidence not composed of, nor generated by, our use of the particular categories as basic, but by means of evidence available to any thinker whether he uses our categories or others as basic. For we can describe anything encountered or imagined, and its found or supposed context and operations, *with precise equivalence of content* in our descriptions (though with considerable differences of nomenclature) , whether we describe it by stating its resemblances and differences with respect to a structure imagined and so far as we know not otherwise existent, or by stating its resemblances and differences with respect to a kind of structure of which instances have been found to exist (in *any* specified sense of the term "existence") .

We may wish to use as categories terms that name kinds of traits, structures, or operations which we suppose to be exceptionally pervasive of nature—or the kinds of traits, structures, or operations so named. But again our supposings and our choice of categories imply nothing whatever as to how pervasive of nature any sort of trait or structure or operation may be. For have we any seriously defensible way of determining how widespread in existence any factor is except by exploring areas of existence—and in any relation whatever to those sorts of operation which we call experiments? People who use the opposed categories of organicism or naturalism are sometimes (perhaps often) more interested respectively in similarities or in differences; in fused dynamic complexes or (some say, although I know of no impressive supporting evidence in the history of philosophy) in distinguishable ingredients of the various fusions. Of course we may, if we wish, thus change the subject and discuss the personalities and biographies of philosophers. But if we do, what we discover to be their differing interests can hardly be taken as entailing or as supporting different hypotheses about the distribution in the world of the various factors in which they are interested. It may be extremely difficult for some men to discriminate traits noticed by others. But this is not a consequence of the traits being intrinsically cognizable only by some—say those who employ as basic categories the kinds of traits in question or the names of those kinds of traits. If there were traits such that only one philosopher or one sect of philosophers could cognize them or their likes, and only another philosopher or another sect of philosophers could cognize other traits or their likes, then it would be impossible for such individuals, or for the members of such sects, to conceive that they differed, since the conception by each, of the traits cognized by the others, is ruled out. Conflict develops when partisans neglect logic and science and philosophical distinctions and allow enthusiasm (or inertia) to prompt them to say that qualities or configurations found here and here and here must necessarily be the fundamental (or the really real, or merely the *de facto*) traits of everything everywhere.

The same story seems to hold of genetic or causal priority. We cannot add one iota of support to a belief that matter and motion are in some sense primary existents, whereas qualities are derivative from them, by taking matter and motion as basic categories and discussing and interpreting all that we find or imagine by its resemblances to, differences from, and its spatiotemporal correlations with, specific instances of moving bodies. The time has surely long since passed when anybody would argue that causal or any other kind of relation could imply, or justify, the reduction of one of the sorts of relata to any other sort. If certain growing organic structures are found to precede, to follow, to include, or to be included by, certain approximate mechanical regularities, then a scrupulous account of one in terms of its relations to the other will be exactly equivalent in content to a scrupulous account of the second in terms of its relations to the first. Hence the complete ineptitude of the common criticism that we are thus resolving philosophical conflicts only by asking others to accept our categories, or to translate their hypotheses into terms of those categories—as Johnny discovers that everybody in the crowd is out of step . . . with *him;* and recommends that they all get into step! Dealing with entities of any sort as related to one categorial frame or another does not make the entities one whit more or less like (or unlike) the constituents of either frame, or change in any way their relations to one another or to anything else. Choice of a set of categories makes no legitimate difference in the content of any opinions. If any A differs in any respects from any B, or resembles it in any respects, then the scrupulous description or interpretation of A as a function of B will be identical in content with an equally scrupulous description or interpretation of B as a (roughly converse) function of A.

But when we go beyond the little area of findings—in whatever way the term "finding" is defined or used—to the immense areas about which we construct the hypotheses for which we take findings to be evidence, favorable or otherwise—then surely no finding, no qualited and structured event or complex of events is, *in and of itself,* evidence for anything other than itself. We are therefore often tempted to say, that whatever else than itself anything is evidence for, must depend upon the interpreter's philosophy, upon his notion of the general hang of things in the world, or at least upon his notion of evidence. But what notion of evidence can we seriously defend except the notion that an occurrence of the sort A is evidence for an occurrence of the sort B, so far as the likes of A have been found to be accompanied by the likes of B, or constituents or phases or analogues of the one with constituents or phases or analogues of the other (proper allowance being made, of course, and by the same procedure, for all other known significant relations in the field)? We have every one of us at one time or another objected to such an account as "pedantry." In moving experiences of poetry and religion and friendship, and of everyday doings like saddling a horse or felling a tree, we have all felt nisus, continuities with the past and tendencies pushing into the future, which prompt us to regard these experiences as evidence of a better sort than the correlations mentioned. That we have such experiences is indisputable. That they induce confident beliefs is widely recognized. But that they are evidence for that, the belief in which they induce, we cannot establish by the vividness of our feelings or the strength of our convictions. Men felt vividly that the earth is at absolute rest; that such and such favorite paintings and poems *must* express to all men of all ages the most precious of all insights or convey to them the greatest delight; that their countries were bound to triumph in wars (some of which, in the event, they have won, some lost); that there just could not be a shift in the activity of a physical system, or of any part of a physical system, without "an impressed force." But can we say that these feelings or convictions were themselves evidence for what men thus believed, except so far as a positive correlation is established between such convictions and things turning out as the propositions (constituent of those convictions) assert? If what we experience is something distinguishable as B developing in, or out of, A, and an aura of felt nisus that pervades the development, what would justify us in regarding A plus the nisus as evidence for B (so long as the nisus does not actually include the occurrence of B), except our observing a positive correlation of the kind discussed between these factors? For we often experience effort that fails of result; and there is little reason to suppose that felt effort is involved in those gravitational relations between moon and ocean called the tides (to take one example from millions). Yet in the light of correlations well established, the fact that the moon is in a certain phase is exceedingly good evidence for certain states of the tides.

Again we sometimes offer as a better interpretation of the evidence-relation, the thesis that the structure of nature (or of the world), so far as we understand it, justifies us in regarding A as evidence for B, if that structure is such as to include a configuration of A's and B's regularly associated in one way or another. But what way have we of determining what the structure of nature probably is, except precisely by exploring the similarities and differences and various other correlations of the occurrences of as many of the various strands of existence as we can? Thus this last notion of the evidence-relation seems to be an illustration of, rather than an alternative to, the "correlation" interpretation. If we attempt to use an *a priori* theory of the structure of nature in order to determine what is evidence for what, we can get no farther than saying that if nature is structured thus and so, then restricted areas of nature must accord with that structure. But that procedure could never yield any slightest grounds for believing that nature is so structured, or for believing anything rather than its opposite about the traits of the restricted areas. For the only serious ground we could have for the probable truth of the above protasis would be the truth or probability of the apodosis stated (along with various other apodoses).

As for basic categories as reflecting evaluations, if a man's evaluations are essentially expressions of his approvals, then there need be no theoretic conflict between Jones and Smith when Jones approves and Smith disapproves of any sort of event, structure, plan or operation. And if Jones' and Smith's different philosophical categories essentially reflect such differing approvals, so far they neither express nor entail any conflicting beliefs. If on the other hand a man's evaluations are reports, or hypotheses, to the effect that certain entities have (or would have if they came into existence) the traits or structures which he means by the word "valuable," then the determining whether his opinion is correct is a matter of ordinary scientific finding and inference, and is not affected by his using as basic frames of reference in description and explanation the traits which he means by "valuable." If his neighbor means some different class of characters by the term "valuable," the two are not thereby in theoretical conflict; and moreover they will see that they are not if each will make clear which specific class of traits he thus means. One says that X is more valuable than Y; the other reverses the judgment. But if they mean different sorts of traits by the term "valuable," then determining how much of each sort of trait X and Y may exhibit, or how much the occurrence of X and the occurrence of Y may favor the manifestation in various L's and M's and N's of what each means by "value," is a problem to which exploration and evidence are relevant, but not dispute. And if Jones and Smith mean either the same sorts of traits or different sorts of traits by "valuable," then unless we hold that there is evidence available to one which is intrinsically incognizable by the other, the two cannot be justified in holding conflicting opinions by any of the four sorts of work of reason which we have considered. If Jones and Smith are antagonistic, but neither we nor they are able to make approximately clear whether each is expressing emotional attitudes or is asserting that various objects have (or lack) in various degrees certain sorts of traits which he means by "valuable," then neither Jones nor Smith nor any of the rest of us is in a position to say that there is theoretical conflict here.

In reasonably mature scientific and scholarly disciplines the holding of conflicting opinions about areas of their subject matters is not regarded as a virtue but rather as a sign that the function of evidence has been neglected or that analysis of meanings has been omitted or confused. It is in some of the so-called social sciences, in some psychological discussions, but particularly in philosophy, that we often find divergence of explanatory hypotheses welcomed as such. A distinguished economist has lately written, "The maximum development of differences of opinion in

all fields of thought is eminently desirable." Now if no two people
in the world ever agreed in any opinion, and if nobody ever agreed
with his own earlier opinions for five minutes running, we should
only be *approaching* (but by no means achieving) the maximum
development of differences of opinion. Is that *really* a desirable
or a defensible objective?

But if my economist friend means by his statement that we should
all recognize that possibilities are logically infinite (that is, that the
denial of their infinity is self-contradictory); that no matter how
much we might ever come to know, the variety of further possibilities of internal structure and of external context of what was
known must remain unlimited; that, as C. I. Lewis has reminded
us in writing of postulate sets, if any one of them is "sufficient
for a mathematical system, then there will be any number of
alternative sets . . . which likewise are sufficient"[7]—if my economist
friend means to convey such advice by his statement, then his celebration of maximum differences of opinion is a way (but a misleading way) of emphasizing a truism of elementary logic. For
what is it of which we can say with logical necessity that it could
not be? Nothing; that which literally and completely is, and is
not, anything whatever. And of what seeming propositions can
we say that it is logically impossible that they be true (or indeed
false), except the self-contradictory propositions which, in totally
denying whatever in one part they assert, assert nothing.

To turn from the possible to whatever is contrasted with it as
in some sense actual, how much should we have to know of what,
among infinite possibilities, actually exists or has existed, in order
to know that certain sorts of relations or qualities are (and will be)
nowhere realized in events? What we should have to know in
order to do this is all events and all their qualities and relations,
and besides this the truth of the proposition that what we know
is absolutely all—that there was never and will never be anything
more or other. But to know the truth of this latter proposition
has been shown by dozens of philosophers to be logically impossible.

We must therefore insist that every occurrence is compatible
with an unlimited number of alternative explanatory hypotheses.
But does it therefore follow that it is desirable, or at all defensible,
that men should take sides, one holding that one hypothesis is the
most probable and every other man holding that some other hypothesis is the most probable, and all changing their beliefs as fast
as they can? So far as different evidences are intrinsically inac-

cessible to different interpreters they could not even imagine that they differed with respect to "they knew not what." So far as, of accessible evidence, one man deals with one section, another with another, the different inferences they may make, when geared to their supporting evidence, must be entirely compatible. And if the different interpreters use, let us say, one of them one method of reckoning probabilities, another another, then for both it will be equally true that on evidence E, by probability method P_1, inference I_1 will enjoy thus much support; whereas on the same evidence E, but by probability method P_2, inference I_2 will enjoy so much support. And if one asks which is the better method of reckoning probabilities (logical inconsistency, of course, ruled out in both cases), have we any serious way of approaching an answer except by finding which method supports inferences the more commonly confirmed by further exploration and observation?

Philosophy considered as peacemaker, as we have done here, does and can in no way limit the possibilities of what may exist, of what may be meant, or of the range of hypotheses that might be true. It carries with it no logical or theoretical restrictions upon the free play of imagination, intellectual or poetic. But would our analysis, if accepted, nevertheless in fact remove a major stimulus to intellectual advance? Is the strife of partisans the best seedbed for new hypotheses and new discoveries? In asking these questions we are again changing the subject of discussion from the nature of theoretical conflict to the temperaments and psychological proclivities of thinkers—of scientists and philosophers. The serious way to ascertain the probabilities with respect to our changed subject would be not by debate but by the fullest sort of historical and psychological investigation. I, of course, do not know the answer. But if theoretical conflict is in fact incompatible with the careful prosecution of the procedures of reason which we have discriminated, then would it not be a very odd thinker who understood this situation and yet could stimulate himself by participating as a partisan in such conflict? He would be much the same kind of person as the man who could actually encourage himself by holding a belief when he was convinced that he had no other ground for the belief except that it thus encouraged him. Undoubtedly there are some persons of such temper, and even among our ablest scientists and philosophers.

Such pacifism of philosophical reason is not an empty gesture of crying "Peace, peace," when there is no peace. It is something to achieve (or to approach) by hard work. If the interpretation is theoretically acceptable it is a summons to such philosophers as are not merely informed but are also in the ancient sense lovers of wisdom, a summons to jobs, almost innumerable jobs, that need doing. For, if the view is satisfactory, theoretical conflicts are largely wasteful of men's intellectual energies, and if they are actually conflicts of opinion and not merely oppositions of interests or of passions, they are resolvable by the kinds of work of reason which we have distinguished and illustrated. At the best, such conflicts tend to fog over our practical oppositions and to distract us from the work of understanding them;—as the insufficiently examined, seeming opposition between national interests and international government (to cite one instance from thousands) may easily prevent our discovering the probability that international government is needed, if nations are to survive at all, and even have *any* interests, high or low, let alone satisfy them. At the worst, theoretic conflicts nourish and greatly increase practical antagonisms. And where groups of human beings share any basic preferences—even for life over death or for health over disease—many of their practical disagreements will be found to reflect conflicting opinions about the probabilities that various policies will secure or enhance what they are agreed in approving and desiring. In such cases the resolution of theoretical conflicts, and the making clear how that resolution can be effected, fulfills the ancient faith in reason. And it could be a chief contribution of philosophy to the fruitful reconciliation (as contrasted with the mere brute suppression) of the oppositions—economic, political, and military—which remain threats to the very existence, and hence (as Aristotle observed generally of threats to our existence) necessarily also threats to all the precious sorts of achievement, of creatures of our kind.

This essay is adapted from a slightly longer version which appeared in *The Philosophical Review* of July, 1946, and is reprinted with the permission of the editors.

1. *Ethica*, III, Prop. 15 et Cor., Prop. 51; IV, Prop. 8.
2. P. Pavlov, *Conditioned Reflexes*, Oxford Press, 1927, p. 148 and elsewhere.
3. New York, 1940, p. 55.
4. *Ibid.*, p. 66.
5. H. Woodrow, *Psychological Bulletin*, Vol. XXXIX, No. 3.
6. Gunnar Myrdal, *An American Dilemma* (Harper & Bros., N. Y., 1941), Vol. I, p. 145.
7. C. I. Lewis, *Philosophy and Phenomenological Research*, Vol. IV, p. 236.

EVERETT W. HALL

Mill's "Proof" of Utility

One need not be a worshiper at the shrine of one's intellectual ancestors to feel a slight sense of distaste at the sight of every author of an elementary textbook in logic or ethics scurrying to chapter iv of Mill's *Utilitarianism,* "Of What Sort of Proof the Principle of Utility Is Susceptible," for examples of fallacies sufficiently blatant to be grasped at a glance by the untrained mind. It is just too obvious that the relation of "desirable" to "desired" is only suffixally similar to the relation of "audible" to "heard" ("audited"). And who cannot spot the error of deriving "everyone desires the general happiness" from "each desires his own happiness"? And so we might go down through the traditional list. But were we to try to understand Mill's argument as a whole and in the simple and obvious sense in which, when so viewed, it seems only fair to take it, we might find a core worth serious consideration.

We must charge this tendency to force Mill's proof of the principle of utility into a set of the most patent fallacies to really first-line philosophers. For example, F. H. Bradley, in *Ethical Studies,*[1] excuses himself for taking time to point out the tissue of inconsistencies that, so he claims, is Mill's argument. "I am ashamed," he writes, "to have to examine such reasoning, but it is necessary to do so, since it is common enough."[2] I shall, however, be mainly concerned to scrutinize the criticisms of another first-rank philosopher, partly because I think he is probably the most influential source of the traditional disparagement of Mill's argument and partly because he has stated the supposed case against Mill's proof most clearly and cogently. I refer to G. E. Moore, and specifically to chapter iii of *Principia Ethica*.

Let us see what Moore's criticism is. For purposes of analysis it is well to have Mill's argument before us, familiar as that argument is. For the moment we shall note only what Moore calls the "first step" and, in fact, only the first half of the first step, which I shall designate "IA":

> (IA) The only proof capable of being given that a thing is visible, is that people actually see it. The only proof that a sound is audible, is that people hear it; and so of the other sources of our experience. In like manner, I apprehend, the sole evidence it is possible to produce that anything is desirable, is that people do actually desire it. If the end which the utilitarian doctrine proposes to itself were not, in theory and in practice, acknowledged to be an end, nothing could ever convince any person that it was so.[3]

Of this, Moore says: "Well, the fallacy in this step is so obvious, that it is quite wonderful how Mill failed to see it."[4] What fallacy? A fallacy Moore calls "the naturalistic fallacy." "Mill has made as naïve and artless a use of the naturalistic fallacy as anybody could desire. 'Good,' he tells us, means 'desirable,' and you can only find out what is desirable by seeking to find out what is actually desired. . . . The important step for Ethics is this one just taken, the step which pretends to prove that 'good' means 'desired.' "[5]

And just what is this naturalistic fallacy that Mill committed so naïvely and artlessly?

> It may be true that all things which are good are *also* something else, just as it is true that all things which are yellow produce a certain kind of vibration in the light. And it is a fact, that Ethics aims at discovering what are those other properties belonging to all things which are good. But far too many philosophers have thought that when they named those other

properties they were actually defining good; that these properties, in fact, were simply not "other," but absolutely and entirely the same with goodness. This view I propose to call the "naturalistic fallacy" and of it I shall now endeavor to dispose.[6]

Now to return to the issue. I think that Moore intends to accuse Mill of identifying two properties that are different, *viz.,* desirableness and desiredness, and this, perhaps, as a step toward identifying goodness with pleasure. I happen to believe, however, that Mill does mean to accept desirableness and desiredness as different properties and that his argument makes this clear and that he does not commit the naturalistic fallacy.

Turning back to step IA, we find Mill saying, "The sole evidence it is possible to produce that anything is desirable is that people actually do desire it." Moore himself correctly paraphrases this in one place, ". . . you can only find out what is desirable by seeking to find out what is actually desired." But then, later, he makes the astounding assertion, without any foundation, that Mill has pretended "to prove that 'good' means 'desired' "! I can only account for this flagrant reading into Mill of the naturalistic fallacy by supposing that Moore could not grasp any other sense to Mill's argument and so thought that Mill *must* have committed this fallacy. But *there is* another and an obvious sense to any interpreter not debauched with verbal casuistry, as I hope to show.

To proceed—Moore continues his attack as follows:

> The fact is that "desirable" does not mean "able to be desired" as "visible" means "able to be seen." The desirable means simply what *ought* to be desired or *deserves* to be desired; just as the detestable means not what can be but what ought to be detested and the damnable what deserves to be damned. Mill has, then, smuggled in, under cover of the word "desirable," the very notion about which he ought to be quite clear. "Desirable" does indeed mean "what it is good to desire"; but when this is understood, it is no longer plausible to say that our only test of *that,* is what is actually desired.[7]

This passage is a classic. Does it not show the complete bankruptcy of Mill's proof of utility? But there is one small question. What reason is there to suppose that Mill was not perfectly aware that "desirable" does not mean "able to be desired" and so, in *this* respect, was not at all analogous to "visible"? Could there be no other way in which the evidence for desirability must be like the evidence for visibility than in the suffixes of the adjectival designations? I think a glance at the whole argument shows that there is. And on what grounds does Moore so peremptorily continue: " 'Desirable' does indeed mean 'what it is good to desire'; but when this is understood, it is no longer plausible to say that our only test of *that* is what is actually desired"? Does he mean to make the astounding assertion which he seems to make, that anyone who says that the only test of the occurrence of A is the occurrence of B must be identifying A with B? This would force everyone who admits the extensional equivalence of two properties into a commission of the naturalistic fallacy!

Let us continue with Moore's criticism:

> Is it merely a tautology when the Prayer Book talks of *good* desires? Are not *bad* desires also possible? Nay, we find Mill himself talking of a "better and nobler object of desire," . . . as if, after all, what is desired were not *ipso facto* good, and good in proportion to the amount it is desired.[8]

Heaven forbid that an English philosopher should espouse a position that makes something in the prayer book a trivial tautology! I shall not undertake to defend Mill in general against such a serious charge, but on the particular point at issue I think I can clear his name. Apparently Moore's argument (which is here mostly suppressed, which perhaps accounts for its mounting vehemence) is that, since the desirable just is the desired for Mill, every desire must be good (desirable). Note, first, that this again assumes that Mill has committed the naturalistic fallacy. Now, even supposing that he had, Moore's argument breaks down; for this fallacy would identify the desirable with the desired, not with desire. A desirable desire would be a desired desire, and not every desire is desired (in fact, even if it were, to state this would require a synthetic sentence). And, still on the assumption that the naturalistic fallacy has been committed, it would be appropriate to define "bad" as "being the object of an aversion," so that it could be plausibly held that there are bad desires. However, all this is outside the utilitarian framework of ideas. That framework requires that a motive be judged good or bad not by the goodness or badness of its object but by the goodness or badness of its tendency, that is, of its total probable consequences if its objects be realized. It is true that Mill rejects the hedonic calculus of Bentham (if that means that the morally good man must calculate the probable effects of every alternative in every choice-situation) in favor of living by traditional moral rules in most situations, but this is only a concession as to a tool for ascertaining probable consequences, and does not entail giving up the position that desires can be judged good or bad only by the test of their total probably consequences.

This leads immediately into a consideration of Moore's next thrust:

> Moreover, if the desired is *ipso facto* the good; then the good is *ipso facto* the motive of our actions, and there can be no question of finding motives for doing it, as Mill is at such pains to do. If Mill's explanation of "desirable" be *true,* then his statement . . . that the rule of action may be *confounded* with the motive of it is untrue: for the motive of action will then be according to him *ipso facto* its rule; there can be no distinction between the two, and therefore no confusion, and thus he has contradicted himself flatly.[9]

The reference here is to the following passage from chapter ii of *Utilitarianism:* Some objectors to utilitarianism

> . . . say it is exacting too much to require that people shall always act from the inducement of promoting the general interests of society. But this is to mistake the very meaning of a standard of morals, and confound the rule of action with the motive of it. It is the business of ethics to tell us what are our duties, or by what test we may know them; but no system of ethics requires that the sole motive of all we do shall be a feeling of duty; on the contrary, ninety-nine hundredths of all our actions are done from other motives, and rightly so done, if the rule of duty does not condemn them.[10]

This is in manifest contradiction with the naturalistic fallacy of identifying good with desired (on the assumption, probably correct, that "motive of action" refers to the object desired) —so much so, in fact, that it should have at least raised the suspicion that Mill's argument for the principle of utility does not reduce to a commission of that fallacy.

Finally, Moore formulates his criticism of Mills' step IA in the form of an accusation that Mill has committed the fallacy of ambiguous middle:

> Well, then, the first step by which Mill has attempted to establish his Hedonism is simply fallacious. He has attempted to establish the identity of the good with the desired, by confusing

the proper sense of "desirable," in which it denotes that which it is good to desire, with the sense which it would bear if it were analogous to such words as "visible." If "desirable" is to be identical with "good," then it must bear one sense; and if it is to be identical with "desired," then it must bear quite another sense. And yet to Mill's contention that the desired is necessarily good, it is quite essential that these two senses of "desirable" should be the same.[11]

I take it Moore is saying that Mill's argument can be formulated as a syllogism in *Barbara*:

> The good is identical with the desirable.
> The desirable is identical with the desired.
> Therefore, the good is identical with the desired.

And in this syllogism, says Moore, the middle term, "desirable," is ambiguous. Here the naturalistic fallacy would appear as the conclusion of a fallacious line of proof. But what evidence is there that Mill meant to use such a syllogism? I find none. Of the whole syllogism, it is clear only that Mill would accept the minor premise, that the desirable and the good are identical.

It is now time to turn to the second half of Mill's first step, which I shall name "IB":

> (IB) No reason can be given why the general happiness is desirable, except that each person, so far as he believes it to be attainable, desires his own happiness. This, however, being the fact, we have not only all the proof which the case admits of, but all which it is possible to require, that happiness is a good: that each person's happiness is a good to that person, and the general happiness, therefore, a good to the aggregate of all persons. Happiness has made out its title as *one* of the ends of conduct, and consequently one of the criteria of morality.[12]

Moore does not specifically criticize this passage, though it is easy to guess how he would criticize it by reference to his method of dealing with step IA and his discussion (without special reference to this passage) of egoistic hedonism.[13] But there is no need to construct a hypothetical criticism; we can fill in the lacuna in Moore by turning to Bradley, who, in this particular conflict, is clearly an ally. Referring to step IB, Bradley writes:

> Whether our "great modern logician" thought that by this he had proved that the happiness of all was desirable for each,

I will not undertake to say. He either meant to prove this, or has proved what he started with, *viz.* that each desires his own pleasure. And yet there is a certain plausibility about it. If many pigs are fed at one trough, each desires his own food, and somehow as a consequence does seem to desire the food of all; and by parity of reasoning it should follow that each pig, desiring his own pleasure, desires also the pleasure of *all*.[14]

And in a footnote he adds:

Either Mill meant to argue, "*Because* everybody desires his own pleasure, *therefore* everybody desires his own pleasure"; or "Because everybody desires his own pleasure, *therefore* everybody desires the pleasure of everybody else." Disciples may take their choice.[15]

Somehow the warning that Mill put into step IB—"all the proof that the case admits of"—did not make any impression. Bradley, like Moore, is assuming that our "great modern logician," as he derisively characterizes Mill, *must* be presenting in his "proof" of the principle of utility a strict, logical deduction. It is high time that this whole interpretation be fundamentally and decisively challenged.

If we turn back to chapter i of *Utilitarianism,* we find Mill unequivocally rejecting any such interpretation:

On the present occasion, I shall, without further discussion of the other theories, attempt to contribute something towards the understanding and appreciation of the Utilitarian or Happiness theory, and towards such proof as it is susceptible of. It is evident that this cannot be proof in the ordinary and popular meaning of the term. Questions of ultimate ends are not amenable to direct proof. Whatever can be proved to be good, must be so by being shown to be a means to something admitted to be good without proof. . . . If, then, it is asserted that there is a comprehensive formula, including all things which are in themselves good, and that whatever else is good, is not so as an end, but as a mean, the formula may be accepted or rejected, but is not a subject of what is commonly understood by proof.[16]

And the very first sentence of chapter iv reverts to this disavowal of any strict proof of the principle of utility: "It has already been remarked, that questions of ultimate ends do not admit of strict proof, in the ordinary acceptation of the term."[17] Not only does Mill thus explicitly disavow any attempt to give a strict proof of the principle of utility, but he makes it clear that the "proof" which he offers is quite another sort of thing. Returning to chapter i, we find him continuing:

> We are not, however, to infer that its acceptance or rejection must depend on blind impulse, or arbitrary choice. There is a larger meaning of the word proof, in which this question is as amenable to it as any other of the disputed questions of philosophy. The subject is within the cognizance of the rational faculty; and neither does that faculty deal with it solely in the way of intuition. Considerations may be presented capable of determining the intellect either to give or withhold its assent to the doctrine; and this is equivalent to proof.
>
> We shall examine presently of what nature are these considerations; in what manner they apply to the case, and what rational grounds, therefore, can be given for accepting or rejecting the utilitarian formula.[18]

The very title of chapter iv is illuminating, "Of What Sort of Proof the Principle of Utility Is Susceptible." Apparently, Mill considered that he was not so much giving a proof of the principle of utility as discussing the question of the meaning of "proof" when applied to an ethical first principle. So we find him asking, concerning the principle of utility, "What ought to be required of this doctrine—what conditions is it requisite that the doctrine should fulfill—to make good its claim to be believed?"[19]

So much, then, is obvious. Mill utterly disavows any attempt to give a strict proof of the principle of utility. Thus steps IA and IB cannot be interpreted as Moore and Bradley have interpreted them; for then they would be simply attempted strict deductions that, unfortunately, are failures because of the commission of fallacies that any schoolboy can detect.[20]

This result is final and quite unassailable. We now come to the more interesting and hazardous task of trying to ascertain just what is the nature of those considerations which, Mill thinks, are capable of determining the intellect to give assent to the principle of utility. And first let us call to mind the well-known, but not on that account wholly irrelevant, fact that Mill was an empiricist, an opponent of all forms of intuitionism and a priorism. That Mill himself thought this relevant is clear from chapter i of *Utilitarianism,* which is devoted precisely to its reiteration in application to ethics:

According to the one opinion, the principles of morals are evident *a priori,* requiring nothing to command assent, except that the meaning of the terms be understood. According to the other doctrine, right and wrong, as well as truth and falsehood, are questions of observation and experience.[21]

Yet Mill is clear that a peculiar problem marks off ethical questions from factual. It is not possible to determine what is right or wrong in individual cases by direct perception. It is necessary, in making ethical judgments, to apply general principles that go back to an ethical first principle: ". . . the morality of an individual action is not a question of direct perception, but of the application of a law to an individual case."[22] Thus this serious question faces the ethical empiricist: How can one's ethical first principle (such as the principle of utility) be established? Self-evidence is not available, for appeal to it would be an embracing of intuitionism; nor is inductive generalization, since the rightness or wrongness of individual acts is not open to direct perception.

In this situation Mill makes use of two considerations, both of which he got from Bentham, not to *prove* the principle of utility but to *make it acceptable* to reasonable men. One of these is essentially an appeal to men's honesty. When ordinary men try to justify their moral judgments rationally, they do so by the tacit use of the principle of utility. When an ethicist attempts to show why his ethical first principle (if it differs from that of utility) should be accepted, he does so by utilitarian arguments.[23] This is not, I am convinced, the old *consensus gentium* argument, nor does it rest on a social-agreement theory of truth. If it were and did, a strict proof of utility would be possible. It is rather, as I have said, an appeal to intellectual honesty. It says, "My dear ethicist, whenever you are caught off guard, either in everyday situations or in arguing for some ethical principle, you find your reasons go back to a tacit assumption of utility as the first principle of ethics. What more does the utilitarian need to do than to bring this clearly to your attention?"

I do not, however, think that this was the main consideration that Mill wished to present in developing a favorable attitude toward the principle of utility. In the first place, it is not in any special sense empirical. In the second place, he adverts to it briefly in chapter i, but not at all in chapter iv, which, as we have seen, is devoted to the task of showing "of what sort of proof the principle of utility is susceptible." Chapter iv is, I wish to urge, simply an explication of a certain sort of consideration that an empiricist can use to gain acceptance for an ethical first principle, the first principle in this instance (though it is not used as a mere illustration, for Mill does wish to get his readers to accept it) being, of course, that of utility.

Let us recall that an empiricist cannot hold that we directly perceive ethical attributes of particular actions. Thus he cannot establish his ethical first principle by an inductive generalization. This, however, is true of any first principle.[24]

> To be incapable of proof by reasoning is common to all first principles; to the first premises of our knowledge, as well as to those of our conduct. But the former, being matters of fact, may be the subject of a direct appeal to the faculties which judge of fact—namely, our senses, and our internal consciousness. Can an appeal be made to the same faculties on questions of practical ends? Or by what other faculty is cognizance taken of them?[25]

It is in answer to this question that Mill gives us step IA. Now just what is the analogy that he wishes to urge upon us between visible and seen, on the one hand, and desirable and desired, on the other? I submit the following as an interpretation that at least makes sense of Mill's argument as a whole.

In the area of knowledge the empiricist cannot strictly prove his first principle. He cannot prove, by induction or by deduction from any more ultimate principle, that there are no visible things never seen, audible occurrences never heard, and so on. But he can set it up as a plausible principle (as a "meaning criterion," as a later positivist put it) that any epistemological theory that requires visible or audible entities that are never seen or heard is talking nonsense. The only test anyone can seriously propose that a thing is visible is that it actually is seen. A theory that conflicts with this requirement will just not be accepted by reasonable people. Similarly in ethical theory. A theory that sets up, as ends desirable in themselves (*i.e.*, good, *not* simply capable of being desired), states of affairs that nobody ever desires is just being academic and unrealistic. "If the end which the utilitarian doctrine proposes to itself were not, in theory and practice, acknowledged to be an end, nothing could ever convince any person that it was so." That is, if no one appealed to the greatest happiness to justify ethical judgments or ever in practice desired the greatest happiness, no considerations capable of getting reasonable people to accept that principle as ethically ultimate could be presented. Let us call this the requirement, directed toward any ethical first principle, of "psychological realism." Since a first principle is incapable of proof, anyone could arbitrarily set up any ethical first principle he chose, and there would be no basis for deciding between this and any other (if we eschew the intuitionist's self-evidence) unless some such requirement as that of psychological realism were set up.

Step IB is to be interpreted in similar fashion, with the addition that Mill is here assuming the truth of psychological hedonism. Now, whatever one's opinion as to this latter doctrine (I believe it to be false), the design of Mill's argument is not affected. "No reason can be given why the general happiness is desirable, except that each person, so far as he believes it to be attainable, desires his own happiness." Let us remember that, for Mill, the desirability of the general happiness is a first principle that cannot be proved. The sentence just quoted, therefore, sets down no requirement as to strict proof. It rather shows what sort of consideration must be presented to lead to the acceptance of this first principle. One cannot sensibly present general happiness as desirable if it is completely unrelated to what individual people actually desire. Mill cannot and does not argue that each seeks the general happiness or that society as a whole somehow has its own motives, over and above those of its members, and that these are directed toward the general happiness. Rather, Mill simply says (anticipating the outcome of step II and the acceptance of the pleasure of each individual as a good) that, since the pleasure of each is a good, the sum of these must be a good: "each person's happiness is a good to that person, and the general happiness, therefore, a good to the aggregate of all persons."[26] Or, as he explains in a letter, "I merely meant in this particular sentence to argue that, since A's happiness is a good, B's a good, C's a good, &c., the sum of all these goods must be a good."[27] This may be incorrect; it may be that goods cannot be added, though surely it is not just obvious that Mill is mistaken in this matter. However that may be, Mill is clearly *not* trying to prove that "*because* everybody desired his own pleasure, *therefore* everybody desires the pleasure of everybody else."[28] He is not (if the reader will tolerate another reiteration) trying to *prove* anything. He is attempting simply to present the general-happiness principle in a way that will make it seem acceptable as an ethical first principle to people who, rejecting self-evidence in this matter, still wish to be intelligent.

The test of psychological realism condemns any ethical theory that would set up as good in themselves ends which no one actually ever seeks. The principle of utility comes through this test, in Mill's first step, unscathed. Now comes the second step as a clincher. No other ethical theory can pass this test successfully, since the only thing people ever desire is happiness. Suppose, now, for a moment, that Mill does make this out. Then, clearly, the principle of utility holds the field alone. Any acceptable ethical first principle must meet the test of psychological realism. Only the principle of utility can meet this test. When and as this is shown, utilitarianism will, as a matter of fact, be accepted. No other kind of proof is required or possible.

Mill himself admits that people do desire as ends many things besides pleasure. He tries to square this with his contention that "there is in reality nothing desired except happiness" by appeal to the sort of associationist account that goes back to John Gay. Frequent association of these other things (e.g., money or moral virtue) with pleasures to which they give rise has set up an inseparable association. Whenever we think of these things, we think of them as pleasant, and so we seek *them*, not some pleasant effect.

This line of thought bears different possible interpretations. It may mean simply that, though we do desire other things than pleasure, (associated) pleasure is the cause of our doing so. This is a plausible account of motivation, but it does not show that only pleasure is desired; it shows only that pleasure is the cause of our desiring whatever we do desire. Thus it is not to the point, for psychological realism does not require of an ethical theory that what it posits as good must be the cause of our desires but rather that it be something actually desired. And it is clear that Mill wants to show that only pleasure is desired for its own sake.

Again Mill may mean to say that we are mistaken; we think we seek other things, but we really seek the pleasure so indissolubly associated with them that we do not, consciously, separate it. It seems, however, rather obvious that this is not what he means, as he reiterates that we do seek these other things than pleasure for their own sakes. Moreover, he says that we seek them as parts of happiness.

Tentatively, then, I suggest the following: Only that which is experienced as pleasant is sought for its own sake. Many things originally not themselves experienced as pleasant come to be so through association with pleasant effects. Thus money or virtue really are desired as ends, but only so far as they are experienced as pleasant. This can then be expressed loosely by saying only pleasure is desired, yet other things are also—as concrete parts of it. It would be better to say: Only things experienced as pleasant are desired for their own sakes. Now, if this be accepted, then what does it involve if we are to suppose that the principle of utility successfully passes the test of psychological realism? It requires that that principle, when it says that happiness is the sole good, mean not that pleasantness is good but that things experienced as pleasant, and they alone, are good. Pleasure, as a property, is not good, and certainly not the sole good. Is this a tenable interpretation? I think it is. But this carries us away from the question of the proof of the principle of utility to the nature of that principle.

One last word, and I am done with my criticism of the traditional way of disposing with Mill's argument. Moore finishes off his criticism of Mill's step II as follows:

> Mill, then, has nothing better to say for himself than this. His two fundamental propositions are, in his own words, "that to think of an object as desirable (unless for the sake of its consequences), and to think of it as pleasant, are one and the same thing; and that to desire anything except in proportion as the idea of it is pleasant, is a physical and metaphysical impossibility." Both of these statements are, we have seen, merely supported by fallacies. The first seems to rest on the naturalistic fallacy; the second rests partly on this, partly on the fallacy of confusing ends and means, and partly on the fallacy of confusing a pleasant thought with the thought of a pleasure.[29]

It is clear again that Moore is thinking of Mill's argument as a strict proof. Had he read it in context, even going back one paragraph, he would have had to give up this whole interpretation. Let me set down the paragraph that immediately precedes the passage Moore quotes:

> We have now, then, an answer to the question, of what sort of proof the principle of utility is susceptible. If the opinion which I have now stated is psychologically true—if human nature is so constituted as to desire nothing which is not either a part of happiness or a means of happiness, we can have no other proof, and we require no other, that these are the only things desirable. If so, happiness is the sole end of human action, and the promotion of it the test by which to judge of all human conduct; from

whence it necessarily follows that it must be the criterion of morality, since a part is included in the whole.[30]

This, so it seems to me, is just a summary of what step II purports to do. It says that, if there is only one sort of thing that is ever desired, then psychological realism requires one's ethical theory to square with this. This sort of plausibility is all that can be required of any ethical theory.

Turning, now, to the paragraph which is the immediate context of the passage that Moore quotes, we find that Mill simply summarizes his contention that there is only one sort of thing ever desired, that this is happiness, that utilitarianism alone, therefore, is acceptable to ethicists who are honestly realistic. However, he does fall into a loose manner of speaking, upon which a casuist is able to capitalize. He writes, "to think of an object as desirable," when the context makes clear that he meant "to desire an object." He has just written, in an earlier part of the same sentence, "desiring a thing and finding it pleasant . . . are phenomena entirely inseparable," which he then reiterates in different words, "to think of a thing as desirable . . . and to think of it as pleasant, are one and the same thing." All this means is that any object desired (for its own sake) is inseparably associated with pleasure. I find no evidence that this commits the naturalistic fallacy. Mill does use the infelicitous term "desirable" here. But he could have used "good" in the same loose and colloquial sense; *i.e.,* he could have said, in accordance with frequent popular usage, "to think of an object as good" when he meant "to desire an object."

In summary, the argument of chapter iv of Mill's *Utilitarianism* is extremely simple and (in the main) sensible. To an empiricist who eschews all intuitive self-evidence, no ethical first principle can be strictly proved. All that one can do is to present considerations that will lead honest and reasonable people to accept such a principle. These considerations, for an empiricist, must turn on what people actually desire. Each person desires his own happiness. Therefore, a first principle that makes happiness good will prove acceptable to honest men when they consider it. And if the happiness of each is good, then the sum of happiness of all is good. Thus the principle of utility is something that men, constituted as they are, can honestly accept. But no other ethical first principle can meet this simple test of psychological realism; for (and here the reasoning is not too clear) the only thing people seek (for its own sake) is happiness. At least a plausible interpretation of this last consideration is that happiness is not a sum of pleasures in the sense of an amount of sheer pleasantness but is a sum of things experienced (whether by one's original nature or through long association) as pleasant.

It must be admitted that this whole interpretation presupposes a fundamental distinction, a distinction which intuitionists[31] like Moore, thinking they can rest their case on the self-evidence of their first principles, apparently ignore. I refer to the distinction between a statement in a theory and a statement about a theory, which here takes the form of the distinction between a proof within an ethical system and a proof of an ethical system. A first principle in an ethical system (or in an epistemological or ontological system) obviously cannot be proved in that system. In fact, to say that a principle is self-evident may mean just that it is a first principle; in *that* system in which it is self-evident it is not to be questioned; the possibility of its falsehood would just be the possibility of a contradiction in the system. In any other sense the self-evidence of a first principle takes us outside the system. But that brings up the serious question of how a whole ethical system can be established, a question that such an intuitionist as Moore never clearly faced just because he never saw this ambiguity in the concept of self-evidence.

Mill, in his loose, commonsensical way, is trying to distinguish between proof in a system and proof of one and to answer the question, "What kind of proof of an ethical system is possible?" He is saying that an ethical system as a whole cannot be established in any other way than by making it acceptable to reasonable men; and this is done just by showing that it and it alone (in its first principles, though not as theoretically elaborated) is actually accepted by men when outside the philosopher's closet. Mill simply asks ethicists to square their professionally elaborated ethics with the common-sense ethics of every man, including themselves.

Originally part of an article, "The 'Proof' of Utility in Bentham and Mill," appearing in *Ethics*, Vol. LX, No. 1 (October, 1949). Reprinted with permission of the University of Chicago Press.

1. F. H. Bradley, *Ethical Studies*, 2d ed. (Oxford, 1927), pp. 113–24.
2. Bradley, *op. cit.*, p. 115n.
3. Quoted by Moore,*Principia Ethica*, p. 66.
4. *Ibid.*, p. 67.

5. *Ibid.*, p. 66.

6. *Ibid.*, p. 10.

7. *Ibid.*, p. 67.

8. *Ibid.*

9. *Ibid.*

10. G. E. Moore, *Utilitarianism* ("Everyman's" ed.), p. 17.

11. Moore, *op. cit.*, pp. 67–68.

12. Quoted by Moore, *ibid.*, p. 66.

13. Cf. *Ibid.*, pp. 96–105. His object of condemnation here is Sidgwick.

14. Bradley, *Ethical Studies*, p. 113.

15. *Ibid.*, pp. 113–14n.

16. Moore, *op. cit.*, p. 4.

17. *Ibid.*, p. 32.

18. *Ibid.*, p. 4.

19. *Ibid.*, p. 32.

20. It would do no good were the critic of Mill to say that Mill's disavowal of strict proof applies only to his whole proof, that this latter includes step II, which is inductive, and that therefore it is permissible to treat steps IA and IB as attempts at strict deduction. First, Mill would call such a combination of deduction and induction a strict proof "in the ordinary acceptation of the term." Second, his disavowal of strict proof is re-emphasized within both steps IA and IB.

21. *Ibid.*, p. 2.

22. *Ibid.*

23. Cf. *ibid.*, pp. 3–4.

24. The critic can rightly urge that this does not square with the traditional interpretation of Mill's justification of induction (by the use of induction). On this point the critic has, I fear, firmer ground to stand on.

25. *Ibid.*, p. 32.

26. *Ibid.*, p. 33.

27. Hugh S. R. Elliot, *The Letters of John Stuart Mill* (1910), Vol. II, p. 116.

28. Bradley, *op. cit.*, p. 114n.

29. Moore, *op. cit.*, p. 72.

30. Mill, *op. cit.*, p. 36.

31. Sometimes by "intuitionistic ethics" is meant not an ethics whose first principles are taken to be self-evident but simply an ethics that claims that there is some value term (such as "good") whose reference is uniquely nondescriptive. In this sense, I claim, Mill was an intuitionist.

HORACE M. KALLEN

Of Humanistic Sources of Democracy

Each of the three words in the title—*humanistic, source, democracy* —is a word of many meanings. Each is extremely ambiguous. In usage, each is rendered specific and singular by the business and desire of the user. The critical term of the three is *source*. What do we mean by *source*? A consensus of the dictionaries would give us *spring*, a locus of origination or spontaneity. When this meaning is transposed into a universe of discourse called philosophy or metaphysics or theology, *source* becomes an alternate for *first cause*. The empirical equivalent for a *first cause*, least open to challenge, is probably the biologist's *gene*. So far as our knowledge presently goes, the *gene* is the one item in nature which consistently repeats itself and on occasion, alters itself. It not only reproduces itself in identical form, but varies spontaneously and then reproduces the variant together with its variations in identical form. The *gene* as cause appears to be a self-reproducing identity capable of change without self-liquidation. Although its altering and mutations present themselves as discontinuous, they come as accretions to its own continuity, as accretions, that is, to a persistent identifiable nature and existence.

1

Now I shall take the term *source,* as applied to *humanism,* to mean a cause resembling a *gene.* I assume that what I am to do in this talk is to identify either a continuing or recurrent cause, called *humanism,* in the generation and upkeep of an effect, called *democracy.*

Inquiry into causes is today *par excellence* the enterprise of the scientist. Identifying causes is his vocation, even when the field is theology. The use of scientific method in theology and the treating of theology as a field for the scientific vocation are, I know, not exactly popular in certain circles, but they have their friends, who are a growing company. They are a growing company because the method of science has proved itself to be of all methods, the most fruitful in that basic phase of the human enterprise which seeks to sort out and define those events which invariably bring about certain other events which someone feels to be of great moment for the life of man.

An undertaking beset with hazards and doubts in all the sciences, the designation of causes is particularly so in the social sciences, where the variables are countless and the constants are few, if not altogether lacking; and where a student may select any one or any group of the current components of an institution or an event, attribute to them causal efficacy, and support his attribution with rationalizations and statistical tables whose mathematics are infallible. This can be done even if the elected components are in fact not at all sources or agents; it can be done with the greatest of ease wherever the uses of things which are at once consequences and modifications of the natures of those things are treated as the origins, the springs whence their natures have drawn or draw their existence. For example, it is well known that many great and influential democratic originals, such as Thomas Jefferson, made considerable use of certain classical writers whose productions are conventionally allocated to the humanities. But whether these humanities made a democrat of Jefferson and were causes of the beatitudes of democracy which we call the Declaration of Independence cannot be decided on the basis of use or purpose. It is no more likely that Jefferson, having studied the humanities, became a democrat, than that Jefferson, being a democrat, chose from the humanities those utterances which would nourish and sustain his democratic works and ways. But the disposition to call an event which preceded another event the cause of that which follows is inveterate, and the temptation to do so is particularly strong in history and the other social sciences, so that it is hard not to call certain of the humanities which figure in Jefferson's spiritual history causes of his democracy *post hoc propter hoc.* I shall try not to be led into this temptation, either with respect to Jefferson or with respect to any of the diverse sequences of humanistic and democratic ideas.

I shall also hope to bypass a number of other temptations. One of these consists in declaring different meanings to be one and the same because they are communicated by means of a single term, word or sign. It is as if oil and vinegar and water and wine and peroxide and quicksilver should be declared the same because they are carried in identical bottles. The identity of the vehicle contaminates the diversity of the passengers and their variety and multitude are masked by its unity. One of the most significant instances of such contamination of meanings by symbols which usage provide is of course the familiar word *God.* It is a word employed by Plato, by Cleanthes, by Plotinus, by St. Augustine, by St. Thomas, by Spinoza, by Jefferson, by Calvin, by Edward Scribner Ames, by Mordecai Kaplan, by William James, by Sitting Bull, and by countless other psychologists, metaphysicians and theologians. However different the language of these men, the dictionaries make their words for God equal and interchangeable, and translate each as the alternate of any. But how can the men's meanings be made equal and interchangeable without terrible violence to the integrity of those separate meanings? Such violence can readily be done to the meanings of *humanism* and *democracy* when verbal illations mask fundamental divergences of intention. Such identifications are produced, as a rule, whenever we are passionately concerned with the survival and domination of one intention, regardless of the consequences to all others. For example, such a passionate concern is attributable to many who insist on deriving the democratic idea from Thomas Aquinas. As a matter of logic and history the derivation is, to say the least, highly debatable; as a postulate of passion it isn't debatable, nor is the passion debatable. Affirming itself, it involves either the ignoring or the overriding of that which is different from itself or the identification of the different with itself. At its most likely it confuses resemblance with sameness, analogy with identity.

This mode of mistakenly attributing causes is another one of the temptations into which the social scientist is all too often led. His sciences abound in analogical thinking, and a great deal of it is striking and some of it is fruitful. There is no need to quarrel with it. But there is great need to be extremely cautious about employing it as a method for bringing to light sources, causes or agencies, be they enduring and supporting or transitory and lapsing. Transitory and lapsing causes occur in the social process at least as frequently as parents. Parents beget and get children, and not even the most intransigent theologian would hesitate to regard them as the sources or causes of at least the bodily being of their children. And so they are; they originate, they give rise to, and with this their parental efficacy consummates itself. It consists in a single act, largely contingent. It does not and cannot persist. After it has occurred parents are only the conditions and occasions of the being of their child, not its enduring and sustaining causes.

Beside these two meanings of the term *source* we must place another, which recurs frequently in certain types of scientific inquiry. This third meaning identifies source with *premise* or *ground*. When *source* is employed in this way, the connection between that which is spring and that which is flow is logical, not dynamic. Thus, if the relationship between *humanism* and *democracy* is considered dynamic, *democracy* will be an effect of *humanism,* not a conclusion from *humanism; humanism* will be a necessary antecedent of *democracy,* but *democracy* will not be a necessary consequence of *humanism.* If, on the other hand, the relationship between *humanism* and *democracy* be the relationship of a syllogistic ground or premise to a syllogistic conclusion, then *humanism* implies *democracy* and *democracy* is a necessary inference from *humanism.* To those who think of the term *source* in this way, *democracy* can exist only if and as *humanism* exists; the historic passage from *humanism* to *democracy* is incidental, is only an explication in time of an implication eternally present in the nature of human events. Many writers treat the relation between *humanism* and *democracy* as if it were of this character. As I read the record, the treatment is not an insight into the nature of the facts but the operation of a desire to conform the facts to a certain interest; it seems to me fundamentally debatable.

2

So much, then, for the term *source*. Let us now discuss the terms *humanism, democracy*. Their meanings, too, are diverse and conflicting, and each is, especially in these times of ours, subjected to too much variation, to make it possible to elicit, in the manner of a physicist or chemist or mathematician, the quality of cause, agency or ground in their relations to one another. The most that I can honestly do is to choose one or more of these meanings, review their sequence, their similarities, their divergences with a view to discovering what is cause and what is effect, and warn you that the choice cannot but express my own social passion and personal interest. Other people make other selections, as is their right. But mine is the only one about which I can speak with any degree of certainty, and over which I hold such authority as it is decent to hold.

Since the task is to discern the nature of the relation between *humanism* and *democracy,* it is proper to seek first a meaning for *democracy.* The term appears early. Plato used it, Aristotle used it, Jefferson used it, and spokesmen of all sorts of interests and pretensions are using it today. The multitude of meanings are not reconcilable. That which I choose for discussion is Jefferson's. His meaning of democracy is unique.

Now the conventional birthday of democracy was July 4, 1776. On that day a conception was made flesh in an act, and the course of human events took a new turn. A war for independence and freedom was justified and its goals were defined by the signing of the document known as the Declaration of Independence, for the support of which the signers mutually pledged each other their lives, their fortunes and their sacred honor. Seven propositions of this Declaration compose the unique beautitudes of the democratic faith of our times. Verse by verse, they read as follows:

1. We hold these truths to be self-evident (Jefferson had written "sacred and undeniable," but the phrase had been replaced with self-evident.);
2. that all men are created equal;
3. that they are endowed by their creator with certain unalienable rights (Jefferson had written "inherent and unalienable," but the Congress struck out "inherent and" and stuck in "certain.");
4. that among these are life, liberty and the pursuit of happiness;
5. that to secure these rights governments are instituted among men,
6. deriving their just powers from the consent of the governed;
7. that whenever any form of government becomes destructive of these ends, it is the right of the people to alter or abolish it,

and to institute new government, laying its foundation on such principles, and organizing its powers in such form, as to them shall seem most likely to effect their safety and happiness.

This is the all of the modern democratic faith and a man can learn it, as a certain gentile once wanted to learn Judaism, while standing on one leg. When, however, we come to the business of interpreting and implementing the articles of this faith in the works and ways of the daily life, the case is different. A great deal of confusion obtains. One such confusion turns upon the meanings which different interpreters undertake to give to the term "equal" in the proposition "that all men are created equal." To some it is nonsense, a glittering generality flung obviously in the face of all experience. To others it expresses a metaphysical truth and is "self-evident" alone as such; namely, that the manifest differences between men are but appearances, unsubstantial and unimportant, that in truth and in reality men are identical and not different, each and every one being the same with each and every other and as interchangeable as machine parts.

The first interpretation, when brought to action, leads to a struggle to perpetuate the modes of human association which the Declaration challenged and denied; it leads to asserting and preserving invidious distinctions; to dividing the people as masters and servants on the basis of differences in faith, race, sex, birth, occupation, possessions and culture; to penalizing the different for being different by shutting them into the servant class and keeping them there.

The second interpretation brought to action leads to a struggle to bring out the hidden metaphysical equality or sameness, by demanding of the different in faith, race, sex, birth, occupations and possessions and culture that they shall liquidate their differences and conform their being to some type or standard defined by power and commanded with authority. Many *soi-distant* "Americanization" movements have been enterprises of this kind, purporting to transform the different into the same. In the actualities of the daily life their methods and results have not been distinguishable from those of the interests which treat the idea that all men are created equal as a glittering generality. Both merely penalized the different for being different. Both made difference a ground of the invidious distinctions essential to setting up and maintaining a citizenship of the second class.

But it was precisely against this invidiousness, this penalization of the different that the Declaration set the nation's will. When it was framed, men and women were being penalized for being what they were everywhere in the world. Women, being female and not male, had no rights that their male relatives needed to respect; Catholics penalized Protestants and Protestants penalized Catholics and each other—all but the Quakers who were penalized for being Quakers by all the other Christian denominations, while the Jews were penalized for not being Christians everywhere in the Christian world. Negroes were penalized for their color; poor men for their poverty; men who worked with their hands, and were thus no gentlemen, for working with their hands. With the proposition "that all men are created equal," the Declaration nullified all that. The men who wrote and signed the Declaration and the men and women who fought and suffered and died for it did not intend by that proposition either to abolish or to penalize differences. They intended to vindicate differences, to acknowledge and to defend their *equal* right to life, liberty and the pursuit of happiness. They affirmed the right to be different and the parity of the different as different. They did not look to any hidden metaphysical equality; they looked to the common, everyday experience that people who are different from each can and do live together with each other on the basis that each has an equal title to the rights of life, liberty and the pursuit of happiness, and that these rights are inherent and unalienable in each.

The Declarants were neither ignorant of nor ignored the historic and present fact that much of such living together consists in mutual alienations of life and liberty and happiness. They knew that the family, the field, the workshop, the school, the playground, the hall of government, the battlefield, all too often show themselves separately and together, as very much like the jail and the gallows, techniques of such mutual alienations of these putative unalienable rights. But the Declarants never meant by "unalienable" that men and women did not kill and maim and frustrate each other, fence each other in and fend each other off. They meant "unalienable" to be a synonym for "inherent," for "constitutive." They meant that the nature of any and every human being, whatever his color, sex, race, faith, occupation or social status, is constituted by these rights as a triangle is constituted by three sides and three angles; they meant that life, liberty and the pursuit of happiness make up the substance of human nature, as the angles and sides of a triangle make up the being of the triangle; that hence, so long as a man is alive he will struggle to go on living, to be free and to seek happiness; that this, his characteristic mode of being, may be attacked, may be mutilated, may be destroyed, but that he cannot behave otherwise than so. Alienation of these unalienable rights, then, is like cutting off a limb or a head, an attack on the inward human essence, not the withdrawal of something called a right that can be put on and put off like a garment or granted and withheld like a gift.

If there is any *humanism* in the Declaration, it is enfolded in this, its affirmation that rights are inherent and unalienable, that they constitute the nature of men, each different from the others and each equal with the others; that as such they are both the spring and the goal of human societies. The proposition, "to secure these rights governments are instituted among men" retains today much of the revolutionary intent it had when it was announced. For those who hold the powers of government, often even in democracies, reveal an inveterate propensity to regard these powers as those of a master, not of a servant, and to treat government as an autonomous end and not a means to other ends. The rationalizations of this propensity are many, but the most ancient and respectable is that which names God as the source and sanction of any power, good or evil. Kings and popes, nobles and clergy rule over the common man by divine right, their authority may not be challenged, nor their commandments disobeyed, because they speak in God's name and as his delegates on earth. When the Declaration was made, nearly all the political and ecclesiastical establishments of the world operated on a general assumption that men were made for governments, not governments for men, that men owe them obedience and service by God's will.

Against this prevailing assumption the Declaration set its principle "to secure these rights governments are instituted among men." It declared the inherent and unalienable rights of man to be the end, government only a means; it made the people the master, government the servant; it made life, liberty and the pursuit of happiness the purpose, government an instrument to attain this purpose.

3

Such, in sum, is the meaning which I find *democracy* to draw from the propositions of the Declaration of Independence. As I read the record, it involves a definite break with the entire tradition of the western world, including much of what is usually regarded as *humanism*. Before the insurgence of this idea of *democracy* neither the ancients nor the moderns failed to penalize this or that section of their own community and all the members of every other community for being different. Let alone the fact that chattel slavery was universal and endemic, the Greeks drew invidious distinctions between themselves and those whom they called barbarians; the Jews between themselves and the Gentiles; the Romans between themselves and their subject peoples; the Christians between themselves and the Jews, the heretics and the infidels. In each case the different must not be equal but subordinate, second-rate, worthy only of subject-status and servile occupation. Alike, the pagan and the Judaeo-Christian tradition affirmed some sort of supernatural sanction for their discriminations against other human beings. John Calvin brought this sanction to the ultimate height of metaphysical authority. He made a dogma of the proposi‧tion that, as Jefferson wrote in 1822 to Benjamin Waterhouse, "God, from the beginning, elected certain individuals to be saved, and certain others to be damned; and that no crimes of the former can damn them; no virtues of the latter save."

The attitude which this consummates is a component of the Greek view of life no less than of the Jewish, but the irony of history made it with the Jews an automatic compensation for their frustrations as a people. It is to them that the tradition attributes, not wrongly, the pretension of being *the chosen people*. Similar pretensions were and are operative among all the peoples of the world, but their expressions have not received equal importance. The Hellenes were not less elect to Plato and Aristotle than the Hebrews were to their prophets and rabbis, but the pagans did not erect this sentiment into a dogma of religion whence they might draw consolation and reassurance. The Jews did. Their God was God omnipotent and just, yet he was capable of playing favorites and choosing out of the infinite multitude of his creatures one group to be his particular people and he to be their particular God, without, however, any fundamental detriment to other peoples, who were also declared to be God's creatures and care. If I understand the prophetic and Judaist view correctly, it was more psychological than logical. The election of Israel did not mean the rejection of the other nations; it meant, not that the nations were rejected but only that Israel was preferred. The Christian employ-ment of this dogma of reassurance and consolation carries its logic

to the limit. Christian dogma changes the status of the Jews from
that of the Chosen People to that of the Rejected People. According to it, just and omnipotent God chooses only those human
beings who believe on the Christ and rejects and condemns to
eternal damnation those who do not believe on the Christ. Calvin
modified this classical view by adding that our finite minds cannot
know whom, in the Christ, infinite God's omniscience and omnipotence has elected and whom rejected.

But whether we think of divine election after the manner of
the Jews or after the manner of the Christian, we see the dogma
as exercising a dominating influence in Judaeo-Christian culture.
We see it as a means of making and supporting invidious distinctions between man and man, as a rule for penalizing the different because it is different. In the climate of opinion where this
dogma figures, equality is the synonym for similarity or identity;
difference is condemned and rejected. Although holders of this
dogma have recently discoursed eloquently and at length about
"the infinite value of the human personality," they have not really
meant any and every personality, with all its differences on its head.
They have really meant personality that agrees or that is persuaded
or that is tortured into agreeing, and is thus become a member of
God's elect who alone can be infinitely valuable; the otherwise-
minded personality, being God's reject, is punished for its difference by being only infinitely valueless and damned.

But this is precisely what *democracy* negates. Democracy sanctions and encourages differences and confirms the equal right of
each and all to life, liberty and the pursuit of happiness. It alone
affirms, without any fear of challenge or contradiction, "the infinite value of human personality." The practical working of its concept of equality may be best illustrated from the attitudes, opinions
and conduct of Thomas Jefferson, foremost of the builders of
democracy into the works and ways of the American people. "No
man," he wrote in his Notes on Virginia, "has power to let another prescribe his faith. Faith is not faith without belief." He held
that no church can claim jurisdiction over any other nor be forced
to pay for the upkeep of any other; that membership in a church
cannot be a condition prior to receiving civil rights or a basis of
withholding or withdrawing civil rights. The value of a religion,
he contended, is to be judged neither by the origins claimed for
it nor the powers it pretended to; the value of a religion was to
be judged by its consequences to the liberties and happiness of

men. Writing in 1803 to Dr. Benjamin Rush, he called attention, with approval, to a vote of the Pennsylvania legislature rejecting a proposal to make belief in God a necessary qualification for public office, "although there was not a single atheist among the voters." Such a law would violate democracy by penalizing citizens for not sharing the beliefs of the majority. He opposed successfully a ministerial undertaking to get the phrase, "Jesus Christ, author of our holy religion," inserted in the Virginia Statute of Religious Liberty —this, not because he failed to appreciate Jesus, but because it would violate the very idea of the Statute.

Jefferson's appreciation of Jesus was singular and unparalleled: its consequence is what is called the Jefferson Bible, which it would repay all Americans to study. This *Bible* is a *democrat's* re-creation of "the life and morals of Jesus of Nazareth," and cannot be correctly understood except in the frame of reference of democracy. Its author constructed it by taking together the Greek, Latin, French and English versions of the gospels, and the gospels only. He cut parallel passages from each, in order to compare them for agreements and differences, and he pasted them accordingly in his notebook. The result was a document which he called "the philosophy of Jesus of Nazareth." What emerges as important in this document is not what is regarded as important in Christian dogma. Jefferson lays no emphasis on the death and resurrection of Jesus; he lays all his emphasis on the social teachings of Jesus. And significantly, he brings these teachings together with certain of the teachings of Epicurus. Rejecting all but the words of Jesus that he believes to be authentic, he writes to John Adams, "I am a real Christian . . . a disciple of the doctrines of Jesus." Elsewhere he speaks of himself as an Epicurean and sees only harmony in the real Christian and Epicurean faiths. His contemporaries, all the clergy and the Federalist laymen, denounced his views of Jesus as blasphemous and atheistic. But they were views alone consistent with the propositions of the Declaration of Independence, views which enabled him to contribute with equal generosity to the Episcopal and Presbyterian churches of Charlottesville, both bitterly inimical to him; and to an enterprise for the purchase and free distribution of Bibles. They were views which, though he held a low opinion of Judaism, enabled him to write to Mordecai Noah: "Your sect by sufferings has furnished a remarkable proof of the universal spirit of religious intolerance inherent in every sect, disclaimed by all when feeble, and practiced by all when in power.

Our laws have applied the only antidote to this view, protecting our religious, as they do our civil rights, by putting all on an equal footing. . . . It is to be hoped that individual dispositions will at length mold themselves on the model of the law, and consider the model bases, on which all religions rest, as the rallying point which unites them in a common interest."

This rallying point was to Jefferson the unalienable right to be different. To be different, therefore to doubt, to inquire, to study and compare alternatives, a right no less unalienable to minorities than to majorities, also when a minority consists of one person only! Jefferson's deepest commitment was to the "illimitable freedom of the human mind to explore and expose every subject susceptible of its contemplation!" He had sworn, he once declared "upon the altar of God, hostility to every form of tyranny over the mind of man." Set this Jeffersonian conception of human relations beside that of an official of the city of Boston, commenting upon assaults made against Jews and Negroes in that sometime Athens of America. Said the official, "Democracy means majority rule, and Jews and Negroes are in the minority." The implication is that minorities have no rights that majorities need respect. A more complete contravention of the democratic idea and the Jeffersonian faith could hardly have been expressed by a public official, nor an attitude more consistent with the tradition of privilege and authority.

The full, practical meaning of the democratic faith as a program of conduct is exemplified by nothing so much as its repudiation of slavery. Neither the classical world nor the Judaeo-Christian ages of faith in fact rejected slavery. There were certain Stoic expressions against it, but no efficacious overt action. Thomas Aquinas, currently a much-cited authority in justification of democracy, was no more opposed to slavery than Aristotle or Luther or Calvin; the enslavement of the different was a testimony to the rightness and power of the elect. True, the history of the predemocratic world records many slave and serf uprisings—whether in Greece or Rome or Northern Europe or the Americas—uprisings in which the slaves fought for their own freedom; it does not record a single instance of free men fighting for the liberation of slaves. This does not occur until the democratic revolution. Jefferson had written a denunciation of slavery into the Declaration of Independence which powerful interests in the Continental Congress erased; and the same interests succeeded in writing safeguards of property in human beings into the Constitution. But there was not room in the same nation for both democracy and slavery. From democracy's first day free men waged a war against slavery by tongue and pen, by stratagem and force. The war finally became a great civil war in which free men staked their all to set slaves free; and having done so, wrote their victory into the fundamental law of the land, as one more step toward the conversion of the ideals of the Declaration of Independence into realities of the American way of life.

4

Now, given this meaning for *democracy*, what has *humanism* contributed to it? Replies to this question will depend, obviously, on which of the many meanings of *humanism* one chooses to consider among the sources of *democracy*. Current discussion gives the conventional meaning a factitious potency. The conventional meaning is the academic meaning. It designates as *humanism* a concern with the humanities and the humanities as the secular literature, and sometimes the graphic and plastic arts of the "pagan" Greeks and Romans. This literature is "classical." It is written in ancient Greek and Latin. It bulks large among lists of "hundred best books," which as a rule do not include anything written in Hebrew. The emphasis falls on its being secular. Thereby it is opposed to the Greek and Latin religious texts of our Judaeo-Christian cults. Humanism began as a cultivation of those works of pagan man in preference to works produced by nonpagan men as glosses upon the revelations of Judaeo-Christian God. It set those humanities against that divinity. It made secular society the peer and better than the peer of churchly. It exalted this-worldliness over other-worldliness, preferring the discourse of human reason to ukase concerning superhuman salvation. By and large, it was anticlerical, even in the church itself. Very many of the early humanists were ordained priests or monks. They were secretaries, librarians, prelates, popes. Others were officials, merchants, courtiers, princes. Their minds were first allured, then liberated by the alternatives to the authoritarian tradition which they encountered in the undogmatic thinking, varied contents and perfect expression of such writers as Cicero, as Tacitus, as Ovid or Pliny or Varro, as Quintilian, as Plato, as Aristotle, whom they had come to read at first hand at last.

That which the humanists found in the Scriptures of the

original tongues was not what authority had drawn from them. An impulse which had first been simple curiosity developed quickly into free inquiry challenging authority. The perusal of the sources at first hand revealed difference and variation in the sources themselves. The discovery of difference and variation led automatically to comparison, and then to the exaltation of the free movements of reason over the conformities of faith. These free movements created in the course of time what is today known as higher criticism. Its technique consisted in the direct observation, the watchful analysis, the careful comparisons and reorderings, the continuous overall scrutiny which pertain to the methods of science.

The classical instance of a humanist according to this meaning of *humanism* is, of course, Erasmus. His *In Praise of Folly* is a judgment upon all users of authority of his day—the soldiers, the priests, the philosophers, the rhetoricians, the pedants, the landlords. His sense of the humanities makes him one of the great ironists of divinity, whose popes he regards as tyrants of the City of the World rather than servants of the City of God, whose friars sell salvation in the market place, whose scholastics find the choice between killing a thousand men and mending a beggar's shoe on Sunday a vital option; who are so learned that the apostles couldn't understand them, as they argue of how one body occupies two places, heaven and the cross, the right hand of God the Father and the consecrated wafer, and as they expound that Mary escaped Adam's sin. Erasmus not only read the New Testament in Greek, he undertook to translate it for the uses of the common people. To make his translation which, in 1516, he dedicated to Leo X, the most accurate in his power, he collated the best available manuscripts, comparing them verse for verse and chapter for chapter, recognizing inconsistencies, seeking the true version instead of the authorized one. Willy-nilly he found himself raising questions concerning the Epistle to the Hebrews, the Epistle of James, the Book of Revelation, the second and sixth chapters of John, the second of Peter, and so on. His concern was, like Jefferson's, the philosophy of Jesus. He prized the spirit, which is without price, more highly than the relics whose magic uses brought good prices. That which defined Erasmus as a humanist as distinguished from the champions of divinity was not merely his delighted knowledge of the classics. It was his method of treating differences with respect. It was his readiness to accept the so-called unauthoritative on the same level as the authorized, to treat authority as a claim only that must make good by merit and not by rule, to exalt free inquiry and to cultivate the toleration which such inquiry postulates. Thereby he gave Martin Luther sufficient cause to call him the "greatest enemy of Christ" and to proclaim that whoever crushed Erasmus would crush a bug that would stink even more when dead than when alive. Thus he gave the conformist churchmen sufficient cause to brand him as a heretic and to place all his works on the Index.

This sort of *humanism* is the antithesis of another kind which has had a certain vogue in the academic arcana of our time. Why its protagonists call it humanism has never been clear to me. I presume that they do so because their central concern continues to be the humaner letters of Greece and Rome which excited and liberated the humanists of the Renaissance; that they disregard the Hebraic originals of our Judaeo-Christian tradition, and fix their attention on Plato and pre-Christian Platonism, and to a lesser degree on Aristotle. Their spokesmen in the United States have been the late Messrs. Paul Elmer More and Irving Babbitt. Mr. T. S. Eliot is a perverse half-English variant, and I do not doubt that many would associate with him our charming and eloquent French colleague, M. Jacques Maritain. Although they call themselves humanists, their preoccupation is not, however, man nor the humanities, but God as conceived and defined by certain classical writers of whom the foremost is Plato. Their method, far from being that of the sciences of our day, is not even the overall scrutiny, the careful observation, the free inquiry of Erasmus. Their method is authoritarian and dialectical. To them man's nature is dual and not one. It has a superior and an inferior part, a soul and a body, and the body is all animal impulse and unchecked desires, while the soul is a unitary principle of human nature inwardly harmonious to, if not a derivative of, the universal and eternal being of God. Over against the multiplicity, the variety, the this-worldliness, of the modern sciences of man, these soi-distant humanists set a hidden single, indivisible eternal, universal human nature, which acts as an "inner check" on the phenomenal multiplicity and variety and holds them together and directs their ways by its infallible force.

Prof. Werner Jaeger has written an illuminating and very sympathetic interpretation of the original of this species of humanism as it took form in the dialogues of Plato, with their antidemocratism, their racism, their doctrine and discipline of authority, stated firmly but somewhat gently in the *Republic*, fiercely in the *Laws*, drawn from the "divine order." This has recently been published in English translation as volumes II and III of *Paideia, the Ideals of Greek Culture*. They bring to us the authentic root of what M. Jacques Maritain opts to call "theocentric humanism." And no democrat could take exception to it, if only it didn't, in Plato, explicitly condemn and excommunicate democracy; if only it didn't serve, after Plato, as a sanction for all the the ways of penalizing the different of which democracy is the rejection. Not alone are the great religions of the world different from each other in countless specific ways, but each great religion is diversified into denominations, sets and cults, everyone with its own characteristic singularity of imagining God and what he requires of man. There is the God of the theists and the God of the deists; these are the Gods of the polytheists and the God of the pantheists; there is one God who is all reason; another who is all love; another who is all will; there is a God who is all spirit and a God who is no less body than spirit. The *theos* of the theocentric humanist differs from sect to sect and man to man and land to land. The center of his humanism is not one but many.

If our theocentric humanist accepts this fact, if he does not presume to excommunicate all other centers but his own as false and evil; if he does not undertake to compel other men to center on his one as *the* One, laying upon them all the penalties of the record should they refuse; if he acknowledges the equal right of different men to think their Gods in such a manner as shall to each seem best for enhancing his life, liberty and pursuit of happiness, then his center is in fact not God but men. Then the *theos* is not invoked as the justification of coercion and tyranny, but becomes the agency "to secure these rights;" then the human being is set free by means of the *theos*. Then the idea or image or being of God is taken honestly and openly for that which in the history of civilization it actually is—a function of mankind's struggles for life, liberty and happiness. The God upon whom a man centers becomes then like the wife of his bosom, the hearth of a home of his own, instead of the noble lady whose beauty and virtue it is his knightly mission to compel other men to acknowledge by the force of his infallible sword. The fascist's State, the Nazi's race, the Japanese' goddess, the Communist's dialectic of matter, cannot offer themselves as rivals and substitutes of this God. He is plural, not singular; multitudinous, not totalitarian; man is the measure of him, not he the measure of man. He is the God of the tradition of Protagoras, not the God of the tradition of Plato. He is the figure of a humanism which stems from the *humanitas* that, during the second century before the Christian era, came to existence among certain Romans of sensibility and sense after their minds had been awakened and their hearts opened by the impact of the philosophy of Epicurus, with its social detachment, its charity and its intellectual freedom. *Humanitas* was the humanism of the Scipionic circle. It comes—altogether accidentally, perhaps—to its high place of expression in a comedy by a member of that circle, the African Terence, who had been a slave, and had been manumitted. In this play, based on one of Menander's (*Heauton Timoroumenos*), trivial in plot, for the most part trivial in utterance, a character pronounces lines that have become part of the wisdom of aspiration of our western world. They are: *Homo sum, humani nihil a me alienum puto.*

Legend has it that the audience which first heard this line rose in tumultuous applause. The line had stopped the show. But its meaning, which has haunted the hearts of men ever since, did not get beyond the show until the democratic revolution, nor lightly, nor without blood and sweat and tears since. This meaning is at the center of still another conception of *humanism* which, being a consequence and function of *democracy,* knowingly prefers among the thinkers of classical antiquity Protagoras the plebeian to Plato the aristocrat. The *humanism* is sometimes identified with the pragmatism of William James. Its spokesman is the late F. C. S. Schiller, one of William James' foremost and most original disciples. In his *Plato or Protagoras,* Schiller throws into a fresh perspective the debate between the former Asiatic self-taught porter and inventor, friend of Pericles and Euripides, bait of Aristophanes, and the Athenian nobleman. The works of Protagoras are lost to us. Some were burned by the Athenians; others have perished. What remains are a few sentences which indicate why. They point to a man-centered humanism, to *humanitas.* "Man," wrote Protagoras, "is the measure of all things, of things that are, that they are, of things that are not, that they are not." The point of importance is that man is the *measure,* not the creator. Whatever his philosophy, he has to take things as experience brings them to him, and he has to value them in terms of their bearing on his life and liberty and pursuit of happiness. Before he can say that this does exist, or that that does not exist, he must have some impression, some idea, of this and that. They must be present somehow, to be declared nonexistent; even as they must be present, somehow, to be declared existent. The presence must make itself felt, and as felt, may be measured. This measurement is a human art; it is the all of the method and the content of science; the spring of the body of knowledge. Considering the Gods as objects of measurement, Protagoras declares in another fragment, "with regard to the Gods, I cannot feel sure that they are or they are not, nor what they are like in figure. For there are many things that hinder sure knowledge; the obscurity of the subject, and the shortness of human life."

These are presumably passages from Protagoras' book *On Truth*. He had read from it in the house of Euripides to a company of free minds of the Greek enlightenment. To some theocentric humanist there present it must have been blasphemy. Protagoras was denounced and condemned to death. He fled Athens, but the book was burned.

As I read the record, an ultimate statement of this meaning of humanism is to be found in the Book of Job, which is itself an assimilation of Greek form to Hebraic insight. There is a familiar, oft-repeated English verse, "Though he slay me will I trust in him." The Hebrew original, correctly translated, reads: "Behold, he will slay me; I shall not survive; nevertheless will I maintain my ways before him." Another verse declares: "Mine integrity hold I fast and will not let it go; my heart shall not reproach me so long as I live." These are words which the author puts in the mouth of Job in reply to his theocentric comforters, who argue that since his torture must be from God, he can be relieved of it only if he looks upon himself as God looks upon him, admits his sin and repents. But Job will not repudiate his human dignity. He contends for the integrity of his human essence even against the inscrutable absoluteness of omnipotent God. Between him and that God there is no common measure, for what measure has man save his human passions and human values, and how can these be applied to omnipotence and omniscience without limiting and belittling it? In consequence, Job, the symbol of all men, must stand up on his own feet alone, working out his destiny by his own measure, recognizing that a just and omnipotent God cannot indulge in a chosen people, cannot elect a favorite, but must maintain all his creatures with an equal providence, thus vindicating the right of each to his different integrity. For the claimant to election by omnipotence also claims the rule of omnipotence; it becomes a pretension to mastery over all mankind and thus a threat of war and slavery to the different, and ultimately of disaster to the pretender himself, be it a single person, a state or a church.

Humanism in this meaning has a certain kinship with *democracy*. But it was elicited from the Book of Job after the democratic revolution. Before that revolution Job was treated as a vindication and proof of the authoritarian ways of an authoritarian God.

5

I think we may now come to some conclusion concerning humanistic sources of democracy. Certain *humanisms* provide obvious analogies with *democracy;* others, no matter what is claimed for them nor who claims it, are altogether incommensurable. Analogic *humanisms* are such because of certain techniques or attitudes or processes which occur also in the ways of *democracy*. But the authentic humanists of history to whom those pertained, such as Erasmus, had no inkling of modern *democracy* and in all likelihood would have been shocked by it. Their *humanism* was not a source of *democracy* because their end, their goal, their stopping place was this *humanism,* not *democracy*. Again, it was not a source because while *democracy* follows, it does not follow from this *humanism*. The latter is chronologically prior; only however, in so far as certain of its aspects are a dynamic common to both itself and *democracy,* may it be designated as a source. Those aspects, we have seen, are not the intellectual or aesthetic content of this *humanism;* they are the methods of the humanists, in the degree that they consist in observation, free inquiry, unrelaxing scrutiny of thoughts and things. The *humanism* which works by the methods of authority, which sets dogma above observation, rationalization above reason, and belief and obedience above scrutiny and free choice cannot be said to contribute anything to *democracy*.

Lastly, there is also a *humanism* which may be taken as a synonym for *democracy*. But it would be as correct to hold that that *democracy* is the source of this *humanism,* as that this *humanism* is a source of *democracy*. For *democracy* is chronologically prior to this *humanism*. Even though it does employ Protagoras and Terence to support its vision, it comes to expression in a social atmosphere, in a climate of culture, where the propositions of the Declaration of Independence are the gradients for human relations and the methods of science for human discourse. This *humanism*, hence, is pluralistic, empirical and libertarian. Its spokesmen acknowledge, they respect, they endeavor sympathetically to understand differences, and the co-operation of differences. They hold with William James in his *The Will to Believe,* "no one of us ought to issue vetoes to the other, nor should we bandy words of abuse. We ought, on the contrary, delicately and profoundly to respect one another's mental freedom." Instead of demanding or exacting conformity, they endeavor to live and let live, to live and help live. God, some of them argue, is, on the record, either a name for companies of many "divine" beings struggling for survival as human beings struggle, and forming their association with other species, not the human only, according to its role in this survival; or else God is a name for an all-powerful entity, differently imagined by different men, that brings forth impartially all the infinite diversities of experience, not men only, nor what men find good and what men find evil; and that just as impartially sustains and destroys them all. God so conceived, these humanists hold, cannot favor man over any other species; nor any race or cult of man over any other; nor any human doctrine and discipline over any other. All maintain themselves or perish, under such a God, not by favor, but by their own dispositions and abilities. According to these humanists each form of existence, has, under such a God, its own different type of life, liberty and happiness; each has an equal right with every other to achieve its type. Among men, each comes together with others to form societies—churches, states, economies, civilizations—because by these means each can "secure these rights" more aptly, more abundantly, than he could alone. The means become the One, generated by the Many. Institutions and governments are at their best when their oneness is thought of and treated not as organism but as organization; when they express not unity but union; when they consist not in integration but orchestration; when they are modes of the free association of the different—organizations of liberty whose just powers are the hearts and the heads of all the human beings whose organizations they are.

There may be other, and as apt, orchestrations of *humanism* with *democracy*. If there are, I must regretfully declare that I have missed them. But I do not think there are; for when humanism is taken thus humanly, democracy is humanism, humanism is democracy.

Reprinted with minor omissions from *Foundation of Democracy*, F. Ernest Johnson, ed., (New York, 1947), with permission of the author and the Institute of Religious Education, New York, N. Y.

ABRAHAM KAPLAN

Obscenity as an Esthetic Category

My problem is not what to do about obscenity, but what to make of it. Control over the arts in this country—whether by official power or by unofficial influence—rests largely on allegations of obscenity. But patterns of social control cannot reasonably be appraised without some conception of what it is that is being controlled. Accordingly, I ask what constitutes obscenity in relation to the arts: Can a work of art be obscene and still be esthetic in status and function? What part, if any, does the obscene play in the esthetic experience? What characteristics of the art object mark its occurrence?

These questions are meant as belonging to the philosophy of art, not to its psychology or sociology. To answer them is not to assert matters of fact, but to clarify relations of ideas. Such a clarification must take facts into account, of course—but its outcome, if successful, is a clear conception rather than a true proposition. Still less does an answer to these questions entail a social policy or a procedure for implementing policy. I do not pretend that the distinctions to be drawn in this essay can be directly applied in a court of law. I shall be content if they throw light on the problem of obscenity for the artist, his audience, and the critic who interprets each to the other.

1

Many people anxious to defend freedom of expression in the arts attack the suppression of obscenity on the grounds that obscenity has no objective existence, but is to be found only in the mind of the censor. I share the conclusion which this argument is intended to bolster—namely, that censorship is to be condemned; but the argument itself appears to me to be fallacious. Its premise is the undeniable proposition that judgments of the obscene vary with time and place. But from this true premise, the invalid inference is made to a subjectivist conclusion: All that can be common to such varying judgments is simply a subjective emotion of disapproval. "Obscenity exists only in the minds and emotions of those who believe in it, and is not a quality of a book or picture."[1] To think otherwise, so this logic runs, is to be guilty of a superstition which is "the modern counterpart of ancient witchcraft."[2]

Now those exercised over obscenity do perhaps resemble the old prosecutors of witchcraft in their fanaticism and irrationality.[3] The emphasis on the relativism of obscenity thus exposes the narrowness and rigidity of traditionalist morality. But the belief in witchcraft was simply false. The belief in obscenity is false only if its rational character is overlooked. What is superstitious is an absolutist conception,[4] alleged to apply universally whether it be recognized or no. The alternative to absolutism is not subjectivism, but an insistence on objectivity *relative to a specified context*. The rationality of a belief is similarly relative to the evidence available for it. But this relation is not only compatible with objectivity, but even defines it. Such a standpoint has come to be known as *objective relativism* or *contextualism*.[5]

Judgments of obscenity vary because they are contextual. I mean more than that "dirt" is misplaced matter, *i.e.*, that property varies with circumstances. I mean that obscenity is to be found in words or pictures only in so far as these can be interpreted to have a certain meaning; and meaning itself is contextual. D. H. Lawrence has protested against objectivism that "it is the mind which is the Augean stables, not language."[6] But language has no content at all, obscene or otherwise, without mind. It means what it does only because it is interpreted as it is in definite contexts, and it is in just such contexts of interpretation that its obscenity is to be localized. So far as the facts of relativity are concerned, obscenity is no more subjective than is any esthetic quality whatever.

What is sound in the relativist position is preserved in the recognition of the difference between an art *object* and the *work* of art which results when the object is responded to in an esthetic context. The art experience is not a passive one, but requires the active participation of the respondent. And obscenity is a property of the resultant work and not of the object out of context. When people disagree whether something is obscene, they are likely to be judging different works of art (constructed, as it were, from the same object), rather than reacting differently to the same work. The important problem posed by relativism is, then, *which* work we are to judge when confronted with a particular art object: it is the problem of interpretation. Of course, standards of propriety may differ, just as there are differences in, say, what would amuse us and the Greeks. But when we read the comedies of Aristophanes, these differences either enter into the interpretation we give to the plays (the art objects), and so give rise to different works of art for us than for his contemporaries, or else the differences are not esthetically relevant at all. Once such differences are explicitly brought into the context, the relativism is objectified.

Now all art is essentially ambiguous, in the sense that the interpretation it calls for is an imaginative one. The object cannot be so fully specified as to leave no room in its reading for our own creative activity.[7] But what allows for an imaginative reading also makes possible a reading which is wholly our own projection. It is this danger, and not subjectivism, which is the point of the truism that "to the pure all things are pure." But not all interpretations *are* merely projective. The qualifications of the reader may make all the difference. A pure mind is just as likely to miss an entendre in Shakespeare as an ignorant one is to misread his Elizabethan usages. A proper judgment of obscenity in the arts can only be made by an informed and sensitive reader—not necessarily because only he can decide whether a work *is* obscene, but because only he can decide *what* work it is that is being judged.

I say a "proper" judgment, but more accurate is: a judgment made in the *ideal* context—ideal, that is, from the standpoint of esthetic appreciation and criticism. But there are other sorts of contexts in which a judgment might be made. There is the *personal* context, constituted by the judger himself. And there are various *standard* contexts (specified statistically or in other ways) which also occur and have their uses. Which context is to be chosen depends on the purpose for which the judgment is being made. I know of no principle of selection or evaluation apart from such purposes. To the question "Who is to judge whether a work is obscene?" we can reply only with the counterquestions, "What is to be done with the judgment when it is made? And why is it being made at all?"

Yet, I do not mean to pretend that the principle of contextualism leaves us with no difficulties in practice. On the contrary, it allows us to become clearly aware of just how serious the difficulties are. Competent critics disagree sharply among themselves. The ideal context is as difficult to achieve as ideals usually are. But it is not true that from the nature of the case the ideal is a hopeless one. Beauty and obscenity alike are in the eye of the beholder. But if —as artists, critics, and lovers of the arts, not as censors—we are prepared to enter into interpretation and evaluation in the one case, why not in the other?

2

Contextualism has brought us to the position that obscenity may be an objective property of a work of art, provided that the work itself be recognized as being relative to some context of response to the art object. Now many people deny that obscenity is an attribute even of the work of art, localizing it instead in the mind of the artist, by way of his "intention." But what are we to understand by artistic "intention"? Are there not different *sorts* of answers appropriate to the question why a particular art object was created?

We may answer, first, in terms of the artists' *motive:* money or glory or whatever ends external to his efforts he expected to be served by them. The legal judgment of obscenity sometimes considers motive—apparently, a work is more likely to be obscene if the artist expected to make money from his labors. But plainly, motive as such is completely irrelevant esthetically. A poet may write to pay for his mother's funeral (Johnson's *Rasselas*) or to seduce a woman who reminds him of his mother, but neither motive has much to do with *what* he writes.

Second, artistic "intention" may be construed as *purpose:* a specification in terms of the artist's medium of how his motive is expressed. The purpose may be to satirize the clergy, to expose the madness of chivalric romance, or to proclaim the rights of women. Unquestionably, purpose must be conceded an esthetic relevance—it is what the artist tried to do *in* his work, not *by* it. Many artists accused of obscenity have defended themselves by insisting on their moral purpose.

But more important than what the artist tried to do is what in fact he *did* do, and this may be taken as a third sense of "intention"—the *intent* of the work itself. A specification of purpose may define an esthetic genre, but never a particular work of art. Every work has its own unique intent: the purpose as embodied in its own specific substance. When Judge Woolsey speaks of Joyce's not "exploiting" obscenity, he is referring to Joyce's artistic purpose, perhaps also to his lack of a monetary motive.[8] But when he refers to the absence of "the leer of the sensualist," it is intent which is involved.[9] What is at question is as much an experienced quality of the work as is the "ring" of sincerity, which is to be contrasted with sincerity itself—the latter being a matter of motive and purpose but not of intent.

Motive, then, helps localize obscenity only in so far as it determines purpose, and the latter, in turn, only as it is embodied in intent. But this brings us back once more from the mind of the artist to the perceived characters of the work of art itself.

The alternative remains to be considered of localizing obscenity in the mind of the audience, *i.e.*, in the effect of the work. The obscene, in the classic legal conception, is what tends to corrupt. This criterion is thought to be more "objective" than reference to the artist's intention. But such reference, at least in the sense of intent, is inescapably involved in the criterion. For the effect might otherwise have been the result of a purely projective interpretation, in which case it is not *that* work which is being judged to be obscene. To resort to the effect of the work is to commit oneself to distinguishing between its causal agency and its operation as a trigger mechanism, *i.e.*, as providing an occasion for projecting onto itself a corruption already present in the reader.

Plainly, which context is selected becomes crucial. The courts may choose as standard context Judge Woolsey's "*l'homme moyen sensuel,*"[10] but unless this standard is carefully specified (by Dr. Kinsey?), there is the serious danger that it will be replaced unwittingly by the personal context of the man passing judgment.

To compare it with the standard of "the reasonable man" in the law of torts is to overlook the fact that "reasonableness" can, in principle, be intersubjectively specified (at least in part)—in terms of probabilities and their logical consequences. But where is the logic of sexual sensitivity that corresponds to the "reasonableness" of inductive and deductive inference? This question is especially embarrassing in view of the claim sometimes made that "familiarity with obscenity blunts the sensibilities,"[11] so that on the criterion of effect, the standard context invites a circular argument: the work is obscene because it *would* produce the effect if only it were not such familiar obscenity!

In the ideal context, the test of effect is wholly inapplicable. For the esthetic experience requires a kind of disinterest or detachment, a "psychic distance," which is incompatible with the corruption in question. Only when we hold the work of art at arm's length is it artistic at all. The work brings emotions to mind or presents them for contemplation. When they are actually felt, we have overstepped the bounds of art. Sad music does not make us literally sad. On the contrary, the more vividly and clearly we apprehend the specific quality of "sadness" of the music, the less sorrowful our own emotions. Of course, art evokes feelings; but it is *imagined* feeling, not what is actually felt as a quality of what we do and undergo. And art works against the translation of imagined feeling into action. It does so partly by providing us insight into feeling, and so allowing us to subject passion to the control of the understanding, as was urged by Spinoza;[12] and partly by providing a catharsis or sublimation of feeling, as in the conceptions of Aristotle and Freud.[13] In sort, "there is a high breathlessness about beauty that cancels lust," as Santayana put it.[14] To be sure, the extreme of psychic distance is also incompatible with esthetic experience, as in the case of the intellectual or—what is more to the point—the philistine. But to ignore altogether the role of distance is to confuse art with promotion—advertising or propaganda.

Now *pornography* is promotional: it is the obscene responded to with minimal psychic distance. Fundamentally, therefore, it is a category of effect. To say that a work is pornographic is to say something about the feeling and actions which it produces in its respondents. We may, of course, identify it by its purpose rather than by direct observation of effect. Its motive—monetary or sexual or whatever—it is likely to share with most art. But as to esthetic intent, this is lacking altogether in so far as the object is being read as pornographic. For in this case, it is not itself the *object* of an experience, esthetic or any other, but rather a stimulus *to* an experience not focused on it. It serves to elicit not the imaginative contemplation of an expressive substance, but rather the release in fantasy of a compelling impulse.

Pornography as such, therefore, is no more esthetic than is an object of sentiment, which has no intrinsic interest but is responded to by way of associations external to its own substance, though not external to the references it contains (as in the words "Souvenir of San Francisco" on the bottom of the tasteless ashtray). But though the pornographic as such is never artistic, contextualism warns us that an art object in a particular context—like that of the schoolboy with the Venus—may serve pornographically rather than as a basis for co-operation with the artist in creating a work of art. Indeed, the converse is also possible: a Pompeian wall painting or a Central American sculpture may have been deliberately produced as pornographic but may constitute for us a work of art. In our culture, pornography masquerades as art with sufficient frequency to deserve a special designation—I suggest *erotica*. It is a species of what artists call "kitch": the vulgarities that hide behind a label of Art with a capital "A." Erotica consists of works that lack even the decency of being *honestly* pornographic.

The distinctions among these categories, however, have been made here on only the conceptual level. As a matter of fact, little is known concerning the actual effects—either stimulation or sublimation—which can be produced by words and pictures. But when obscenity is distinguished from pornography by reference to effect, it follows that art as such is never pornographic (though it may be obscene and in several senses is very likely to be). The effect of art on life is not so specific and immediate as is comprised in the concept of pornography. Action flows from impulses, habits, and predispositions which are not so easily changed as puritans both fear and hope. At most, an art object might trigger a process already primed. But in so far as this is its manner of working, it ceases to be art.

Obscenity, then, so far as it relates to art, can be localized neither in intention nor in effect, but only in the expressive substance of the work of art itself. Ultimately, to be sure, the content of a work of art, as of any vehicle of communication, is an abstraction from both intention and effect. Whether a word is insulting depends, at bottom, on its being used in order to convey an insult and its being responded to as conveying one. Yet, when this usage is established, the word is insulting even when spoken in innocence or to an insensible hearer; it has been misused or misunderstood, that is all. The question is one of the ideal context of its occurrence, not the personal context, nor yet a standard context selected to serve some extraneous interest.

I do not mean to say that obscenity is a matter of the occurrence of "dirty words." On the contrary! It is the work as a whole which must be considered. For it is an important characteristic of a work of art that it cannot be interpreted piecemeal. Each element affects the content of all the others. The work is an integrated, coherent whole whose expressive quality cannot be additively constructed from what is expressed by its isolated parts. Judge Woolsey's position is esthetically unassailable when he says of *Ulysses* that, although it contains "many words usually considered dirty. . . . Each word of the book contributes like a bit of mosaic to the detail of the picture which Joyce is seeking to construct for his readers."[15] Indeed, isolated words may easily lose their expressiveness by mechanical repetition, to be restored to artistic potency only by skillful exploitation of a fresh setting in a complex work. The obscenity that occurs in a work of art may be as shocking to some as army talk; but it is wholly different in quality. The one is expressive; the other marks both the failure of expression and the lack of something to express.

It is a further consequence of this conception that obscenity in art not only does not lie in a baldness of sexual reference, but is, in fact, incompatible with wholly explicit statement. Explicitness may be pornographic, but it has no place in art. Where nothing is left to the imagination, the reading of the art object may stimulate an experience but does not itself constitute one. No opportunity is provided for that sharing in the act of creation which alone makes an experience esthetic. Nothing is a work of art for *me* unless I have been able to put something of my deeper self into it. The art object invites me to express something of that self and guides me in my efforts to do so; but the effort must be mine. Hence the popularity of the merely pornographic: it makes so few demands. Genuine expression is replaced by a spurious consummation.

As an esthetic category, obscenity is, by contrast, of the very stuff of imagination. In one etymology, "obscene" is from "obscurus"—

what is concealed. Now expression is concealment as well as revelation. Art speaks in symbols, and at the core of every symbol is a secret which only imagination can fathom. The symbol itself thus takes on the mysterious quality of what it hides. It is experienced as charged with feeling and produces tension by at once inviting and resisting penetration. Both art and obscenity have a single genetic root: the infantile capacity to endow a mere sign with the affect that belongs properly to what it signifies.[16] A creature incapable of obscenity is also incapable of art. Magic, too, avails itself of the same capacity: words themselves become things, imbued with mysterious powers over other things. Psychologically, obscenity stands between art and magic—neither wholly make-believe like the one, nor yet wholly believing like the other. In many cultures, obscenity has an important role in magical rituals. In our own, its magical character is betrayed in the puritan's supposition that words alone can work evil, and that evil will be averted if only the words are not uttered.

3

Because there is, after all, a difference between a symbol and what it symbolizes, obscenity is a matter, not of what the work *refers* to, but rather of the *expressive* substance of the work. Puritans may condemn a work for presenting certain aspects of life; artists may defend it because what is presented are certain aspects of *life*. Truth is used both as a mark of obscenity and as a mark of its absence. In fact, it can serve as neither. The question whether the world *is* as art (referentially) presents it to be is irrelevant to esthetic quality in general, and to the quality of obscenity in particular. Art is not obscene by virtue merely of its subject, nor does it cease to be obscene merely because its subject is virtuous. A verse attributed to D. H. Lawrence complains, "Tell me what's wrong with words or with you, that the thing is all right but the word is taboo!" But there is nothing wrong with recognizing that words and things are different, and that properties of the one cannot necessarily be imputed to the other. Words are public, for instance, and easy to produce, and can occur in contexts where the things they refer to would not be appropriate and could not occur. The Stoics argued that "there being nothing dishonest in the conjugal duty, it could not be denoted by any dishonest word, and that therefore the word used by clowns to denote it is as good as any other."[17] The question is, however, whether clowning is not different from conjugal life as the Stoics themselves conceived it, and whether the language used is not in fact part of the clowning.

In short, obscenity, like art itself, is not a matter of referential, but of expressive meanings. What is relevant is not subject, but substance; not an isolable message, but an embodied content. The artist does not bodily translate a subject into the work, but transforms it—he selects from it and gives it form. Thereby the work becomes more than merely an instrument of communication; it commands intrinsic interest because of its own inherent qualities. No subject as such can be obscene (one can always talk about it in Latin!). To be sure, the subject of a work of art contributes to its substance—reference enters into the service of expression—and so has an indirect relevance.[18] But the indirectness is crucial. A sexual subject (or similar reference) is a necessary condition for obscenity but not a sufficient one; only for pornography, as for propaganda, does the referential message suffice.

Thus, though censorship may extend to themes as well as treatments, obscenity does not. The immorality of the actual characters and conduct which provide the novelist with his material is alike irrelevant to the charge of obscenity and to the defense against it. For words are not the things they mean; art is not life. Art supplements life and does not merely duplicate it. The question of obscenity is a question of what the novelist is bringing on the scene, and the first answer to that question must be "a novel"; a sequence of incidents *with form and expression*. The qualities of the work are not determined by the traits of its subject matter. Truth, therefore, in the sense of depicting life as it is, neither produces nor precludes obscenity.

4

Obscenity, then, is an experienced quality of the work of art and can no more be localized in the subject matter of the work than in its intention or effect. But *what* quality is it? There are, in fact, several species of the obscene, which must be distinguished from one another because they differ so widely in their esthetic status and function.

First, is what I call *conventional obscenity:* the quality of any work which attacks established sexual patterns and practices. In essence, it is the presentation of a sexual heterodoxy, a rejection of accepted standards of sexual behavior. Zola, Ibsen, and Shaw provide familiar examples. The accusations of obscenity directed against them can be seen clearly—in retrospect!—to have been social rather than moral. The guilt with which they were charged was not sin, but a violation of good taste and, even more, of sound judgment. For sexual heterodoxy is frequently generalized, by the writer and his readers alike, to an overall radicalism. To attack established morality in any respect is to undermine the authority of every established pattern. It surprises no one that the author of *Nana* also wrote *J'Accuse;* of *Ghosts, An Enemy of the People;* and of *Mrs. Warren's Profession, Saint Joan.* It is a commonplace that mores tend everywhere to be moralized, so that unconventionality of any kind is condemned as immoral, and if sexual, as obscene.

The dual vocabulary for sexual subject matters, to be found in many cultures besides our own, is a device to preserve the conventions. The four-letter word is a scapegoat which allows the rest of the language to be free of sin.[19] The use of a foreign language (especially Latin) for questionable passages conveys a detached point of view which leaves the conventions undisturbed. More important, the foreignness restricts the work to a well-educated elite, whose conformity is not in doubt or who may, indeed, feel privileged to stand above the mores altogether. Conventional obscenity is not too good for the masses. It is too dangerous for them. If they begin by attacking accepted standards of sexual behavior, so the theory runs, they will end by rejecting all social constraints in an orgy of anarchic egoism.

Accordingly, it is conventional obscenity which is the main concern of the censor—not, say, the pornography of night-club entertainment. From the viewpoint of the censor, the tired businessman may call "time-out," but he mustn't change the rules of the game. It is one thing for him to declare a moratorium on his debt to society, but quite another for him to repudiate his honorable obligations. In short, he may be wicked but not scandalous; and scandal consists in open revolt against sexual constraints rather than covert evasion of them. Pope Paul IV was consistent in expurgating Boccaccio by retaining the episodes but transforming the erring nuns and monks into laymen:[20] thereby scandal was averted.

Now it might appear that conventional obscenity has nothing to do with art as such, but only with propaganda. For a work is usually identified as conventionally obscene on the basis of its message, not its expressive content; and art does not convey messages. As Sidney long ago pointed out in his defense of poesie,[21] the poet does not lie because he asserts nothing. He therefore does not assert that sexual conventions must be changed, but at most presents for imaginative contemplation the workings of our or other conventions. Some artists, however, consciously adopt a propagandistic stance. Yet, conventional obscenity does not depend upon a literalistic approach to art by way of subject, reference, and message rather than substance, expression, and embodied meaning. Both puritan and propagandist overlook the more subtle morality in the content of a work of art, in terms of which conventional obscenity is not limited to a reformist purpose, but plays an important role in all artistic intent.

The artist's integrity requires that he present the world as he sees it; his creativity, that he sees it afresh, in his own terms. The new vision is bound to be different, and as different, is judged to be wicked by the conformist morality of the old. The Hays production code requires that "correct standards of life" be presented, "subject only to the requirements of drama and entertainment"! But if they are subjected also to the requirements of honest and creative art, their "correctness" is likely to be challenged. Again and again in the history of art, the creative artist has had to take his stand against the Academy, as the repository of tradition not merely in art, but in life as well. Clive Bell is scarcely exaggerating when he warns that "of all the enemies of art, culture is perhaps the most dangerous."[22] The academic artist is likely to be free of conventional obscenity, but also to be innocent of esthetic quality. The artist who creates new forms and exploits new techniques— who develops, in a word, a new style—does so because he has something new to say; and in art, whatever is said needs its own language. The very newness is then felt as an attack on established patterns. The hostility to "modern art" evinced by the pillars of church, state, and society is not a product of insensitivity. On the contrary, it displays a realistic awareness of the threat which art has always posed to sheer conformity. The charge of obscenity directed against the arts is strictly comparable to the moral depravity regularly ascribed to heretical religious sects. "Thou shalt have no other Gods before me!" and a new vision of God—so says the priesthood—can only be a visitation of the Devil.

Art, in short, is a matter of inspiration as well as of skill. And inspiration—from the standpoint of the conventional—is a demonic corruption of the old rather than a new revelation of the divine. The "genius" is one who is possessed and hence dangerous. Mann's *Faustus* embodies a recurrent myth of the artist: he has sold his soul to the Devil to enjoy the fruits of the sin of *hubris* committed in imitating the Creator. A vicious circle is thus engendered. The philistine distrust of the artist leads to his rejection by established society, which provokes a counterattack that in turn is taken to justify the initial reaction. The situation, then, is not that we can generalize from sexual heterodoxy to a wholesale radicalism. It is rather that we can particularize from the artist's rejection of convention—because for him it is stale, flat, and unprofitable—to a sexual heterodoxy, and thus to conventional obscenity. The representation of pubic hair, for instance, is commonly regarded as obscene. But this is largely because it did not appear in the classic nude; and it did not appear there because the prevailing custom was to remove the hair from the body.[23] This is not our custom; but it is the custom in our art, and to depart from it is, therefore, to be obscene.

Now it is easy to exaggerate the danger to established patterns from art. We have already seen that there is no ground for supposing the effect of art on life to be immediate and direct. On the other hand, it is easy to exaggerate also the contribution to society which conventional obscenity makes. Traditional morality may be sound even if conformist, and in many respects surely *is* sound. Society needs stability as well as change; some changes *are* for the worse. Stability cannot be identified with stagnation and death, as Herbert Read has rashly claimed in defense of the artists as *advocati diaboli*.[24] The part of reason, it seems to me, is to reject both the sterile conformism which condemns art for its conventional obscenity and the destructive individualism which takes pride in standing above "the law of the herd."

5

A second type of obscenity I call *Dionysian obscenity*. It consists in what society regards as "excessive" sexualism. Familiar examples are provided by Aristophanes, Boccaccio, Rabelais, and the Elizabethans. As a quality of the work of art, it is an expression of an exuberant delight in life. Dionysian obscenity is present in its clearest form in the old Greek comedy where its connection with fertility rites and phallic ceremonies is obvious. It has played a part in such rites and ceremonies in many cultures.

Its occurrence in art forms is equally widespread. For art rests above all on a delight in color, sound, texture, and shape. The appeal of art is first sensuous; and between the sensuous and sensual the difference is only in the suffix not the root. The art object presents for enjoyment an esthetic surface in which formal and expressive values are present, to be sure, but only as fused with an immediate sensory appeal. The work of art may lead us, as Plato and Plotinus hoped,[25] to the world beyond sense; but it can do so only *through* sense. And sense must delight us in the passage. This fact was at the bottom of the iconoclastic controversy and has led some strict puritans to condemn all art as essentially immoral. The premise from which the condemnation springs is a sound one, even if the conclusion is not. We cannot consistently worship beauty and despise the pleasures which the bodily senses can afford. Matthew Arnold was distressed at the "vulgarity" of some of Keats' letters to Fanny Brawne; but more realistic critics have recognized that if he were incapable of such letters, he would not have written *The Eve of St. Agnes*.[26] Dionysian obscenity in art is of a piece with the enthusiasm which the artist displays over the delightful qualities of his medium.

But the artist is not merely celebrating the joys of esthetic perception. He is also providing a symbolic consummation for the entire range of human desire. It is the artist who can truly say that, being human, nothing human is alien to him. He is forever drawing the circle which takes in what man and nature reject. He himself is wounded by such rejection, and in comforting himself he pleases everyone. It is scarcely accidental that so much art, in all cultures and in all media, has to do with love. The human interest of love, in all its phases and manifestations, is the inexhaustible riches from which art unceasingly draws beauty. Can anyone doubt that if the human mammal gave birth in litters, painters and sculptors would find in multiple breasts the exquisite forms that the female nude now provides them? Whatever art touches it transfigures. But though the poet makes of love the divine passion, it remains *passion*. And when he presents it for what it is, in its full-bodied vigor, we call him obscene.

Whatever else art may be, it is an intensification of emotion. And when the emotion is a sexual one, the result is Dionysian obscenity. It cannot be pretended that the poetry, painting, sculpture, and even music of love owe nothing and repay nothing to our sexuality. We may recognize this debt without reducing beauty altogether to an effusion of sex. But art is not confined to the bare surface of human feeling. It enriches experiences only because its roots penetrate to the depths of feeling and so bring our emotional life to flower.

The consummations of art, however, are symbolic. It is for this reason that "excessive" sexuality so often finds a place in art: there is no other place for it to go. The symbol is possible when the reality is not. Dionysian obscenity is a symbolic release of impulses thwarted in fact. It compensates us for the frustrations imposed by rigid conventions. It is not merely a device to elude external repression; it is a mechanism whereby we can admit our feelings to ourselves. Sex becomes permissible when it is esthetically symbolized. We condemn it as obscene only when being brought face to face with our own impulses overwhelms us with anxiety and guilt.

On this basis, Dionysian obscenity not only need not be immoral, but may even serve as a moral agent. By providing a catharsis or sublimation, art may act as a safety valve without which libidinal pressures become explosive. This is especially suggested by the comic quality so characteristic of Dionysian obscenity. Modern burlesque, from a historical viewpoint, is a pathetic attempt to recapture this quality. Comedy releases in laughter tensions which might otherwise prove no laughing matter. The comic spirit detaches us from our impulses and their frustration to allow a satisfaction on another level.

It is for this reason, too, that Dionysian obscenity is so seldom pornographic. Pornography is grim and earnest and feeds only on frustration. In art, sexual energies are not gathered up for a desperate assault on social restraints, but are canalized so as to structure an esthetic experience which is in itself deeply satisfying.

The protest against Dionysian obscenity is essentially a protest against sexuality as such. It is a denunciation of the innate depravity of human nature, which finds satisfaction in "the lure of the senses and the evils of the flesh." The Dionysian, on the other hand, refuses to regard the act of love as inherently sinful. On the contrary, for him it is the supreme manifestation of what is good in life: the indomitable creative impulse. This same impulse finds expression in art. In Dionysian obscenity, art and life join in vigorous, unrestrained laughter.

6

Completely different in quality is a third kind of obscenity, which I call *the obscenity of the perverse*. Unlike conventional obscenity, it is not an attack on accepted standards, nor is it, like Dionysian obscenity, an affirmation of impulse despite restraints. It is rather a rebellion against convention which at the same time acknowledges the authority of received standards. In the obscenity of the perverse, the artist "accepts the common code only to flout it; conscious of sin, he makes sin attractive; his theme is the 'flowers of evil.' "[27] Baudelaire himself, as he claimed, does make sin hideous. The truly perverse finds sin attractive *because* it is sin (*e.g.,* Huysmans, de Sade). His obscenity lacks the naïveté of the Dionysian; it is likely to be lewd in a sophisticated fashion. The effect is that of calculated indecency.

Dionysian obscenity celebrates sex; conventional obscenity is neutral toward sex, being concerned primarily with the social evils of particular sex patterns; for perverse obscenity, sex is dirty, and it occupies itself with sex for the sake of the dirt. In viewing all obscenity as "smut" and "filth," the puritan only betrays his own perversion. There is here a profound ambivalence, a rebellion which is also a submission. Satan is not a free spirit, but a rebel divided against himself. In freedom, there is vigor and forthrightness, an enlargement of the soul, which is the antithesis of evil. In perverse obscenity, we have the pathetic spectacle of the Black Mass—worshipers without a God, seeking in hatred and rejection what they are incapable of accepting in love.

At bottom, the obscenity of the perverse is sheer hypocrisy; it is not so black as it paints itself. While pretending to rise above morality, it abjectly submits to it and only thereby becomes truly immoral, in playing false to its own dignity and freedom. While pretending to delight in sex, in fact it abhors sexuality, being convinced of its sinfulness and seeking it out only for the sin. For the perverse, sex is desirable only because it is forbidden; but it remains in the end a bitter fruit. Paradoxically, it is the puritan who creates such obscenity. For its foundation is secrecy and shame. The obscene is what is off the scene, hidden, covered. And shame, as ethnologists have long recognized, is not merely the cause of covering, but the effect.[28] The secret becomes shameful because of its secrecy. To be perverse is to uncover it merely because it is hidden. This is the obscenity of the leer and innuendo. The asterisks and dashes of the supposed puritan serve in fact to convey unambiguously the perverse content.

Basically, what perverse obscenity expresses is fear—fear of the great power of the sexual impulses. It is because of this power that prohibitions and constraints have been imposed upon it in all societies. But just because it is hidden, it looms larger and more threatening. What is perverse is not the concern with being overwhelmed by brute desire; it is the part of reason to look to the defenses of rationality. The perversion consists of purchasing freedom from anxiety by assuming a burden of guilt, selling one's soul to the Devil for fear of being rejected by God. Perverse obscenity tries to cope with the forces of sexuality by a symbolic denial of their potency. It plays with fire in a childish effort to convince itself that it cannot be burned. But what is most manifest in it is only the futility and the fear. By contrast, Dionysian obscenity triumphs over impulse by freely yielding to it, while conventional obscenity resolutely sets itself to canalize impulse more effectively than custom permits.

There is thus a close connection between the obscenity of the perverse and blasphemy. Historically, indeed, it was only on the basis of this connection that the early strictures against obscenity proceeded.[29] The obscenity of the perverse simultaneously makes too much of sex and too little; just as the blasphemer acknowledges God by denying Him, profanes the holy to damn himself. Diabolism, after all, is just another religion. Perverse obscenity does not wish to profane love in order to remove the taboo from it. Just the contrary; it pretends to ignore the taboo so as to destroy what is, for it, the fearful holiness of love. It is perverse obscenity, not the Dionysian, which is likely to be exploited in pornography; for pornography, as D. H. Lawrence has noted, is "the attempt to insult sex, to do dirt on it."[30] In the obscenity of the perverse, sex is no more than a disgusting necessity; the perversion lies in finding pleasure in the disgust.

Such an attitude is plainly foreign to art and could enter into esthetic experience only to drain it completely of esthetic quality. It is approximated, however, by a type of obscenity which lies between the Dionysian and the perverse—what might be called *ro-*

mantic obscenity. This is the category, exemplified in Swinburne and the "fleshly" school, which preserves the sense of sin yet celebrates sexuality in spite of it. It lacks the pagan innocence of the Dionysian but also the lust for evil of the perverse. It is romantic, as expressing a felt need to cover the nakedness of sex with sentiment and estheticism. This need is nowhere more apparent than in the strident insistence on being unashamedly sensual. The art in which romantic obscenity is to be found has something of the pathos of adolescent bravado.

7

In one of its etymologies, the word "obscene" is given the sense of the inauspicious and ill-omened.[31] This is the sense appropriate to the obscenity of the perverse, for its content is hate, not love. It seeks in sexuality only what is life-denying, finding in sinfulness the great Nay which it struggles to express. Its impulse is to destroy itself, though it contents itself with a stylized gesture toward the self-castration which some fathers of the church performed in fact. Obscenity may thus become linked with symbols of violence.

Aggression is as much repressed and controlled by society as are libidinal impulses. Murder is as universally condemned as incest, hostility as rigidly patterned as sexuality. Aggressive impulses, therefore, also seek expression in the symbols of art. Corresponding to the sexuality of Dionysian comedy is the violence of Greek tragedy. The impulses of love and hate may become confused and intertwined and sex patterned into sado-masochistic perversion. In the expression of this content, psychic distance can no longer be maintained, but is submerged in emphatic identifications both with brutality and with its victims. A new category of the obscene emerges: the *pornography of violence.*

In this type of obscenity, sexual desire finds symbolic release only as transformed into acts of aggression.[32] A phenomenally popular series of novels is constructed according to a rigid pattern of alternation of violence and sex which coincide only at the climax when the virile hero is allowed to shoot the wicked beauty. More sophisticated in style and structure, but essentially the same in substance, is the work of the "realistic" school sometimes associated with the name of Hemingway. Death in the afternoon prepares for love at midnight. There is no question that writing of this genre is effective; the question is only whether the effect is esthetic—an abattoir can also provide a moving experience. Esthetic or not, this genre is enormously successful; taking into account the "detective" story and the crime "comic," the pornography of violence is more widespread in our culture than all the other categories of obscenity put together.

It is, perhaps, banal to associate this fact with the role of violence in our culture, as a source even of recreation for the spectator. Yet, Henry Miller's denunciation must be taken seriously: "Fear, guilt and murder—these constitute the real triumvirate which rules our lives. *What is obscene then?* The whole fabric of life as we know it today."[33] It is easy to dismiss so sweeping a judgment. Yet, it remains true that the pornography of violence enjoys an immunity denied altogether not only to Dionysian obscenity, but even to the fundamentally respectable conventional obscenity. A noteworthy exception is the action of the British Board of Film Censors in prohibiting the showing of Disney's *Snow White* to children, on the ground that it might frighten them, at a time when all the children in London were being taught how to wear gas masks.[34]

8

Moral issues, as such, fall outside the scope of this essay. Yet, esthetics cannot ignore the moral content of art, and the esthetics of obscenity must finally face the question of how obscenity, in its various species, affects that content.

The moral content of art is plainly not a matter of doctrinaire messages, but something more fundamental. As I conceive it, it is nothing less than the affirmation of life, a great yea-saying to the human condition. In mastering its medium and imposing form on its materials, art creates a microcosm in which everything is significant and everything is of value, the perfection of what experience in the macrocosm might be made to provide. In this capacity, art may serve as the voice of prophecy and, like all prophets, go unheard or be stoned when its teaching is at variance with a law no longer alive to the demands of life. If, as in literature, human life itself is the subject to be artistically transformed, art insists on seeing it whole, for only thus can it understand and revitalize it; but when art uncovers what men wish to keep hidden, it is despised and condemned. And always, art remains a challenge to evil and death, forcing enduring human value out of the sadly deficient and evanescent material of experience.

In this conception, conventional and Dionysian obscenity, and perhaps also romantic obscenity, all play their part in the performance of the esthetic function; but not pornography, not the obscenity of the perverse, and especially not the pornography of violence. For these are in the service of death, not of life. They belong to that monstrous morality and taste of the burial ground where death is glorified and the sculpture of Michelangelo is given a fig leaf. The god of such obscenity is not Eros, but Thanatos. Not the wages of sin, but sin itself, is death.

Originally published in *Law and Contemporary Problems* (Durham, N. C., Fall, 1955), and reprinted with permission of the Duke University School of Law.

1. Theodore Schroeder, *Freedom of the Press and "Obscene" Literature,* (1906), p. 42; and *"Obscene" Literature and Constitutional Law,* (1911), pp. 13–14.

2. Morris L. Ernst and William Seagle, *To the Pure . . . A Study of Obscenity and the Censor,* (1928), p. x.

3. See Vilfredo Pareto, *The Mind and Society,* (Livingston ed., 1935), Vol. 2, p. 1010.

4. See Mortimer J. Adler, *Art and Prudence,* (1937), p. 126.

5. See John Dewey, *Art as Experience,* (1934).

6. D. H. Lawrence, *Sex Literature and Censorship,* (1953), p. 59.

7. See Kaplan and Kris, "Esthetic Ambiguity," in Ernest Kris, *Psychoanalytic Exploration in Art,* (1952), chap. 10.

8. United States v. One Book Called "Ulysses," 5 F. Supp. (S.D.N.Y. 1933), pp. 182, 183, aff'd, 72 F.2d (2d Cir. 1934), p. 705 (the court's decision is reprinted as a preface in James Joyce, *Ulysses* (Random House ed., 1934)).

9. Joyce, *op. cit.,* p. 183.

10. *Ibid.,* p. 184.

11. United States v. Harmon, 45 Fed. (D. Kan. 1891), pp. 414, 423.

12. See Benedictus Spinoza, *Ethics, passim.*

13. See *The Poetics of Aristotle, passim;* Sigmund Freud, *A General Introduction to Psychoanalysis* (1938), pp. 327–28.

14. George Santayana, *Reason in Art* (1934), p. 171.

15. United States v. One Book Called "Ulysses," 2 F. Supp. (S.D.N.Y. 1933), pp. 182, 184, aff'd, 72 F.2d 705 (2d Cir. 1934). See also James T. Farrell, "Testimony on Censorship," in *Reflections at Fifty* (1954), p. 212.

16. See Sandor Ferenczi, "On Obscene Words," in *Sex in Psychoanalysis* (1950), chap. 4.

17. Pierre Bayle, *The Dictionary Historical and Critical* (1837), p. 850.

18. See Kaplan, "Referential Meaning in the Arts," p. 12; *Journal of Aesthetics and Art Criticism* (1954), p. 457.

19. See Herbert Read, *An Obscenity Symbol,* 9 American Speech (1934), pp. 264, 267.

20. See A. L. Haight, *Banned Books,* (1935), chap. 8.

21. Philip Sidney, *The Defence of Poesie.*

22. Clive Bell, *Art* 267 (1927).

23. See Havelock Ellis, *Studies in the Psychology of Sex* (1936), Vol. IV, p. 94.

24. See Marjorie Bowen, *Ethics in Modern Art* ix (1939).

25. See *The Symposium* of Plato *passim;* Plotinus, *On the One and Good,* being the treatises of the sixth Ennead *passim.*

26. *E.g.,* Bell, *op. cit. supra* note 22, at 271–72.

27. Albert Guérard, *Art for Art's Sake* (1936), pp. 189–90.

28. See, *e.g.,* Edward Westermarck, *The History of Human Marriage* (3d ed. 1901), p. 211.

29. See, *e.g.,* Alpert, *Judicial Censorship of Obscene Literature,* 52 Harv. L. Rev. 40, 43–44 (1938).

30. D. H. Lawrence, *op. cit. supra* note 6, at 74.

31. See Havelock Ellis, "The Revaluation of Obscenity," in *More Essays of Love and Virtue* (1931), p. 99.

32. See generally Gershon Legman, *Love and Death* (1949); George Orwell, "Raffles and Miss Blandish," in *Critical Essays* (1946), p. 142.

33. Miller, "Obscenity and the Law of Reflection," *Tricolor,* Feb. 1945, p. 48, reprinted in Henry Miller, *The Air-Conditioned Nightmare* (vol. 2, Remember to Remember) 274, 286 (1947).

34. See H. L. Mencken, *The American Language Supplement One,* 644 (1948).

CHARLES MORRIS

The Science of Man and Unified Science

In 1939, at the Fifth International Congress for the Unity of Science, held at Harvard University, I read a paper with the title "Semiotic, the Socio-Humanistic Sciences, and the Unity of Science."[1] This paper suggested that "the theory of signs (semiotic) furnishes the key to the incorporation of the socio-humanistic sciences in the structure of unified science." The proposal made was to develop the theory of signs upon a biological base, to use this theory in the construction of a biologically based theory of value, and then to approach the whole domain of man's cultural activities in terms of semiotic and axiology so constructed. In this way it might be possible to build a bridge between the natural sciences and the science of man, both of which would then fall within a single system of knowledge. Such a program may be represented in the following diagram:

| science of man |
| science of values |
| science of signs |
| physical and bio-
logical sciences |

In the last decade much scientific work has been done which is relevant to the carrying out of this program. It is these developments which I wish to comment upon at this time.

The Science of Signs

The author's book, *Signs, Language, and Behavior,* published in 1946, was an attempt to show that semiotic could be given a biological foundation such that scientific methods could be applied to the whole domain of meaning. The suggestion was made that the analysis of any sign might be given by stating the things to which it directs behavior and the behavior which it prepares to these things. The interpretant of a sign (the effect of the sign of an organism) would then be a disposition to react to something or other in a certain way, and the signification of the sign would be given by specifying the reaction thus prepared and the things to which the reaction is prepared. On this approach the basic terminology of semiotic would be constructed upon terms of the physical and biological sciences, and in principle the whole domain of meaning woud be open to study by scientific methods.[2]

In this book it was further argued that such a behavioral approach to semiotic would allow a proper place for formal logic and logical analysis, since the approach itself furnished the basis for a distinction between analytical and nonanalytical sign combinations. Symbolic logic could then be conceived as the analytical portion of semiotic. And since logical analysis is not a theory of meaning but an analysis of given or entertained meanings, it does not itself decide between various theories of meaning; hence it is compatible with a biologically grounded semiotic. Further evidence for this compatibility may be found in the work of Charles Peirce (especially volumes II and V of his *Collected Papers*) since Peirce too ultimately viewed the interpretant of a sign as a disposition to respond; in Book II of C. I. Lewis' *An Analysis of Knowledge and Valuation,* which grounds the ultimate distinctions needed by symbolic logic upon their Peircean view of meaning; and in Hans Reichenbach's *Experience and Prediction,* which finds no conflict between the pragmatist's theory of meaning and the analyses made by the logical empiricists. Here at a critical point in theory the approaches of the pragmatic and logistic wings of the unity of science movement seem to have converged through the development of a study of meaning.

Among the many steps toward a scientific semiotic which are taking place today, three may here be noticed. The basing of linguistics upon the theory of signs, as in the work of Roman Jakobson, locates linguistics within semiotic, and this, taken together with the similar movement in respect to formal logic, augurs closer co-operation between the linguist, the logician, and the semiotician. Hans Reichenbach's attempt in *Elements of Symbolic Logic* to apply symbolic logic to the analysis of the everyday language is an instance of the direction of such co-operation.

The application of quantitative methods to content analysis by Harold D. Lasswell and his co-workers, while at present restricted to political discourse, is of sufficient generality to provide a model for the quantitative analysis of all types of discourse (see *Language of Politics,* by Harold D. Lasswell, Nathan Leites, and associates). Content analysis, so conceived, falls within the empirical or descriptive part of semiotic, and makes more precise its methods of study.

The elaboration of the theory of communication by mathematical, physical, and engineering techniques (as in Norbert Wiener's *Cybernetics;* Claude Shannon and Warren Weaver's *Mathematical Theory of Communication*) is further evidence that semiotic has now been linked to the basic scientific and technological disciplines. It is possible that the concept of feedback mechanisms stressed by Wiener and his associates may provide, in the form of circular neural processes, an approach to a fundamental problem of semiotic: the nature of the interpretant of a sign.[3]

The Science of Value

A central stimulus toward building a science of value on a behavioral basis has been the work of John Dewey. In his *Theory of Valuation*[4] he envisaged the task of the theory of value as the study of the nature and relation of prizing and appraisal. In his article "The Field of 'Value,'" in *Value: A Cooperative Inquiry* (edited by Ray Lepley) Dewey uses the term "selective-rejective behavior" to characterize the general field of behavior within which the study of values is to be carried on; and in this article he maintains that an appraisal (or evaluation) does not differ in kind from a statement, and hence is controllable by scientific methods. In an article in the same book, following the general direction set by Dewey's work, I suggested that axiology might be regarded as the science of preferential behavior. Since a study of such behavior would of course include the way it affects and is affected by signs, this characterization of axiology embraces the study of preferences (prizings, selection-rejections), appraisals (evaluations, judgments of value), and their interrelations. So conceived, the field of value is open to scientific study.

As examples of studies of prizings in line with this approach reference may be made to the monograph by Henry A. Murray and Christiana D. Morgan, "A Clinical Study of Sentiments";[5] and to the various papers by Jerome S. Bruner and his associates.[6] For some years the author has been making a study of the preferences of various kinds of persons in various cultures. While the study has been mainly concerned with preferences among various possible ways to live, some attention has been given to preferences as to paintings and philosophies, and to the interrelation of these three sets of preferences. It is possible in this way to isolate empirically various value patterns, to ascertain their number, to study their relative strengths in various cultures, and to investigate what kinds of persons accept which patterns under what conditions. The detailed results of this study have not yet been published, but an indication of the methods and the type of results can be found in an article "Individual Differences and Cultural Patterns" in the volume *Personality*, edited by Clyde Kluckhohn and Henry A. Murray, and in my book, *The Open Self*.[7]

The empirical study of appraisals has been slower in getting under way, since it required a theory of signs sufficiently developed to handle such signs and to compare them with other kinds of signs. It is my belief that the analyses given in *Signs, Language, and Behavior*, in Book III of C. I. Lewis' *An Analysis of Knowledge and Valuation*, and in C. L. Stevenson's *Ethics and Language*, have gone a considerable way toward meeting this need, and hence to prepare the ground both for the scientific study of appraisals and the scientific making of appraisals.

The situation seems to me to be something like this: appraisals are signs the evidence for whose applicability is in the last analysis found in prizings. As such, appraisals are cognitive (true or false) since they make predictions which can be tested; but they differ from certain other kinds of signs whose applicability does not involve the occurrence or nonoccurrence of prizings as evidence. It is true, as Stevenson maintains, that conflicts of prizings are not necessarily resolved by the increase of knowledge; it is even true that a certain diet or way of life good with respect to some persons may be bad with respect to others. But these facts force us only to qualify our appraisals with respect to certain persons under certain conditions, and to admit that knowledge of values does not insure their attainment; they do not force us to abandon the view that appraisals are empirically meaningful and capable in principle of being controlled by scientific methods.[8]

If prizings and appraisals are subject to scientific study, then so is the problem of their relation. It is possible to investigate the influence of certain prizings in the formation or acceptance of appraisals, and the reverse effect upon prizings of appraisals formed by an individual or known to be held by other individuals. Similarly, the relation of prizings and appraisals to nonevaluative knowledge is open to experimental determination. My study of paintings has touched upon these matters, but serious work on such problems is yet to be done.

It is often maintained that preferences are not values, and that consequently a study of preferences has nothing to do with the study of values. To admit the first part of this thesis does not, however, require an acceptance of the conclusion. It is true that when we ascribe value to something we often mean that it is value-able, *i.e.*, able to support a prizing, or able to support continued prizing, or more able to do either of these than is something else. These are, to be sure, claims made about an object, and not a description of existing prizings. But since they are claims to *prizability*, they can only ultimately be tested by observing whether, under stipulated conditions, the objects are prized or continue to be prized. So without claiming that preferences and values are the same thing, it is possible to maintain that axiology, conceived as the study of preferential behavior, is a study of values. I, indeed, know of no other way that values can be studied.

The Science of Man

We must now note a third growing tendency in the scientific study of man: the tendency to regard any particular human trait as a function of many factors or variables, *i.e.*, to think in terms of fields. This attitude contrasts with the tendency to look at man only in terms of physique or environment or culture or language. Each of these approaches has often been carried on in isolation, and indeed in competition with the other approaches; now we seem to have come to the point where we must realize that any of these approaches when carried far enough involves all of the others.[9]

The trait to be studied may be anything whatsoever: clothes worn, philosophies accepted, schizophrenia, aggressiveness, literary preferences, and so forth. In studying this trait in individuals one seeks to find the conditions of the field under which the trait appears. Thus if one is studying schizophrenic traits from this point of view one would try to find out what types of organisms, in what environments, under what social relations, and equipped with what symbols, become schizophrenic. In seeking to uncover such laws, many individuals would have to be studied and many factors considered. The methods of factor analysis developed by L. L. Thurstone (in his *Multiple Factor Analysis*) furnish one important way by which the complex interrelations of such data can be handled.

The field approach to the study of man provides the context in which the science of signs and the science of values are themselves to be carried on. These sciences, conceived as behavioral sciences, are linked in the ways previously indicated with the biological and physical sciences. Putting them within the field approach brings out this relation in another way, for this approach requires that data on physiques and physical environment be included in the study of human traits. The science of man is in this way linked methodologically with the biological and physical sciences to form a single scientific system.

One of the merits of William H. Sheldon's important work (as reported in *The Varieties of Human Physique, The Varieties of Temperament,* and *The Varieties of Delinquent Youth*) is that his constitutional emphasis has forced us to take account of the biological differences in the individuals whose traits are being studied. He has supplied constitutional data on many of my subjects, and at a later time detailed reports will show how this research on psychoses, ways to live, and paintings in various cultures has confirmed his basic thesis as to the importance of considering differences of physique in the study of human beings. Here it is only necessary to add that Sheldon's work is of significance in helping to bridge the gap between the biological and the human sciences by reinserting the physique into the total field. The same service with respect to environmental factors has been performed by Ellsworth Huntington, whose lifework was brought to a focus in *Mainsprings of Civilization.*

The constitutional and environmental factors link the science of man with the biological and physical sciences. At the same time, the recognition in personality development of the role of social factors and the role of symbols which individuals produce, ensures us that nothing distinctively human will be lost. The science of man is linked with the biological and physical sciences but not reduced to them. For as sign processes, the ideas and ideals of individuals enter as formative factors in the total field; they are the way in which man in a genuine sense is one factor in the making of his own future, transforming his body, his physical environment, and his culture.[10]

Conclusion

Such are some of the ways in which the work of the last decade has advanced the program of integrating the science of man and bringing it within the framework of unified science. Further and rapid developments in this direction may be expected in the next decade. Such developments will not be of scientific interest alone; they are of importance for the integration of man as man. They help to destroy at the root the opposition of man's scientific and humanistic concerns. In integrating science we at the same time integrate and liberate ourselves.

This article originally appeared in the *Proceedings of the American Academy of Arts and Sciences,* Vol. 80 (1951), pp. 37–44, and is reprinted with permission.

1. An abstract of this paper was printed as part of the article "The Significance of the Unity of Science Movement," *Philosophy and Phenomenological Research,* Vol. 6 (1946), pp. 508–15.

2. References to criticisms of this approach, and my reply to these criticisms, may be found in "Signs About Signs About Signs," *Philosophy and Phenomenological Research,* Vol. 9 (1948), pp. 115–33.

3. See the papers by Warren S. McCulloch and Walter Pitts, *Bulletin of Mathematical Biophysics,* Vol. 5 (1943), pp. 115–33; Vol. 9 (1947), pp. 127–47. Also, D. O. Hebb's book, *The Organization of Behavior.*

4. In *International Encyclopedia of Unified Science,* Vol. II, No. 4.

5. *Genetic Psychology Monographs,* Vol. 32 (1945), pp. 3–149, 153–311.

6. Such as "Value and Need as Organizing Factors in Perception," *Journal of Abnormal and Social Psychology,* Vol. 42 (1947), pp. 33–44; "Personal Values as Selective Factors in Perception," *ibid.,* Vol. 43 (1948), pp. 142–54.

7. An article, "Comparative Strength of Life-Ideals in Eastern and Western Cultures," is to appear in a volume of proceedings of the second East-West Philosophers' Conference, to be edited by Charles A. Moore. [This volume has since been published under the title *Essays in East-West Philosophy* (Honolulu, University of Hawaii Press, 1951).]

8. This issue is of such basic importance that it deserves to be made a central topic of discussion by the Institute for the Unity of Science. Philipp Frank's position in *Relativity—A Richer Truth* seems in accord with the position taken; but I am not sure that Reichenbach or Stevenson would agree.

9. This point of view provides the basis of organization of the anthology, *Personality,* edited by Kluckhohn and Murray. Murray has sometimes called this the "multiform method." Laura Thompson had come to a similar methodological position as a result of her work on the Hopi Indians; see her book, *Culture in Crisis.* I had been led to the same result in the study of signs and values. This view facilitates the integration of the science of man, including therein the social sciences. A comprehensive attempt at such integration is found in the volume, *Toward a General Theory of Action,* by members of the Harvard Department of Social Relations and their collaborators. [This book appeared in 1951, Harvard University Press, with Talcott Parsons and Edward A. Shils as editors.] The point of view is an extension and elaboration of that found in Talcott Parsons' *The Structure of Social Action.*

10. See *The Open Self;* G. H. Mead's *Mind, Self, and Society;* F. S. C. Northrop's "Ideological Man in His Relation to Scientifically Known Natural Man" in *Ideological Differences and World Order,* of which he is the editor.

ARTHUR E. MURPHY

The Common Good

The problem I propose to investigate in this paper is *prima facie* a modest one, for it concerns the meaning of a well-known expression in a use with which both practical men and philosophers are familiar. The expression is "the common good" as it occurs in statements which affirm that "the common good," "the public interest," or "the welfare of the community" requires or warrants one sort of action or another. The context of such use is that in which reasons are asked for and given in support of orders issued, claims presented or policies recommended, and in which a distinction is made between good reasons and bad. In raising the question of meaning here I have no special analytic or metaphysical ax to grind. Most of us on many occasions have considered and discussed claims thus supported as if we understood them and have accepted some and rejected others on what we took to be good grounds. It is difficult to see how the intelligent discussion of social policies could go on if we did not. Our present trouble is that on fundamental issues the discussion of social policies is by no means as intelligent as it ought to be. Some part of this failure is due,

I think, to the fact that in the social situations in which our talk of "common good" arises we are not clear in our minds as to what it is that we are trying to say or how properly to test the cogency of what is offered as a reason. Hence one more effort to reach a better understanding is perhaps worth making.

1

The natural starting point for such an inquiry is a closer look at the context in which, prior to any intrusion of philosophical analysis, these words are used with conviction and practical effect. One such use, at least, is obvious. Like other expressions that invoke ideals for purposes of social action, "the common good" is a term of praise and an instrument of power. In the public speech of those who are expert in its practical use, it is a potent factor in the mobilization of mass support for policies requiring a considerable effort of voluntary co-operation for their successful prosecution. The larger undertakings of modern society, both in peace and war, do require such co-operation, and words thus used are essential links in the process that unites a multiplicity of individual responses in a pattern of co-ordinated behavior. Moved by appeals to the righteous claims of a common cause men have willingly worked and died together as they would not have worked or died for more tangible and less exalted ends. In a world once more preparing itself for total war, this use of the language of ideals has an unmistakable significance and "the common good" a "social reality" that even the most hardheaded of social realists can appreciate.

So far, then, we may safely say that the context in which the expression we are examining has an authentic use is that in which emotively potent language is employed to elicit agreement in attitude on the part of those addressed. The analysts who have recently paid most attention to the uses of "ethical language" have properly observed and stressed this fact.[1] In so doing they have emphasized in an illuminating way the likeness of the verbal procedures of moralists and politicians to those of advertisers and other social experts in persuasive discourse. Men are thus moved by appeals to "common good" and also by the words of praise in which a popular radio comedian expresses and incites approval for the brand of cigarette he has been hired for a season to delight in. In each case a large-scale social agreement is achieved by the use of words designed to influence attitudes, not merely to convey information, and in each the language used is to be understood in the light of that distinctive interest and intent. So far the procedures are alike and the same rules of interpretation should apply to both.

This authentic if somewhat rudimentary insight is a genuine contribution to our subject. It helps us locate the meaning of a questionable term by tracing it to the social neighborhood in which it works, and it calls our attention to some of its less genteel relations, to whom it bears a family resemblance. So far so good. But there are persuasions *and* persuasions, and for some of our purposes the difference between them may be at least as important as their similarity. An analysis that ignores or underestimates these differences through its reiterated insistence that words designed to influence our practical decisions are all alike persuasive in intent will advance our understanding at one point only to obstruct it at another. I believe that current inquiries into the "emotive" uses of language are frequently in this way obstructive. Our present concern, however, is not to refute these theories but accurately to describe the situation of which we have so far given an adequate account. Having therefore duly noted, in the fashion of time, that appeals to "common good" are, and are meant to be, persuasive, let us now inquire more specifically what kind of persuasion this is and what sort of agreement is required if it is properly to do its work.

It is at least, and essentially, a persuasion offered to support and justify a decision or command. It is presented as a reason why something or other ought to be done or left undone, and its apparent cogency as thus understood is intrinsic to its effectiveness in eliciting agreement in attitude from those to whom it is addressed. This does not mean, of course, that those who understand and are moved by it will stop on each occasion to ask for evidence of the genuineness of the good it promises or the good faith of those who claim to speak for it. But it does mean that talk of this sort functions, like paper money, in terms of confidence and credit. The question of its warranted validity can meaningfully arise. When it does arise, the answer wanted is in terms of the rightness of its claim, not of the *de facto* efficacy of its emotive use. And until its cogency is re-established it will not for the questioner be persuasive as it was before. That is why the masters of totalitarian propaganda are at such pains to see to it that such questions do not arise. A managed credulity is the only proper atmosphere in which to preserve the emotive efficacy of words that sound or look like reasons but will not bear the examination of an inquiring mind. Even here, however, the words must sound or look like reasons, for it is only as thus understood and accepted that they can perform their distinctive function.

What is this function, and how are reasons relevant to its fulfilment? To elicit agreement, to be sure. But to elicit agreement by reference to goods which those addressed will recognize as worth having, for whose attainment they acknowledge a shared responsibility, and with respect to which some decisions are warrantable as reasonable and right while others can properly be rejected as arbitrary or unwise. The language in which an approval thus substantiated is expressed is that of shared ideals, of loyalty and fair-dealing, of goods authentically worth the effort that is called for to secure them. This is a normative use of language; it answers questions about excellence and right and justice in terms of what, by relevant criteria, is reliably accredited as excellent or right or just. There are advanced thinkers who find this usage esoteric and occult. If we would only tell them what we mean in terms that transform a justification into a description, a command or a verbal enticement, if we would just say plainly and with no nonsense what kind of an *is* an *ought* is supposed to be, *then* they would know what we were talking about and we could do "meta-ethics" together.

But in that case we should not any longer be talking about the subject that here concerns us. For a justification is not a decription, nor a command, nor a verbal enticement, and to talk about it as though it were, is to talk, however meticulously and elaborately, about something else, with which for analytic purposes it has been mistakenly identified. Fortunately the more discerning analysts are coming to see that this is so and to direct their formidable powers, in consequence, to the elucidation of the logical structure of specific subject matters to which particular types of reason are relevant rather than to the imposition upon all alike of a pre-fabricated "clarity" borrowed from mathematical logic and the preconception of a positivistic epistemology.[2] I propose, within the limits of my competence, to follow their example.

In what sort of situation, then, would a question about the *reasons* for a practical decision, phrased in terms of common good, significantly arise, and how, in such a situation, could a relevant and cogent answer be identified? It would be a question about what ought to be done, asked by men who were capable of recog-

nizing some obligations and were concerned in their common behavior to see to it that these obligations were met. It would refer
to the conditions that made moral sense of their shared social concerns, to benefits received or anticipated and responsibilities in-
curred, and it would ask that a particular decision, on which agreement was sought, be justified by its contribution to some good they
were thus jointly concerned to secure. If there were no disagreement with respect to such goods and obligations the request for
justification would not, save rhetorically, arise. If there were no
agreement there would be no common ground on which it could
be reasonably discussed. The offering and testing of practical
reasons, the reasons that justify a decision with respect to right
and good, presuppose a tension of disagreements mediated by the
shared commitments of a working understanding. A common good
is the ideal content of this presupposed understanding functioning
as a standard for the adjudication of conflicting claims and the
justification of questionable decisions. The language that invokes
it is significantly addressed to men who, in such situations, ask
for reasons and for whom an authentic obligation in a cause worth
serving is a good and sufficient reason for the action called for in
its name. To persuade, in this usage, is to convince, and the criteria
that distinguish a warranted from a spurious claim are presupposed
in the determination of the moral relevance and cogency of language used.

There are, then, as we noted, persuasions *and* persuasions, and
the differences between them are important. The agreement in
attitude evoked by the successful advertiser of cigarettes is casual,
mindless, and irresponsible. It may appropriately be achieved by
any means conducive to this end. Those who share a preference for
Chesterfields, for example, need agree on little else to respond appropriately to the verbal bait presented to them. Nor is it essential to their enjoyment or the advertiser's profit that they judge or
justify their approval of his product, though even here a form of
words is used that panders to man's insatiable desire for reasons.
Perhaps Chesterfields really are milder, and this is somehow a good
thing, of which a discriminating smoker ought to take account.
Nor, finally, does their shared addiction carry with it any further
commitments that they need be seriously concerned to respect.
A man may switch his brand of cigarettes or whiskey without
prejudice to his position as a man of distinction.

The requirements for the agreement in attitude in which the

language of common good has a distinctive use are more exacting. Here considerations are offered to persuade men to agree in what they recognize as right and reasonable, when they judge the issue fairly on the ground of shared benefits and responsibilities and are prepared to accept a verdict thus arrived at as a commitment to such further conduct as is warrantably called for on its accredited authority. This is properly described as ethical agreement because an ethical standard is presupposed in the determination of the pertinence of the considerations offered to support it and the moral authority of the decisions in which it is embodied. An agreement in attitude maintained in this way and at this level of responsible behavior is what makes a social group a community in the sense in which that term has a significant moral use. The common good is an ideal or represented good thus acknowledged and operative in rationally self-controlled behavior, and it is as thus united that men constitute a community in which the persuasive claim of social agencies to moral authority makes honest and examinable sense.

We are now in a position to sum up the first stage of our inquiry in one negative and one positive conclusion. In quest of clarity concerning potent words of questionable import we looked for their meaning in their use, and found this usage in the process in which a language that invokes ideals asks for ethical agreement from those to whom it is persuasively addressed. So far our findings are in harmony with the analytic orthodoxies of the day. But we have found in *ethical* agreement rather more than the analysts of "ethical language" have been prepared to bargain for. For this turns out to be a normative use of language. The persuasions that support its claims are addressed to men as capable of moral understanding and call for justification on the terms it sets. An agreement to which the examinable validity of the persuasions offered make no difference, or in which moral relevance and cogency meant no more than the causal efficacy of "emotive" language in influencing attitudes by any means and for any ends the speaker found effective, would not be ethical agreement. That, on the contrary, is the way in which agreement in attitude is secured in situations in which the persuasion offered is not addressed to men as moral agents and in which, in consequence, the questions to which a moral reason is an answer do not significantly arise. It is not surprising that those who seek in such "emotive meaning" the pattern of significant ethical discourse make only nonsense of the claims and pro-

cedures of practical reason. This confirms their positivistic preconceptions, rules out hard questions with which their methods are
not competent to deal, and sends them rejoicing on their way.
Since our aim is to make sense of ethical agreement in the use and
on the terms appropriate to its specific nature and intent, their
way cannot be our way.

We must therefore look elsewhere for the understanding which,
by the very nature of their method and intent, they cannot give us.
Nor is there longer any doubt as to where we are to look. Following the well-known semantic directive to point to the referent, we
have, to the best of our ability, pointed. And what we are now
plainly pointing at are the processes of communication in which
moral authority is invoked, supported and used as an instrument
of control in the ordering of group behavior. A community, whatever else it may be, is at least a social nexus within which such
processes occur and are to some degree effective. Here at last our
idealistic terminology appears to make connection with substantial fact and the "ought" of ethical language to find its locus
in the existential context of an identifiable social process. From
now on we should at least know what we are talking about and
where to look for reliable answers to our questions.

2

Our inquiry has so far specified the context in which the claims
of common good arise and can significantly be discussed, but it
has not shown us how they can properly be tested. The language
here employed is normative; it speaks of justification and makes
pretensions to validity. If we are to understand its cogency, we
must distinguish between its right and wrong use *for moral purposes,* when both are social facts. Nor can we simply appeal to
"society" to make this distinction for us, for any such appeal yields
morally equivocal results.

The gist of our difficulty is this. When we address men in the
morally authoritative language of community we speak to them
as if our mutual behavior were to be governed by the common
purposes and responsibilities which give our claims a moral meaning, and as if they would so understand and respond to them. In
fact, however, this is often not even approximately the case. "Society" as such is not community, in the sense in which community
is a term of justification or 'he claims and interests of "common

good" a valid moral reason. George Herbert Mead used to illustrate the wide range of "sociality" by instancing the "conversation of gestures" of a dogfight in which each participant adapts its behavior to the other in carrying out the social act in which they are mutually involved.[3] It is hardly necessary to stress the point that the sociality thus identified is not community nor the conversation involved in it the basis for a common understanding. Nor is this merely because the gestures are nonverbal. Words, too, can be weapons, and the political equivalent of the dogfight on the human level is not made more irenic by the capacity of the participants to verbalize their animosities. A conversation of verbal gestures can be used either to further moral understanding or to defeat it by trading on its authority for selfish and divisive ends. In the societies that we know both these uses do patently occur and the latter is no less socially effective than the former.

The current manner of speaking of "society as a whole," as a locus of moral authority sounds promising but is, as it stands, misleading. An actual social group is not made a moral whole, a community, by its numbers or power or by the orthodoxy of opinion that prevails within it. Its members are united by some loyalties and interests, antagonistic with respect to others. It is just because they disagree on some issues that an appeal to ethical agreement is needed to elicit a kind of co-operation not otherwise attainable. A society becomes a moral whole to the extent that the ideals that articulate this presupposed agreement are embodied on the whole and for essential purposes in the procedures of its corporate life. Hence, it is not "society as a whole" that defines the "ought"; it is the ought of ethical agreement as exemplified in procedures of good faith and fair dealing that constitute a society a whole for which moral authority can significantly be claimed. The reference to "society" as a ground for valid moral judgment must, if it is to be rationally discerning, be a reference to society as moral, to community. And whether the claims of any given society are genuinely entitled to such respect will have to be decided not on merely "social" but on moral grounds.

If "society as a whole" is unavailing here, the "group mind" is no better case. For the "group" for moral purposes is mindless save as its members achieve some kind of ethical understanding and know how to use it. One of the most impressive attempts yet made to work out a moral theory in such terms is Mead's social behaviorism. As a description of the manner in which the current norms of group approval are carried over as the voice of "the generalized other" into the socially conditioned individual's responses to his own behavior, this theory is remarkably illuminating. As an account of the moral authority of a community as embodied in the behavior of individuals who respond to it as selves or persons, it is patently inadequate. When the generalized other whispers "lo, thou must," the "me" repeats "I must." But the "me" that thus responds is so far not a moral self at all, nor is the group whose standardized responses it reflects a community. Neither the one nor the other has a mind of its own, for the "self" has only what the group has given it and the group, made up of other "me's," similarly conditioned, had none to give. A society thus constituted is more accurately characterized as a "lonely crowd" in which each individual vainly looks to others to supply him with a selfhood none of them has got.[4]

Nor does the addition, in Mead's theory, of an "I," an "emergent" factor in individual behavior which may conflict with and resist group pressures, really help.[5] For if, as he insists, the only principles by which the individual can judge his conduct ethically are those of "the group," then the "I" has nothing to judge with, no moral standpoint from which to make a judgment. Morality at this level is simply conformity to the internalized pressure of standardized group opinion and while the aberrant individual may rebel against these standards and in time remake them, his rebellion is not moral until it has succeeded in imposing itself on others as a new group pressure and is "right" then only as it was "wrong" before, by reference to the generalized opinion that in fact prevails.

Stripped of the generous liberalism of Mead's own personal philosophy this doctrine can be used to rationalize but not to justify a prevalent contemporary state of mind. So accustomed have we grown to the naturalistic fallacy in its sociological form, to the identification of the moral *ought* with the *is* of group approval or aversion, that we hardly understand what else than socially dominant opinion (in our group, of course) moral authority might be. Surely the man who presumes to set his private judgment against the verdict of his "peer group" *must* be wrong, for is not that just what being wrong consists in, at least for those of us who have learned, like Sidney Webb, to "think in communities"?[6]

No it is not, if we know what we are talking about when we speak of a community in which moral authority has an honest moral meaning. If the verdict of "the community" means the mass or dominant attitude of approval or aversion in some assigned social group, however arrived at and by whatever means maintained, then the verdict of "the community" may very possibly be wrong by any standard entitled to our respect as moral agents. If on the other hand, the authority we are asked to respect is one which is prepared to justify its claims at the level of examinable understanding, on the grounds of common good which those who share its benefits are bound in justice to support, then it is precisely to the judgment of responsible individuals that its claims are properly addressed. If such judgment were *merely* "private," if it were not grounded in publicly examinable reasons, it would not be a judgment at all, but an appetite, animus or whim, and the question of its validity would not meaningfully arise. But if it were not "private" as *personal,* as the individual's own reasonable decision which he alone can make and for which he makes himself responsible, then again it would not be a judgment, but the appetite, animus or whim of others, re-enacted at a level of behavior in which the criteria appropriate to moral judgment no longer have a rational use.

The distinction between these two meanings of "community" has practical as well as analytic significance. There are few uglier forms of cynicism than that of the politicians who, having demoralized the public mind with fear, suspicion and misrepresentation, triumphantly acclaim the result as the moral judgment of "the community" whose righteous verdict somehow justifies their performance. We have seen enough of this in recent times to feel its danger. It is not yet clear that we have the intellectual and moral stamina to expose it for the imposture that it is.

Who, then, speaks for the community in which a common good is a justifying reason for the conduct called for in its name? There are, of course, the duly constituted authorities whose legal competence is ordinarily not difficult to determine. In the performance of their duties such men are entitled to command and to admonish and to be respected and obeyed. But they speak with moral authority only as representatives of a public interest committed to their keeping as a public trust, and are properly to be understood accordingly. What makes this interest public is no *de facto* generality; it is not what everybody wants when each is concerned to please himself or all have been made submissive to the same mass pressures. It is the interest that can justify itself as public on terms of equity that apply to all, the terms of ethical agreement that distinguish a community from a manipulated crowd. To maintain the ethical agreement vital to such community it is indeed essential that its members "think alike" on fundamentals. That does not mean, however, that they must hold identical opinions on controversial issues, opinions maintained by indoctrination in all the varied media of managed mass credulity. That is not to think alike, for so far it is not to think at all. It is, rather, the way in which men agree when they do not think, when their minds are the passive instruments of social forces that they do not understand. To think alike, where doubt has arisen and a justification is called for, we must first of all think, and to think is to judge, to submit divergent claims and opinions to the test of examinable reasons and to decide, not arbitrarily, but fairly, on the merits of the case. An agreement thus maintained is an ethical agreement and the society that preserves and defends it a community. Claims based upon it are addressed to men as individuals, at the level of social behavior at which they recognize a valid claim as a practical reason and respond to it as such. The morally authoritative verdict of the community is the concensus maintained and validated in this process. Where there are no such individuals, there is no such community.

All this, we shall be told once more, is far too good to be true. Of course, if community is defined in moral terms, then only a society that satisfies those terms will be, in this queer way of speaking, a community. But actual societies are not like that. Strip away the unscientific verbiage and what is left of social behavior in a clearheaded last analysis is custom, credulity and conflicting interests held in balance in some areas by organized power. The rest is talk. So speaks the enlightened realist who looks for facts, not theories, and is determined not to be imposed upon by words. Since there is some truth in what he says, though little understanding, he deserves an answer here. It is, at this stage in our inquiry, not difficult to give.

Of course it is the case that if we cut away all ideal language, and all that language stands for and evokes in human behavior, we are left in a world in which such language has no cogency, and, indeed, no sense. For it is only through the processes of communication in which men come to understand their social life as serving common ends and relate their wills responsibly to a good thus shared that they constitute the community which is the referent and justification of their ideal claims. As Josiah Royce was fond of insisting, a society thus constituted is and must be a community of interpretation.[7] Take away the interpretation, the attitude of will involved in it and the conduct in which its claims are embodied and there is nothing left to which, in actual social behavior, the description we have given would literally apply. Where such communication is rudimentary, there is but rudimentary community. Where it is perverted to divisive ends our talk of common good becomes as empty of rational cogency as the cynics take it to be. And where it breaks down altogether, we are left in the state of nature which the realist's last analysis sufficiently describes. That is just what I have been insisting on; it is the same fact seen, as it were, from the under side. And that, from where he stands, is all the social realist can see of it.

Nor is it difficult to see why the temptation recurs to speak of his as in some ultimate and privileged sense the last analysis. These are disillusioning times. Over wide areas of what we used to call the civilized world, communication at this level simply does not exist, and we have come to look on the liberal philosophers of our tradition as naïve in supposing that it ever did or could. The trust and trustworthiness that make community a fact require an act of faith, a faith too often disappointed in the recent past to leave much room for hope and charity. We do not propose to be deceived again and therefore look with growing favor on philosophers who ask us to retreat to a position invulnerable to deception because, from the standpoint it defines, there is no longer anything of moral import to be deceived about. That is one way, after all, to be secure in our minds, and we now place a high value on security.

Nothing, however, could be more unrealistic than the notion that a language free of moralistic implications could provide a working basis for effective social action. In times of crisis men do not surrender the language of ideals; they go on using it with increased urgency and vehemence. Our present disillusionment is full of righteous indignation; the hope of a better world, we say, has been betrayed by evil men, and we appeal to the judgment of "the free world" to justify our cause against them. This, too, is moralistic talk. Is it mere talk, that masks a drive for power in the persuasive rhetoric of high sounding words? We emphatically reject that suggestion, not as an analytic inaccuracy but as slander. But what then? What truthfulness is there in our claims, and what is the reality behind them? It can only be the reality embodied in processes of rationally self-controlled behavior, in professedly common purposes faithfully maintained, in pledges kept and hoped for goods achieved in co-operative action. Where these processes operate and are effective there is community and those who speak its language need deceive neither their fellows nor themselves, for it is precisely by these means that they achieve a kind of understanding not elsewhere or otherwise attainable. Where these processes fail there is still tall talk, and its "emotive" use, but the means of determining its veracity are gone. Hence those who look for the justification of a language of ideals outside the commitment and procedures in which that justification can in fact be made will assuredly not find it. There is no submoral or metaethical substitute for moral understanding, and it is only in terms of such understanding that the distinction between good faith and deception can intelligibly be made out.

The processes that constitute a community are real, and ultimately real, not at all in the sense that they are existentially ubiquitous or socially unconditioned or guaranteed to prevail in "Ultimate Reality" against confusion and ill will. They are real in the quite simple sense that they sometimes do operate in actual human affairs, that there is no better way of doing the work they do than in the way they do it and that this is a work which, for essential human purposes, we cannot do without. There is a level of human behavior at which men ask for justifying reasons, and to the question thus asked nothing but a reason can be an answer. In the asking and answering of such questions they sometimes achieve an understanding that makes moral sense of their social relations. They speak, then, in terms of common good and in so speaking they are not, or need not be, deceived. For the common good is the good of a community and community is actualized in the lives of men who seek and find a common good. It is through the procedures of communication in which ideals are invoked as reasons and claims justified on their authority that they do thus seek and find it.

There is, then, for those who would use with moral cogency the persuasive language of a common good, no escape from the commitments and the risks that use entails. The commonness of the common good is not like that of the common cold, a contagion spread in crowds by indiscriminate association. It is shared as ideals are shared by those who honor them and kept, if it is well kept at all, as promises are kept. There is, in consequence, endless opportunity for deception and confusion in the social use of the language that ostensibly appeals to it. We should be glad, of course, if there were some value-free standpoint or some fool-and-knave-proof method to which we could refer for the clarification and justification of our ideals. But there is none and from the nature of the case there cannot be. We must work with such moral understanding as we have, with men who, like ourselves, are sometimes knaves or fools, and within a social process in which the quest for better understanding is faced by un-ideal obstructions which no amount of mere well-wishing can remove. Wherever in this shared enterprise we do the best we can, in the service of the best we know, and know what we are doing, there the work of practical reason does go on, and sometimes justifies itself in the process that defines its meaning. It has, and needs, no better justification.

Main section of presidential address delivered before the forty-seventh annual meeting of the Eastern Division of the American Philosophical Association at the University of Toronto, December 28, 29, 30, 1950.

1. For the best brief account of this procedure see C. L. Stevenson, "The Nature of Ethical Disagreement," in Feigl and Sellars, *Readings in Ethical Analysis* (Appleton-Century-Crofts, 1949).

2. C.F., for example, S. E. Toulmin's *The Place of Reason in Ethics* (Cambridge University Press, 1950).

3. George Herbert Mead, *Mind, Self and Society* (University of Chicago Press, 1934), p. 42 ff.

4. David Riesman, *The Lonely Crowd* (Yale University Press, 1950), p. 265.

5. Mead, *op. cit.,* p. 173 ff.

6. As quoted in Beatrice Webb, *Our Partnership* (Longmans, Green and Co., 1940), p. 222.

7. Josiah Royce, *The Problem of Christianity* (The Macmillan Co., 1913), Vol. II, Chap. III.

F. S. C. NORTHROP

Ethical Relativism in the Light of Recent Legal Science

Anthropology and sociological jurisprudence have extended the study of ethics to the cultures of the entire world. Two things result: (1) the relativity of ethics and philosophy to culture, and (2) the relativity of culture to philosophy. The distinctions necessary to clarify these two conclusions are the concern of this paper.

Its approach is through three developments in American legal sciences. They are (1) Legal Positivism, (2) Sociological Jurisprudence, and (3) Natural Law Jurisprudence.

Legal Positivism

Legal positivism received its fullest American expression in Thayer, Langdell, and Ames. It is exemplified today in Mr. Justice Frankfurter and Judge Emeritus Learned Hand. Philosophically it derives secondarily from Wright, Peirce, and James[1] and primarily from Austin, Bentham, and Hume, supplemented with Hobbes. From Hobbes it takes its criterion of the effectiveness and sanction of law—namely in the power of the sovereign.

From Hume, Bentham, and James it receives its psychological ethics and its positivism.

Its positivism means that one need study only the positive law to make correct judicial decisions or to practice properly. By positive law is meant the statutes and judicial decisions. The positive law being declared, ethics is foreign to the judge's judgment. His duty is to accept the ethical content of the positive law, not questioning why. Ethics is assigned consequently to the theory of legislation.

This assignment of ethics to the private citizen, expressing himself through legislation, derives from the subjectivism of any psychological ethics, such as that of Hume, Austin, James, and Learned Hand.[2] Its only meaning for the "social good" is the pooling of the private "goods" in the legislative market place. Were the judge, therefore, to introduce his ethical judgment into his legal decision, he would be guilty of confusing private with public justice.[3]

This leaves no basis for the judicial review of legislation. Judge Learned Hand draws this conclusion, interpreting the Bill of Rights merely as "counsels of moderation" to the legislature.[4] Justices Douglas and Black, however, in accord with Locke, Jefferson, and Marshall, interpret the Bill of Rights in civil liberty cases as positive law which the judge must use to measure both the executive and the legislature.[5] This is to affirm a meaning of "socially good" other than the pooling of private goods in the legislature and to reject both ethical subjectivism and legal positivism.

But where is this trans-legislative meaning of "socially good" to be found? An obvious answer is: In an empirical study of the norms of social behavior. In short the basis of law is not introspective psychology but empirical social science. This is the point of the legal philosophy of Savigny, Ehrlich,[6] Roscoe Pound,[7] and Underhill Moore[8] and of the Yale Law School's policy, initiated in the 1920's when Mr. (now Justice) Douglas was a professor there, of calling nonlegally trained social scientists[9] and even a philosopher of culture to its faculty. Thus legal positivism gave way to:

Sociological Jurisprudence

Its thesis is that positive law cannot be understood apart from the social norms of the "living law." Ehrlich defined the latter as "the inner order of the associations of human beings"[10] and described it as "the law which dominates life itself even though it has not been posited in legal propositions [*i.e.*, the positive law]."[11] Ehrlich's "inner order of associations" is equivalent to what the anthropologists call "the pattern of a culture."[12] Thus Ehrlich's theory might equally appropriately be called anthropological jurisprudence.[13]

For both the sociological jurist and the anthropologist, the inner order or pattern, which is the living law, is empirically and inescapably ethical. Thus in summarizing an appraisal of their science by some fifty anthropologists, Professor Kroeber writes: "Values evidently are intimately associated with the most basic and implicit patterning of the phenomena of culture."[14] Similarly, Ehrlich speaks of the "social norms" of the "inner order" of society, which provide the sanction for and determine the effectiveness of the positive law.[15]

Note that Hobbes is dropped. The sanction for positive law and the criterion of its effectiveness is not power, but the correspondence between its ethical content and that of the living law. When, as with the Prohibition Amendment or Chiang Kai-shek's Western constitution applied to Confucian China,[16] the norms of the positive law fail to correspond to those of the living law, the positive law fails even though plenty of power is at hand. Thus instead of positive law deriving its sanction from something ethically neutral, such as power, both power and positive law derive their sanction and effectiveness from the ethical content of the living law.

Sociological jurisprudence also provides a standard for judging legislation, thereby validating judicial review of majority legislation. Ethics is not consigned to the theory of legislation which is outside the judge's province.

Furthermore, the "social good" that measures majority legislation is neither vacuously abstract, after the manner of the neo-Kantians, nor subjectively arbitrary. Instead, it is given by the anthropologist's or sociologist's objective determination of the norms embodied in the inner order of associations or pattern of the culture in question. Hence, social ethics is a cognitive science. The sentences, describing the normative "is" of the living law, which sociological jurisprudence uses to judge the goodness or badness of the positive law, being empirically testable, are not hortatory.

Sociological jurisprudence also shows the prevalent assertion that the "good" cannot be derived from the "is" to be meaningless unless the context is specified. Law as conceived by the legal positivist provides a context in which the assertion is true. Clearly, one cannot obtain the standard for judging the "is" of a given subject matter, such as the positive law, from the "is" of that subject matter itself. It does not follow, however, as sociological jurisprudence clearly shows, that the "good" or standard for judging the "is" of one subject matter, such as the positive law, cannot be found in the "is" of some other subject matter, such as the living law. When this is possible, the statement, "It is impossible to derive the 'good' from an 'is,' " is false.

The sociological jurist's way of using the "is" of the living law as the standard for measuring the goodness or badness of the positive law is as follows: According to his theory, today's positive law is the deposit of yesterday's living law. But whereas the former tends to remain static, due to the principle of *stare decisis,* the living law may change. Then the positive law becomes bad, in the sense of the word "bad" as defined by sociological jurisprudence, as in need of reform. The specific ethical content of the reform is determined by an empirical study of the normative inner order of today's living law. This is then used to define the positive legal statutes that correspond to it. These statutes specify the respect in which the traditional positive law is to be reformed.

But if this method of using the "is" of the living law, as the standard for measuring the goodness or badness, and attendant reform, of the positive law, is not to be circular and question-begging, the method of determining the living law must not appeal to the positive law. It was the great merit of my predecessor, the late Professor Underhill Moore, (1) to have noted that the traditional sociological jurisprudence did not meet this requirement, and (2) to have devised a method which does meet it. He showed that so long as introspective psychological terms were used in describing the living law, different empirical observers gave quite different reports concerning its supposedly objective character. This led Moore to use the spatiotemporal concepts of Hull's behavioristic psychology to describe the living law.[17] It then became defined as the high-frequency, spatiotemporal behavior of the people in question.

Certainly this method gives objectivity. It is practicable,

however, only for societies containing a small number of persons. Also, it is not clear that the spatiotemporal differences in the observable behavior of Hindus and Muslims in British India would be subtle enough to distinguish the living law norms of the two groups. Yet these norms were so different that the people found it necessary to divide into Pakistan and Free India. Some other method is required.

Cultural anthropology and the comparative philosophy of cultures reveal this way. Both disciplines have shown that the spatiotemporal social habits and ordering of people in any culture and its objective buildings, art forms, and positive legal procedures for settling disputes are the deposit of an implicit or explicit common set of meanings for describing, integrating, and anticipating the raw data of human experience. As Professor Kluckhohn has written:

> The publication of Paul Radin's *Primitive Man as a Philosopher* did much toward destroying the myth that a cognitive orientation toward experience was a peculiarity of literate societies. . . . Every people has its characteristic set of "primitive postulates." As Bateson has said: "The human individual is endlessly simplifying and generalizing his own view of his environment; he constantly imposes . . . his own constructions and meanings; these constructions and meanings are characteristic of one culture as opposed to another."[18]

When these primitive postulates or meanings were discovered or learned by a people initially in the distant past, the anthropologists call that philosophy implicit; when the philosophy is discovered or brought to the consciousness in the present they call it explicit.[19]

The method of anthropological jurisprudence for determining the norms of the living law without appeal to the positive law is that, therefore, of specifying the implicit or explicit philosophy, or complex of philosophies, of the society whose positive law is being judged. Professor Kluckhohn has shown how this is done in a homogeneous culture where the philosophy is implicit.[20] The writer has indicated how it is to be done in a heterogeneous culture, such as contemporary Western Continental Europe, whose living law is a complex deposit of several diverse and even conflicting, explicitly recorded philosophies.[21] The latter study shows that in such cases the method must be both qualitative and quantitative. Qualitatively it must specify the philosophy, including religious, economic, and cultural assumptions, of each major association of individuals. Quantitatively it must determine the number of adherents which each qualitative philosophy enjoys.[22]

When one approaches the living law of the entire world in this manner, one fact becomes clear: It is heterogeneous and pluralistic in its normative content. The living law norms of one people are not those of another. This fact has important implications.

First, it reveals why traditional positive international law is so weak. The reason is not, as the legal positivists asserted, because there is no *de facto* supranational power. The reason instead is that, being modeled on the homogeneous living law of late medieval Europe, its norms failed to correspond sufficiently to the changing and pluralistic living law of the world, to draw unto itself the ethical vitality and power necessary to be effective. Conversely, this means that a more effective positive international law is possible providing we so formulate its normative content that it draws upon the ethical heterogeneity and pluralism of the entire world's living law.[23]

The latter fact also points up the sense in which each philosophy and its particular ethics is culture-bound. Why are there so few, if any, nondualistic Vedanta philosophers in our American Philosophical Association and so many in its Indian counterpart? Is it not because the Indians have been born in Hindu culture and we in Anglo-American culture? To many Mexicans, viewing us from their culture with its Spanish philosophy of individualistic uncompromising passion and its Roman Catholic religious and Continental Rationalistic secular tradition, most Anglo-American culture seems simple-minded, mediocre ethically, and devoid of seriousness, spiritual subtlety, and depth—all the consequence of the unfortunate accident of having been born in a culture whose living law was formed by the rather poverty-stricken set of meanings provided by normalistic British empirical philosophy. If we answer that such Mexican judgments are the accident of the culture of their birth, we may answer truthfully, but in doing so are we not like the pot that calls the kettle black?

Is there any way out of this predicament? This question brings us to the third development in contemporary legal science.

Natural Law Ethics and Jurisprudence

What forces us to take this development seriously is not merely that legal scientists of Roman Catholic religious faith and Latin

European legal training, such as Professor A. P. d'Entrèves of Oxford are ably defending it,[24] but also that those of Protestant or Jewish religious background, trained in law schools teaching only legal positivism or sociological jurisprudence, are turning toward or to it—men such as Professor Lon L. Fuller and Dean Emeritus Roscoe Pound of the Harvard Law School,[25] Professor Friedrich Kessler[26] and Dean Emeritus Robert Hutchins of the Yale Law School, Dr. Mortimer Adler[27] of the Columbia and University of Chicago Law Schools, and Sir Arthur L. Goodhart, Regius Professor of Jurisprudence Emeritus at the University of Oxford, who initially was a staunch Austinian legal positivist.[28]

The major reason is clear. One must judge the living as well as the positive law. The living law of Hitler's Germany forced us to do this; that of Communist Russia is now requiring it again. In fact, everywhere, especially in Asia and Africa, people are reforming their domestic living as well as their traditional positive law. Any theory of ethics and law which cannot provide a measure or standard for judging and reforming the living law is, therefore, inadequate. Is there such a standard? Clearly sociological jurisprudence alone cannot give the answer, since one cannot find the standard for measuring the "is" of the living law in the "is" of the living law itself.

Yet, judge the living law we must. The urgent question, therefore, arises: Is there any standard, objectively determinable, and hence an "is," other than the positive and the living law, against which the goodness and badness of the living law can be measured, after the manner in which the "is" of the living law measures the goodness or badness of the positive law? Natural law ethics and jurisprudence is the thesis that there is such a standard.

The clew to it is already implicit in the aforementioned method of sociological jurisprudence. This method consists in making explicit the meanings or concepts held in common by the people of a given society for conceiving, remembering, integrating, and anticipating the raw data of their experience and ordering their social associations and behavior. In short, the living law of a given society is the deposit in cultural artifacts and in social human habits of a specific way of conceptualizing the raw unconceptualized data of anybody's experience. This conclusion has two components. Attention to the first generates sociological jurisprudence and the relativity of each philosophy and its particular ethic to culture. Attention to the second generates natural law jurisprudence and the relativity of culture to philosophy.

The former factor shows itself in the philosophical pluralism embodied in the many living laws of the world. All of us are members of a culture which is the deposit of a particular composite of traditional philosophies. Hence, in so far as any person, or group of persons, without deeper philosophical analysis and criticism, allows the traditional philosophy of his culture and its particular ethic to determine his evaluations, his professional judgments are culturally relative and the doctrine of the sociology of knowledge holds.[29] The likelihood of this occurring should make one slightly suspicious about the number of British empiricists at Oxford and Cambridge and in this Association today.

But to stop here is to overlook the second factor in the living law of sociological jurisprudence: Any set of primitive assumptions, which a people use to describe, remember, order, and anticipate the raw data of their experience and to guide their social behavior, refers to those raw data for its validity. In this sense man's empirically validated philosophy and its particular ethic makes culture and the living law norms of culture.

It becomes necessary, therefore, in order to specify (1) the sense in which culture is relative to philosophy, and (2) the different sense in which philosophy is relative to culture to distinguish two types of fact, which the writer elsewhere has called "first order facts" and "second order facts."[30] First order facts are the introspected or sensed raw data, antecedent to all theory and all cultures, given in anyone's experience in any culture. Second order facts are cultural artifacts, *i.e.*, they are the result in part at least of human theory of first order facts. Nature and natural law are the names for all first order facts and their relations. Culture and living law are the names for all second order facts and their inner order. To the extent, therefore, that any philosophy appeals to second order facts for its meaning and verification, it and its ethic are relative to culture. To the extent that any philosophy (1) derives its meaning and verification from first order fact, and (2) guides human behavior to create second order facts, culture is relative to philosophy and to its ethic.

Conditions (1) and (2) above entail a clear distinction between science and art. The discipline for discovering and verifying theory of first order facts is natural science. The discipline by which men, given an assumed theory of first order facts, use this theory as the standard for guiding their behavior in the creation of second order artifacts is called art or practical wisdom. Where the initial theories of first order facts differ, there are different artifacts and hence different living laws and cultures. The discipline by which men discover and verify the theory of second order facts is social science. It presupposes both art, or practical wisdom, and natural science, when it does not commit the error of confusing second order with first order facts. The opinion that *all* philosophical and ethical judgments are culturally relative is the result of the latter error.

Stated more precisely, therefore, natural law jurisprudence is the thesis that scientifically verified theory of the "is" of first order facts provides the cognitive standard for measuring the goodness or badness of second order artifacts. Thus just as sociological jurisprudence uses the scientifically verified theory of the "is" of the living law to judge both legislation and the cases of positive law, so natural law jurisprudence uses the empirically verified theory of the "is" of first order facts to judge the goodness or badness of the living law.

Natural law jurisprudence recognizes, with sociological jurisprudence, that contemporary man observes the second order facts of culture as well as the first order facts of nature. It affirms, however, that it is possible and necessary, if a cognitive standard for judging and reforming the living law is to be found, to push the artifacts of culture aside and to use only first order facts of nature and natural man in formulating and verifying a set of basic assumptions, which, since they do not derive from the "is" of the living law, can be used to judge and reform the living law.

Such a procedure is possible for two reasons. First, there was a time before human beings and, hence, before any culture. This would be impossible were there only cultural facts or were all facts culturally conditioned. Second, all science involves specialization. Specialization means neglecting certain facts to concentrate on others. Natural philosophy and its ethic is, therefore, both possible and scientific.

Additional distinctions are necessary if certain misconceptions are to be avoided. Natural law ethics is frequently described as the thesis that conduct and its fruits are good when they express "man's essential nature." Put this way, a difficulty arises. Since man's essential nature is what it is, how can man or anything else avoid expressing its essential nature? Clearly, unless one dis-

tinguishes two different senses of the "essential nature" of anything, there is no answer to this question. Not having made such
a distinction, many critics have concluded that natural law ethics
entails a *reductio ad absurdum:* Were it true, men would be good
automatically and there would be no possibility, and hence no
problem, of good or evil. We would be like the initial Adam and
Eve in the Garden of Eden, entirely innocent of either good or
evil in our natural behavior.

To meet this misconception, many defenders of natural law
have fallen into the second misconception of supposing that this
theory entails a teleological physics and metaphysics of becoming
in which potential entities are being modified by their ideal final
causes. Were this so, natural law philosophers, such as Hobbes
and Locke, who do not affirm such a physics and metaphysics could
not have an ethics. This is clearly false.

Both of these misconceptions evaporate when two additional
distinctions are made: (1) between the essential nature of first
order facts *qua* fact and their essential nature *qua* theory, and
(2) between (a) those natural entities whose behavior is completely the expression of their essential nature *qua* fact, and (b)
those natural entities whose judgments and behavior are in part at
least the expression of what they think all first order facts are
qua theory. Stones are examples of natural entities whose behavior is completely the expression of their essential nature *qua*
fact. This is the case because they do not have the capacity to
frame theories of what they and other first order facts are *qua*
theory. Human beings are natural entities which have an essential nature both *qua* fact and *qua* theory. This is the case because they have the capacity to frame theories of their essential
nature *qua* theory. This they do by appeal to first order facts
alone.

The thesis of natural law ethics and jurisprudence, therefore,
is not that any first order natural entity is good if it expresses its
essential nature *qua* fact. It is, instead, the thesis (1) that there
are certain natural entities, namely human beings, whose judgments and behavior are in part at least the expression of what they
think all first order facts are *qua* theory,[31] and (2) that such
judgments and behavior are good when the theory in question is
true as tested empirically by reference solely to first order facts *qua*
fact.

Concretely what this means is that any person, confronted with the countless first order facts from within and from without himself, selects, probably with hypothetical trial and error, certain facts as elementary and the key to the defining, remembering, ordering, and anticipating of all the others. Then the explicit or implicit set of symbols or ideas, designating the totality of human knowledge as thus understood, constitutes that person's, or people's, system of meanings. To look at all the first order facts which are taken thus as elementary and fundamental, is to evaluate in the manner of natural law ethics. Consequently its evaluations are good or bad to the extent that its implicit or explicit set of meanings is true or false.

It is to be emphasized that the symbols can obtain their meaning by pointing to existential, intuitive factors such as a particular pain or passion as well as by axiomatically expressing formal, rationalistic relations. The contention that natural law theory is excessively rationalistic is, therefore, erroneous.

The question, also, whether first order facts *qua* human theory entail a particular physics and metaphysics, or any metaphysics at all, is an empirical question for natural science to decide. In the days of Aristotle it seemed to do so. There is nothing, however, in the method of natural law ethics to require such a conclusion. Moreover, there is considerable evidence in contemporary mathematical physics to the contrary. All that natural law ethics requires or assumes in its method is that there is an empirically verified theory of first order facts with some specific content.

The importance of the distinction between the essential nature of first order facts *qua* fact and their essential nature *qua* theory is that, whereas first order facts *qua* fact merely are and can be neither true or false nor good or bad, *theories* of first order facts are true or false and hence may be in error. Consequently behavior which is in part at least the consequence of primitive assumptions concerning first order facts *qua* theory may be in error also. This is why Adam and Eve had to eat of the tree of human knowledge and guide their behavior, in creating second order artifacts, by this knowledge before there was any meaning for them to be, or know, good or evil. This meaning is that the second order artifacts of human behavior are good or bad if the human theory guiding this behavior is true or false as tested empirically by appeal to the first order facts of anyone's experience. Of three natural law theories with different theoretical content that one is the "best" which accounts for (1) all the first order facts accounted for by the other two, and (2) additional first order facts as well.

This definition of the "best" theory of first order facts prescribes the two methods of natural law ethics. One proceeds through cultural anthropology and the comparative philosophy of the world's cultures and consists (a) in making explicit the implicit philosophy, or complex of philosophies, of each culture, (b) in seeking, in each culture, the first order facts in anyone's experience which led its initial sages or scientists, and the people generally following their sages, to regard their particular philosophy as empirically verified, and (c) in specifying a single consistent set of assumptions which accounts for all the first order facts at the basis of the traditional cultural philosophies. Procedure (b) rests on the assumption that no philosophy, or its ethic, ever captured a vast body of people unless it seemed to be required by specific first order facts in their experience, *i.e.,* unless it was a natural law theory.[32] Procedure (b) may also guide one to first order facts in one's own experience which our Western theories of natural science and philosophy have missed or neglected.[33]

The second method of natural law jurisprudence proceeds through the verified theory of first order facts of contemporary natural science. Such theory is "best," in the sense defined above, because it takes into account facts never faced, and probably unexplained, by any previous philosophy of culture or nature. The procedure consists in making explicit, by philosophical analysis, the implicit theory of meanings and of mind which the verified theory contains. Any verified theory of first order facts, even of introspected ones, focuses attention, as it comes from the natural scientist, on the object of knowledge. Nevertheless, any first order theory, even Einstein's theory of the motion of a stone, tells us implictly that the human mind is such that it can discover, construct, and verify the type of conceptual and propositional meanings which the theory explicitly illustrates and contains. Consequently, the frequent assertion that the theory of natural science takes care of the object of knowledge to the neglect of the subject, its meanings and mind, is erroneous, providing, by philosophical analysis, its implicit theory of ideas and of mind is made explicit.

By combining the results of these two methods of natural law jurisprudence it should be possible to specify an empirically verified theory of first order facts including mind, which is scientifically truer than any traditional natural philosophy, in the sense that it

(a) accounts for any first order facts accounted for by any traditional theory, and (b) is the only theory accounting for the first order facts of all theories, including those of contemporary mathematical physics. This, to be sure, is a difficult, though not an impossible, undertaking. But one should not expect an easy solution of the problem of the cultural relativity of ethical values.

Such an approach through the comparative philosophy of culture and the philosophy of contemporary natural science is essential for two additional reasons. We are children of culture as well as nature. Second order facts and their meanings not merely impress us daily, but are also built into our habits and personality structure. As sociological jurisprudence shows, to act as if tradition does not exist is to fail. Also the major influence transforming today's living law, the world over, is scientific technology. This transformation is as much a living law fact as is the traditional living law itself. Technology derives from the primitive concepts and the mentality of mathematical physics. Hence only by combining the explicitly stated philosophical assumptions of both approaches can sociological jurisprudence make its own contemporary subject matter intelligible or find the standard for measuring what to preserve and what to modify in that subject matter.

It remains to specify the distinction between "good" and "ought" in natural law ethics. "Good" is the name for the empirically verifiable theory of first order facts when this theory is taken as the theoretical standpoint for guiding human behavior and evaluating its artifacts. The "good," therefore, is not a primitive concept, but is a predicate, applicable only to second order artifacts, that is defined in terms of scientifically true theory of first order facts. "Ought" is the *for-me-ness* of such theory. The making of a true theory mine occurs when, by appeal to first order facts which are *mine,* I find the theory to be empirically verified *by* or *for me.* In short, goodness calls merely for empirically verified theory of first order facts, whereas oughtness requires in addition the for-me-ness, by way of discovery or rediscovery, and verification, of that truth.

Natural law ethics, because of its distinction between first and second order facts, and its thesis that second order facts are the deposit, by way of art, of implicit or explicit theories of first order facts, entails sociological jurisprudence and its living law. The living law, however, with its second order facts can bring its inner norms to bear in deciding concrete disputes, especially in a technological law of contract society,[34] only if its inner order is given operational definition in terms of a positive constitution, a Bill of Rights, legislative statutes, and positive legal procedures. Hence, just as understanding of legal positivism leads to sociological jurisprudence, which in turn leads to natural law jurisprudence, so the latter needs first the living law of sociological jurisprudence and then the positive law of legal positivism to make itself effective.

Reprinted with permission of the editors of *The Journal of Philosophy*, 1955.

1. Jerome Frank, "A Conflict with Oblivion: Some Observations on the Founders of Legal Pragmatism," *Rutgers Law Review*, Vol. 9, pp. 425–63.

2. Learned Hand, *The Spirit of Liberty*, 2nd ed., (New York, Alfred A. Knopf, 1953), pp. 41, 58.

3. Hand, *op. cit.*, pp. 51, 54, 209–19.

4. Hand, *op. cit.*, p. 73. See also: Thayer, James B., Vol. 7, *Harvard Law Review* (1893), p. 129.

5. "Beauharnais vs. Illinois," *United States Supreme Court Reports*, Vol. 343 (1951), pp. 250–306, esp. pp. 267–68. "Adler vs. Board of Education of the City of New York," *ibid.*, Vol. 342 (1951), pp. 485–512, esp. pp. 485, 496–97, 508–11.

6. Eugen Ehrlich, *Fundamental Principles of the Sociology of Law*, Walter L. Moll, translator, (Cambridge, Harvard University Press, 1936).

7. Roscoe Pound, "Law and the Science of Law," Vol. 43, *Yale Law Journal*, pp. 525–36; *An Introduction to the Philosophy of Law* (Yale University Press, 1946), pp. 1–143; "The Scope and Purpose of Sociological Jurisprudence," *Harvard Law Review*, Vol. 24, pp. 591–619; Vol. 25, pp. 140–68, 489–516.

8. Underhill Moore, and others, *Yale Law Journal*, Vol. 38, pp. 703–19; Vol. 40, pp. 381–400, 555–75, 752–78, 928–53, 1055–73, 1219–50; Vol. 42, pp. 817–62, 1198–1235; Vol. 54, pp. 260–92; Moore and Charles C. Callahan, "Law and Learning Theory," *ibid.*, Vol. 53, pp. 1–136.

9. The economist Walton Hamilton and the sociologist Harold D. Lasswell.

10. Ehrlich, *op. cit.*, p. 37.

11. *Ibid.*, p. 493.

12. Clyde Kluckhohn, "Universal Categories of Culture," in *Anthropology Today*, prepared under A. L. Kroeber (University of Chicago Press, 1953), pp. 507–23; also Kroeber, A. L., *Configurations of Culture Growth* (University of California Press, Berkeley and Los Angeles, 1944).

13. F. S. C. Northrup, "Philosophical Anthropology and World Law," *Transactions of The New York Academy of Sciences*, Ser. II, Vol. 14, pp. 109–12.

14. A. L. Kroeber, "Concluding Review," in Tax, Sol, etc., editors, *An Appraisal of Anthropology Today* (University of Chicago Press, 1953), p. 373.

15. Ehrlich, *op. cit.*, pp. 39–136.

16. Chiang Monlin, *Tides from the West* (Yale University Press, 1947), pp. 137–40. Cf. Northrop, *The Taming of the Nations* (hereafter T/N) (New York, Macmillan, 1952), pp. 108–48.

17. Underhill Moore and Charles C. Callahan, *op. cit.*, pp. 61 ff.

18. Clyde Kluckhohn, "The Philosophy of the Navaho Indians," in F. S. C. Northrop, ed., *Ideological Differences and World Order* (hereafter *ID&WO*) (Yale University Press, 1949), p. 356. Cf. Pitirim A. Sorokin's "logico-meaning causality" in his *Society, Culture, and Personality* (New York, Harper & Bros., 1947).

19. A. L. Kroeber and Clyde Kluckhohn, *Culture, a Critical Review of Concepts and Definitions,* Papers of the Peabody Museum of American Archaeology and Ethnology, Harvard University, Vol. XLVII (1952), p. 181.

20. Clyde Kluckhohn, *op. cit. supra* note 18, pp. 356–84.

21. F. S. C. Northrop, *European Union and United States Foreign Policy, a Study in Sociological Jurisprudence* (hereafter EU & USFP) (New York, Macmillan, 1954), pp. 75–137.

22. *Ibid.*, pp. 126, 133; see also E. Adamson Hoebel, *The Law of Primitive Man,* (Cambridge, Harvard University Press, 1954), Chap. I, especially p. 14.

23. For suggestions of how this is to be done, see F. S. C. Northrop, *Yale Law Journal,* Vol. 61, pp. 623–54, and T/N, pp. 259–309.

24. A. P. D'Entrèves, *Natural Law* (London, Hutchinson's University Library, 1952).

25. Lon L. Fuller, *The Law in Quest of Itself* (Chicago, Foundation Press, 1940). Roscoe Pound, "Toward a New Jus Gentium," in Northrop, *ID&WO,* pp. 1–47.

26. Friedrich Kessler, "Natural Law, Justice and Democracy," *Tulane Law Review,* Vol. XIX, pp. 32–61; also *University of Chicago Law Review,* Vol. 9, pp. 98–112.

27. Mortimer J. Adler, *What Man Has Made of Man* (New York, Longmans, Green and Co., 1937).

28. Sir Arthur L. Goodhart, *English Law and the Moral Law* (London, Stevens & Sons, Ltd., 1953. Note also: John Wild, *Plato's Modern Enemies and the Theory of Natural Law* (University of Chicago Press, 1953).

29. Karl Mannheim, *Ideology and Utopia* (London, Routledge & Kegan Paul, Ltd., 1948); and *Man and Society* (London, Routledge & Kegan Paul, Ltd., 1948); Jacques J. Maquet, *The Sociology of Knowledge* (Boston, Beacon Press, 1951).

30. F. S. C. Northrop, "The Theory of Types and the Verification of Ethical Theories," in Charles A. Moore, ed., *Essays in East-West Philosophy,* (Honolulu, University of Hawaii Press, 1951), pp. 371–82.

31. For contemporary scientific theories of how this can be, see: Northrop *ID&WO,* pp. 407–28.

32. Cf. Edward F. Barrett, ed., *University of Notre Dame Natural Law Institute Proceedings 1951,* University of Notre Dame, Vol. V (1953); and Northrop's review in *Northwestern University Law Review,* Vol. 48 (1953), pp. 396–400; also Joseph Needham, *Human Law and the Laws of Nature in China and the West* (Oxford University Press, 1951). For a description and analysis of the scientific method by which the norms of culture are related to the philosophy of nature, see Northrop, *The Logic of the Sciences and the Humanities* (New York, Macmillan, 1947), pp. 328–47.

33. F. S. C. Northrop, *The Meeting of East and West* (New York, Macmillan, 1946), pp. 312–404.

34. Sir Henry S. Maine, *Ancient Law* (London, John Murray, 1908), p. 151; and F. S. C. Northrop, "The Philosophy of Natural Science and Comparative Law," *Proceedings and Addresses of The American Philosophical Association,* Vol. XXVI, pp. 5–25.

CHARNER M. PERRY

The Rationale of Political Discussion

Democratic government is sometimes characterized as government by discussion. This characterization is as much a reflection of hope as a statement of fact; but as some mixture of ideal and fact it indicates basic aspects of democratic politics. The two parts of the phrase qualify each other. The ideal of discussion requires a kind of government, an institutional context, within which discussion may occur and be effective; and democratic government requires a kind of discussion, the kind, namely, that will eventuate in social decisions, ideally, in wise or reasonable decisions. Though my concern is with the characteristics of political discussion and especially with the factors which might move it toward reasonable or just decisions, let me emphasize by brief comment the importance of the problems I am here disregarding.

The character and fruitfulness of political discussion depend on the institutions within which it occurs, on the abilities and habits of mind of the participants, on knowledge available. Graham asserts, not too pessimistically, that "History reveals no society which has gained a consciousness of the mechanics and dynamics of its institution sufficient to prevent their operation to ends quite different from those for which they were devised and quite alien to any comprehensible purpose."[1] Certainly we do not know much that we badly need to know about the conditions necessary for successful political discussion; but several important rules of thumb have been stated.

One of the most important is found in Hobbes. Hobbes' basic insight, briefly translated into my own words, is that when an established order—government and laws—is inadequate to enforce agreements, discussion becomes ineffectual. What is reasonable and prudent for one man to propose or to do depends in large part on his estimate of what other men will do; and unless estimates can be based on operating institutions or customs, discussion deteriorates because of uncertainty.

Another fundamental consideration is stated in the *Federalist Papers*. Unless existing institutions keep factions broken up into many small ones, discussion is likely to be ended by a dominant faction or frustrated by the sharp oppositions of interest and ideals between two or three large groups.

It has been also plausibly suggested that political discussion has most chance of success when it occurs in an institutional order which settles most problems, especially those involving conflicts of interests, by nonpolitical processes, channeling only the residual and general problems to the jurisdiction of politics. This suggestion is one of the strongest arguments for so-called laissez faire economic organization.

However these rules of thumb may be evaluated, they serve as reminders that political discussion does depend on an institutional order, perhaps a complicated and fragile one, as well as on intellectual and moral virtues, and that we know very little of what we need to know about the minimum and optimum conditions for political discussion. Having emphasized these problems, I now leave them.

With respect to political discussion itself the questions I wish to examine are those arising when we consider what reasons we may or should present to other people in political argument, how we should evaluate arguments directed to us, and by what process or pattern these arguments and counterarguments are, or should be, combined to move toward political decision, ideally to decisions that are in some sense wise, reasonable, or just. These, in general, are the questions; but there are so many misconceptions and false or partially false assumptions about reasons, reasoning, and discussion that it is difficult to state the questions clearly and properly. The manner of stating a problem provides at least part of the criteria for evaluating solutions. Some specification, if not removal, of misconceptions will at least throw some light on my own preconceptions and thus clarify my remarks if not my problem.

The misconceptions to which I refer run through popular thought but they may conveniently be specified in terms of philosophical doctrines. First, let me remind you that both philosophers and small children ask "why" at most inconvenient times; and that the asking of "why" can be and frequently is continued indefinitely. Children, fortunately, outgrow this but philosophers usually do not.

Many philosophers, especially since the seventeenth century, have attempted to find for their theoretical constructions a base or starting point which would in some sense be certain or beyond question, that is, an absolute beginning in regard to which it would be impossible or improper to ask "why." Such a firm beginning might be simple ideas, or impressions, or sense data, or protocol sentences, or a completely formalized logical structure. Such an attempt does, in some way, involve a misconception; and it is misleading as well as frustrating. To be sure, we should examine critically both our beliefs and our methods; but it is just a fact that we must start from where we are, in the middle of things; and as we search for steady footing and test what seems available we are already using and dependent on complicated intellectual equipment. We cannot answer reasonably many of a child's "whys" because his knowledge and reasoning are not sufficiently developed. If a philosopher attempts to become a child again, divesting himself of his acquired ideological equipment, his questions become unanswerable.

The problem of reasons in political discussion should not, then, be thought of as a search for an absolute beginning, for a reason such that no further question could be asked about it. The problem is rather how, beginning in the middle, wherever we happen to be, we can find relatively dependable stopping points.

Two related misconceptions may be suggested by the general remark that philosophy in recent times has had a strong Utopian orientation. F. S. C. Northrop assures us that professors of English have displaced philosophers as the unofficial chaplains of the universities; but if we have given up beauty, goodness, and parts of truth, we believe that linguistic analysis will yet make us free. We are still children of the Enlightenment; and we have a deep faith that removing superstition and error will permit the truth to shine by its own light. Almost all modern skeptics seem convinced that their skepticism, if accepted, would do much to improve life and society. The sociological relativists see a tolerant and peaceable society built on the insight that values are relative to cultures and that none can claim superiority; naturalists and emotivists imply, do they not, that if we would recognize that desires are just desires and attitudes are just attitudes, we could see through a lot of nonsense and manage our affairs with detachment and good sense? Hume argued explicitly that if men would see that trying to determine what any man deserves is an impossible project and merely occasions endless disputes, they could then settle matters of property on more stable and socially advantageous principles. Keynes remarks perceptively of Bertrand Russell: "Bertie in particular sustained simultaneously a pair of opinions ludicrously incompatible. He held that in fact human affairs were carried on after a most irrational fashion, but that the remedy was quite simple and easy, since all we had to do was to carry them on rationally."[2]

I do, myself, value skeptical criticism highly; but surely we are mistaken if we assume that the skeptical removal of proposed political reasons leaves in operation a set of good and natural ones. No political reason which is critically examined can, I suppose, survive a determinedly skeptical analysis; but life and politics go on and are guided by the reasons left untouched, that is, merely by the ones that have not been examined. I think, then, consideration of political discussion should be a critical examination of how we do reason rather than an ambiguous skepticism.

Our philosophical Utopianism is not always skeptical. Frequently, it is affirmative and surmounts all obstacles in its flight. Indeed, the skeptical and the affirmative moments are likely to be fused into the same doctrine, as Keynes suggests is the case with Russell. In our positive mood, however, we are too much inclined to think in terms of ideal limits. Now, the attempt to think through processes to their ideal limits *is* an essential philosophic technique. It is frequently involved, as in many recent linguistic analyses, when the study undertaken seems merely a scrutiny of the actual. Nevertheless, ideal limits are tricky; and when we use them we need to know how far we are departing from what is actual or possible. Moreover, many processes vanish or lose their distinctive characteristics as an ideal limit is reached or approached. Consider discussion, for instance, purged of all its impurities and freed of its obstacles. Remove prejudices, conflicting interests, coercion, ignorance, and assume a group of men who are open-minded, skilled in expression and understanding, impartial, and possessed of all possible wisdom and knowledge. In such a case, one participant might briefly sketch a problem or perhaps give a bare hint of it; and then everyone would see all the pros and cons and the resolution of them; and the sense of the meeting would be reached; or perhaps, if there really are alternative logics, the wise men might talk indefinitely, each equally cogent in his own way, but never really touching each other. In either case, discussion would have become useless or impossible or both.

Political discussion, certainly, is an impure mixture. It involves ignorance, prejudice, conflicting interests, and varying amounts of coercion. It can hardly be thought of as much like philosophical discussion, which is in some sense directed to truth or an approximation thereto; but there is some similarity, too.

Finally, and perhaps most important, there is, in both popular thought and philosophy, an extreme assumption about the separation of facts and values. This assumption is reflected in the disjunction between ethics and social science. Such separation and disjunction are perhaps examples of misuse of an ideal limit. Within reason the separation between philosophy and social science has some utility and sense; but taken too seriously it creates insuperable problems for both philosophers and social scientists. If social philosophers, or indeed philosophers of any brand, do not have some subject matter, some data, some facts, then their reasoning, if it can be called that, must be a priori in a bad sense. And if there is one proposition that is true a priori I suggest that it is this, that when one has nothing to talk about there is nothing to say.

The abstraction which the social scientist attempts is different but equally unfortunate. The attempt to describe action in abstraction from the ends and values which give it direction and organization would cut off and ignore whatever lies beneath the surface of opaque events. Social scientists do not usually go very far in this direction. What they do, when they push beyond modest limits their intention of achieving a value-free description of society, is to use without acknowledgment or critical examination various distinctions and principles.

Since values do occur in action as effective patterns or principles of organization and since action without organization or direction cannot be described as fact, questions about cogent reasons in political discussions should not be construed as postulating a region of pure, nonfactual values, or, on the other hand, as directing our attention to facts which are value-free but nevertheless adequate grounds for political decisions. No doubt both of these extremes are, in some good sense, truly there; but they are ideal limits, lying far to either side of what we can grasp and examine in political discussion.

The reasons, then, that I seek are not initial certainties, nor a residuum to be hoped for after the acids of skepticism have dissolved everything brought into contact with them, nor yet the high, thin reasons which we dimly see as we think such processes as discussion through to ideal limits. They are, rather, the reasons which have firmness, compounded perhaps of cogency and effectiveness, to support arguments directed to others and to move us toward agreement when presented in arguments of other people. Such reasons are to be sought by plunging, so to speak, into the middle of discussion, and then looking and feeling around us for something that will give us direction and help us move forward.

That political discussion begins in the middle of things involves that it takes for granted as given a great deal that does not enter explicitly into the discussion. What is given and taken for granted is not explicitly stated; and what is not explicitly stated is not accurately known and is to some extent indeterminate.

To philosophers it may seem intolerable that what is given should not be "laid on the line" as explicitly stated assumptions. That this demand cannot be fully met is one of the major theses I am presenting. What we can explicitly know or even explicitly assume is like the small part of an iceberg showing above the surface of the water. We know the base is there because it supports what is above the surface; but we do not know just what are its shape, size, and composition. Any plausible and understandable statement of some assumptions depends on a large remainder that is merely given.

It is not only impossible to meet fully the demand that what is taken for granted should be translated into explicit assumptions; it is imprudent, at least in political discussion, to push the demand very far, because a precise and explicit statement of what is given becomes an assumption, raises issues, and is no longer taken for granted.

What is given for political discussion may be somewhat artificially divided into two main parts. Figuratively, we may say that discussion is bounded on one side by the results of past actions, for brevity the status quo, and on the other by principles. Because political discussion always starts from, and takes for given, the existing order, the status quo, it must always be to some extent conditioned by the "vested interests," by mistakes that have been made, and by a distribution of power resulting in part from luck, force, and fraud. Even after a revolution (which is, of course, not a discussion) discussion would have to be resumed from the positions, advantageous or disadvantageous, which people then occupied by reason of chance or shrewdness. It must be remembered, however, that the status quo, though given, is to some extent unknown and indeterminate.

On the other side political discussion is bounded by principles, which also are given, and cannot be brought fully to explicit statement. Let me here acknowledge a problem, whether or not I can dispel it. The notion of principles is difficult and perhaps not very fashionable nowadays. Principles lie at or near an ideal limit. They are what our rules and patterns of thinking and action would be if they could be brought completely to explicit statement and abstracted from irrelevant content. To speak of principles as I do is to assert that rules are developed from an underlying matrix, part of which always underlies and guides the explicitly stated rules.

That political discussion depends on principles is easy to see but difficult to prove. Let me aim at attaining moderate plausibility by a few examples.

The participants in political discussion, I presume, must to some extent know what they are trying to do. They take for granted the principles of relevance and evidence which they use in discriminating facts relevant to their purposes and in evaluating evidence as to what alternative actions are possible and what means are available of shaping them toward their own objectives. Some of these principles may be embodied in explicit rules but not much; most of them will be embedded in skill and judgment.

Some of the principles of the participants may also be said, in a sense, to be principles of or for the discussion. The principles of considering projects in terms of relevant evidence and available facts will be reflected in the way in which arguments are presented and the discussion organized, even though many of the participants aim at deceit or withholding information. Similarly the schema of ends and alternative means, and the principles of weighing means in terms of efficiency and economy impose themselves on any consideration of action; and this schema with its principles provides one of the main patterns of political argument.

Finally, there are principles which function in the discussion as a social fact in a way somewhat different from analogous principles in participants. Since political discussion is aimed at decision and action, there is a presumption that the decision will or should be acted on. This is not a prediction. Political decisions are typically somewhat ambiguous, leaving some leeway for judgment and for acts of God in an uncertain future. On the other hand it is not a tautology. Nevertheless, it would seem inappropriate to discuss whether we shall do what we decide to do. Another principle is suggested by the phrase "limitation of coercion." Politics does involve considerable amounts of coercion; but that coercion is to be limited by "rules of the game" in a way never explicitly stated is a principle without which discussion cannot proceed.

An existing order, the status quo, and principles, then, are given. Political discussion starts from the status quo and is guided by principles. This much is important; but it does not tell us how reasons to function within political argument and to move it toward reasonable decisions are to be found or recognized. Insofar as the status quo and principles are not made explicit, and in that sense are unknown and indeterminate, they do not provide content or premises for arguments. How, then, do we construct arguments which contain as much reasonableness as can be attained without too much sacrifice of effectiveness?

Let me again use negative considerations to narrow the area in which answers to this question may be sought. Political discussion has been thought of as being guided, ideally if not yet actually, by the canons of scientific inquiry. Some such analogy has been deeply and persistently influential, especially since the development of modern science, appearing in Bentham and Dewey as well as many social scientists. That all relevant knowledge, natural, social, or supernatural, should be utilized in practical affairs seems obvious; but nevertheless it seems equally clear that the analogy between discussion and scientific inquiry does not hold. If it did, experts would sooner or later assume the functions of government and discussion would be replaced by public information and acquiescence. Utilization of scientific results for political action requires some prior consensus; and because of basic conflicts of interests and conflicts of ideals in society and between societies, such agreement cannot be achieved or bypassed by scientific inquiry.

Consider, now, whether the movement of political discussion may be thought of as similar to the deduction of a conclusion from premises, whether a set of practical premises or a combination of "prescriptive" and "descriptive" ones. This, also, has been a persistent and misleading analogy. It corresponds, perhaps, to a vulgar conception of "natural law," though none of the major exponents of natural law, with the possible exception of Locke, had quite such a simple doctrine. In any case, the deductive analogy is clearly wrong. Even in legal reasoning, where the Constitution and statute law seem to provide premises, deduction has only a limited application; and outside this favorable region the deductive analogy breaks down completely; and we have the familiar and insoluble puzzles as to how significant value premises may be established and the less familiar but even more difficult problem as to how individuals and groups diversified by their different histories, faced in various directions by their customs, interests, ideals, and commitments, could from timeless premises deduce solutions to their problems. This view persists despite its obvious difficulties because there are indeed principles which are given. Principles, however, are how we reason, not what we reason from. When made into premises they are empty; they can never be made fully explicit as premises or rules; and a residue always remains unstated for use and interpretation of the rules. Political discussion is not deduction, though deduction does on occasion appear within it.

If we rule out just one more possibility, the remaining territory is so limited that the answer to our problem can be plainly seen. The possibility to be ruled out is that political discussion has no rationale, no movement, even in ideal, toward decisions that are better than they might have been without it. This possibility is contrary to experience, since all of us from time to time engage in political discussions, large or small, with the intention of influencing them to some extent in the direction of reason, prudence, good sense, or fairness.

What we actually do in practice and should sooner or later recognize in theory is to cut out and construct reasons, some more, some less, compelling, from what lies on either side of political discussion and in the middle of it.

From the existing body of institutions, customs, and prior agreements, given in indeterminate fashion as the status quo, we take what has been made, or may be made, explicit as law and tradition. Law and tradition may be appealed to as good though not always sufficient grounds for present decisions. Tradition is the less determinate part of this complex. It includes precedents and heroes, the Monroe Doctrine, Jefferson and Lincoln; and both precedents and heroes may be squeezed into arguments pointing in different directions.

From principles, by making them partly explicit and adding material from institutions and from contexts in which the principles have been used, we construct ideals—liberty, equality, justice, democracy. Ideals are colored by the society in which they were developed; and they are to some extent changeable in response to new situations, institutional changes, and even the exigencies of an argument. They nevertheless have a component, not easily identifiable, which persists through time and across cultural boundaries.

In the middle of discussion, because it has participants who are agents and who contribute to the shaping of action, are interests. Interests are channeling of malleable and shifting impulses by custom, precept, example, and previous action. They reflect plans that have been made and are a projection of action into an uncertain future in terms of objectives and means believed useful to attaining the objectives.

Law and tradition, interests, and ideals provide the reasons which function in political discussion. Though discriminated for specification, these factors are interdependent and interacting. Interests are shaped by tradition and by ideals; laws and traditions are molded by and embody interests and ideals; and ideals are given part of their content by tradition and interests. And the process of interaction continues as all of them are reshaped by political discussion and receive new deposits of it.

Again, I notice an objection which I may not be able to remove to everyone's satisfaction. Granted, it might be said, that law, for instance, does constrain people, should it, has it any right, so to speak, to claim moral authority? Notice, at least, that law and existing institutions embody as much of our interests and ideals as we have so far been able to put into them. Consider also that political discussion would be a silly seam continuously unraveled as fast as sewn if the results of past decisions lost their claim on us as fast as they are made. Undertand, too, that I am not saying that law presents a compelling or conclusive reason; but merely that it provides a good reason which may or may not be met by reasons, perhaps stronger, drawn from interest or ideals.

This introduces the point which is most important. Political discussion is not, and cannot be, a linear process. It moves back and forth between law, interests, and ideals, none of which contains the sole or the soundest or the most compelling set of premises. Any sound or cogent political argument would contain a minimum of all three components, and in the high points of political argument a statesman may bring them into a dramatic unity. Depending, however, on the problem and the situation, emphasis may fall here or there. When interests are in stubborn conflict, tradition and ideals may be utilized. If there is conflict of ideals, participants may look for real or apparent way of harmonizing interests. In general, political discussion succeeds by achieving a partial or temporary equilibrium among the three components. The equilibrium is never, or hardly ever, stable; its maintenance always depends at least in part on coercion and the inertia of custom. Unless, however, the equilibrium moves, however slowly and irregularly, toward wisdom and justice, government by discussion is not likely to be a successful experiment.

If, now, I have given you a plausible account, you may agree that political discussion has the elements I have indicated. But I suspect that you will still be asking, despite my assurance, Is it moral? is it right? is it ethics? My answer is yes; and the only conclusive test I can conceive is that political discussion coincides point by point with the deliberation by which the individual decides his own problems. What, indeed, could political discussion as a mixture of ideal and fact be except a projection on a large canvas, with its own texture and coarseness, of the reasoning which the individual knows as his own?

Presidential Address delivered before the fifty-third annual meeting of the Western Division of the American Philosophical Association at the Michigan State College, East Lansing, Michigan, April 28, 29, and 30, 1955.

1. Frank D. Graham, *Social Goals and Economic Institution* (Princeton 1942), p. 5.

2. John Maynard Keynes, *Two Memoirs,* (New York and London, 1949), p. 102.

WILMON H. SHELDON

The Absolute Truth of Hedonism

How wrongheaded and time-wasting are the "refutations" of hedonism that spot and blot the pages of the history of ethics! There is no better example of the needless antagonisms of philosophers.

For of course in ethics as in metaphysics there are schools that disagree; but there is more of emotion in the moralist's attitude, less of the cool survey which might appropriate from all the schools whatever truth they have gleaned. Morality is a practical affair; the opposition between moral systems has direct consequences in the lives of men, consequences leading to fights btween individuals and between groups and wars between nations. Whereas metaphysic—in the West if not in the East—is usually conceived in a more theoretical spirit and without immediate effect on man's life. The moralist's vision is the more likely to be obscured by indignation at what he deems the immoral counsels of his opponent.

Now of all the oppositions within the field of ethics, the chiefest and stiffest is the opposition to hedonism, the gospel of pleasure. Always there in the past to be sure, this antipathy has increased and multiplied with the increasingly socialized mentality of modern man, until today there is scarcely a self-confessed hedonist to be found. For pleasure, the hedonist's moral good, is clearly an individual matter. One directly enjoys his own pleasures only; if as a good neighbor he is pleased by the pleasures of his fellows, that enjoyment is still his alone. Whence the hedonist is called self-seeking, egotist—the worst of vices for our time. Yes, hedonism is in bad repute today, the underdog of ethics. Could we possibly expect to persuade the sincere moralist in respect of the claims here to be made?

True, some of our moralists do claim to include a degree of hedonism in their codes. They are a little more synthetic than the moralists of the past. If Kant, for instance, declared all desire for pleasure immoral, probably few today would go so far. Remember that F. H. Bradley, prince of rationalists, said he would accept an "intelligent" hedonism. And most of our ethical treatises assign pleasure a place in the scale of moral values, though a rather low place. What we have now to see is that it deserves not only the highest place but the only place—yet, strangely enough, in a sense which admits other criteria of moral goodness as well. Indeed, for conscious beings, of whom alone we are here treating, all good, be it moral, aesthetic, ontological, or whatever, is identical with its pleasantness. As Aquinas says of beauty, the cognitive good, that it is what pleases when seen, *quod visum placet,* so we should say of any and all good: it is what pleases when experienced. That is hedonism's thesis: the goodness of the good is the pleasantness of it, pleasantness explicit at the moment or implicit for the future. In fact, as we are to see, hedonism is a tautology. And it is a waste of time to try to refute tautologies. For all that, they have their uses in reminding us of what we are committed to. And the present reminder is much needed to quiet this quarrel of the schools.

Naturally, pleasure is not to be understood as sensual pleasure only. There lies the danger of hedonism for the common unreflecting man, even more for the youth, whose more delicate and enduring pleasures have yet to be developed. And no doubt the moralists have felt this danger and modeled their teaching accordingly. But it is one thing to say that a certain doctrine should not be taught to everybody, and another thing to say it is false. "I have many things to say unto you," said Jesus to the disciples, "but ye can not bear them now." Yet even so, we may come to see that hedonism clearly understood can safely be taught to all who really want the truth. Nor on the other hand is pleasure to be thought of as a quiescent state with no contents but the indefinable pleasure quality. A pleasure is the experience of a pleasant object, even if sometimes the object be something in one's own ego; happy self-consciousness is a contradiction only to the abstract dialectician. Nay more, pleasure is never a quite passive state. An anticipated or hoped-for pleasure belongs to an object which we wish to gain, and wish is incipient action. Likewise a contemplated future pain belongs to an object which we wish to avoid. And a present pleasure applies to an object which while experiencing it we wish and tend to retain, a present pain to an object which while we have it we would remove. Enjoying sweet music we would say with Faust, "Oh, moment stay, thou art so fair"; suffering the pain of a harsh discord, we squirm or ejaculate as if to dodge or eject it. Pleasure *contains* desire, desire satisfied, realized, but none the less present. The very goodness of the pleasure lies in the fact that we want the object while we have it. Then there is no longer the single state of the want—where want means lack—nor merely the present actuality of the goal; we have the marriage of the two, both equally present in the realizing moment. The realization is good only as we want it; which means that we tend to retain it. We have our cake and eat it too. True, many pleasures come unsought: the gift from a friend, the native health of the young. But these are wanted while they are enjoyed, we dwell on them, roll them under the tongue, if only for an instant. Pleasure is the wantedness of the present object. Always we want our happy moments to last—until they begin to pall on us as so frequently they do. For it seems to be a condition of man's make-up that his common pleasures usually evaporate rather quickly; fatigue sets in, the beauty of the landscape diminishes for the continued gaze, the joy of a task accomplished fades all too soon. None the less would we keep them if we could. See then that the pleasure-pain quality is definable in terms of wish or desire toward or away from some object, future or present, possible or actual; and as wish is incipient action or tendency to action, definable in terms of action or tendency thereto. The good—and not merely the moral good—is that which we seek to obtain and retain, the bad that which we strive to avoid or remove. So it is then with voluntary behavior, the subject-matter of ethics; reflex action is out of the picture except as it may be voluntarily

controlled. Thus did James Ward define these supposedly irreducible qualities, pleasure and pain, in terms of action and object of action. (Let process-philosophy agree.) And for us the
point is: pleasure, the goal of hedonism, cannot be treated in abstraction from desired objects; it is an active state, it contains desire within it, never does it leave activity quite behind, never does
it lose sight of the object consciously envisaged.

Here lies the error of Thomas Hill Green's attempt to refute
hedonism. Green argued that we do not desire pleasure for or by
itself but rather some object that yields pleasure. A quibble to be
sure; but see its source. He failed to see that pleasure *means* the
luring object gained. What is lure but the promise of pleasure
in the object? Green was unwittingly arguing for hedonism.
But his method was the all-too-frequent method of the school-
philosophers, interpreting the opponent in a too narrow way and
then finding him wrong. Certainly it is the pleasantness of the
object, the pleasure-giving object, that is desirable. For brevity
however we shall in what follows use the single term "pleasure."

Did we just now say desirable rather than desired? This re-
calls another misunderstanding. Remember how Mill was blamed
for identifying *desired* with *desirable*. Desirable, said the critics,
means *ought to be desired,* something more than actually being
desired. Hence the moral aim is beyond pleasure. But of course
the hedonist understands "ought to be desired" to mean "would
be desired if we knew how to gain the maximum of pleasure."
There is no logical implication of a mysterious and indefinable
ought; our wishes and our ignorance of the means of satisfaction
are enough to describe the situation. The Greeks said that sin
is action in ignorance. So it is, but they didn't see that a good
deal of the ignorance is due to our own free choice to ignore. But
Mill, the economist of India House, being of a rather overly practical cast of mind, did not see the full meaning of the pleasure doctrine. The same failure to do justice to his own position is found in
his statement that some pleasures have a higher quality than others.
It is better, he admitted, to be Socrates dissatisfied than a pig
satisfied. Enemies seized upon the word "quality"; it pointed
to a distinction outside the pleasure zone. But again, Mill might
have seen that higher quality means greater intensity of pleasantness or greater extensity of pleasantness—greater number or variety of pleasant objects—or both. Obviously Socrates dissatisfied
is better than a pig satisfied because Socrates has or could have

a thousandfold more pleasures—those intrinsic to intelligent humanity—than the pig can have. That is the hedonist doctrine: the *summum bonum* for morality is maximum intensity and extensity of pleasure. Maximum, because if something is good, more of it is better, and the maximum the best. Quantity elucidates quality in respect of good. True indeed, other things may interfere. To eat is good, to eat more is not always good, to eat most is bad. Thus it is with man's conditioned pleasures. But that doesn't deny the supreme goodness of the maximum attainable; it shows only that with us men the maximum of one pleasure often interferes with other pleasures, as eating too much interferes with the pleasures of health. All the same, what we want is the greatest *possible* number and intensity of pleasures now and forever. That is the direct and observable trait of man's natural quest for pleasure: we all *do* want as much as we can get—*provided no harm is done thereby*—which provision itself confirms the hedonism, as harm means injury, pain. And as greater intensity of pleasure is of itself good, so is greater extensity. Variety is the spice of life. Mere number of different pleasures is a good in itself, a pleasure added to the collection, a summation which is a degree of consummation. There is the insight of the process-metaphyic, of Whitehead, Bergson, Dewey; the rolling snowball, increase, progress such that the future contains the past, life more and more abundant. Greatness, majesty, magnanimity, —do we not ascribe these to Deity? Quantity is of the essence of the good. And if the good is pleasure, that essence means quantity unlimited, maximum pleasure.

Nor need we distinguish between pleasure, happiness, joy, bliss, satisfaction, and the like. The blissfulness of bliss, the satisfactoriness of satisfaction, and so on, is precisely the pleasantness of pleasure; what we here mean by pleasure is just the common element in all these, the gratification they afford. We use the term because it is so unassuming. The moralist, keen for the dignity of morality, must have honorific names; they enlist man's emotion and desire for them as noble ends. Which is to say that the reward of attaining them is esteemed deeper, greater, than if they were *mere* pleasures. So well-nigh inevitable it is that we think of pleasure in terms of our common sensual gratifications. So hard it is to realize that the pith and marrow of all these ends is ever one and the same; plain, homely, simple childlike pleasure, joy, happiness—call it what you will—in possessing them, the more noble being the more durable, more productive of further pleasures, and such. The very fact that the typical moralist stresses nobility reveals his basic hedonism. He appeals to man's love of the higher: what is this love but ardent longing for the *bliss* of possession?

Some may, perhaps unwittingly, confess their hedonism by their very words; certainly most would not admit. Take an example or two. When the Advaita Vedantist declares that Brahman-Atman is maximum bliss, he is a professed hedonist, even if he would repudiate the name. So, though without profession, are all the other Eastern systems; their practical animus drives thereto. For the Buddhist of whatever sect the goal is escape from the pangs of the wheel of existence, for Hinduism the like, as also the attainment of the blessed peace of Atman, for the Neo-Confucianists of China, the happiness of a balanced life in one's station. If some Buddhists and even some Vedantists assert that Nirvana or Brahman is above the distinction of bliss and misery, their conduct in pursuing these goals shows that they seek the joy of attainment. Relief from misery is itself a positive joy. There is no separation between the two motives claimed by hedonism, the positive motive of pleasure and the negative motive of release from pain. There is only a distinction in the way of gaining the pleasant experience; the one way is to seek it directly and by itself, the other way is to seek it as the happy release from pain. What these good Orientals long for is certainly not nothingness: it is impossible to desire *mere* extinction. To desire nothing is not to desire. What the disciple craves is to *experience* nothingness, if that were possible; or at least nothingness in the sense of release from the miserable conditions that make up man's mortal existence. We judge him by his deeds rather than his words; he acts as if the experience he calls negation were a maximum satisfaction. And surely it is obvious that what makes satisfaction satisfactory is the happiness which attends the fulfillment of longing.

Really the position of the hedonist seems so simple that it needs but to be stated to be believed. Not only is it the instinctive view of the natural man; we verify it constantly in everyday life. Men *do* seek things that bring pleasure, avoid those that give pain. The hopes of mankind embodied in religion—religion the treasury of man's ultimate goods—verify it when they picture the bliss of heaven and the torments of hell. Man's invincible sense of justice assigns pain as the reward of sin, happiness as the reward of virtue.

Significant it is that Kant, archopponent of hedonism, affirmed as a postulate of morality that God rewards with happiness those who follow the exclusive imperative of duty for duty's sake. So lurks hedonism in the bosom of the enemy. Indeed the intrinsic value of discipline, self-control, self-sacrifice, of every one of the sterner virtues, lies in their soul-satisfying power to overcome the seduction of the lesser, more ephemeral pleasures, "pleasures that while tasted cloy," pleasures that will be followed by pains, to overcome it for the sake of the deep and durable happiness of a balance that cannot be upset—a happiness which itself transmutes the pangs of discipline into positive joys. Stoicism is at heart hedonism.

True enough, the good man who chooses the hard way doesn't usually put it thus to himself. Does the martyr submit to be burned because he anticipates pleasure therein? No, more often than not, nine times out of ten perhaps, the moral conflict is rather between repelling pains than luring joys. On the one hand the pains that follow the righteous course, on the other hand the torture, for the good man a greater torture, of a conscience that knows its guilt: such is the alternative where the moral issue stands out in its nakedness. "I cannot do otherwise," said Luther, "God help me!" Such is man's moral handicap that he must so often fail to sense the proper lure of the right and choose it only because he is terrified of his self-torturing conscience. Even so, he is hedonist through and through.

Whatever be one's theory, it is in practice impossible for him to avoid the search for pleasure and removal of pain. And the reason is of the most elementary: whenever we want something, be it duty for duty's sake, or knowledge for itself alone, or just a tasty morsel, we want the joy of getting it; whenever we dislike anything we hope for the joy of its absence. We wish for the fulfillment of our desire; fulfillment of desire we anticipate as a joy; we wish for a joy. This is in fact a tautology, nothing more. Not, of course, that in seeking anything we always *think* of the pleasure it will confer, though sometimes we do. The underlying motive is usually behind the scene, the lure of pleasure is the power behind the throne. Hedonism does not say that every man is conscious of his hedonism; only that he acts it. The athlete, striving his hardest to win the race, isn't thinking of the pleasures of victory; he is thinking of the tape, the speed he needs, the closeness of his rival. But what is the motive power, forgotten during the struggle, that gave rise to the struggle? It is the joy of victory. Because the motive is usually beneath the surface-consciousness of the moment, the critic overlooks it; and because hedonism seems to be a doctrine dangerous for the unthinking crowd he gladly believes he has refuted it.

True enough, we often yield to the pleasure of the moment— markedly with respect to pleasures of sense and of triumph over an opponent—when reason tells us that so doing will give more pain than pleasure. Does this give the lie to hedonism, this rejection of the greater pleasure for the less? Now notice that in such a case the choice is our own. Confronted with the alternatives, we *permit* our attention to be held by the more immediate and lesser pleasure till it looms larger than the more remote but greater. That is where enters our freedom of choice, our blame or merit. We do not passively endure the lures of possible goods; we play our part, we respond to them by opening our hearts to the one, not to the other, thereby ourselves lessening the lure of the other. Shall I drink the fifth cocktail you offer me? Doctor says I should not, with my blood pressure. I want that pressure reduced, want it badly. On the other hand, think of the delicious taste, the joy of a mild intoxication, the wealth of ideas, all seeming good, that will enter the mind. I choose the latter. The determinist is right when he says that we always follow the stronger lure. But he forgets that often, too often, we ourselves make it the stronger by choosing to dwell on it. Freedom of will, at least in morals, is freedom of attention. Yes, we always seek pleasure in our voluntary acts; psychological hedonism is correct. And did we but realize it, deep in our hearts we want maximum pleasure, lasting and manifold; but since what is deepest is farthest from the surface, we seldom do realize it with sufficient force and clearness, and we choose pleasures that work against it. Here enters the truth and the import of ethical hedonism. We *ought* to choose the most fruitful pleasures, even if for the present that means choosing the painful. Yet the oughtness of the ought is only the fact that ever the motive is at work within us, the subconscious drive toward maximum happiness—if only we would let it succeed! To sin is but to frustrate freely our deepest wishes.

Such then is hedonism's claim. No more than a tautology; true. But, as said above, tautologies are useful, they are needful to our weak human nature; they remind us of what we too easily forget. And this tautology should remind us that it is a waste of time to try to persuade men not to seek happiness. They will inevitably do it. The only caution needed is: seek the pleasures which will permit or give rise to other pleasures, not those that lead, in our sorry world, to the exclusion of other pleasures or to pains. How does the parent persuade the growing mind of the youth, *really* persuade him and not just compel him by fear of punishment, to do what is right, to play fair, not to lie, cheat, steal, and such? Never by saying in the bass voice of authority, "It is wicked!" Why, asks the youngster, is it wicked? And the wise parent shows him that it is wicked because it leads to trouble —trouble for others, trouble for himself. Then only is the youth genuinely persuaded, for his intelligence is satisfied. Authority is needed only where intelligence is lacking. Hedonism banks on intelligence. In brief, man's goal is maximum pleasure and minimum pain, and his task is to discover the means thereto—maximum, of course, as said, in the sense of the greatest possible *intensity* of pleasantness, and also the greatest possible *extensity* or number of different pleasures. As it is often put, man wants the fullest and richest possible life. Nor can he help wanting it, subconsciously if not consciously. Hedonism is but man the wisher coming to self-consciousness. Yet though he may become quite aware of this his wish in a general way, he will not necessarily do the deeds which lead to the goal. Too often he will of his own free choice persuade himself that some particular pleasure conduces to the goal when such is not the case. Ethical hedonism banks on man's freedom.

Hedonism is true, so far as man is concerned absolutely true, true without qualification, everywhere and always, never denied in any degree. Pleasure—experience of things, events, objects which are desired—that is the only good, the only value in and for itself, known to man or animal. Everything else which we call good is good just so far as it tends toward pleasure, leads to happiness. Yet while this is absolutely true, it is not in *practice* enough for morality, morality being practical. What are the means, the rules of conduct which will guide us ignorant mortals to this final goal and end? For surely in this law-abiding universe, there are some fixed principles of conduct, following which we approximate, abandoning we frustrate, our dearest wants. There lie the contributions of the other types of ethical theory, the rigorists, self-realizers, and so on. Let us now consider some of these, and see how they verify the truth of hedonism, yet at the same time add truths of their own, which hedonism by itself does not discover even though it gives the impulse to their discovery.

Take first the one that appeals most to the modern socialized consciousness, the creed of altruism: live for others, for all mankind, for animals too, let no selfish pleasures interfere. Grant its rightness. Pleasure, this view correctly sees, is an individual affair; as no one man is another man, his pleasure is not another's pleasure. Then the conclusion is drawn: the cult of pleasure is inevitably selfish. Now we might answer that hedonism doesn't imply *exclusive* self-keeping. It might be the case, as Herbert Spencer argued, that the egotist can enjoy the fullest and deepest happiness only by coming to delight in the happiness of all creatures, and actively working therefor. Hedonism doesn't contradict altruism. But the altruist makes a good practical reply. Human nature is weak and corrupt, and if the egotist is told to seek his own happiness he will not make the tremendous effort required to realize that his happiness does depend on the happiness of all men, still less on the happiness of animals. He will perhaps work for the good of the limited circle on whom his prosperity obviously depends; as the politician tries to please his constituents in order to be kept in office. But that is very far from the morality of altruism. Man needs more than counsels of prudence; he needs an imperative, an Ought, an authoritative urge and drive. With human nature as it is, the pleasure motive simply will not suffice. So speaks the altruist. And no doubt this is true. Man is but a child in respect of ultimate good; as a child needs the guidance of a parent, adult man needs authority of one sort or another. If not of another person or group of persons, then at least of the law of the land, and above all human laws of the moral law within. But of course the question is: what is this moral law? The altruist, flaming with indignation against the selfishness of avowed pleasure seekers, goes to the exclusive extreme and declares the happiness motive intrinsically inadequate. Inadequate indeed it is for much of our human nature; but why not because we weaklings tend to interpret the pleasure motive itself in an exclusive way? It is not the motive that is wrong; it is the radical evil of our nature that we *will* take it in the exclusive sense of a search for one's own pleasure or the pleasure of one's group, regardless of others. As just said, that is no implicate of hedonism.

But we may go further, much further. Hedonism sees that every wish finds its good in the joy of fulfillment, its evil in the frustration thereof. No matter what bad consequences may later follow, the joy of fulfillment is *so far* good, and its goodness consists in its pleasantness. This holds of every wish, of any man or any animal. To wish *means* to look forward to its fulfillment as a joy, its frustration as a pain. This is, again as said, a tautology; there is no escaping it. As such, it is a universal truth. For every conscious being it holds and must hold. The good of the fulfillment is the joy of the realized wish. But the good is that which ought to be. That is the axiom of morality, itself a tautology. See, then, the consequence: *every wish ought to be fulfilled.* And as wishes are always wishes of individuals, *every individual ought to have his own wishes fulfilled as being just his own private personal wishes.* To be sure, in this vale of tears many wishes when fulfilled prevent the realization of other wishes. Mine fulfilled may prevent yours being fulfilled. Evil, as St. Thomas teaches, is privation, frustration. The good for man, as St. Thomas also teaches, is the fulfillment of his natural wants. The means of fulfillment constitute the moral law. But the point to be stressed is this: hedonism is intrinsically, inevitably universal. You as a reflecting hedonist see that in the absence of evil consequences from either, my pleasure ought to be realized just as your own should be, wherefore you adopt it into the system of ends for which you live. To be sure, the objector here asks: how do *you* come to wish for *my* pleasure which just *is not* your pleasure? You see that my pleasure is my good, yet that is far from seeing that it is *your* good, object of *your* wish for which you will work. But the objector fails to see that *ought* and *wished for* are identical. When you come to understand that my happiness ought to be, *because* it is wanted by me, you have seen a universal truth: whatever is wanted (other things not interfering) should come to be, and no matter who brings it about. You hope it will be brought about, and to hope is to wish. Thus do you come to wish for my happiness. It all turns on the absolute identity of goodness or oughtness with wantedness. The minute we realize that something is good and ought to be, do we to the degree of our appreciation of its goodness wish it to exist. There is no need here of an organic theory of interlocking human interests, though the theory may be true. Nor is there need to posit, with some of our naturalists, the sharing of experiences between fellow men, your enjoyments and mine, your wishes and mine shared in common, egoistic privacy denied. A private mind may see a universal truth, a rule of con-

THE ABSOLUTE TRUTH OF HEDONISM 479

duct valid for all private minds. And here that truth is: every wish of every conscious being deserves gratification to the degree in which it doesn't frustrate other wishes. He who sees the goodness of the fulfillment *ipso facto* wishes for it, to however slight a degree. That is why every conscious being we know of, man or animal, is an end in himself, though he or it is more than that. That also is why the sum total of many men's pleasures may become the object of your private pleasure—which the critic, failing to see that oughtness is wantedness potential or actual, has called an unwarranted assumption of the hedonist.

But alas that this all-inclusive wish is so often weaker, far weaker, than the wish for a pleasure restricted to one's self; alas that these so often conflict! When they do, of course the consequences of each alternative must be weighed, if the direction toward the maximum is to be followed. It is for us working human beings to judge as best we may what the consequences will be. In any case, however, hedonism *is* altruism. Even so, the teaching of altruism is needed to make explicit the full meaning of hedonism.

But now the objector will say: suppose I get an intense pleasure, a sadistic delirious joy, by inflicting pain on you and seeing you squirm? Suppose the degree of my pleasure is far greater than the degree of your pain? Have I not then by tormenting you increased the sum total of human happiness, and so done a good moral deed? And if so, we ought to train ourselves to become expert sadists. Of course the objection doesn't see that hedonism means, as just said: every *individual* should have maximum happiness. Individuals alone are wishers; the maximum total of human pleasure is no good end except as constituted by the maximum in and for each person. The sadist, delighting in another's pain, breaks this hedonist rule. As the utilitarians used to say, "every one to count as one, none as more than one": good Christian doctrine too.

Other types claim to refute hedonism; not so much by appeal to the heart-warming gospel of love as by certain cold logical implications. The good, all grant, is what ought to be; surely then it follows that the good which is pleasure ought to be. But is pleasure the only good? Altruism has dwelt on the happiness of others; may not the service of mankind come to reveal other and better goods? Already mentioned is Kant's categorical imperative; even if he fell away when he tacked on at the end the hedonist reward, was it necessary to do that? Surely he was right when he declared that the only unqualified good is a good will, firm and unyielding in the performance of duty for duty's sake. Surely the Ought is above all natural wishes, with its unshakable independence. Still, independence is strength, and who says we do not enjoy being strong? "Duty," wrote Kant, "thou sublime and mighty name. . . . We love, we want to have and to own, the sublime and mighty." *There* lies the secret of the appeal, the appeal which indeed we all feel, of the Kantian and the Stoic ethic. *There* is its lure. We sense a deeper-going joy in the austere beauty of the stern daughter of the voice of God than in the pleasant graces of the sirens of this world. Yet even admitting so much to the hedonist, the rigorist will not be persuaded. He will return to the charge, declaring that however true be the above, there is still, there must be, something in the notion of Ought which defies description in terms of the pleasant, something too high and good to be reduced to the level of the common commodity pleasure. He will ask: *ought* we to follow duty for duty's sake because we love the sublime independence of it? And he will reply: No! We should put away that emotion, and follow the call of duty because it is *right*. Not because of its austere beauty, not for its aesthetic refinement, not even because of the longing for a conscience at peace with itself, still less for the consequences to human happiness; just do the right because it is right, no *arrière pensée*, no sullying of the purity of motive. Such is the lofty teaching of the idealist.

How then do we know what is right? No test is given us; not even the Kantian (really pragmatic) test of working as a universal rule in man's social life should be permitted in this perspective. But no test is needed, we are told. Values are directly felt. We know the right by intuition if our mind is free from search for pleasure and such. Adapting the poet's words:

> Right is an angel of so lovely mien
> As to be worshiped needs but to be seen.

If we are pious we shall say God reveals it to us; if not pious, we shall just call it a pure intuition. But the right is not deducible from the facts of nature, from the ways of the natural man. It is self-guaranteeing. The Ought cannot be defined in terms of natural process. Value, moral value at least, is indefinable, underivable, ultimate. And we are warned against the "naturalistic fallacy" of deriving the good from the facts, the ideal from the actual, right from might.

Suppose, then, that men disagree in their intuitions of what is right. Certainly to an extent they do. A Nietzsche asserts that power is the moral good, a Hitler that the German race and its way of life is the moral good, a Stalin that the rule of the proletariat and the ensuing classless society is the ideal, an American that it is democracy. In such a situation there is bound to be a pragmatic test. Which mode of life will survive? And as survival is the dearest wish of each type, this is hedonism. But these are political or social ideals; perhaps there is more agreement in respect of the individual in relation to other individuals. Most men would agree that it is wrong to lie, to steal, to murder, and so on, unless possibly these acts are required for the sake of some greater good to come. Even here, to be sure, as the qualification just added suggests, there is some disagreement. The pacifist believes it is *never* right to fight, no matter what; the rigorist that it is *never* right to lie; by no means would all moralists agree to these. Yet on the whole there is a fairly widespread agreement on general principles; it is good to cure sickness, to promote fellow-feeling, to cultivate the arts and sciences, and so on. See, then, the significance of this agreement. It is *human beings* that agree—and why do they agree? Because they are alike, of the same nature as human. Which means that their intuition of the right is in accord with human nature. It is not an insight into some value whose meaning has nothing to do with the natural wants of man. It is the expression of those wants. Fundamental, not ephemeral, wants, to be sure; those just named are basic needs, conditions required for man's life and life more abundant. Moral values, for us men at least, are the objects of our deepest and most inclusive needs. What no one ever desires or would desire if he knew of it, has and can have no value for him. No value, no good of any sort, without desire actual or potential. Indeed the very imperative of duty for duty's sake implies the same. That imperative means the performance of duty such that it will give opportunity for continued performance of duty, and in more and more ways. If it is a universal rule, binding upon man forever and not self-defeating, it demands the continuation and broadening of man's life that he may more and more realize this absolute imperative. It was the merit of the rigorous moralist Fichte, in his lectures on the *Vocation of Man,* to emphasize this. But such continuation and enrichment is precisely what the hedonist urges. There is, there can be, no separation between moral values and the satisfaction of man's *natural* craving for a full and rich and continued life, for the joyous exercise of his faculties—always, of course, so far as not interfering with their further exercise in one's self or fellows. And this, after all, is through and through the pragmatic test, which test is surely hedonist. No; moral values are not *wholly* indefinable. They are to be defined in practical terms as means of fulfilling our basic needs. For that matter, nothing is wholly indefinable or wholly definable; any description is some degree of definition and no definition includes all to which the term is liable. Thus the moral law is pragmatically defined as that which would, if obeyed, help us to adapt ourselves to our human and natural environment so as to gratify our deepest wants, and to the maximum. And if those wants are summed up as life, liberty, and the pursuit of happiness, notice that life and liberty are the indispensable means to the pursuit of happiness, happiness the goal of all human endeavor.

But certainly the axiologist who asserts that value is indefinable in terms of actual being, is right in this: nothing is good unless actually or potentially an object of desire, and desire is not to be defined in terms of what *is,* being typically an urge to what *is not.* Right, for us human beings, can never be derived from might.

The Thomist ethic has seen clearly this unison of objective values with our subjective desires, well brought out of late in Fr. Walter Farrell's *Companion to the Summa,* Vol. I, a commentary on the ethics in Part II of the *Summa Theologica.* As this writer says, *man wants what he wants;* behind these wants he cannot go. If the Thomist sees them implanted by the Creator in the very essence of man, his substantial form-matter, no less should the naturalist who views them as product of a long and slow evolution, see them to be essential to the species *homo sapiens.* Even the idealizing Germans, Kant and Fichte, had to appeal to man's desire for a continued and prosperous society to discover the content of the moral law—as Hegel so clearly saw. But have the other types of ethical theory seen the same?

On the one hand the idealist, witnessing the ideal goods eternal in the heavens, fears their eternal validity will be lost to view if they are defined as objects of our desire: we change our wishes so often, we wish for so many bad things, things that defeat other desires. So he declares that desire merely of itself gives no clue to the right; the right is what we *ought* to desire. True indeed; but that doesn't involve the irrelevance of desire to the ideal goods. What he should say is: we all inevitably, inescapably, at least subconsciously, desire maximum happiness, maximum in intensity and extensity, while actually, consciously, or even subconsciously perhaps, we also desire many things that work against this maximum; whereby we go against our own desire. Man is a very inconsistent animal. Let him then choose the courses which so far as he can see point toward the realizing of the maximum for each and all. The urge to this choice is what he calls the Ought; but the whole thing can be put in terms of desire and their objects. *Ought* is but an awesome name for the authority weak mortals need to keep them straight. (Of course we are all weak mortals.)

On the other hand the analytical epistemologist, whose gaze is focused not upon eternal verities or validities, but on man's mind, seeing quite correctly that nothing can be deemed good by man unless man sees it as what he would like to be or have, tends to lose sight of the stability of nature's laws, even of human nature's, and go to the opposite extreme, asserting that whatever we may desire is made good by our desiring it. (Or as R. B. Perry has said, by our interest in it—obviously the same point, interest being a desire to see or know or have and the like.) As the idealist affirms that we desire a thing because it is good, the epistemologist and subjectivist insists that a thing is good because we desire it. And as we have a degree of freedom in respect of particular desires—we may suppress the desire to help a fellow man and follow the desire to cheat him—so the subjective theorist would seem to allege that there are no fixed moral standards. After all, does not the older morality of the eternal laws smack of Toryism, of the supernatural, the mysterious authority of the Divine command? Such authority is anathema to this modernist—also, it seems, to the so-called humanists of today. Man, they seem to say, is master of his fate, creates his own morality. Perhaps few would go so far as that, but their opponents accuse them of it and it may be implied in some of their statements. Even if so, however, the subjectivist is, like most philosophers, right except for his exclusions. The morally good would not for us men be good unless it commanded our admiration, unless we should *like* to realize it. It surely has that "emotive" trait, as some of the analysts have said. But that, as the acute analyst, C. L. Stevenson, has written, does not in the least deny its validity as an eternal principle of the way of happiness for us, for all conscious beings. And the simple fact is that *any* satisfied desire, be it ever so trivial, so petty, so at odds with other more lasting and fruitful satisfactions, is quite of itself good *so far*. St. Thomas says that the murderer's blow is good in so far as it shows the strength of the murderer, bad in the effect of destroying life. Equally may we say that there is no pleasure which *merely* by itself is bad. The rule of hedonism is never broken.

So, then, as regards the claims of these opponents, the objective and the subjective views: both are right, each is wrong. It is senseless to say that we desire a thing *because* it is good; it is just as senseless to say a thing is good *because* we desire it. Good and desire, for us human beings, for all conscious beings presumably, are the two sides or phases of one and the same event or state or entity. Neither phase generates the other. Nor are our desires arbitrary; they are ingrained in our given nature which we did not make. It is not we who make a thing good by wanting it, for what made us want it? The lure of the object, be it health, wealth, knowledge, power, or whatever, is not put there by ourselves. Who could wish to commit suicide just for the fun of it? Our part is only to choose between lures, or desires. For what is a lure without our desire? The alluring object would not draw us, did not something in our nature respond or correspond to it. To repeat then: as is so often the case, each claim is right in respect of the positive assertion that *its* phase is present, wrong when it insists that the other is generated by its phase, this phase alone being the essence of the matter.

Originally published in *The Journal of Philosophy*, 1950; reprinted with permission of the editors. Some omissions have been made here.

T. V. SMITH

Philosophy and Democracy

Everyone is aware that about some things we are agreed, whereas about other things we differ . . . when anyone speaks of justice and goodness we part company and are at odds with one another and with ourselves.—PLATO *Phaedrus* 263.

Of the three great stages for the theater of life, two body forth the distinctively human show. First, however, there is the more elementary behavior of man—the stage of animal urgency. Then there is action guided by ends—the stage of political endeavor. Finally, there is contemplation of ideals or of whatever else—the stage of philosophic wonder and worth. Our present preoccupation is with the political and the philosophic. The lower stage of purely animal behavior is here remarked for perspective and as a reminder that the human spirit has no final immunity from the heats of body and the fumes of earth. The vocation of man advances through political sublimation of animal urgency to contemplation as catharsis for action, political or animal.

Without prejudging other means than the natural for this advance, let us focus attention upon man's predicament at its worst to see whether ideal potencies of real promise may not lie submerged in the mud and scum of things merely mortal. Let me ask you graciously to bear, though not necessarily to share, the assumption that our human journey is from elemental nescience through momentary prescience to ultimate nescience. The lights that flash across our little day of dim reason are lurid but lost in a sky of primeval and of eventual darkness. Historic afterimages get confused with premonitory gleams from a future rising out of the unknowable, like dawn from a night that is spent; and neither the after- nor the fore-images can clearly and surely be distinguished from the vague but indigenous glows of our own animal heats.

This inability finally to distinguish is the propaedeutic for promotion from animal impetuosity to civilized forbearance. It marks the firmest foundation for the tolerance which is characteristic of democracy alone. Animals heated with the scent of the prey brook no opposition without compulsion and abide no delay short of bondage. When such urgencies of action intersect, battle ensues; and the fittest for the quarry is merely the survivor from the fray. That is the story of man the animal. Man the political animal permits a biography that is better without reaching the level of the story that is best. His political career line rises highest where it turns democratic; but the line passes from better to best as the demand for political action transforms itself into the contemplation of norms as self-justifying eidola.

This is indeed a convenient division between politics and philosophy. Politics is concerned with ideals as agencies of action; philosophy is concerned with ideals as objects for inner celebration. Democracy is the political form which requires and feeds upon some philosophic flair among its citizens. This is the core of what is now to be clothed with argument and subdued to rhetoric.

1. *Frustration of the Ideal in Action*

Political knowers and political doers are both alike often heard to talk of truth, of goodness, and even of beauty—these anciently nominated representatives of the whole domain of the ideal. But the atmosphere of action always hovers over such political talk. Truth is something to be caught and proclaimed; goodness something to be achieved; beauty a thing to be created or a body to be embraced. Each is something that a man can grab, and, once grasped, something that can be used to expedite endeavor. "Truth," said Justice Holmes, speaking when he had reached only the midstage of self-mastery—"truth (I used to say when I was young) was the majority vote of that nation that could lick all others." Truth so conceived serves as convenient cover for coercion, as Holmes was destined to write into a great decision: "Persecution for the expression of opinion seems perfectly logical. If you have no doubt of your premises or of your power and want a certain result with all your heart you . . . naturally sweep away all opposition."

Now, fortunately for America, Holmes was too young for subversive action when he felt sure of his premises and too old when he felt certain of his power. But, unfortunately for the peace of the world, Mussolini has felt certain of both his premises and his power at once, and Stalin of both at once, and Hitler of both at once [1937]. Persecution for the expression of opinion seems perfectly logical to all of them. Let the propaganda minister for the most fanatical of the three articulate for all of them the function and fate of truth when seized upon by men of action: "Christ cannot possibly have been a Jew," says Goebbels, that great logician, this moment arbiter of truth in Berlin. "I don't have to prove that scientifically. It is a fact." If that seems unduly even Teutonically crass, what above that can we make of the suborned philosopher Gentile who, for the sake of Italian fascism, glorifies what he calls "holy violence" and states as his final theory of knowledge this: "that the true doctrine is that which is expressed in action rather than in words and books"? Nor is the world in need of words to make recurrent deeds in Russia mean other than this same taking of the kingdom of truth by storm.

The trouble with truth as agent of action is that we can never be certain what cause it represents. As Holmes put it, we lack a knowledge of the "truth of truth." That lacking, all that we need is lacking, unless we are willing surreptitiously to substitute for certainty our private feelings of certitude. That will is easier than the wit to give the substitution effect; for we meet other identical chiselers who feel certitude, alas, over the opposite from our convictions. Such logical chiselers can always frustrate one another's cause without anyone thereby being able to further his own.

But to summarize this in a systematic word, let us observe that the tests of certainty arising from the three prevailing theories of truth—idealism, realism, pragmatism—are severally and jointly unable to promote any of our certitudes into objective certainty.

1. *The coherence theory of truth offers no adequate test for truth.*—Only an absolute point of view to give vision to all things as a whole can reveal adequate coherence, and such a point of view is not available to man. What is not available can neither test nor be tested by finite frailty. Of coherence, then, I remark simply that it is only when men know not what to trust that they trust they know not what.

2. *The correspondence theory offers no adequate test of truth.*—One must already know what is true before he can know what beyond his ideas corresponds to his ideas. Of correspondence, then, I remark simply that it is only when men must say something that they say something which they themselves do not understand.

3. *The prediction theory is no adequate test of truth.*—If truth is prediction, then no idea ever is, but merely always is to be, true; for prediction cannot *be* what it is *of* without confounding confusion of hope and the hoped for. Of this theory I remark, finally, that it is only men who despair of truth who call prediction of truth, truth itself.

No one of these theories can adequately test itself, much less anything else. How, indeed, can coherence test the coherence theory? And to what, pray, does the correspondence theory correspond? And what solvent prediction validates the prediction theory of truth? The unspoken reliance of all schools alike, no less so than the reliance of the plain man, is some feeling of certitude. And that, we have seen, is not enough; it is logically irrelevant to certainty. This doubtful reliance it is which sustains the faith in truth of the idealist, short of the absolute unity which is his ever unavailable official test of coherence; of the realist, short of the ubiquity which would be the necessary condition for his correspondence; of the pragmatist, short of either social universality or of temporal infinity, which two are, jointly or alternatively, required but vainly sought, to save his theory from solipsism. Certitude is the reliance of which all these are rationalizations; and certitude, I repeat, is not enough. It more easily marks the beginning of coercion than the end of demonstration. The cowardly will assume certitude sufficient for action; the intellectually unscrupulous will feign a certitude; the ignorant will stubbornly feel a certitude; the conscientious will coin a certitude of their moral impetuosity; and all alike, though with motives diverse, will risk a battle, leaving the conscientious and the stubborn to shed their blood in the name of a cause which in pathetic retrospect may well appear only a case of private belief lifted to specious certainty by one's poor animal heat or by the prideful mistake of some superior giving orders of the day. Such certitude, however, is all that men intent upon action require to justify suppression of fellow men in the name of and for the sake of truth. Such validation is clearly not enough to save action from infamy.

Communism has taught us anew, and fascism has enforced this lesson, that self-admitted truth is not enough for political action. The only insurance the modern world has against the recurrence of the age old debacle of persecution for opinion is the presence in it of a sufficient number of men of such character as will mollify assertions of truth with the restraints of tolerance. The primary test of such character is a superphilosophic caution in identifying certitude with certainty, in asserting self-evidence as a test of truth.

The development of civilization has meant, among other things, the disciplining of character into such caution. Only good men can and will practice such forbearance. Generosity becomes thus the savior of Truth, but its salvation is conditioned upon a certain categorical obscuration, the metamorphosing of truth into goodness. Unabashed assertions of truth short of the general agreement which alone bespeaks certainty are suicidal to mankind. Agreements, however, in many important matters upon the scale required and at the depth necessary have so far proved impossible. Catholics and Communists are not likely, for instance, to agree upon a philosophy of history; nor are Fascists and Democrats upon the meaning and value of liberty. Something more, therefore, than motivation to truth is required to prevent, short of impossible agreement, the assumption of certainty and the menacing gestures which tend to follow therefrom. Beyond truth lies goodness, and civilization requires the advance. Generosity of spirit is the indispensable condition for this advance; for only the generous actor will mitigate with mercy his animal heat precipitated as political convictions.

But let the scrupulous man beware of premature fixation upon the new galaxy of goodness, if he would continue to lessen the penalty constantly invited by a mind housed in an animal body. Though the Good saves Truth, itself it cannot save from the urge of action. As by enveloping Truth, Goodness somehow obscures it, so it in turn darkens the vision of him who admiringly beholds it. When this narrowing has grown chronic, it reinforces the drive for truth which threatens civilization itself through the premature substitution of certitude for certainty, and furnishes an impenetrable rationalization of righteousness for animals' deeds steeped in infamy. Truth-fixation suffused and succored by vision of the good may easily become the moral bigotry which among all bad things modern men have rightly come to deem the worst. Worship of the Good too easily generates as its earthly active fruit an inversion of spirit semipathological. A developing love of discipline for its own sake marks the spread of this moral paralysis, and asceticism is the end result of a love of goodness which insists upon burying its ideal goal in the living tomb of action.

If, however, generosity lifts its wings toward the empyrean, the soul finds itself mounting to magnanimity; and borne above on these spreading plumes, it lands at last on the threshold of Beauty. All dross purged by this arduous passage, the soul might now lose the narrowness acquired in the first realm and all impetuosity, assertive or regressive, hanging over from its sojourn in the second realm of ideal being.

But if still pushed by animal heat, the soul, though deep in the domain of the philosophic, may yet count ideals as prescriptions and still insist, like political reformers, upon doing something. Then Beauty, succumbing to the fate of Truth and Goodness, will be turned into a sales slogan or crumpled into the puerile pulchritude of some other prostitution of ideality to action. The danger here is indeed twofold, as in the case of Goodness. For to this exploitation of Beauty is to be added a too lustful embrace of it. There is an inversion of action which takes the form not of asceticism but of voluptuousness. If in adoration of Beauty the soul grows infatuated and sinks sighingly down until accustomed to amorous indolence, the effulgence of the ideal grows gray through wont, luxury begets softness, and the soul, losing its orientation, begins to doubt whether there is any supporting goodness and proudly to proclaim that there is no truth but beauty. Inspiration survives as intoxication, and inebriation leads to madness. Beauty, the catalyzer of goodness and truth, is reduced to impotence by this demand upon her, and the soul is then left only with her discontents feeding upon their own fumings. This is the direst vengeance self-inflicted upon a soul rendered alien to ideality by her own overdevotion to action—to have successive reliefs from previous narrownesses culminate in the ennui that is worse than all narrowness, sick satiety from surfeiting upon Beauty. To the grief of frustration in action, which visits all men everywhere, is now added the greater grief superinduced from failure to face the ideal for what it is in its own right and realm. Hear Housman's plaintive call for help from this grief universal of Everyman, of *every man,* the actor who wants to be artist, the artist who must play at acting whether he wants to or not.

Sons of landsmen, sons of seamen, hear the tale of grief and me,
Looking from the land of Biscay on the waters of the sea.

Looking from the land of Biscay over Ocean to the sky
On the far-beholding foreland paced at even grief and I.
There, as warm the west was burning and the east encoloured cold,
Down the waterway of sunset drove to shore a ship of gold.
Gold of mast and gold of cordage, gold of sail to sight was she,
And she glassed her ensign golden in the waters of the sea.

Oh, said I, my friend and lover, take we now that ship and sail
Outward in the ebb of hues and steer upon the sunset trail;
Leave the night to fall behind us and the clouding countries leave:
Help for you and me is yonder, in the havens west of eve.

Under hill she neared the harbour, till the gazer could behold
On the golden deck the steersman standing at the helm of gold,
Man and ship and sky and water burning in a single flame;
And the mariner of Ocean he was calling as he came:
From the highway of the sunset he was shouting on the sea,
"Landsman of the land of Biscay, have you help for grief and me?"

When I heard I did not answer, I stood mute and shook my head:
Son of earth and son of Ocean, much we thought and nothing said.
Grief and I abode the nightfall; to the sunset grief and he
Turned them from the land of Biscay on the waters of the sea.

2. *Philosophy as Retreat from an Succor for the Life of Action*

Thus the ashes of action for all the sons of men who think action enough. Action is necessary for man the animal, but action is not enough for the animal Man. Action goes awry for mere animals; action goes sour for political animals. Politics as end-guided endeavor requires some ideality as retreat from action and as succor in action. The philosophic mind concerns itself with this surplusage of ideality over action: it finds in the contemplation of ideals both relief and replenishment. To fail to see the problem generated for man by this plethora of the ideal is the final stupidity. To declare the problem beyond remedy is cynicism, that human vice which leans least toward virtue's side. To come directly to terms with the problem will almost certainly involve some half-concealed acceptance of frustration as the final fruit of man's efforts to make through action the best of the worst. This latest frustration can be lessened—can even be well nigh cured, as we hope to show—by a conspiracy of will and wit to promote the heroism involved in this making through politics the best of the worst to some high magnanimity of making through philosophy the best of the best.

So far I have spoken as though politics were concerned with one set of norms and philosophy with another set. Such has, it appears, been all too often the historic conviction. And such may be the case, for all that I know for certain. Such, however, is not my best guess. There is, I dare say, one set of ideals, not two; but the one set may be taken in these two ways: as patterns for practice and as objects of appreciation. Fate, which when taken wrongly becomes frustration, when taken rightly offers vocation and opportunity for the wise. Only citizens innocent of philosophy will take ideals wrongly and thereby reap frustration. Citizens intent upon philosophy know that ideals, which for animals are mere prescriptions, may become self-rewarding objects of contemplation for spirits who know a worth transcending use. Politics is preoccupation with norms as programs of action; philosophy is preoccupation with norms as producers of serenity. The proper preface to philosophy, and the wise propaedeutic to politics, is acquaintance with and appreciation of "the law of nature," as Plato called it, "that performance can never hit the truth as closely as theory."

Politics need not "hit the truth" at all, as Plato conceived truth. What the politician wants, he goes and gets—or learns why: learns who stands in his way, what his price is, and then pays the price of compromise necessary to give both a part of what each wanted altogether. If the politician rises above the economic, it is usually to broaden out only to such other kindred motives as safety, then to security, and perhaps at last to deference as the price of universal pride. Such motives mark the very outer reach of politics. But these motives, even when exploited to the full, hardly touch the periphery of philosophy, concerned as it is with ideals as such; and with hardly any ideal level lower than Truth. The utility motif of politics ends its quest for truth by grabbing it and then passing it out as political patronage wrapped in cellophane of palaver or, under sufficient provocation, hurling it like a brickbat at the heads of opponents. This is to take the kingdom of philosophy by violence in a fit of frenzy for action prescribed by the ideal of Truth. Thus has room been made for the custom-built truths of Nazi Germany, and the action-assimilated truths of Fascist Italy.

Nor is America without historic and present witness to the indigenous presence of this impetuous will. For every Roger Williams who writes "the tenet of bloody persecution" against intolerance, there is a John Cotton to indite "the tenet of bloody persecution washed and made white in the blood of the Lamb." "No," shouted Cotton to Williams, "we did not drive you from Massachusetts because you followed your conscience, but because you refused to follow your conscience in doing what you well knew to be right!" Such is the final offense of all political isms that prostitute philosophy to urgency, whether they appear as brown, black, or red. If man's response, however, be a more reticent, not to say a more reverent, appropriation of the pure ideal and a more strategic approach in proper season to it from, and from it to, the life of action—then he may with some reason expect out of what Wordsworth has called "wise passiveness" some purgation from the passions of politics and some recreation in action from the much-too-much for any animal of incessant contemplation of pure Beauty. Indeed from the aesthetic zenith of ideality a soul that has lovingly communed with Beauty without desire to battle about it may come down the dialectical ladder without recession of the luster beholden on the topmost rung. He may preoccupy himself with Goodness once more but now with lessened desire to break somebody's head out of deference to some moral Ought. Indeed, still farther down the ladder which connects all normative levels of being, he may halt unhurried before the ideal of Truth without too much temptation to yell every opponent down with the shrill animal cry of "self-evidence," when all that is evident is that the issue is in dispute.

3. *Democracy as Politics Transformed*
by Philosophy

It is here and thus that the political enterprise is transformed into the democratic process. Democracy is politics no longer innocent of philosophy. The democrat will not announce political truth short of achieved agreement. He will not publicly call action good which is good merely for him. And in the social field he will not denominate beautiful what arrives other than through consent. Democracy is such reverence for persons and such respect for toleration as will suffer all things short of coercion.

Such forbearance is, it appears, not possible for those who believe that truth for action, goodness in action, beauty through action is all the ideality there is for man. Too little of perfection is collectively achievable for that faith ever to flourish. To believe that is so to affront the hungry human spirit as to humiliate man into the desperation of trying for ideality through coercion. If all is lost by withholding action, then all must be forgiven action to the uttermost. The democrat, however, has learned, or is learning, that opportunities for action lost, not all of ideality is lost. There remains the Truth-for-me, the Goodness-for-me, the Beauty-for-me. These are not invidious forms of the ideal, as so many timid minds think. They are, on the contrary, the most absolute forms of the ideal ever yet vouchsafed to man. Suppression of beliefs discrepant from Truth-for-me, coercion of fellow men into acceptance of Goodness-for-me, disdain of differences from the Beautiful-for-me—these animal procedures do not enhance ideals, nor objectify them. Such procedures indeed degrade spirits into animals, and poison with motives of counteraggression the springs of generosity from which, and from which alone, persuasion can enlarge the boundaries of the second-best type of objectivity, that created through agreement.

Democracy as a governmental form is primarily concerned with maintaining the conditions under which citizens may try for some objectification of the ideal in and through action. It encourages and implements with sanctions that narrow but substantial meeting of minds known at law as contract. It encourages, by withholding sanctions, that larger meeting of minds called free association. It even permits hierarchies to flourish—economic, religious, cultural: permits them to perpetuate themselves through esoteric nurture of the young, to protect themselves by the right of exclusion, and to disseminate themselves through the propaganda of the word. Democracy is not jealous of these save as these become hamperingly jealous of one another. It is not jealous of any of the provincial idealisms, for democracy enshrines a faith in ideality that includes and transcends all the faith of all the sectaries. Else how proclaim in the name of "the people, yes" equality when there is no equality, liberty when men remain so unfree, fraternity when competition is the common fate of men; and especially how proclaim all these all at once when no one of them is at any time fulfilled? Veritably democracy arises from and perpetuates a faith in the reality and in the transmuting power of ideality as the end of man. The final glory of this faith of faiths is that it can allow for hierarchies without itself becoming a hierarchy. It is a faith in the horizontal versus the vertical type of social organization.

This faith in ideality leads America to offer to all through a common education direct access to the realm of imagination, that domicile of all ideals. What men can think and feel privately is of no jeopardy so long as it remains unsuborned to action. The perpetuation of the superiority of worth to use is the final validation and protection of the democratic way of life. This is its substitute and catharsis for the hierarchies which democracy permits to flourish. For democracy is the enshrinement of the principle of aristocracy in a field and fashion noncompetitive. Democratic theory makes every man an aristocrat, and those who measure up to the theory become at the same time real aristocrats and true democrats. This means, however—what has ever shown faintly through all its denials—that real aristocracy is a thing of taste rather than of property, that true democracy is a matter of feeling rather than of pretense. They are both qualities of the inner life showing themselves in the outer order first and foremost as a will to depreciate false pretensions. The elevation and cultivation of the inner life of imagination, the luxury land of the spirit, is the final glory of democracy and its chief guaranty of perpetuation so long as men still hear and attend the aristocratic prompting.

With the loosening of all other bonds, the bounds of fancy are enlarged; and there may proliferate freely from the securing of minimal animal wants—which the aristocrat must insist upon as *noblesse oblige* no less than the democrat as elemental justice— the lofty life of the human spirit, fed from direct confrontation with the ideal as such. The field of fancy is free, and all favors there are self-favors. And what favors does the self not bestow upon itself in that no man's land of utter privacy! Publicly we blush to remember how partial we have been to ourselves in that retreat. Every man a king—there, clothed in the habiliments of royal purple! Every man his own pope—there, speaking to himself with finality upon faith and morals! Every man his own logician— there, relying for truth at last upon certitude without the jeopardy which attends the conversion of certitude into certainty through claimed, but disputed, self-evidence! What a world, open and free to every humblest democrat! How easy the access! Only engage in the action-abnegating action of putting your chin in your hand; and, presto, you have crossed the threshold from the mediocrity of ideals-compromised-in-action to the domain of pure ideality; and your progress, once in, is limited only by your capacity to concentrate attention upon what nature freely furnishes to the humblest mind.

If some candidates hardly enter this bright domain of supreme worthfulness, they abstain from choice. If some, once in, are not promoted to the inner sanctuary of the trinity Truth-Goodness-Beauty, it is because in the secret balloting they blackball themselves. Those who elect to enter beyond the periphery of idle reverie and who promote their progress among the élite of the self-chosen, spreading the mantle of imagination over even action itself by mastering the trick of arresting any and every immediate, these become for their very aristocracy the hope of democracy. For those who have sojourned for even a season in the presence of the ideal will have little enough avidity, as Plato saw, for the denizenship of the dark. They have tasted the pleasures of the aristocracy of the light. And yet when they return to action, as they seasonally must out of deference to their animal nature, they bring with them the memory of mortal experience at its most majestic and retain sensitization to the lure of a gold too precious to glitter. For it is these devotees of imagination, and they alone, who have discovered and loved possessions which for some to have more of does not mean for others to have less of. Here then is the most fertile field for democratic equality to blossom into flower. Here is the chance at last for liberty without the limit elsewhere imposed by the equal rights of others. Here is fruition for fraternity—a fraternity of the equal and the free.

Not only is the truest democracy found in this aristocracy of the imagination, but this aristocracy makes it possible to have a semblance of democracy in the world of action, through the instrumentality of politics. Devotees of the ideal can, as political actors, arrange compromises between those who still find the meaning of life in competition, feeling little lust themselves for the gold whose division among men it is their privilege to facilitate. They can budge the education of the young toward the philosophic mind. They can become self-respecting buffers to protect against fate those doomed to frustration in action. And by being what they are, more than by anything they say or do, they can bear steadfast witness to the superiority of the imagined over the actual for animals who want above all wants simply to become spirits.

Whether these be contrite spirits of historic piety or scientific saints of the newer secularity, they constitute the aristocracy of democracy. Disdaining power aristocracies of the past, this élite is fed and furnished with such ideality as leaves it pliable with reference to ownership of the means of production of all external goods. It is the business of philosophers, good shepherds as they are of their own thoughts, to exemplify, to celebrate, and to promote the noncompetitive life by devotion to goods themselves not competitive. The beginning of this wisdom is for philosophers to be what they would have others to become. Civilization represents man's slowly maturing aspiration to universalize such an aristocracy of the spirit as cause of and cure for the democratic will.

Reprinted with permission of the editor, and University of Chicago Press, from the *International Journal of Ethics*, 1937.

Biographical Notes

ALICE AMBROSE, born November 25, 1906, Lexington, Illinois. A.B., 1928, James Millikin University; M.A., 1929, Ph.D., 1932, University of Wisconsin; Ph.D., 1938, Cambridge University. Professor of Philosophy, Smith College. Author of *Fundamentals of Symbolic Logic* (with Morris Lazerowitz) (New York, Rinehart, 1948); contributor to *Philosophical Analysis, The Philosophy of G. E. Moore,* and to various philosophical periodicals.

MAX BLACK, born February 24, 1909, Baku, Russia. American citizen. Educated Cambridge, Gottingen, and London. A.B., Ph.D., D.Lit.(London). Susan Linn Sage Professor of Philosophy, Cornell University. Vice-President, American Philosophical Association, 1953. Co-editor, *Journal of Symbolic Logic,* 1945-1951. Co-editor, *Philosophical Review,* 1946–. Author of *The Nature of Mathematics* (1933, 2nd ed. 1950), *Critical Thinking* (1946, 2nd ed. 1952), *Language and Philosophy* (1949), *Problems of Analysis* (1954). Edited *Philosophical Analysis* (1950), and *Philosophical Writings of Frege* (with P. T. Geach, 1952).

BRAND BLANSHARD, born 1892. Educated University of Michigan, B.A., 1914; Columbia University, M.A., 1918; University of Oxford, B.Sc., 1920; Harvard University, Ph.D., 1921. Taught at University of Michigan, 1921-25, Swarthmore College, 1925-45, Yale University, 1945–. Rhodes scholar, 1913-15, 1919-20; Guggenheim fellow, 1929-30. Gifford lecturer, St. Andrews, 1952-53; Hertz lecturer, British Academy; Adamson lecturer, Manchester University; Howison lecturer, University of California; Dudleian and William Belden Noble lecturer, Harvard University; Hon. Fellow, Merton College, Oxford. President, American Philosophical Association, Eastern Div., 1942-44. President, American Theological Society, 1955-56. Lecturer on American thought, Salzburg Seminar for American Studies,

1953. Hon. Litt.D., L.H.D., LL.D. Author of *The Nature of Thought* (1939) 2 Vol.; co-author, *Preface to Philosophy* (1945), *Philosophy in American Education* (1944), etc.

RUDOLF CARNAP, born May 18, 1891, Wuppertal, Germany. Studied at Universities of Jena and Freiburg i.Br., Dr. Phil., Jena, 1921; Hon.Sc.D., Harvard University, 1936. Instructor, University of Vienna, 1926-31; Professor of Philosophy, German University of Prague, 1931-36, University of Chicago, 1936-52, University of California at Los Angeles, 1954—. Member, Institute for Advanced Study, Princeton, 1952-54. Author of *Der Raum* (1922); *Physikalische Begriffsbildung* (1926); *Der logische Aufbau der Welt* (1928); *Abriss der Logistik* (1929); *Logische Syntax der Sprache* (1934), English Transl., *Logical Syntax of Language* (1937), Italian transl. in preparation; *Foundations of Logic and Mathematics* (1939); *Introduction to Semantics* (1942); *Formalization of Logic* (1943); *Meaning and Necessity* (1947), 2nd enlarged ed. (1956); *Logical Foundations of Probability* (1950); *The Continuum of Inductive Methods* (1952); *Einführung in die symbolische Logik* (1954).

JAMES COLLINS, born July 12, 1917, Holyoke, Mass. Educated Catholic University of America, A.B., A.M., and Ph.D., 1944. Research Fellow in Philosophy, Harvard University, 1945. Professor of Philosophy, St. Louis University, 1945—. Member of Phi Beta Kappa, American Philosophical Association, and past president, American Catholic Philosophical Association (1953-54). Author of *The Existentialists: A Critical Study* (Chicago, Regnery, 1952); *The Mind of Kierkegaard* (Chicago, Regnery, 1953); *A History of Modern European Philosophy* (Milwaukee, Bruce, 1954); and articles in philosophical journals.

WILLIAM RAY DENNES, born April 10, 1898, Healdsburg, California. A.B., 1919, M.A., 1920, University of California; D.Phil., 1923, Oxford University; LL.D., 1951, New York University. Professor of Philosophy and formerly Dean of the Graduate Division, University of California, Berkeley. Sometime Associate Professor of Philosophy at Yale University and Visiting Professor at Harvard and Stanford Universities. Author of *The Method and Presuppositions of Group Psychology;* with others: *The Philosophy of George Santayana; Naturalism and the Human Spirit;* editor and contributor: twenty volumes of the *University of California Publications in Philosophy.*

CURT JOHN DUCASSE, born July 7, 1881, Angouleme, France. A.B., 1908, A.M., 1909, University of Washington; Ph.D., 1912, Harvard University. Instructor in Philosophy and Psychology, 1912-16, Assistant Professor of Philosophy, 1916-24, Associate Professor, 1924-26, University of Washington. Associate Professor, 1926-29, Professor, 1929—, Brown University.

Past president, American Philosophical Association (Eastern Div.), Association for Symbolic Logic, American Society for Aesthetics. Paul Carus Lecturer, American Philosophical Association. Author of *Causation and the Types of Necessity*, 1924; *The Philosophy of Art*, 1930; *Philosophy as a Science*, 1941; *Art, the Critics, and You*, 1944; *Nature, Mind, and Death*, 1951; *A Philosophical Scrutiny of Religion*, 1953. Also chapters contributed to several books; and numerous articles, discussions, and book reviews in philosophical journals and in magazines.

NELSON GOODMAN. Ph.D., Harvard, 1941. Military Service, U. S. Army, 1942-45. Instructor in Philosophy, Tufts College, 1945-46. Professor of Philosophy, University of Pennsylvania, 1946–. Author of *The Structure of Appearance* (Harvard University Press, 1951); *Fact, Fiction and Forecast* (Athlone Press, University of London, 1954, Harvard University Press, 1955); and numerous articles in philosophical periodicals.

EVERETT W. HALL, born April 24, 1901, Janesville, Wisconsin. A.B., 1923, Lawrence College; A.M., 1925, Ph.D., 1929, Cornell University. Professor of Philosophy and Head of the Department, State University of Iowa, 1941-52; Kenan Professor and Chairman of the Department of Philosophy, University of North Carolina, 1952–. Author of *Twentieth Century Philosophy* (co-author), Dagobert Runes, ed. (New York, Philosophical Library, 1943); *What Is Value? An Essay in Philosophical Analysis* (London and New York, Routledge and Kegan Paul, Humanities Press, 1952); *Modern Science and Human Values: A Study in the History of Ideas* (New York, Van Nostrand, 1956).

CHARLES HARTSHORNE, born 1897, in Pennsylvania. Haverford College, 1914-17; private in U. S. Army Medical Corps, 1917-19; A.B., 1921, A.M., 1922, Ph.D., 1923, Harvard University. Sheldon Traveling Fellow in Germany, 1923-25. Instructor and research fellow, Harvard University, 1925; Professor of Philosophy, University of Chicago, 1943-55; Professor of Philosophy, Emory University, 1955–. Terry lecturer, Yale University, 1947; Fulbright lecturer in Melbourne, Australia, 1952. President, American Philosophical Association (Western Div.), 1948-49; president, Charles Peirce Society, 1950-51; president, Metaphysical Society of America, 1954-55. Author of *The Philosophy and Psychology of Sensation* (1934); *The Divine Relativity* (1948); *Reality as Social Process* (1953); *Philosophers Speak of God* (with William L. Reese) (1953); and other books. Editor of *The Collected Papers of Charles S. Peirce* (with Paul Weiss) (1931-35).

SIDNEY HOOK, born December 20, 1902. B.S., City College of New York; M.A., Ph.D., Columbia University. Professor and Chairman, Department of Philosophy, Washington Square College; Head, Division of Philosophy and

Psychology, Graduate School of Arts and Science, New York University. Author, among other works, of *Metaphysics of Pragmatism; From Hegel to Marx; John Dewey; Religion, Social Myths and Democracy; The Hero in History; Heresy, Yes—Conspiracy, No;* editor (with Konvitz), *Experience and Freedom,* and *John Dewey, Philosopher of Science and Democracy.*

HORACE M. KALLEN, born 1882. Ph.D., L.H.D., Litt.D. Research Professor in Social Philosophy; Professor Emeritus, Graduate Faculty of Political and Social Science, New School for Social Research. Visiting Professor, Claremont College, summers, 1938-40, 1947; University of Wisconsin, summer, 1943; Harvard University, summer, 1955; taught at Harvard University, Princeton University, Clark University, University of Wisconsin; sometime member, Mayor's Committee on City Planning of New York City, President's Commission on Higher Education, and other public bodies. Author, among other works, of *William James and Henri Bergson, Chapter in Creative Intelligence; The Book of Job as a Greek Tragedy; The Structure of Lasting Peace; Culture and Democracy in the United States; The Philosophy of William James; Why Religion; Individualism, An American Way of Life; A Free Society; The Decline and Rise of the Consumer; The Future of Peace; The Liberation of the Adult; Frontiers of Hope; The Education of Free Men; Ideals and Experience; Art and Freedom; The Liberal Spirit.*

ABRAHAM KAPLAN, born June 11, 1918, Odessa, Russia; American citizen since 1930. B.A., 1937, College of St. Thomas; graduate study, University of Chicago, 1937-40; Ph.D., 1942, University of California at Los Angeles. Research Associate, Division Wartime Communications, 1942-43; Guggenheim Fellow, 1945-46; Consultant, Rand Corporation, Division of Social Science and Mathematics, 1947—; Research Associate, Rockefeller Project on Language and Symbolism, 1951-52; Visiting Professor, University of Michigan, 1951-52; Visiting Professor, Columbia University, 1955; Professor, University of California at Los Angeles, 1946—. Author of *Power and Society* (with H. D. Lasswell) (Yale University Press, 1950, Kegan Paul, 1951); "Must There Be Propositions" (with I. Copi), *Mind* (1939); "A Framework for Empirical Ethics" (with B. Ritchie), *Philosophy of Science* (1939); "Are Moral Judgments Assertions," *Philosophical Review* (1942); "Definition and Specification of Meaning," *Journal of Philosophy* (1946); and other articles.

CLARENCE IRVING LEWIS, born April 12, 1883, Stoneham, Mass. A.B., 1906, Ph.D., 1910, Harvard University; D.H.L., 1941, University of Chicago. Assistant Professor, Associate Professor and Professor of Philosophy, Harvard University, 1921-53; Carus Lecturer, 1945; Professor of Philosophy Emeritus, Harvard University, 1953–; Hibben Research Fellow in Philosophy, Princeton University, 1953-54; Lecturer in Philosophy, Stanford University, 1954–. Author of *Survey of Symbolic Logic* (University of California Press, 1918); *Mind and the World-Order* (Scribner, 1929); *Symbolic Logic* (with C. H. Langford) (Appleton-Century, 1932), reprinted (Dover, 1952); *An Analysis of Knowledge and Valuation* (Open Court, 1946); *The Ground and Nature of the Right* (Columbia University Press, 1955).

CHARLES MORRIS, born May 23, 1901, Denver, Colorado. B.S., Northwestern University, 1922; Ph.D., University of Chicago, 1925. Lecturer in Philosophy, University of Chicago; Fellow, American Academy of Arts and Sciences; Fellow, American Association for the Advancement of Science. Author of *Six Theories of Mind* (1932); *Logical Positivism, Pragmatism and Scientific Empiricism* (1937); *Foundations of the Theory of Signs* (1938); *Paths of Life* (1942); *Signs, Language, and Behavior* (1946); *The Open Self* (1948); *Varieties of Human Value* (in press).

ARTHUR E. MURPHY, born September 1, 1901, Ithaca, N. Y. A.B., 1923, Ph.D., 1926, University of California, Berkeley. Taught at University of California, Berkeley, University of Chicago, Brown University; Chairman of Department of Philosophy–University of Illinois, 1939-45, Cornell University, 1945-53, University of Washington, 1953–. Paul Carus lecturer, Tenth Series, 1955. President, American Philosophical Association, Eastern Div., 1950; Fellow, American Academy of Arts and Sciences. Editor, *The Philosophical Review*, 1950-53. Author of *The Uses of Reason* (Macmillan, 1944); co-author, *Philosophy in American Education* (Harper, 1946); *American Scholarship in the Twentieth Century* (Harvard University Press, 1953).

ERNEST NAGEL, born November 16, 1901, Novemesto, Czechoslovakia. B.S. in Social Science, 1923, City College of New York; M.A., 1925, Ph.D., 1930, Columbia University. Instructor in Philosophy, City College of New York, 1930-31, Columbia University, 1931-37; Assistant Professor of Philosophy, 1937-39, Associate Professor of Philosophy, 1937-47, Professor of Philosophy, Columbia University, 1947–. President, Association for Symbolic Logic, 1947-49, American Philosophical Association (Eastern Div.), 1954; Vice-President, American Association for the Advancement of Science (Section L), 1951. Fellow of the American Academy of Arts and Sciences. Editor, *Journal of Symbolic Logic*, 1940-45, *Journal of Philosophy*, 1939-56. Author of *On the Logic of Measurement* (1930); *Introduction to Logic and Scientific Method* (with M. R. Cohen) (1934); *Principles of the Theory of Probability* (1939); *Sovereign Reason* (1954).

F. S. C. NORTHROP, born November 27, 1893, Janesville, Wisconsin. B.A., 1915, Beloit College; M.A., 1919, Yale University; Ph.D., 1924, Harvard University. Honorary degrees: Hon.Litt.D., 1946, Beloit College; L.L.D., 1949, University of Hawaii; L.L.D., 1955, Rollins College; Profesor Extraordinario, 1949, La Universidad Nacional Autenoma de Mexico. Guggenheim Fellow, 1932-33, Trinity College, Cambridge, and the University of Göttingen, Germany. Also studied at University of Freiburg, Germany; Trinity College, Cambridge; and Imperial College of Science and Technology, London. Taught at Yale University since 1923: Master of Silliman College, 1940-47; Sterling Professor of Philosophy and Law, Law School and Graduate School, 1947–. Author of *Science and First Principles* (1931); *The Meeting of East and West* (1946); *The Logic of the Sciences and the Humanities* (1947); *The Taming of the Nations* (1952); *European Union and United States Foreign Policy* (1954).

STEPHEN C. PEPPER, born April 29, 1891, Newark, N. J.; father, Charles Ovey Pepper, an artist, mother, Frances Coburn, both originally from Maine. Lived in Paris until 1899. Parents then settled in Concord, Mass. Taken around the world, 1901-02, visiting Japan, China, Java, India. A.B., 1913, M.A., 1914, Ph.D., 1916, Harvard University; L.H.D., 1950, Colby College. Taught at Wellesley College, 1916-17. U. S. Army, 1917-18. At University of California since 1919 as teaching Assistant, Instructor, Assistant Professor, Associate Professor, Professor; Chairman of Art Department, 1938-53; Chairman of Philosophy Department, 1954–. Author of *Aesthetic Quality; World Hypotheses; A Digest of Purposive Values; The Basis of Criticism in the Arts; Principles of Art Appreciation; The Work of Art.*

CHARNER MARQUIS PERRY, born March 15, 1902, Franklin, Texas; son of William Charner and Ola Cox Perry. B.A., 1924, M.A., 1925, University of Texas; Ph.D., 1926, University of Chicago. Instructor in Philosophy, University of Michigan, 1926-27; Adjunct Professor of Philosophy, University of Texas, 1927-33; Fellow, Social Science Research Council, 1931-32; Professor, 1951–, Acting Chairman, Department of Philosophy, 1940-47, Chairman, Department of Philosophy, University of Chicago, 1948–. Editor, *Ethics*, 1934–.

WILLARD VAN ORMAN QUINE, born June 25, 1908, Akron, Ohio. A.B., 1930 (summa in mathematics), Oberlin College; A.M., 1931, Ph.D., 1932, Harvard University; M.A., 1953, Oxford University; Litt.D., 1955, Oberlin College. Lieutenant and Lieutenant Commander, USNR, 1942-46. Rockefeller Postwar Fellow, 1946-47. Consultant, Rand Corporation, 1949. Chairman, Department of Philosophy, Harvard University, 1952-53. George Eastman Visiting Professor, Oxford University, 1953-54. Harvard University since 1936, Professor of Philosophy and Senior Fellow of Society of Fellows, 1948–. Member, Institute for Advanced Study, 1956-57; Vice-

President, American Philosophical Association (Eastern Div.), 1951; President, Association for Symbolic Logic, 1953-55. Consulting Editor, *Journal of Symbolic Logic*, 1936-41, 1946-52. Author of *A System of Logistic* (1934); *Mathematical Logic* (1940 and later editions); *Elementary Logic* (1941); *O Sentido da Nova Lógica* (1944); *Methods of Logic* (1950); *From a Logical Point of View* (1953).

HERBERT WALLACE SCHNEIDER, born March 16, 1892, Berea, Ohio. A.B., 1915, Ph.D., 1917, Columbia University; L.H.D., 1948, Union College. Professor of Philosophy and Religion, Columbia University, 1931—. Research Fellow, Italy, 1928, 1937; Fulbright Fellow, France, 1950; Secretariat, Unesco, 1953-56. President, American Philosophical Association (Eastern Div.), 1948. Author of *Making the Fascist State* (New York, 1930); *The Puritan Mind* (New York, 1931); *Meditations in Season* (New York, 1938); *History of American Philosophy* (Columbia University Press, 1946); *Religion in Twentieth Century America* (Harvard University Press, 1952); *Three Dimensions of Public Morality* (Indiana University Press, 1956).

WILFRID SELLARS, born May 12, 1912, Ann Arbor, Mich. Attended Lycee Louis le Grand, 1929-30; B.A., 1933, University of Michigan; M.A., 1934, University of Buffalo; 1937-38, Harvard University; M.A., 1940, Oxford University. Taught at State University of Iowa, 1938-46 (on leave, 1943-46); University of Minnesota, 1946—. Co-editor of *Readings in Philosophical Analysis* (with Herbert Feigl) (New York, Appleton-Century-Crofts, 1949); *Readings in Ethical Theory* (with John Hospers) (New York, Appleton-Century-Crofts, 1952). Founder and co-editor (with Herbert Feigl), *Philosophical Studies*, a journal published by the University of Minnesota Press.

WILMON H. SHELDON, born 1875, Newton, Mass. B.A., 1895, M.A., 1896, Ph.D., 1899, Harvard University. Assistant in Philosophy, University of Wisconsin, 1899-1900; Austin Teaching Fellow, Harvard University, 1900-01; Assistant in Philosophy, Columbia University, 1901-05; Preceptor in Philosophy, Princeton University, 1905-09; Stone Professor of Philosophy, Dartmouth College, 1909-20; Professor of Philosophy, Yale University, 1920-43, Emeritus, 1943—. President, American Philosophical Association, 1920-21. Author of *Strife of Systems and Productive Duality* (1919); *America's Progressive Philosophy* (1942); *Process and Polarity* (1944); *God and Polarity* (1954); *Sex and Salvation* (1955).

T. V. SMITH, born 1890, Blanket, Texas. B.A., M.A., University of Texas; Ph.D., 1922, University of Chicago. Professor of Philosophy, University of Chicago, 1927-48; Maxwell Professor of Citizenship and Philosophy, Syracuse University, 1948-56, Emeritus Professor, 1946-56. Editor, *Interna-*

tional Journal of Ethics (now *Ethics*) for a decade and a half. State Senator, University of Chicago district, 1934-38; Illinois Congressman at Large 1938-40. A founder of the University of Chicago Round Table of the Air, and of CBS book program, Invitation to Learning. Author of *Democratic Way of Life; Philosophic Way of Life; Legislative Way of Life; The Promise of American Politics; Discipline for Democracy; Beyond Conscience; The Ethics of Compromise and the Art of Containment; Politics and Public Service* (with L. D. White); *Foundations of Democracy* (with Senator Robert A. Taft).

WALTER T. STACE, born 1886, London, England. B.A., Litt.D., Trinity College, Dublin. In British civil service in Ceylon, 1910-1932, holding posts as magistrate, district judge, major of Colombo, etc. Lecturer and Professor of Philosophy, Princeton University, 1932-55. Retired, 1955. Author of *A Critical History of Greek Philosophy* (1920); *The Philosophy of Hegel* (1924); *The Meaning of Beauty* (1930); *The Theory of Knowledge and Existence* (1932); *The Concept of Morals* (1936); *The Destiny of Western Man* (1942); *The Nature of the World* (1946); *Time and Eternity* (1952); *Religion and the Modern Mind* (1952); *The Gate of Silence* (1952).

CHARLES L. STEVENSON, born 1908, Cincinnati, Ohio. Undergraduate work, Yale University, 1926-30; studied at Cambridge, England, 1930-33, and at Harvard University, 1933-35. Taught for several years at Harvard University and Yale University; with University of Michigan since 1946, now as a Professor of Philosophy. Author of *Ethics and Language* (Yale University Press, 1944); also a number of essays on philosophy, including "Interpretation and Evaluation in Aesthetics," in *Philosophical Analysis,* Max Black, ed. (Cornell University Press, 1950).

PAUL WEISS, born May 19, 1901. B.S.S., 1927, City College of New York; A.M., 1928, Ph.D., 1929, Harvard University. Sears Traveling Fellow, 1929-30; Professor at Yale since 1946. Founder and editor, *Review of Metaphysics* (since 1947); Advisory Board of *Philosophy of Science.* Contributor to *American Philosophy Today and Tomorrow* (1935); *Moral Principles of Action* (1952); *Approaches to World Peace* (1944); *Perspectives on Troubled Decade* (1950); Co-editor, *Collected Papers of Charles S. Peirce;* contributor to technical periodicals.

DONALD CARY WILLIAMS, born May 28, 1899, Crows Landing, California. A.B. in English, 1923, Occidental College, Los Angeles; graduate student of Philosophy and English, Harvard University, 1923-24, of Philosophy and Psychology, University of California, Berkeley, 1925-27, and of Philosophy, Harvard University, 1927-28; A.M., 1925, Ph.D., 1928, in

Philosophy, Harvard University. Studied Philosophy in Germany and France as a Sheldon Fellow from Harvard, 1928-29; a Guggenheim Fellow in 1928. Taught English at Occidental College, 1924-25; and Philosophy at Harvard University, 1929-30, at University of California at Los Angeles, 1930-39, and at Harvard University, 1939—. Author of *The Ground of Induction* (1947); and numerous essays.

Index